Spinoza on Monism

Philosophers in Depth

Series Editors: **Stephen Boulter** and **Constantine Sandis**

Philosophers in Depth is a series of themed edited collections focusing on particular aspects of the thought of major figures from the history of philosophy. The volumes showcase a combination of newly commissioned and previously published work with the aim of deepening our understanding of the topics covered. Each book stands alone, but taken together the series will amount to a vast collection of critical essays covering the history of philosophy, exploring issues that are central to the ideas of individual philosophers. This project was launched with the financial support of the Institute for Historical and Cultural Research at Oxford Brookes University, for which we are very grateful.

Titles include:

Philip Goff (*editor*)
SPINOZA ON MONISM

Leonard Kahn (*editor*)
MILL ON JUSTICE

Arto Laitinen and Constantine Sandis (*editors*)
HEGEL ON ACTION

Katherine Morris (*editor*)
SARTRE ON THE BODY

Charles R. Pigden (*editor*)
HUME ON MOTIVATION AND VIRTUE

Sabine Roeser
REID ON ETHICS

Daniel Whiting (*editor*)
THE LATER WITTGENSTEIN ON LANGUAGE

Forthcoming titles:

Alison Denham (*editor*)
PLATO ON ART

Pierre Destree (*editor*)
ARISTOTLE ON AESTHETICS

Henrik Rydenfelt and Sami Pihlström (*editors*)
JAMES ON RELIGION

Philosophers in Depth
Series Standing Order ISBN 978–0–230–55411–5 Hardback
978–0–230–55412–2 Paperback
(*outside North America only*)

You can receive future titles in this series as they are published by placing a standing order. Please contact your bookseller or, in case of difficulty, write to us at the address below with your name and address, the title of the series and one of the ISBNs quoted above.

Customer Services Department, Macmillan Distribution Ltd, Houndmills, Basingstoke, Hampshire RG21 6XS, England

Spinoza on Monism

Edited by

Philip Goff
University of Liverpool

For William,

A bit of light reading

Philip
xxx

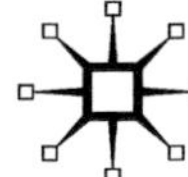

First published 2012 by
PALGRAVE MACMILLAN

Palgrave Macmillan in the UK is an imprint of Macmillan Publishers Limited, registered in England, company number 785998, of Houndmills, Basingstoke, Hampshire RG21 6XS.

Palgrave Macmillan in the US is a division of St Martin's Press LLC, 175 Fifth Avenue, New York, NY 10010.

Palgrave Macmillan is the global academic imprint of the above companies and has companies and representatives throughout the world.

Palgrave® and Macmillan® are registered trademarks in the United States, the United Kingdom, Europe and other countries.

ISBN: 978–0–230–27948–3

This book is printed on paper suitable for recycling and made from fully managed and sustained forest sources. Logging, pulping and manufacturing processes are expected to conform to the environmental regulations of the country of origin.

A catalogue record for this book is available from the British Library.

A catalog record for this book is available from the Library of Congress.

10 9 8 7 6 5 4 3 2 1
21 20 19 18 17 16 15 14 13 12

Printed and bound in Great Britain by
CPI Antony Rowe, Chippenham and Eastbourne

Contents

Acknowledgements

I would like to thank *The Philosophical Review* for kindly allowing us to reprint 'Monism: The Priority of the Whole', and *History of Philosophy Quarterly* for kindly allowing us to reprint 'Spinoza's Demonstration of Monism: A New Line of Defense'.

I am very grateful to Constantine Sandis and Stephen Boulder, the editors of this series, for inviting me to put together this volume, and for their tireless help along the way.

I can't believe how great the chapters turned out, so I would like to thank all the contributors. I am especially grateful to Terry Horgan and Matjaž Potrč who, from the start, were enthusiastic about the project and helped shape it, and to Ghislain Guigon, who provided some much needed assistance at the end.

Contributors

Donnchadh O'Conaill teaches at Durham University. His research interests include phenomenology, the problems of consciousness and subjectivity, metaphysics, the philosophy of perception and the philosophy of action.

Philip Goff is Lecturer in Philosophy at the University of Liverpool. He is currently working on a monograph arguing against physicalism and is passionate about putting consciousness (back) at the heart of metaphysics. His recent publications include "Ghosts and sparse properties: Why the physicalist has more to fear from ghosts than zombies" in *Philosophy and Phenomenological Research*, "A posteriori physicalists get our phenomenal concepts wrong" in *Australasian Journal of Philosophy* and "Does Mary know I mean plus rather than quus? A new hard problem" in *Philosophical Studies*.

Ghislain Guigon is a maître assistant at the Philosophy Department of the University of Geneva. He obtained his doctorate in Philosophy in 2009 from the University of Geneva. His main research interests include metaphysics, early modern philosophy, philosophy of religion and philosophical logic. His publications include 'Bringing About and Conjunction: A Reply to Bigelow on Omnificence' in *Analysis* 69.3 (2009), 'Meinong on Magnitudes and Measurement' in *Meinong Studies* vol. 1, pp. 255–296 (2005).

Richard Healey is Professor of Philosophy at the University of Arizona since 1991. Born in England, he has taught in the USA since 1980. His research centres on the conceptual foundations and philosophical implications of physics. His second book, *Gauging What's Real*, won the 2008 Lakatos Award. He is currently developing a pragmatist interpretation of quantum theory as part of a wider project to explore the relations between science and metaphysics from a broadly pragmatist perspective.

John Heil is Professor of Philosophy at Washington University in St Louis and a honorary research associate at Monash University. He has published many papers on philosophy of mind and metaphysics. His publications include *Philosophy of Mind: A Contemporary Introduction* 2nd ed. (2004), *From an Ontological Point of View* (2003).

Terry Horgan is a philosopher at the University of Arizona. He writes articles in metaphysics, epistemology, mind and metaethics. His co-authored books include *Austere Realism: Contextual Semantics Meets Miminal Ontology* (with M. Potrc, 2007), *Connectionism and the Philosophy of Psychology* (with J. Tienson, 1996).

Mark Kulstad is Professor of Philosophy at Rice University. He is the author of *Leibniz on Apperception, Consciousness, and Reflection* (1991), co-editor (with J.A. Cover) of *Central Themes in Early Modern Philosophy* (1990) and author of numerous articles on Leibniz – often in relation to Spinoza – and other early modern philosophers. He was elected twice as President of Leibniz Society of North America.

Mogens Lærke is Senior Lecturer at the University of Aberdeen and, Marie Curie Research Fellow at the Ecole Normale Supérieure de Lyon (CERPHI UMR 5037) for the period 2011–13. He obtained his doctorate from the University of Paris IV Sorbonne and is a former Harper Fellow at the University of Chicago. He is the author of *Leibniz lecteur de Spinoza. La genèse d'une opposition complexe* (2008), the editor of *The Use of Censorship in the Enlightenment* (2009), co-editor (with M. Kulstad and D. Snyder) of *The Philosophy of the Young Leibniz* (2009) and the author of numerous articles on early modern philosophy.

E. J. Lowe is Professor of Philosophy at Durham University, UK, specializing in metaphysics, the philosophy of mind and action, the philosophy of logic and language, and the history of early modern philosophy. His books include *Subjects of Experience* (1995), *The Possibility of Metaphysics* (1998), *The Four-Category Ontology* (2006), *Personal Agency* (2008) and *More Kinds of Being* (2009).

Yitzhak Y. Melamed is Associate Professor in the Philosophy Department at Johns Hopkins University. He is the author of *Spinoza's Metaphysics of Substance and Thought* (forthcoming), co-editor of *Spinoza's Theological Political Treatise: Critical Guide* (2010), *Spinoza and German Idealism* (forthcoming) and *Eternity* (forthcoming).

Steve Nadler is the William H. Hay II Professor of Philosophy at the University of Wisconsin-Madison. His recent books are *The Best of All Possible Worlds: A Story of Philosophers, God, and Evil* (2009) and *A Book Forged in Hell: Spinoza's Scandalous Treatise and the Birth of the Secular Age* (2011).

Rebecca Newberger Goldstein is a philosopher and novelist. She is the author of nine books of fiction and non-fiction, including *Betraying Spinoza: The Renegade Jew Who Gave Us Modernity* (2009).

Matjaž Potrč is Professor of Philosophy at Ljubljana University, Slovenia. His interests include phenomenology and cognitive science, the common sources of analytic and continental traditions, moral philosophy. Publications include Abundant Truth in Austere World (with T. Horgan), in P. Greenough and M.P. Lynch (eds.) *Truth and Realism,* (2006); *Austere Realism* (with T. Horgan, 2008); *Challenging Moral Particularism* (ed. with M. Lance and V. Strahovnik, 2008); The World of Qualia, in E. Wright (ed.) *The Case for Qualia* (2008).

Jonathan Schaffer earned his doctorate in Philosophy at Rutgers University in 1999, and returned to Rutgers as a Professor in 2010. In the intervening years he has held positions at the University of Houston, the University of Massachusetts-Amherst and the Australian National University. His research has focused primarily on metaphysics and epistemology, with forays into language and science. His interest in monism traces back to an undergraduate fascination with Hegel, and his current research on monism has been supported by grants from the A.M. Monius Institute and the Australian Research Council.

Tuomas E. Tahko is an Academy of Finland postdoctoral researcher at the University of Helsinki, working on metaphysics and metaphilosophy. He is the editor of *Contemporary Aristotelian Metaphysics* (2011).

Introduction

According to a familiar metaphysical view, reality ultimately consists of very small particles, such that all facts about concrete reality are dependent on the intrinsic nature of, and relationships between, those particles. Call this view 'atomism'. If you'll allow me to indulge in theological metaphor, the atomist thinks that all God has to do to sustain the universe throughout time is to determine the facts concerning these tiny particles that make up the world.

We can distinguish between more and less radical versions of atomism. According to the more radical version, call it 'existence atomism', the only things that exist are the particles. There are no tables, plants, people, stars or planets, only particles arranged in various ways. According to a less radical version of the view, call it 'priority atomism', there exist many different kinds of thing – tables, plants, people and stars – but each existing thing which is not a fundamental particle is dependent for its existence on the facts about the particles.

This book is not about atomism, but about monism, the view that reality ultimately consists of one object, generally taken to be the universe. This view is much less familiar than atomism, but is easily understood by analogy with it. Whilst for the atomist all facts about concrete reality are dependent on the facts about particles, for the monist all facts about concrete reality are dependent on facts about the universe. Whilst the atomist imagines God tending to the universe by twiddling with its atoms, the monist pictures God fiddling with the nature of the cosmos directly.

By analogy with the more and less radical forms of atomism, we can distinguish more and less radical forms of monism. Existence monists think that the only thing that exists is the universe: there are no tables, planets or people. They need not, and generally do not, hold that the universe is a characterless blob without structure. In a world where existence monism is true, the universe might instantiate mass in a polka-dotted fashion. But this is not to be taken to entail the existence of parts of that universe, e.g. massy bits of the universe arranged in a polka-dotted fashion.

Priority monists believe in things other than the universe, perhaps tables, people and plants, but hold that these things are dependent on the universe and its properties. In some world where priority monism is true, the universe instantiates mass in a polka-dotted fashion, and in virtue of this there exist massy bits of that universe arranged in a polka-dotted fashion.

Historically, Spinoza is probably the most significant proponent of monism. Spinoza inherited the ontological categories of substance, attribute, and mode from Descartes: attributes (such as thought or extension) defining the nature of substances (such as minds and material bodies), with a mode being a specific way of instantiating an attribute (a specific feeling of pain, a specific instance of sphericity), which is dependent for its existence on the substance which has it. But whilst Descartes believed in a plurality of substances, falling under two kinds – those with the attribute of thought and those with the attribute of extension – Spinoza believed in only one substance, which he called 'God or nature'. Spinoza's one substance had both the attribute of thought and the attribute of extension, as well as an infinite number of other attributes unknown to human beings. Ordinary objects, such as tables, plants, and planets, were not substances in their own right, but modes of 'God or nature,' dependent on the one substance for their existence.

Monism was largely ignored, or even treated with contempt, in 20th century analytic philosophy. But in the 21st century, there has been a growing interest in the view, mainly due to its exposition and defense in the work of Jonathan Schaffer, a defender of priority monism, and in the co-written work of Terry Horgan and Matjaž Potrč, defenders of existence monism. This volume, for the first time in print, brings together these three thinkers to debate the relative theoretical attractiveness of their views.

The first half of the book focuses on monism in contemporary metaphysics, with particular focus on the work of Schaffer and Horgan/Potrč. The second half explores the form of monism advocated by Spinoza, providing fresh interpretation of Spinoza's thesis that there is only one substance, and his argument for it. This choice of ordering – from present to past – may seem strange. But my ultimate interest is in neither the present nor the past, but in the future. By beginning with a critical discussion of monism as it exists today, and against this background re-examining monism as it was understood and defended by Spinoza, I hope some light will be shed on what place, if any, monism will occupy in metaphysics going forward.

Jonathan Schaffer's 'Monism: the priority of the whole', which opens the volume, is the classic contemporary statement and defense of monism. A rigorous presentation of priority monism is accompanied by powerful empirical and modal arguments in its favor. The empirical argument for priority monism goes as follows. We have good empirical grounds for thinking that the world is an entangled system. If the world is an entangled system, then facts about the universe as a whole do not supervene on facts about the intrinsic nature of its parts together with spatiotemporal relations between parts; atomism cannot provide us with a supervenience base for the whole of reality. By taking the whole as a fundamental unit, however, monism can provide us with an adequate supervenience base. Priority monism looks like the best way to make metaphysical sense of contemporary science.

The modal argument for priority monism starts from the metaphysical possibility of 'atomless gunk,' matter such that every part of it has proper parts, so that there are no ultimate parts to form an atomistic base. If the gunky world is one where parts are prior to wholes, there will be no ultimate base from which being is derived: parts will be dependent on smaller parts, which will be dependent on smaller parts, and so on ad infinitum. However, if the gunky world is one where wholes are prior to parts, the largest whole will form the ultimate ground of reality. On the assumption that there must be a fundamental ground for everything that exists, gunky worlds must be worlds in which priority monism is true. On the assumption that metaphysical theses are either necessarily true or necessarily false, the fact that priority monism is true at some world entails that it is true at every world.

Horgan and Potrč accept, at least for the sake of discussion, that Schaffer's empirical and modal arguments for monism are sound, but take them to count equally in favor of existence monism and priority monism. From this starting point, most of their chapter is taken up with an extensive argument for the thesis that existence monism is to be preferred to priority monism. The crucial starting point is an argument for the impossibility of metaphysical vagueness. It is reasonably uncontroversial that the ordinary objects common sense commits to – things like chairs, planets, people, and animals – are vague. Therefore, if the world cannot contain vagueness, it cannot contain such ordinary objects.

Horgan and Potrč provide a way of accounting for the truth of the sentences which quantify over such ordinary objects, in terms of an indirect correspondence between such sentences and the world, and hope that this pays their dues to common sense. But once we have accounted for such common-sense truths, there seems little theoretical role to be played by parts of the cosmos, especially if those parts are not to be identified with ordinary objects (because ordinary objects, being vague, cannot exist). If one thought that the heterogeneity of the world was grounded in the properties of the parts, then this might provide a role for the parts to play. But of course both priority monist and existence monist ground the heterogeneity of the world in the nature of the world itself. If there is no theoretical role for the parts of the cosmos to play, then we may as well not invest in them. Existence monism is to be preferred on grounds of economy.

In the next chapter Schaffer responds directly to this attack. He argues that, even if we accept many of the claims of Horgan and Potrč, there is still an important theoretical role for the parts of the cosmos to play: the parts of the cosmos provide the many candidate extensions of terms required by iterated supervaluationism. Schaffer also casts doubt on the supposed theoretical simplicity of existence monism, on two counts. Firstly, he believes that the view defended by Horgan and Potrč relies on an obscure and complicated semantics, which counterbalances any ontological saving. Secondly, Schaffer argues for an unorthodox understanding of Occam's razor, according to which derivative entities come at no ontological cost. Both priority monism and existence monism agree on the number of fundamental entities, i.e. one, and so there is no advantage of economy – according to this unorthodox view of economy – in going for the latter rather than the former.

The next three papers are critical discussions of the priority monism of Schaffer, or the existence monism of Horgan and Potrč, or both. E.J. Lowe launches a monumental attack on both forms of monism, from a variety of angles. My own paper focuses specifically on Horgan and Potrč, arguing that their view cannot make sense of common-sense truths concerning distinct subjects of experience. Donnchadh O'Conaill and Tuomas Tahko attack Schaffer's attempt to support monism with common sense, arguing on semantic and ontological grounds that the world must contain certain metaphysically distinguished portions.

In the next chapter, Richard Healey critically discusses two versions of the empirical argument for monism in great detail, ultimately rejecting both of them. Support for monism grounded in quantum field theory, the kind of argument favoured by Schaffer, is to be rejected on the grounds that quantum field theories 'do not themselves purport to represent or describe the world'. Healey then goes on to show why this feature of quantum field theory is problematic to Horgan and Potrč's arguments for existence monism.

In the final chapter of the metaphysics papers, John Heil discusses monism and the modal and empirical considerations thought to favor it against the backdrop of a substance/attribute ontology. Whilst Schaffer offers limited defense of the thesis that there must be a fundamental ground of being, Heil offers a more sustained defense of this, in part by drawing out the metaphysical weirdness of actual infinities.

Ghislain Guigon's chapter is the perfect bridge from the metaphysics essays to the historical essays. He offers an interpretation of Spinoza, but frames his interpretation in terms of the categories – 'existence monism' and 'priority monism' – which contemporary metaphysicians use to discuss monism. Guigon disputes Schaffer's categorization of Spinoza as a priority monist, at least if we understand 'priority monism' as the view that (i) every concrete thing distinct from the cosmos or Nature is a proper part of it and (ii) the whole is prior to each of its proper parts. The claim is not that Spinoza was an existence monist – Spinoza believed not only in the existence of the cosmos, but also in its modes – but that Spinoza took the cosmos to be a *mereologically simple entity*: the modes are dependent on the cosmos, but are not *parts* of the cosmos. Although Spinoza does sometimes talk of the whole cosmos as if it had parts, this talk is to be given a fictionalist analysis: useful for certain purposes but not literally true. It is commonly believed that Spinoza was not always consistent in what he said about the priority of parts and wholes. Guigon's paper tries to give, perhaps for the first time, a coherent interpretation of Spinoza's discourse on composition and priority.

Despite denying that Spinoza is a priority monist, Guigon maintains the orthodox view that Spinoza is an existence pluralist of some kind, believing in a plurality of modes as well as a single substance. However, this interpretation cannot be taken for granted. It was disputed for example by Hegel, who read Spinoza as believing that the appearance of plurality in the world is illusory. The next two chapters, by Yitzhak Melamed and Steve Nadler are resolutely in opposition to this Hegelian interpretation. They admit from the outset, however, that the orthodox interpretation is not without problems.

Following a rich philosophical tradition, Spinoza takes there to be a relationship of asymmetric dependence between a substance and its modes: the modes depend for their existence on the substance to which they belong, but not the other way round. This leads to the following difficulty: if the one substance does not need its modes in order to exist, why do they exist at all? Spinoza demands that everything that exists has an explanation of its existence. So what explains the existence of the modes? Of course, for those who follow the Hegelian interpretation of Spinoza, there is a very neat solution to this difficulty: there are no modes, therefore, no need to explain their existence.

Melamed presents a number of arguments against the Hegelian interpretation, and goes on to explain the existence of the modes in terms of the essentially active nature of the one substance. This still leaves us with a difficulty, however. How does the unified indivisibility of the one substance give rise to the divided diversity of the empirical world?

Nadler's piece picks up where Melamed's left off, taking up the question of how an infinite source of being gives rise to a finite series of things. Nadler makes use of the Spinozistic distinction between two kinds of infinite modes of God, immediate infinite modes and mediate infinite modes, distinguished – as the name implies – by their degree of metaphysical distance from God. He goes on to defend a compelling interpretation according to which the immediate infinite mode of extension entails the existence of an infinite series of essences of finite bodies, whilst the mediate infinite mode of extension entails the existence of an infinite series of finite actually existing bodies. In this way Nadler attempts to bridge the gap between the infinite source of being and finite creation.

Whilst Nadler and Melamed are keen to defend the orthodox view that Spinoza is a substance monist, Mogens Laerke is keen to deny it. This is not because Spinoza in his view believed in a plurality of substances. The claim is rather that Spinoza took oneness to be a merely relative or negative idea, and hence not a property which can be ascribed to the essential nature of God. The relative idea of number has application only when there can be several of a given thing, and therefore when it comes to God the idea of number fails to have application.

In the next chapter Mark Kulstad addresses difficulties with how to interpret Spinoza's argument for substance monism, i.e. his demonstration that there is no substance other than God, who is a substance with infinite attributes. After giving an initial reconstruction of the argument, Kulstad raises various problems that he then tries to resolve. For instance, Spinoza's proof of the existence of God is premised on the fact that God is a substance, which contrasts it for example with Anselm's proof which is premised on a more specific feature of God, namely God's property of being that than which nothing greater can be conceived. Because of this, if Spinoza's argument for God's existence is successful, it seems that it would prove the existence not only of the substance with all attributes, but of, say, the substance with only the attribute of thought, for such a thing would share with God the property of being a substance.

But in that case there would be two substances rather than one, which is of course inconsistent with Spinoza's commitment to substance monism (and inconsistent with the premise of his demonstration of monism that no two substances can share an attribute, for God would share with this lesser substance the property of extension). Kulstad's solution to this difficulty involves the claim that Spinoza intended to demonstrate not that there is no substance numerically distinct from God, but that there is no substance which is 'external' to God, i.e. no substance which is neither identical to, nor a proper part of, God.

The volume finishes with Goldstein's essay, which is a passionate and lively celebration of Spinoza's all-encompassing vision in which reality is reduced to logic.

The thesis that there is only one thing, or only one fundamental thing, is unfamiliar, and consequently strikes many as odd. A little familiarity, which I hope is provided by these essays, reveals it to be a view which needs to be taken very seriously indeed. It might even turn out to be true.

Part I

Monism in Contemporary Metaphysics

1

Monism: The Priority of the Whole

Jonathan Schaffer

> Listening not to me but to the Logos it is wise to agree that all things are one.
>
> – Heraclitus

Consider a circle and a pair of its semicircles. Which is prior, the whole or its parts? Are the semicircles dependent abstractions from their whole, or is the circle a derivative construction from its parts? Now in place of the circle consider the entire cosmos (the ultimate concrete whole), and in place of the pair of semicircles consider the myriad particles (the ultimate concrete parts). Which if either is ultimately prior, the one ultimate whole or its many ultimate parts?

The *monist* holds that the whole is prior to its parts, and thus views the cosmos as fundamental, with metaphysical explanation dangling downward from the One. The *pluralist* holds that the parts are prior to their whole, and thus tends to consider particles fundamental, with metaphysical explanation snaking upward from the many. Just as the materialist and idealist debate which properties are fundamental, so the monist and pluralist debate which objects are fundamental.

I will defend the monistic view. In particular I will argue that there are physical and modal considerations that favour the priority of the whole. Physically, there is good evidence that the cosmos forms an *entangled system* and good reason to treat entangled systems as irreducible wholes. Modally, mereology allows for the possibility of *atomless gunk*, with no ultimate parts for the pluralist to invoke as the ground of being.

The debate between monists and pluralists has long occupied philosophical centre stage, with William James (1975, 64) considering it 'the most central of all philosophic problems, central because so pregnant.' The monistic side can claim an intellectual pedigree tracing from Parmenides, Plato, and Plotinus to Spinoza, Hegel, and Bradley. During the nineteenth century, the monistic side had achieved a position of dominance.[1]

Yet today, monism is routinely dismissed as obviously false or merely meaningless. These attitudes are rooted in the philosophical revolts of the early twentieth century. During the early analytic revolt against the neo-Hegelians, Russell and Moore dismissed monism as contrary to common sense.[2] During the positivistic revolt against metaphysics generally, Carnap and Ayer ridiculed the whole debate as mystical nonsense.[3] So the fashions turn.

I will claim that monism was never refuted but only misinterpreted. Monism is now usually interpreted as the view that exactly one thing exists (van Inwagen 2002, 25; Hoffman and Rosenkrantz 1997, 77). On such a view there are no particles, pebbles, planets, or any other parts to the world. There is only the One. Perhaps monism would deserve to be dismissed as obviously false, given this interpretation. *But how uncharitable*!

The core tenet of historical monism is not that the whole has no parts, but rather that the whole is *prior* to its parts. As Proclus (1987, 79) says: 'The monad is everywhere prior to the plurality.... In the case of bodies, the whole that precedes the parts is the whole that embraces all separate beings in the cosmos.' Such a doctrine presupposes that there are parts, for the whole to be prior to them. The historical debate is not a debate over which objects exist, but rather a debate over which objects are fundamental. I will defend the monistic view, so interpreted: the world has parts, but the parts are dependent fragments of an integrated whole.

The plan: In §1 I will clarify the debate as a debate over which objects are fundamental. In §2 I will argue for the monistic view that the cosmos is fundamental, on the basis of considerations from physics and mereology. I will conclude with a brief appendix on historical matters.

1.1 The question of fundamental mereology

The debate between monists and pluralists – as I will reconstruct it – concerns which objects are fundamental. In particular it concerns the connection between the mereological order of whole and part and the metaphysical order of prior and posterior. Monism and pluralism will emerge as exclusive and exhaustive views of what is fundamental.

1.1.1 Whole and part: mereological structure

There is structure to a cat. For instance, the nose is part of the head but not part of the paws. One who noted the existence of the cat, and its nose, head, and paws, but missed the parthood relations between them, would have missed an aspect of the cat. As with the cat, so with the world. One who listed what things exist, but missed the parthood relations between them, would have missed an aspect of the world. Or so I will assume.

In particular I will assume that there is a world and that it has proper parts. More precisely, I assume that there is a maximal actual concrete object – *the cosmos* – of which all actual concrete objects are parts. I should stress that I am only concerned with actual concrete objects. *Possibilia, abstracta,* and actual *concreta* in categories other than *object* are not my concern (deities and spirits, if such there be, are not my concern either). When I speak of the world – and defend the monistic thesis that the whole is prior to its parts – I am speaking of the material cosmos and its planets, pebbles, particles, and other proper parts.

The assumption that there is a world with proper parts may seem modest and plausible, but it is certainly controversial, in at least two respects. First, it is controversial to assume that there are parthood relations at all. The *nihilist* holds that there are no actual – and perhaps even no possible – instances of the proper parthood relation.[4] Second, it is controversial to assume that there is a world. For instance, the *organicist* holds that there are only particles and organisms, and presumably the actual cosmos is neither.[5]

These two points of controversy are independent. One might deny that there are instances of the proper parthood relation but accept the existence of the world. One would then treat the cosmos as an extended simple.[6] Or one might accept that there are instances of the proper part-hood relation but deny that there is a world. The organicist holds this view. If the world is an extended simple, then the monist has won from the start. If there is no world, then the pluralist has won from the start. A substantive debate as to whether the whole or its parts is prior can arise only if the whole and its parts both exist.

Since I will be defending the monistic view, it may be worth saying more in defense of the assumption that there is a world. The existence of the cosmos has both intuitive and empirical support. Intuitively, natural language provides a singular term for this entity ('the cosmos'). The cosmos is hardly the sort of strange fusion undreamt of by common sense. Empirically, the cosmos is the object of empirical study. Indeed it is the primary subject matter of physical cosmology.[7]

The existence of the cosmos can claim further support from mereology. Classical mereology – with its axiom of unrestricted composition – guarantees the existence of the cosmos as the fusion of all actual concrete objects. But any account of when composition occurs that preserves common sense and fits science should recognize the cosmos. It is only the most radical views of composition – views that do not even recognize tables and chairs – that do not recognize the cosmos. Suffice it to say that if the strongest objection to monism is that the world does not exist, then I would think that it is the monist who can claim the mantle of common sense and science.

I should note one further controversial assumption I will be making, namely that *composition is not identity*.[8] In particular, I assume that the cosmos is not identical to the plurality of its planets, pebbles, or particles, or to any other plurality of its many proper parts. If the one literally *is* the many, then monism and pluralism would no longer be opposing views – indeed both 'sides' would turn out to be right.

Putting this together, I am assuming that there is a cosmos, that it has proper parts, and that it is not identical to any plurality of its many proper parts. I consider these assumptions very plausible but cannot defend them any further here. My purpose is just to articulate my assumptions, acknowledge where they may be controversial, and explain their role in the debate.

1.1.2 Prior and posterior: metaphysical structure

The mereological structure of whole and part is not the only structure to the world. There is also the metaphysical structure of prior and posterior, reflecting what depends on what, and revealing what are the fundamental independent entities that serve as the ground of being.

Consider Socrates. Given that he exists, the proposition <Socrates exists> must be true. And conversely, given that the proposition <Socrates exists> is true, there must be Socrates. Yet clearly there is an asymmetry. The proposition is true *because* the man exists and not vice versa. Truth depends on being (Aristotle 1984a, 22; Armstrong 1997, 3). Further, given that Socrates exists, his singleton {Socrates} must exist. And conversely, given that {Socrates} exists, there must be Socrates. Yet – given the iterative conception, on which sets are founded on their members – there is an asymmetry. {Socrates} exists *in virtue of* Socrates and not vice versa. Sets depend on their members (Fine 1994, 4–5). One who noted the existence of Socrates, the truth of <Socrates exists>, and the existence of {Socrates}, but missed the asymmetric dependence relations among them, would have missed an aspect of the world. Or so I will assume.

In particular I will assume that there is a relation of metaphysical priority. Moreover, I assume that this relation can hold between entities of arbitrary category – or at least, I assume that this relation can hold between actual concrete objects, which are my current concern. So I assume that it makes sense to inquire as to the dependence ordering (if any) among Socrates' snub nose, his body, and the cosmos that embodies him.

The assumption that there are priority relations between actual concrete objects is weighty and controversial in at least two respects. First, it is controversial to allow that there is such a relation as priority at all. The *metaphysical skeptic* may well refuse to acknowledge the notion.[9] I think the skeptic has missed part of the structure of the world. Anyone who wants to debate the dependence of truth on being, sets on members, or minds on matter, must understand some notion of priority. Anyone who is interested in what is fundamental – where to be fundamental is to be ultimately prior – must understand some notion of priority. Perhaps the notion of priority is amenable to further analysis (see Fine 2001; Lowe 2005; Schaffer 2009). I am doubtful but will remain neutral on that question here. In any case I think that it would be a mistake to insist that this useful and natural notion is illegitimate unless one can display its analysis. By that standard virtually no philosophical notion would count as legitimate.

Second, it may be controversial to allow for priority relations between actual concrete objects. One might allow that there are priority relations between, say, *properties* but refuse to extend the notion of priority further.[10] (Obviously this second point of controversy only arises if the first is surmounted.) That said, the examples of priority mentioned above span various categories. Socrates is an actual concrete object, {Socrates} is an abstract object, and the truth of <Socrates exists> is a fact. So it seems a gratuitous restriction to disallow the prospect of priority relations holding between actual concrete objects. That said, if there are no priority relations between actual concrete objects – for either of the two reasons just considered – then the entire debate between monists and pluralists should be rejected out of hand.

I will further assume that the priority relations among actual concrete objects form a well-founded partial ordering. Partial ordering structure may be imposed by treating priority as irreflexive, asymmetric, and transitive. Well-foundedness is imposed by requiring that all priority chains terminate. This assumption provides the kind of hierarchical structure against which the question of what is fundamental makes sense. It is a corollary of the well-foundedness condition that there are basic actual concrete objects. Without a well-founded partial ordering, there would be a third option besides monism and pluralism, on which neither the one whole nor any of its proper parts are basic because no actual concrete objects are basic.

The assumption of a well-founded partial ordering may be understood as a kind of *metaphysical foundationalism*, on analogy with *epistemic foundationalism*. Just as the epistemic foundationalist thinks all warrant must originate in basic warrant and rejects limitless chains of warrant and circular warrant, so the metaphysical foundationalist thinks all being must originate in basic being and rejects limitless chains of dependence (*metaphysical infinitism*) and circular dependence (*metaphysical coherentism*).[11] There must be a ground of being. If one thing exists only *in virtue of* another, then there must be something from which the reality of the derivative entities ultimately derives.[12]

Putting this together, I am assuming that there are priority relations between actual concrete objects, in the structure of a well-founded partial ordering. I consider these assumptions weighty though still plausible but cannot defend them any further here. Once again my purpose is to articulate my assumptions, acknowledge where they may be controversial, and explain their role in the debate.

1.1.3 Fundamental mereology: the tiling constraint

So far I have discussed the mereological and metaphysical structures of the world. To characterize the debate between monists and pluralists, it remains to connect these structures. For the debate concerns the correlation between the mereological order of whole and part, and the metaphysical order of prior and posterior. Specifically it concerns what is fundamental (ultimately prior) among actual concrete objects. I will now introduce some formalism, use it to state a constraint on what is fundamental, and then (§1.4) characterize the monistic and pluralistic views.

So, first the formalism. I will use 'P' to express the relation of part-hood, 'D' to express the relation of dependence, and '*u*' as a dedicated constant for the actual material cosmos:

$Pxy = x$ is a part of y

$Dxy = x$ depends on y

$u =$ the cosmos

As I am concerned only with actual concrete objects, I will use 'C' to express this status, which may be defined in terms of being a part of the cosmos:

$$\mathrm{Cx} =_{\mathrm{df}} \mathrm{Pxu}$$

Finally I will use 'B' to express the crucial status of being a basic actual concrete object, which may be defined as being concrete and not depending on anything concrete:

$$\mathrm{Bx} =_{\mathrm{df}} \mathrm{Cx} \,\&\, \sim (\exists \mathrm{y})\, (\mathrm{Cy} \,\&\, \mathrm{Dxy})$$

The central question under discussion is the *question of fundamental mereology,* which is the question of what are the basic actual concrete objects. This is the question of what is the ground of the mereological hierarchy of whole and part. In terms of the formalism, this is the question of which entities x are such that Bx.

Before canvassing possible answers to this question, it will prove useful to introduce a constraint on possible answers. This constraint is *the tiling constraint,* which is that the basic actual concrete objects collectively cover the cosmos without overlapping.[13] In a slogan: no gaps, no overlaps. In terms of the formalism, the requirement that the basics cover the cosmos can be expressed as the requirement that the fusion of all the basic entities is the whole cosmos. Using 'Sum: $x(\varphi\, x)$' to denote the fusion of all entities meeting description φ, this may be expressed as:

Covering: Sum: $\mathrm{x(Bx) = u}$

The requirement that the basics do not overlap is the requirement that no two basic entities have a common part:

No Overlap: $(\forall x)(\forall y)\ ((Bx\ \&\ By\ \&\ x \neq y) \supset \sim (\exists z)\ (Pzx\ \&\ Pzy))$

The reason for requiring *Covering* is *the argument from completeness.* The first premise of the argument is that the basic entities must be complete, in the sense of providing *a blueprint for reality.* More precisely, a plurality of entities is complete if and only if duplicating all these entities, while preserving their fundamental relations, metaphysically suffices to duplicate the cosmos and its contents.[14]

The second premise of the argument from completeness is that any plurality of entities that did not cover the cosmos would be incomplete. They would fail to provide a blueprint with respect to the portion left uncovered. For instance, if the plurality of basics did not cover this cabinet, then they would fail to specify the intrinsic properties associated with this cabinet and its various contents. That portion of reality would be left ungrounded. Duplicating these basics would not metaphysically suffice to duplicate the cosmos and those of its contents associated with this cabinet.

From these premises, it follows that the basic actual concrete objects must collectively cover the cosmos. This provides a useful constraint on answers to the question of fundamental mereology. For instance, Socrates' nose will not serve as the one and only basic object. Indeed it is a corollary of the covering condition that, *if* there is exactly one basic object, *then* it must be the cosmos itself. Nothing less will satisfy *Covering* (A second corollary – which was also a corollary of well-foundedness – is that there are basic objects. Nothing covers nothing.)

The reason for requiring *No Overlap* is *the argument from recombinability.* It begins from the premise that the fundamental actual concrete objects should *be freely recombinable,* serving as independent units of being (building blocks, as it were). Thus each should be, in Hume's words, 'entirely loose and separate' (Hume 2000, 58). Somewhat more precisely, a plurality of entities is freely recombinable if and only if any combination of ways that each entity can be individually is a way that the plurality can be collectively. If entities are metaphysically independent, then they should be modally unconstrained in combination.

The second premise of the argument from recombinability is that overlapping entities are *modally constrained.* Consider two overlapping homogeneously red circles, each of which could individually be homogeneously green. The one circle cannot retain its parts and its redness, while the other circle retains its parts but turns homogeneously green. Otherwise the overlapping part would have to be both red and green. In general, it is not possible to vary the intrinsic properties of the common part with respect to the one overlapping thing, without varying the intrinsic properties or composition of the other.

From these premises, it follows that no basic entities can overlap. Overlap would compromise the modal freedom of the basics. There are *harmony constraints* between overlapping things, concerning their common parts.

The *No Overlap* condition will turn out to be strictly stronger than anything I will need. I will in fact only make use of a weaker condition, which is that no basics are related as whole to part:

No Parthood: $(\forall x)(\forall y)\ ((Bx\ \&\ By\ \&\ x \neq y) \supset \sim Pxy)$

This is a weaker condition than *No Overlap,* insofar as (i) if there are basics related as whole-to-part, then there is overlap among these basics at that part, but (ii) if there is overlap among the basics, there need not be relations of whole-to-part (for instance, conjoined twins overlap but are not related as whole-to-part).

The *No Parthood* condition can be independently supported by a second argument, which is *the argument from economy.* The first premise of the argument is that the basic objects should not be multiplied without necessity. More precisely, the basic objects should not be merely complete, they should be *minimally complete,* in having no proper subplurality that is complete.

The second premise of the argument from economy is that entities related as whole-to-part are redundant. This is because every whole has the *relational intrinsic* property of (i) having so-many parts, (ii) having parts with such-and-such intrinsic properties, and (iii) having parts that are thus-and-so related. For instance, Socrates has the intrinsic property of having a snub nose – any duplicate of Socrates must have a snub nose.[15] Likewise any duplicate of the cosmos must duplicate all of its parts and their intrinsic properties and their relations. Fix the whole, and all its parts are fixed.[16]

From these premises, it follows that the basic objects should not include any entities related as whole-to-part. After all, any complete plurality of fundamentals that includes a whole and one of its proper parts will have a complete subplurality without this proper part, and so fail to be minimal. (Indeed, since duplicating the whole entails duplication of all of its parts, adding the part contributes nothing new to the characterization of reality already provided by the whole.) In general, once a given whole is included among the basics, any mention of its proper parts becomes redundant.[17]

It is a corollary of both the *No Overlap* and the *No Parthood* conditions that *if* there is more than one basic object, *then* the cosmos cannot be basic. For every actual concrete object is part of, and thus overlaps, the cosmos.

Overall, the tiling constraint can be understood as a *partitioning constraint.* Consider all the ways that one may slice a pie. One might leave the whole uncut, or slice it in half, or cut it into quarters, and so forth. One cannot leave any part out. However one cuts, one divides the whole. And one cannot serve any part twice. Each part belongs to one and only one slice. In place of the pie, consider the cosmos. Different answers to the question of fundamental mereology can be seen – in light of the tiling constraint – as different ways of carving up the cosmos into basic pieces. The question of fundamental mereology can be seen as presupposing that there is a metaphysically privileged way to carve up the cosmos, provided by the notion of a basic piece.

1.1.4 Monism and pluralism

Different answers to the question of fundamental mereology – in light of the tiling constraint – correspond to different ways of carving up the cosmos. One way to carve up the cosmos is to leave the whole uncut. On this view there is one and only one basic actual concrete object, and it is the whole world. This is *Monism*:[18]

$$\text{Monism} =_{df} (\exists! x)\, Bx \;\&\; Bu$$

Monism can thus be thought of as the conjunction of the numerical thesis that there is exactly one basic object with the holistic thesis that the cosmos is basic. Given the tiling constraint, each of these conjuncts entails the other. If there is exactly one basic actual concrete object, it must be the whole cosmos since nothing less can cover all of reality. And if the cosmos is basic, there can be no other basic actual concrete object since anything other would be a part of the cosmos. So, given the tiling constraint, the following theses are equivalent to *Monism*:

$$(\exists! x)\, Bx$$

$$Bu$$

Moreover, given the foundationalist assumption of a well-founded partial dependence ordering (§1.2), *Monism* is equivalent to the thesis that every proper part of the cosmos depends on the cosmos. Suppose that *Monism* holds. Given well-foundedness, every actual concrete object must be either basic or dependent on some basic object. By the definition of *Monism*, the cosmos is the only such basis. So every proper part of the cosmos must depend on the cosmos. In the other direction, suppose that every proper part of the cosmos depends on the cosmos. By the asymmetry of dependence, the cosmos cannot then depend on any of its proper parts. By irreflexivity the cosmos cannot depend on itself. So the cosmos must be basic. Moreover nothing else can be basic since by supposition everything else is dependent on the cosmos. So there can be one and only one basic actual concrete object, namely the cosmos. Thus, given metaphysical foundationalism, the following thesis is equivalent to *Monism:*

$$(\forall x)\, ((Pxu \;\&\; x \neq u) \supset Dxu)$$

The second way to carve up the cosmos is to make some cuts. On his view, there are many basic actual concrete objects, all of which are proper parts of the cosmos. This is *Pluralism:*

$$Pluralism =_{df} (\exists x)(\exists y)\ (Bx\ \&\ By\ \&\ x \neq y)\ \&\ {\sim}\ Bu$$

Pluralism can thus be thought of as the conjunction of the numerical thesis that there are at least two basic objects with the partialistic thesis that the cosmos is not basic. Given the tiling constraint, each of these conjuncts entails the other. If there are at least two basic objects, the cosmos cannot be basic, or else there would be whole-part relations among the basics. And if the cosmos is not basic, then there must be at least two basic objects, in order to cover all of reality. So given the tiling constraint, the following theses are equivalent to *Pluralism:*

$$(\exists x)(\exists y)\ (Bx\ \&\ By\ \&\ x \neq y)$$

$${\sim}\ Bu$$

Moreover, given the foundationalist assumption of a well-founded partial dependence ordering, together with the tiling constraint, *Pluralism* is equivalent to the thesis that the cosmos depends on some of its proper parts. Suppose that *Pluralism* holds. Given well-foundedness every actual concrete object must be either basic or dependent on some basic object. By the definition of pluralism proper parts of the cosmos are the only such basis. So the cosmos must depend on some of its proper parts. In the other direction, suppose that the cosmos depends on some of its proper parts. Then the cosmos cannot be basic. By well-foundedness, some of these proper parts must be basic. By the tiling constraint, it cannot be that just one of these proper parts is basic. So there must be at least two basic objects. Thus given metaphysical foundationalism plus tiling, the following thesis is equivalent to *Pluralism:*

$$(\exists x)\ (Pxu\ \&\ x \neq u\ \&\ Dux)$$

It will prove worthwhile to give special mention to a specific form of *Pluralism,* on which the basic objects are all mereological simples. This is *Atomism:*[19]

$$Atomism =_{df} (\exists x)(\exists y)\ (Bx\ \&\ By\ \&\ x \neq y)\ \&\ (\forall x)\ (Bx \supset {\sim}\ (\exists y)\ (Pyx\ \&\ x \neq y))$$

Atomism is the most fine-grained form of *Pluralism,* cutting the world all the way down to mereologically minimal slices. *Atomism* is also the most thematic form of *Pluralism* – where the monist attributes ultimate priority to

At a world that is heterogeneous all the way down, *everything* – including whatever is basic – must be heterogeneous. This shows that it is metaphysically possible for 12 to be false. Further, this scenario shows that the pluralistic strategy of accounting for heterogeneity in terms of differences between internally homogeneous parts is insufficient. As A. E. Taylor (1961, 88) points out by way of tu quoque, if the pluralist's basic units of being 'have internal variety of their own, [then they] simply repeat within themselves the problem they are supposed to solve.'

What remains is the question of how to give a consistent account of basic heterogeneous entities (which both monist and pluralist require). There are at least three consistent accounts. The first account – which I prefer – is via *distributional properties*.[37] A given whole might, for instance, have the property of being polka-dotted. There would be no question of the whole being 'different from itself' or having any other problematic status. The claim that the whole is polka-dotted is a coherent claim, which would entail heterogeneity among its derivative dots and background.

Behind every heterogeneous distributional property winds a bumpy configurational path. A colour, for instance, can be represented as a point in a three-dimensional colour configuration space (with dimensions for hue, brightness, and saturation). The colour of a two-dimensional plane can then be represented as a path in a five-dimensional configuration space, where each point on the plane is represented by <*x*, *y*> coordinates and assigned a location in colour space <*hue*, *saturation*, *brightness*>. A colour-homogeneous two-dimensional plane will trace out a path in this five-dimensional space that is flat along the three colour dimensions, while a colour-heterogeneous plane (such as a polka-dotted plane) will trace a bumpy path. Such a path in configuration space specifies a determinate distributional property.

The representation of the heterogeneous world via a configurational space is not metaphysical trickery but standard fare in physics. For instance, in quantum mechanics, the wave function of the universe is standardly represented as a field in configuration space. The field assigns a complex-valued amplitude to each point in the space. Here again there is no question of the world being 'different from itself' or having any other problematic status.[38]

For the monist, the general fact that the world is heterogeneous is due to the world's instantiating the determinable property of *being heterogeneous*. The specific way that the world is heterogeneous is due to the world's instantiating the determinate property of tracing such-and-such a curve through physical configuration space. Thus the one whole can be parturient.

A second account of heterogeneity is via *regionalized properties*. This account treats seemingly monadic properties as having an extra argument place for a region. So the world might be heterogeneous by, for instance, bearing the redness relation to here and the greenness relation to there.[39]

A third account of heterogeneity is via *regionalized instantiation*. This account, instead of regionalizing properties, regionalizes instantiation (Johnston 1987).

So the world might be heterogeneous by, for instance, instantiating-here red and instantiating-there green. Since the regionalization is incorporated in the copula, it may be expressed *adverbially*, as 'the world is-herely red and is-therely green,' or 'the world is red in a herely way, and green in a therely way.'

In summary, the heterogeneity of basic entities is everyone's problem. Fortunately for everyone, it is a problem that seems to allow many consistent solutions.

1.2.4 Atomless gunk: the asymmetry of existence

I turn now to a final argument, which is that the pluralist cannot provide a decent account of the *possibility of atomless gunk*. Gunk is matter every part of which has proper parts, so that there are no ultimate parts to form an atomistic base.

To begin with, there is good reason for thinking that gunk is metaphysically possible (see Schaffer 2003). Gunk is certainly conceivable. For instance, it is conceivable that everything is both extended and divisible. This generates a Zeno sequence of divisions without limit. Likewise Pascal's hypothesis is conceivable, on which there is an endless nested sequence of microcosms, in which every physical 'atom' of the universe houses a miniature replica universe, every 'atom' of this mini-universe houses its own mini-universe, and so on without limit. Further, if there are extended material objects that can literally touch, they can do so only at gunky junctures (Zimmerman 1996). Since such literal touching is conceivable, gunk must be conceivable. I do not think that conceivability entails metaphysical possibility, but I do think that inconceivability entails impossibility. So at the very least there is no inconceivability argument against gunk.

Further, there are gunky models of classical mereology (see Simons 1987, 41). So to the extent that the models of classical mereology represent metaphysical possibilities, it follows that gunk is metaphysically possible. Indeed, most alternative views of mereology – save the radical nihilist view on which there are no proper parthood relations at all – allow for gunk. For instance, organicism allows for turtles – or any other organisms – all the way down. Thus consider the rhyme:

Great fleas have little fleas
Upon their backs to bite 'em;
Little fleas have lesser fleas,
And so ad infinitum. (quoted in Bohm 1957, 139)

Likewise accounts of composition that require causal integration or spatiotemporal connectedness allow for gunk.

Finally – and perhaps most tellingly – gunk is scientifically serious. Thus Dehmelt (1989) posits an infinite regression of sub-electron structure, Georgi (1989, 456) suggests that effective quantum field theories might form an infinite tower that 'goes down to arbitrary short distances in a kind of infinite regression ... just a series of layers without end,' and Greene (1999, 141–42), noting that 'history surely has taught us that every time our understanding of the universe deepens, we find yet smaller microconstituents constituting a finer level of matter,' allows that even strings might be just 'one more layer in the cosmic onion.' So to the extent that scientifically serious, empirically open hypotheses ought to be accorded the status of metaphysical possibilities, there is further evidence for:

16. Atomless gunk is metaphysically possible.

Now, the monist has no trouble with the possibility of gunk. If the world is gunky, that's the way the world is. It is such that every part of it has proper parts. Likewise if the world is atomistic, that's the way the world is. It is such that every part of it has ultimate parts. Likewise if the world contains a mixture of gunk and atoms, that's the way the world is. It is such that some parts are such that every part of them has proper parts, and some parts are such that every part of them has ultimate parts. The monist can handle any possibility.

But how can the pluralist account for the possibility of gunk (or of a mixture)? There seem to be three main options. First, the pluralist might move to the idea of *endless dependence*, where things get ever more basic without limit. This idea represents the thematic extension of the atomistic motif of part prior to whole.

But endless dependence conflicts with the foundationalist requirement that there be basic objects (§1.2). On this option nothing is basic at gunky worlds. There would be no ultimate ground. Being would be infinitely deferred, never achieved. As Plotinus (1991, 97) argues: 'Atoms again (Democritus) cannot meet the need of a base. There are no atoms; all body is divisible endlessly.' The foundationalist requirement is not supposed to be a merely accidental truth of actuality. It is supposed to follow from the need for a ground of being, from which any derivative entities derive. Indeed, if metaphysical possibility concerns what is compossible with the laws of metaphysics, which govern what ground what (§2.2), then foundationalism will be necessarily true if true at all. Hence the foundationalist should endorse the following modal strengthening:

17. It is metaphysically necessary that there are basic objects.

At the very least, it seems a cost of the move to endless dependence (one not incurred by *Monism*) that it requires abandoning this classic foundationalist picture of metaphysical structure.

As a second option, the pluralist might *go disjunctive*, maintaining *Atomism* as a thesis about what is fundamental at the actual world, while upholding a different – and perhaps even monistic – view of what is fundamental at gunky and mixed worlds.[40] But this idea is at most as plausible as its presupposition that the actual world is non-gunky. As noted above, it is an empirically open question whether the actual world is gunky (Schaffer 2003, 502–6).

Moreover, disjunctivism is objectionably *disunifed*. If *Atomism* is true at the actual world, then all actual mereological composites are grounded in actual simples. But if this is how grounding works, then – given that metaphysical possibility holds fixed how grounding works – this should be a metaphysically necessary truth:

18. If *Atomism* is true, it is necessarily true.[41]

At the very least, it seems a cost of this disjunctive treatment (one not incurred by *Monism*) that it cannot give a unified treatment of gunky and atomistic scenarios.

Finally, the pluralist might reject *Atomism*, maintaining that what is basic is mereologically intermediate. But this seems objectionably *arbitrary*, especially in cases where there is no natural joint in the mereological structure. For instance, in the case of a homogeneously pink sphere of gunk, all the levels of mereological structure (save for the top) are intermediate, and all are homogeneously pink. No layer of decomposition seems privileged. Homogeneous gunk thus emerges as especially problematic for the pluralist since (i) there are no atoms for the atomist, and (ii) there are no privileged molecules for the molecularist. The only privileged level of structure is at the top.

Further the use of basic molecules is already *quasi-monistic*. Given the tiling constraint (§1.3), no proper parts of any basic molecules can themselves be basic. Hence the use of basic molecules involves treating the whole as prior to its parts, with respect to the basic molecules and their derivative parts. So it is hard to see how the molecular pluralist could have any principled objection to monism. For instance, if the objection to monism was the 'commonsense' objection that parts are prior to their wholes, then the molecular pluralist is equally open to the objection. Or if the objection to monism was from heterogeneity, then given that the basic molecules can be heterogeneous – as is needed to cover the case of heterogeneous gunk – then the molecular pluralist is equally open to the objection. Thus the pluralist seems best advised to accept *Atomism*:

19. If *Pluralism* is true, then *Atomism* is true.

Putting this together, given 18 and 19, it follows that if *Pluralism* is true, then *Atomism* is metaphysically necessary. But given 16 and 17, *Atomism* is not metaphysically necessary since there need not be any atoms. Hence *Pluralism* is false. Or at the very least, it is hard to see how the pluralist can provide an account of gunky and mixed scenarios that can rival the monistic account in unity and elegance. As McTaggart (1988, 172) – though himself a pluralist – puts the argument:

> Can we find any fixed points in all this complexity? At present, I think, we can only find one – the universe. If there were simple substances, ... they would also be fixed points, but the existence of simple substances has not been proved .... But the universe does exist, and its position among substances is unique and important .... It has thus, objectively, ... a position much more fundamental than that of most substances, if not all.

A second underlying mereological asymmetry comes to light: *the asymmetry of existence*. The asymmetry is that there must be an ultimate whole, but there need not be ultimate parts. In other words, though atomless gunk is metaphysically possible, *worldless junk* – the converse of gunk, in which everything is a proper part of something – is metaphysically impossible. Classical mereology – with its axiom of unrestricted composition – guarantees the existence of a unique fusion of all concrete objects. Thus there are gunky models of classical mereology, but no junky models. Indeed, a mereologically maximal element is the only individual that classical mereology guarantees on every model. If such models correspond to possibilities, then the only guaranteed existence is the One.

But leaving classical mereology aside, virtually no plausible accounts of when composition occurs allow for junky models. For instance, if composition requires spatiotemporal connectedness, and there is an infinite sequence of connected objects, each one a proper part of the next, then the fusion of these infinitely many objects should itself be spatiotemporally connected.

Moreover, the impossibility of junk also follows from the platitude that a possible object must exist *at a possible world*. No world – provided that worlds are understood as possible concrete cosmoi – could contain worldless junk because a world that contained junk would be an entity, not a proper part of another entity at that world. A world would top-off the junk.

In summary, if the choice is between the ultimate whole and its ultimate parts, and if the choice must be made in the same style at all metaphysically possible worlds, and if there must be a ground of being at all metaphysically possible worlds, then the only choice is the one whole. For only the one whole is guaranteed to exist. Only the monist can provide a unified story of the ground of being for every metaphysically possible world.

This concludes my discussion of arguments. I have maintained that there are physical and modal considerations that favour the monistic view. Physically, there is good evidence that the cosmos forms an *entangled system* and good reason to treat entangled systems as irreducible wholes. Modally, mereology allows for the possibility of *atomless gunk*, with no ultimate parts for the pluralist to invoke as the ground of being. I have also argued that considerations from common sense and from heterogeneity do not favour the pluralistic view. So I conclude that the monistic side has the better of the arguments, or at least the better of the four arguments here considered. *Monism* deserves our serious reconsideration.

Appendix: historical matters

In the main text I have discussed the doctrine that the cosmos is the one and only basic actual concrete object, prior to any of its proper parts, and labeled that doctrine *Monism* (§1.4). I have made only a passing attempt to justify the label. This appendix is for the reader interested in the historical question of whether the label is apt.

Call the interpretation of monism I have offered *the priority reading* and call someone who is a monist in this sense a *priority monist*. Contrast this with the widespread reading on which monism is the doctrine that the cosmos is the one-and-only actual concrete object in existence. Call this *the existence reading* and call someone who is a monist in this sense an *existence monist*. In the formalism I have been using (§1.3):

$$\text{Priority Monism} =_{df} (\exists!\, x)\, Bx \;\&\; Bu$$

$$\text{Existence Monism} =_{df} (\exists!\, x)\, Cx \;\&\; Cu$$

Priority Monism is the very same doctrine as *Monism*, while *Existence Monism* is the doctrine that there is one and only one actual concrete object.[42]

Existence Monism is a strictly stronger doctrine than *Priority Monism*, in that *Existence Monism* entails *Priority Monism*, but not vice versa. If *Existence Monism* holds, then the cosmos is the only actual concrete object. By the irreflexivity of dependence, the cosmos does not depend on itself. So it does not depend on any actual concrete object. Thus it is basic. And no other actual concrete object can be basic because on this view there is no other actual concrete object. So it would follow that the cosmos is the one and only basic object, as per *Priority Monism*. But *Priority Monism* does not entail *Existence Monism* because the priority monist can and should allow for the existence of many derivative proper parts of the cosmos.

Given the distinction between *Priority Monism* and *Existence Monism*, the question arises as to whether various historical monists are best read as priority monists, or as full-blown existence monists (or perhaps as neither). It seems to me that the priority reading should be preferred to the existence reading if the texts in question can sustain it, on grounds of interpretive clarity. After all, *Existence Monism* is a radical view, conflicting with such seeming truisms as Moore's 'Here is one hand ... and here is another'

(Moore 1993b, 166). Not for nothing has monism – when interpreted as *Existence Monism* – fallen into disgrace. *Priority Monism* does not conflict with Moorean banalities. It merely entails – sensibly enough – that Moore's hands are not *fundamental* entities (§2.1).

But textual fit is a difficult issue, for at least three reasons. First, there are many historical monists to consider, including Parmenides, Plato, Plotinus, Proclus, Spinoza, Hegel, Lotze, Royce, Bosanquet, Bradley, and Blanshard. I cannot possibly discuss each of these philosophers in any detail here. Second, each of these philosophers has his own idiosyncratic doctrines, and it is highly doubtful that there is any one precisely formulated monistic doctrine that would fit each philosopher in the tradition. Third, many of the texts in this tradition are notoriously opaque, subject to scholarly controversy, and liable to contradictory impulses.

To establish a prima facie case for the priority reading, I will proceed by tracing three main threads of the monistic tradition and arguing that each of these threads presupposes the falsity of *Existence Monism*, while being perfectly compatible with *Priority Monism*. So a first main thread in the monistic tradition is that of *the priority of whole to part*. Thus recall Proclus's dictum: 'The monad is everywhere prior to the plurality.... In the case of bodies, the whole that precedes the parts is the whole that embraces all separate beings in the cosmos' (Proclus 1987, 79). In this vein Joachim (1906, 9–10) speaks of a 'whole of parts' wherein 'the structural plan of the whole determines precisely the nature of the differences which are its parts.'[43] Notice how Proclus and Joachim both speak freely of the parts of the whole.

The claim of the priority of whole to part – which obviously fits *Priority Monism* – is just as obviously incompatible with *Existence Monism*. For *Existence Monism* denies that there are any parts to the whole. Hence it denies that there is anything for the whole to be prior to. Thus any historical monist who claims that the whole is prior to its parts is committed to the existence of the parts, as derivative entities.

A second main thread in the monistic tradition is that of *the organic unity of the whole*. This is a thread that traces back to Plato's *Timaeus*, with its vision of the cosmos as constructed by the demiurge in the pattern of 'one visible animal comprehending within itself all other animals' (Plato 1961, 1163).[44] This thread winds through Plotinus's cosmology: 'All is one universally comprehensive living being, encircling all the living beings within it,...every separate thing is an integral part of this All by belonging to the total material fabric' (Plotinus 1991, 318–19).[45] As Hegel (1975, 191–92) memorably writes,

> The limbs and organs for instance, of an organic body are not merely parts of it: it is only in their unity that they are what they are.... These limbs and organs become mere parts, only when they pass under the hands of an anatomist, whose occupation be it remembered, is not with the living

> body but with the corpse. Not that such analysis is illegitimate: we only mean that the external and mechanical relation of whole and parts is not sufficient for us, if we want to study organic life in its truth. And if this be so in organic life, it is the case to a much greater extent when we apply this relation to the mind and the formations of the spiritual world.[46]

Notice how Plato, Plotinus, and Hegel all speak of individuals existing within the body of the cosmos.

Such a notion of organic unity is incompatible with *Existence Monism*. The notion of organic unity comes from Aristotle's view of the organism as a substantial whole, whose limbs and organs are dependent on their interrelations within the whole. An organism has parts. Hence any historical monist who speaks of organic unity is committed to the existence of parts to be the limbs and organs (as it were) of the cosmic body. But the notion of organic unity is a perfect fit for *Priority Monism*. Aristotle's view of the organism is that of a unified substantial whole, prior to its parts (like a syllable, not like a heap: §2.1). As such the claim that the whole possesses organic unity is just an expression of the priority thesis that the whole is prior to its parts.

A third main thread in the monistic tradition is that of *the world as an integrated system*. Arguably the seed of this idea can be found in what Spinoza (1994, 82–83) wrote to Oldenburg: 'Concerning whole and parts, I consider things as parts of some whole insofar as the nature of the one so adapts itself to the nature of the other that so far as possible they are in harmony with one another.' And thus: 'Each body, in so far as it exists modified in a certain way, must be considered as a part of the whole universe, must agree with the whole to which it belongs, and must cohere with the remaining bodies' (Spinoza 1994, 84).[47] Royce (1900, 122) argues that any alleged plurality of real objects would be internally related 'so as not to be mutually independent,' such that these must be 'parts or aspects of One real being,' in such a way as to render us as 'only bits of the true Self' (Royce 1967, 416). And Bosanquet (1913, 37) writes, 'A world or a cosmos is a system of members, such that every member, being *ex hypothesi* distinct, nevertheless contributes to the unity of the whole.'[48] Notice how Spinoza, Royce, and Bosanquet all explicitly speak of members of the system.

The idea of the cosmos as an integrated system is incompatible with *Existence Monism*. For *Existence Monism* denies that there is anything other than the cosmos. Hence it denies that there are any things to be integrated into the cosmos. Thus any historical monist who claims that the cosmos is an integrated system is committed to the existence of the parts, as what are integrated in the whole. As Taylor summarizes:

> The world for knowledge must ... be an orderly whole or system.... Therefore it must certainly be one; it cannot be a medley of independent elements which somehow luckily happen to form a coherent collection.

> But again, because it is a system, it cannot be a mere unit; it must be the expression of a single principle in and through a multiplicity of terms or constituents. (Taylor 1961, 94–95; compare Ewing 1934, 87)

But the idea of the cosmos as an integrated system is a perfect fit for *Priority Monism*. For the idea is that the individual parts are fragments that are dependent on their integration with each other into a common whole. As Joachim – in the course of interpreting Spinoza – expresses the idea:

> A single 'extended' thing – a particular body e.g. – is finite and dependent; a fragment torn from its context, in which alone it has its being and significance. Neither in its existence nor in its nature has it any independence. It owes its *existence* to an indefinite chain of causes, each of which is itself a finite body and the effect of another finite body; it owes its *nature* to its place in the whole system of bodies which together constitute the corporeal universe. (Joachim 1901, 23; see Schaffer forthcoming)

I have so far explained why three main threads of the monistic tradition fit with *Priority Monism* but not with *Existence Monism*. I would add that many of the historical monists directly deny *Existence Monism*. For instance, Bosanquet (1911, 260) explicitly acknowledges 'subordinate individuals' and is concerned only to deny that a part can be 'in the full sense a substance' (1911, 253). Perhaps most memorably, Alexander (1950, 347) concludes the first volume of *Space, Time, and Deity* with the words: '[The parts] are not the whole reality but they are real in themselves.... The One is the system of the Many in which they are conserved not the vortex in which they are engulfed.'

I would further add that most historical pluralists have taken themselves to be involved in a debate over what grounds what. Thus Leibniz (1989, 85) maintains that the whole exists in virtue of its parts: 'Every being derives its reality only from the reality of those beings of which it is composed.'[49] James (1977, 33) speaks of going 'from parts to wholes,' claiming 'beings may first exist and feed so to speak on their own existence, and then secondarily become known to each other.' And McTaggart (1988, 271) expresses his commitment to pluralism as follows:

> If it is asked which aspect is more fundamental, the answer must be that pluralism is the more fundamental, because...the primary parts, which are a plurality, have this position of unique significance. It expresses the relations of the universe and the primary parts more appropriately – so far as we can determine those relations *a priori* – to say that the universe is composed of the primary parts than to say that it is manifested in them. And this leaves the balance on the side of pluralism.

Indeed, even Russell (2003, 92) – though sometimes guilty of misreading monists as existence monists – puts his own positive doctrine in terms of dependence: 'The existence of the complex depends on the existence of the simple, and not vice versa.' The pluralist no more need deny the existence of the one whole, than the monist need deny the existence of the many parts.[50]

This concludes my case for the priority reading. I have argued that the priority reading is more charitable and provides a better textual fit. But perhaps closer readings of the relevant texts will reveal that both *Priority* and *Existence Monism* are interwoven into the monistic tradition.[51] If so, then I would suggest that *Priority Monism* is the strand of the monistic tradition worth reviving. Or perhaps closer readings will reveal that the traditional monists – despite the passages I have cited – have all been existence monists after all. If so, I would still recommend the question of fundamental mereology as an intrinsically interesting question in its own right, albeit one with less historical depth.

Notes

My thanks go to the A. M. Monius Institute for their generous support. I am grateful for helpful comments from many, including Frank Arntzenius, Dirk Baltzly, Einar Bohn, Phillip Bricker, Ross Cameron, David Chalmers, Edwin Curley, Michael della Rocca, Ned Hall, Richard Healey, Terry Horgan, Jenann Ismael, James Kreines, Uriah Kriegel, Ned Markosian, Kris McDaniel, Brian McLaughlin, Trenton Merricks, Kristie Miller, Josh Parsons, Susanna Schellenberg, Ted Sider, Brad Skow, Kelly Trogdon, Brian Weatherson, and the *Philosophical Review* referees. I also received useful feedback from audiences at the University of Toronto, Brown, Ohio State, Yale, the Free University of Amsterdam, Purdue, Lafayette, Simon Fraser University, the University of Colorado-Boulder, Monash University, and the University of St. Andrews, as well as at Metaphysical Mayhem and the Arizona Ontology Conference.

This chapter is reprinted from Schaffer, Jonathan 2010. 'Monism: The Priority of the Whole', *Philosophical Review*, 119: 1, 31–76.

1. According to Joad (1957, 428), monism in the nineteenth century commanded 'a larger measure of agreement among philosophers than has been accorded to any other philosophy since the Middle Ages.' As Schiller (1897, 62) once complained, in a reply to Lotze: 'Nothing is cheaper and commoner in philosophy than monism; what, unhappily, is still rare, is an attempt to defend it, and critically to establish its assumptions.'
2. Thus Russell (1985, 36) wrote, 'I share the common-sense belief that there are many separate things; I do not regard the apparent multiplicity of the world as consisting merely in phases and unreal divisions of a single indivisible Reality' (compare Moore 1993a, 107).
3. So Ayer (1952, 146) claimed: 'The assertion that Reality is One, which it is characteristic of a monist to make and a pluralist to controvert, is nonsensical, since no empirical situation could have any bearing on its truth' (compare Carnap 1959, 67).
4. In this vein Rosen and Dorr (2002,169–71) recommend a 'fictionalist agnosticism' about mereology, according to which talk about parthood relations should be understood as prefixed by a tacit 'according to the fiction of mereology' operator.

5. The organicist view is defended by van Inwagen (1990), who later explicitly embraces the consequence that there is no world, paraphrasing 'the world' as a plural term (van Inwagen 2002, 127).
6. Horgan and Potrč (2000, 249) forward a view whose main metaphysical theses are: '1. There really is just one concrete particular, viz., the whole universe (the *blobject*). 2. The blobject has enormous spatiotemporal structural complexity, and enormous local variability – even though it does not have any genuine parts.' In Schaffer 2007a, I argue that the best version of nihilism is the monistic version that only posits the world.
7. Thus Hawley and Holcomb (2005, 5) define cosmology as 'the study of the formation, structure, and evolution of the universe as a whole.' And Hartle (2003, 615) characterizes 'the central question of quantum cosmology' as 'The universe has a quantum state. What is it?'
8. Baxter (1988) is perhaps the main defender of the thesis that composition *is* identity. D. Lewis (1991, §3.6), Armstrong (1997), and Sider (2007) all defend the thesis that composition is *not* identity but is analogous to identity in important respects. I am only assuming the falsity of the Baxter-style view.
9. In this vein, Thomson (1999, 306) decries both ontological and epistemological priority as 'dark notions,' though she does immediately allow that 'we have *some* grip on what [these notions] are.' Similarly D. Lewis (1999a, 29) advertises supervenience as providing 'a stripped-down form of reductionism, unencumbered by dubious denials of existence, claims of ontological priority, or claims of translatability.'
10. For instance, D. Lewis introduces a *naturalness ranking* for properties, but is equivocal as to whether this ranking extends to objects (thus compare Lewis 1999a, 45–46 to Lewis 1999b, 65).
11. Lowe (2005, §3) connects the asymmetry of priority to the general asymmetry of explanation: ''because' *is* asymmetrical, because it expresses an *explanatory* relationship and explanation is asymmetrical,' to which he adds: 'The asymmetry of explanation is, of course, intimately related to the unacceptability of *circular arguments*.'
12. Aristotle (1984b, 1688) characterizes substance as what is ultimately prior and conceives of such substances as the ground of being: 'Substance is the subject of our inquiry; for the principles and the causes we are seeking are those of substances. For if the universe is of the nature of a whole, substance is its first part' (compare Gill 1989, 3; Schaffer 2009). Without such substances there would be nothing at all. As Leibniz wrote to de Volder: 'Where there is no reality that is not borrowed, there will never be any reality, since it must belong ultimately to some subject' (quoted in Adams 1994, 335; compare Aristotle 1984a, 5; Fine 1991, 267).
13. As D. Lewis (1986a, 60) says of the sparse properties, 'there are only just enough of them to characterize things completely and without redundancy.' The natural generalization to mereology is provided by Varzi (2000, 286): 'A good inventory must be complete: everything in the domain of quantification must show up somewhere. But a good inventory must also avoid redundancies: nothing should show up more than once.'
14. This formulation is a generalization of Jackson's definition of physicalism in terms of minimal physical duplicates: 'Any world which is a minimal physical duplicate of any world is a duplicate *simpliciter* of that world' (Jackson 1998, 160). The generalization is to the claim that any world which is a minimal *fundamental* duplicate of our world is a duplicate simpliciter of our world. Though note that

I am not using this definition to define what it is to be fundamental but rather just as a constraint on the fundamental.

15. For further discussion of intrinsicness and parthood, see Weatherson 2008 and Sider 2007. Weatherson (2008, §2.1) provides the following example: 'most people have the property *having longer legs than arms*, and indeed seem to have this property intrinsically.'
16. Thus Armstrong (1997, 12) suggests: 'The mereological whole supervenes upon its parts, but equally the parts supervene upon the whole' (compare D. Lewis 1991, 8). Though note that I have only claimed whole-to-part supervenience and that the argument in the main text only works in that direction (the difference between whole-to-part and part-to-whole supervenience being that the property of having-such-a-part is *intrinsic* to the whole, while the property of belonging-to-such-a-whole is *extrinsic* to the part). I will return to the question of part-to-whole supervenience in §2.2.
17. In classical terms, I have argued that *no substance can have substantial proper parts*. Thus Aristotle (1984b, 1643) maintains that 'no substance is composed of substances' since a substance must be a *unity*, and so anything consisting of two substances must be 'actually two' and so 'never actually one' (1984b, 1640). Likewise Spinoza (1994, 93) argues that no substance can have substantial proper parts, or else 'the whole...could both be and be conceived without its parts, which is absurd.'
18. In this vein Hegel (1949, 301) holds that what is fundamental is 'the organic being...in undivided oneness and as a whole,' and Bradley (1978, 521) adds: 'Everything less than the universe is an abstraction from the whole.' See the appendix for further historical discussion.
19. In this vein, Leibniz (1989, 213) maintains: 'These monads are the true atoms of nature and, in brief, the elements of things,' and Russell (2003, 94) adds: 'I believe that there are simple things in the universe, and that these beings have relations in virtue of which complex beings are composed.' See the appendix for further historical discussion.
20. Mackenzie (1914, 27) suggests the label *Cosmism*: 'A theory may be essentially singularistic, in the sense that it regards the whole of reality as an inseparable unity, no aspect of which is really independent of the rest; and it may yet be pluralistic, in that it recognizes within that unity many fundamental distinctions that cannot be annulled...I propose to call it 'Cosmism'.' Mackenzie nominates Plato, Aristotle, Spinoza, Hegel, Bradley, and McTaggart as fellow cosmists.
21. Russell's argument continues to reverberate. Here is a recent echo from Hoffman and Rosenkrantz (1997, 78): 'Monism has an additional very serious disadvantage: it is inconsistent with something that appears to be an evident datum of experience, namely, that there is a plurality of things.'
22. As Williams (1953, 14) notes: 'At its broadest the 'true' meaning of 'abstract' is *partial*, *incomplete*, or *fragmentary*, the trait of what is less than its including whole. Since there must be, for everything but the World All, at least something, and indeed many things, of which it is a proper part, everything but the World All is 'abstract' in this broad sense' (see Schaffer 2009, §3.3).
23. Thus Proclus (2007, 55–56) maintains: 'The circle is not established from semi-circles but rather the opposite is the case.... [W]hen the diameter is drawn then at that point semi-circles are made. The name itself proves this, since 'semi-circle' has its derivation from 'circle' and not *vice versa*.'
24. Aristotle (1984b, 1634) gives the right angle and the acute angle, and the man and his finger, as examples in which the whole is prior to its part: 'for in formula

the parts are explained by reference to [the wholes], and in virtue also of the power of existing apart from the parts the wholes are prior.'

25. As with the percept, so with other mental unities. And so the philosopher who is an idealist might take the seeming priority of mental wholes over their parts as a further argument for monism. Indeed most of the nineteenth-century British monists were idealists first and foremost, and monists as a result. As Joad (1957, 420) explains: 'We entertain our ideas, we form our plans as wholes.... The wholes of monistic philosophy are in this respect like mental wholes.'
26. In this vein, Dummett (1973, 577) suggests 'the picture of reality as an amorphous lump, not yet articulated into distinct objects.' As Campbell (1990, 154) – who defends 'Spinoza's conclusion, that there is just one genuine substance, the cosmos itself' – notes: 'There seem to be no natural lines along which Nature admits of partition' (Campbell 1990, 139).
27. Indeed, as James (1985, 329–30) points out, monism is a nearly universal feature of religious experiences: 'Mystical states in general assert a pretty distinct theoretic drift.... One of these directions is optimism, and the other is monism' (compare Huxley 1944, 5). The philosopher who takes religious experiences to be evidentiary (such as Alston [1991]) should regard this as further evidence for monism. In this regard, it may be worth noting that one of the standard objections to treating religious experience as evidentiary is the problem of conflicting experiences, which threaten to provide rebutting defeaters to any particular religious view (Plantinga 2000, 439). Monism may be one of the few features of religious experience not troubled by such conflict, and so – for whatever that is worth – may even deserve special status as a feature of religious experiences unthreatened by such defeaters.
28. Schrödinger (1935, 555), who introduced the notion of entanglement, called it 'not *one* but rather *the* characteristic trait of quantum mechanics.' Entanglement is a very general feature of the mathematics and has been empirically confirmed by Alain Aspect and others. To the extent we can reasonably expect any feature of quantum mechanics to survive in future theories, we can reasonably expect entanglement to survive. As d'Espagnat (1981, 1804) remarks in this regard: 'we may safely say that non-separability is now one of the most certain general concepts in physics.'
29. It is controversial whether the Big Bang is to be treated as *physically real*, or as a mere *boundary condition* (a hole in spacetime). If the Big Bang is a boundary, then the assumption I need is that all causal horizons vanish as one moves to the boundary. Indeed, even if there are non-vanishing causal horizons, this would at most yield a pluralism in letter but not spirit, in which the universe contains many vast isolated bubbles. Everything we ever encounter – everything in our bubble – would still form one entangled system.
30. It is controversial whether temporal evolution is always via the Schrödinger dynamics (*unitarity*), or whether there is a further dynamics of wave-function collapse.
31. As Joos (2006, 226–27) explains, 'due to non-local features of quantum theory,' a consistent description of any system 'must finally include the whole universe.' According to Zeh (2004, 115), 'the essential lesson of decoherence is that the whole universe must be strongly entangled,' where apparent particles 'can be dynamically described in terms of a unitarily evolving (hence strongly entangled) universal wave function' (Zeh 2003, 330).
32. D. Lewis's 'Humean supervenience' is a modern variant of Democritean pluralism, on which 'all there is to the world is a vast mosaic of local matters of

particular fact, just one little thing and then another,' these things being interrelated by 'a system of external relations of spatiotemporal distance' (D. Lewis 1986b, ix).

33. In this vein, Toraldo di Francia (1998, 28) writes, 'Since any particle has certainly interacted with other particles in the past, the world turns out to be *nonseparable* into individual and independent objects' (compare Gribbin 1984, 229). Nadeau and Kafatos (1999, 4) maintain that 'an undivided wholeness exists on the most basic and primary level in all aspects of physical reality,' invoking 'a seamlessly interconnected whole called the cosmos' (1999, 5). Esfeld (2001, 258) concludes, 'Only the whole of all quantum systems taken together is in a pure state....Consequently all matter at the level of quantum systems is one holistic system.' And Penrose (2004, 578), from a chapter entitled 'The entangled quantum world,' says, 'A system of more than one particle must nevertheless be treated as a single holistic unit.'
34. According to Rosen (2006, 35), the laws of metaphysics 'specify the categories of basic constituents and the rules for their combination. They determine how nonbasic entities are generated from or 'grounded' in the basic array.'
35. Melissus draws a comparable conclusion, as Sedley (1999, 126) notes: '[Melissus] infers homogeneity (it is 'alike everywhere'), on the ground that anything heterogeneous would thereby be a plurality.'
36. Though Rea (2001, 147) makes the point that a homogeneous world 'does not require us to deny anything that is manifest to the five senses' since these appearances can in principle be written off as false appearances enjoyed by minds that 'are not denizens of the material world.'
37. Here I follow Parsons (2004), who offers examples such as *being polka-dotted* and *being hot at one end and cold at the other* and invokes the possibility of heterogeneity-all-the-way-down to argue against the reductionist view that distributional properties derive from a plurality of homogeneous parts.
38. Indeed Albert (1996, 277) suggests that the most natural ontology of both Newtonian and quantum mechanics is in terms of a single world-atom moving through configuration space: 'The space in which any realistic understanding of quantum mechanics is necessarily going to depict the history of the world as playing itself out is configuration space' (compare P. Lewis 2004).
39. This idea can be thought of as the relativistic extension of the usual endurantist idea that seemingly monadic properties have an extra argument place for a time. Indeed, the problem of the heterogeneity of the cosmos parallels the problem of intrinsic change (temporal heterogeneity) for enduring objects. See Sider 2001 (chap. 4) for further discussion of the problem of intrinsic change.
40. Thus Fine, who is generally sympathetic to the pluralistic view that wholes are constructed out of parts, considers the possibility of 'a universe of indefinitely divisible matter' and concedes here that the whole seems basic: 'Any uniform piece of matter will then be the aggregate of smaller pieces of matter. But all the same, it is reasonable to suppose that the uniform pieces of matter are all basic' (Fine 1991, 266).
41. Leibniz, Russell, and Wittgenstein all endorse the metaphysical necessity of *Atomism*. Indeed, I think Leibniz, Russell, and Wittgenstein are best read as arguing from the metaphysical necessity of *Atomism* to the impossibility of gunk. As Leibniz (1989, 85) puts the point, to Arnauld: 'It will not have any reality at all if each being of which it is composed is itself a being by aggregation, a being for which we must still seek further grounds for its reality, grounds which

never can be found' (compare Leibniz 1989, 213; Russell 2003, 94; Wittgenstein 1990, 35). Thus the arguments for the metaphysical possibility of gunk, as per 16, prove crucial. For they provide *independent* rationale for inferring the falsity of *Pluralism* from the possibility of gunk, rather than turning the argument around and inferring the impossibility of gunk from the alleged truth of *Pluralism*.

42. For a wider taxonomy of monistic views, see Schaffer 2007b (§1).
43. As Joad (1957, 420) summarizes: 'The wholes emphasized by monistic philosophers are, therefore, logically prior to their parts. They are there, as it were, to begin with, and being there, proceed to express themselves in parts whose natures they pervade and determine.'
44. Thus Harte (2002, 279) argues that, in the Timaean cosmology, the parts of the cosmic body are determined by their place in the whole structure. She concludes: 'The claim that parts are structure-laden is thus the claim that there is some sort of metaphysical dependence of the parts on the whole.'
45. O'Meara (1996, 79) comments: 'In Plotinus, as in Plato and Aristotle, the central kind of priority is priority 'by nature'.... It is this kind of priority that is the concern of fundamental ontology as an attempt to identify what is fundamental in reality, that on which things depend,' where for Plotinus, 'The One is that on which all else depends' (1996, 77).
46. See Beiser 2005 for a discussion of the 'ubiquitous organic metaphors' woven through Hegel's corpus, with the conclusion that 'Hegel's thinking essentially proceeds from an organic vision of the world, a view of the universe as a single vast living organism' (Beiser 2005, 80).
47. Elsewhere, Spinoza (1994, 127) speaks of conceiving that 'the whole of nature is one individual, whose parts, that is, all bodies, vary in infinite ways.' See Curley 1969 for further discussion.
48. Thus Blanshard (1973, 145) approvingly describes Bosanquet's thesis in *Principle of Individuality and Value* as: 'the world is a single individual whose parts are connected with each other by a necessity so intimate and so organic that the nature of the part depended on its place in the Absolute.' Blanshard (1939, 516) himself defends the view that 'the universe of existing things is a system in which all things are related internally.'
49. Leibniz's monads are ideal entities that transcend space. So his view is strictly neutral on the priority of the whole to its parts within the cosmos. On this issue Leibniz actually sides with *Monism*: 'In the continuum, the whole is prior to its parts' (quoted in Levey 1998, §3).
50. Indeed, James (1975, 66) ridicules just this sort of confusion coming from monists, in the era when monism was ascendant: 'It is an odd fact that many monists consider a great victory scored for their side when pluralists say 'the universe is many'. 'The Universe!' they chuckle – 'his speech betrayeth him. He stands confessed of monism out of his own mouth'.'
51. I would consider Parmenides (see Owen 1960) and Melissus (see Sedley 1999) to be existence monists, and Horgan and Potrč (2000, 2007) are certainly existence monists.

References

Adams, Robert Merrihew. 1994. *Leibniz: Determinist, Theist, Idealist*. Oxford: Oxford University Press.

Albert, David. 1996. 'Elementary Quantum Metaphysics.' In *Bohmian Mechanics and Quantum Theory: An Appraisal*, ed. James T. Cushing, Arthur Stock, and Sheldon Goldstein, 277–84. Dordrecht: Kluwer Academic Publishers.

Alexander, Samuel. 1950. *Space, Time, and Deity: The Gifford Lectures at Glasgow 1916–1918*, Vol. 1. New York: Humanities Press.

Alston, William. 1991. *Perceiving God: The Epistemology of Religious Experience*. Ithaca, NY: Cornell University Press.

Aristotle. 1984a. 'Categories.' In *The Complete Works of Aristotle*. Vol. 1, ed. Jonathan Barnes, 3–24. Princeton: Princeton University Press.

——. 1984b. 'Metaphysics.' In *The Complete Works of Aristotle*. Vol. 2, ed. Jonathan Barnes, 1552–1728. Princeton: Princeton University Press.

Armstrong, D. M. 1997. *A World of States of Affairs*. Cambridge: Cambridge University Press.

Ayer, A. J. 1952. *Language, Truth and Logic*. New York: Dover Books.

Baxter, Donald. 1988. 'Many-One Identity.' *Philosophical Papers* 17: 193–216.

Beiser, Frederick. 2005. *Hegel*. London: Routledge.

Bell, Eric Temple. 1951. *Mathematics: Queen and Servant of Science*. Washington, DC: Mathematical Association of America.

Blanshard, Brand. 1939. *The Nature of Thought*, Vol. 2. London: George Allen and Unwin.

——. 1973. *Reason and Analysis*. LaSalle, IL: Open Court Press.

Bohm, David. 1957. *Causality and Chance in Modern Physics*. London: Routledge and Kegan Paul.

Bohm, David, and B. J. Hiley. 1993. *The Undivided Universe*. London: Routledge.

Bosanquet, Bernard. 1911. *Logic: Or the Morphology of Knowledge*, Vol. 2. Oxford: Clarendon Press.

——. 1913. *The Value and Destiny of the Individual*. New York: Macmillan.

Bradley, F. H. 1978. *Appearance and Reality*. Oxford: Clarendon Press.

Campbell, Keith. 1990. *Abstract Particulars*. Oxford: Basil Blackwell.

Carnap, Rudolph, 1959. 'The Elimination of Metaphysics through Logical Analysis of Language.' In *Logical Positivism*, ed. A. J. Ayer, 60–81. New York: Macmillan.

Curley, Edwin. 1969. *Spinoza's Metaphysics*. Cambridge, MA: Harvard University Press.

Davies, Paul. 1983. *God and the New Physics*. New York: Simon and Schuster.

Dehmelt, Hans. 1989. 'Triton,...Electron,...Cosmon...: An Infinite Regression?' *Proceedings of the National Academy of Sciences* 86: 8618–19.

d'Espagnat, Bernard. 1981. *Physical Review Letters* 49: 1804.

Dummett, Michael. 1973. *Frege: Philosophy of Language*. Cambridge, MA: Harvard University Press.

Esfeld, Michael. 2001. *Holism in Philosophy of Mind and Philosophy of Physics*. Dordrecht: Kluwer.

Ewing, A. C. 1934. *Idealism: A Critical Survey*. New York: Humanities Press.

Fine, Kit. 1991. 'The Study of Ontology.' *Noûs* 25: 263–94.

——. 1994. 'Essence and Modality.' *Philosophical Perspectives* 8: 1–16.

——. 2001. 'The Question of Realism.' *Philosophers Imprint* 1: 1–30.

Georgi, Howard. 1989. 'Effective Quantum Field Theories.' In *The New Physics*, ed. Paul Davies, 446–57. Cambridge: Cambridge University Press.

Gill, Mary Louise. 1989. *Aristotle on Substance: The Paradox of Unity*. Princeton: Princeton University Press.

Greene, Brian. 1999. *The Elegant Universe: Superstrings, Hidden Dimensions, and the Quest for the Ultimate Theory.* New York: Random House.

Gribbin, John. 1984. *In Search of SchrÖdinger's Cat: Quantum Physics and Reality.* New York: Bantam Books.

Halvorson, Hans, and Rob Clifton. 2002. 'No Place for Particles in Relativistic Quantum Theories?' *Philosophy of Science* 69: 1–28.

Harte, Verity. 2002. *Plato on Parts and Wholes: The Metaphysics of Structure.* Oxford: Clarendon Press.

Hartle, James. 2003. 'The State of the Universe.' In *The Future of Theoretical Physics and Cosmology,* ed. G. W. Gibbons, E. P. S. Shellard, and S. J. Rankin, 615–20. Cambridge: Cambridge University Press.

Hawley, John F., and Katherine A. Holcomb. 2005. *Foundations of Modern Cosmology,* 2nd ed. Oxford: Oxford University Press.

Healey, Richard. 1991. 'Holism and Nonseparability.' *Journal of Philosophy* 88: 393–421.

Hegel, G. W. F. 1949. *The Phenomenology of Mind,* trans. J. B. Baillie. London: George Allen and Unwin.

——. 1975. *Hegel's Logic: Being Part One of the Encyclopedia of the Philosophical Sciences,* trans. William Wallace. Oxford: Oxford University Press.

Hoffman, Joshua, and Gary S. Rosenkrantz. 1997. *Substance: Its Nature and Existence.* London: Routledge.

Horgan, Terence, and Matjaž Potrč. 2000. 'Blobjectivism and Indirect Correspondence.' *Facta Philosophica* 2: 249–70.

——. 2007. *Austere Realism: Contextual Semantics Meets Minimal Ontology.* Cambridge, MA: MIT Press.

Hume, David. 2000. *An Enquiry Concerning Human Understanding,* ed. Tom L. Beauchamp. Oxford: Oxford University Press.

Hüttemann, Andreas, and David Papineau. 2005. 'Physicalism Decomposed.' *Analysis* 65: 33–39.

Huxley, Aldous. 1944. *The Perennial Philosophy.* New York: Harper and Row. Jackson, Frank. 1998. 'Armchair Metaphysics.' In *Mind, Method, and Conditionals,* 154–76. London: Routledge.

James, William. 1975. *The Works of William James: Pragmatism,* ed. Frederick H. Burkhardt, Fredson Bowers, and Ignas K. Skrupskelis. Cambridge, MA: Harvard University Press.

——. 1977. *The Works of William James: A Pluralistic Universe,* ed. Frederick H. Burkhardt, Fredson Bowers, and Ignas K. Skrupskelis. Cambridge, MA: Harvard University Press.

——. 1985. *The Works of William James: The Varieties of Religious Experience,* ed. Frederick H. Burkhardt, Fredson Bowers, and Ignas K. Skrupskelis. Cambridge, MA: Harvard University Press. Joachim, Harold. 1901. *A Study of the Ethics of Spinoza: Ethica Ordine GeometricoDemonstrata.* Oxford: Clarendon Press.

Joachim, H.H. 1906. *The Nature of Truth.* Oxford: Clarendon Press.

Joad, C. E. M. 1957. *Guide to Philosophy.* New York: Dover Books. Johnston, Mark. 1987. 'Is There a Problem about Persistence?' *Proceedings of the Aristotelian Society* 61s: 107–35.

Joos, Erich. 2006. 'Decoherence and the Transition from Quantum Physics to Classical Physics.' In *Entangled World,* ed. Jürgen Audretsch, 203–33. Berlin: Wiley-VCH.

Kim, Jaegwon. 1998. *Mind in a Physical World: An Essay on the Mind-Body Problem and Mental Causation*. Cambridge, MA: MIT Press.

Kirk, G. S., and J. E. Raven. 1962. *The Presocratic Philosophers: A Critical History with a Selection of Texts*. Cambridge: Cambridge University Press.

Kuhlmann, Meinard. 2006. 'Quantum Field Theory.' *Stanford Encyclopedia of Philosophy*, Fall 2006 edition, ed. Edward N. Zalta. http://plato.stanford.edu/archives/fall2006/entries/quantum-feld-theory/.

Leibniz, G. W. F. 1989. *Philosophical Essays*, ed. and trans. Roger Ariew and Daniel Garber. Indianapolis, IN: Hackett.

Levey, Samuel. 1998. 'Leibniz on Mathematics and the Actually Infinite Division of Matter.' *Philosophical Review* 107: 49–96.

Lewis, David. 1986a. *On the Plurality of Worlds*. Oxford: Basil Blackwell.

——. 1986b. 'Introduction.' In *Philosophical Papers*, Vol. 2, ix–xvii. Oxford: Oxford University Press.

——. 1991. *Parts of Classes*. Oxford: Basil Blackwell.

——. 1999a. 'New Work for a Theory of Universals.' In *Papers in Metaphysics and Epistemology*, 8–55. Cambridge: Cambridge University Press.

——. 1999b. 'Putnam's Paradox.' In *Papers in Metaphysics and Epistemology*, 56–77. Cambridge: Cambridge University Press.

——. 1999c. 'Many, but Almost One.' In *Papers in Metaphysics and Epistemology*, 164–82. Cambridge: Cambridge University Press. Lewis, Peter. 2004. 'Life in Configuration Space.' *British Journal for the Philosophy of Science* 55: 713–29.

Lowe, E. J. 2005. 'Ontological Dependence.' *Stanford Encyclopedia of Philosophy*, Summer 2005 edition, ed. Edward N. Zalta. http://plato.stanford.edu/archives/sum2005/entries/dependence-ontological/.

Mackenzie, J. S. 1914. 'The Meaning of Reality.' *Mind* 23: 19–40. Maudlin, Tim. 1998. 'Part and Whole in Quantum Mechanics.' In *Interpreting Bodies: Classical and Quantum Objects in Modern Physics*, ed. Elena Castellani, 46–60. Princeton, NJ: Princeton University Press.

McTaggart John, McTaggart Ellis. 1988. *The Nature of Existence*. Vol. 1, ed. C. D. Broad. Cambridge: Cambridge University Press. Moore, G. E. 1993a. 'A Defence of Common Sense.' In *G. E. Moore: Selected Writings*, ed. Thomas Baldwin, 106–33. London: Routledge. ——. 1993b. 'Proof of an External World.' In *G. E. Moore: Selected Writings*, ed. Thomas Baldwin, 147–70. London: Routledge. Nadeau, Robert, and Menas Kafatos. 1999. *The Non-local Universe: The New Physics and Matters of the Mind*. Oxford: Oxford University Press.

O'Meara, Dominic J. 1996. 'The Hierarchical Ordering of Reality in Plotinus.' In *The Cambridge Companion to Plotinus*, ed. Lloyd P. Gerson, 66–81. Cambridge: Cambridge University Press.

Oppenheim, Paul, and Hilary Putnam. 1991. 'Unity of Science as a Working Hypothesis.' In *The Philosophy of Science*, ed. Richard Boyd, PhillipGasper, and J. D. Trout, 405–27. Cambridge, MA: MIT Press.

Owen, G. E. L. 1960. 'Eleatic Questions.' *Classical Quarterly* 10: 84–102.

Parsons, Josh. 2004. 'Distributional Properties.' In *Lewisian Themes: The Philosophy of David K. Lewis*, ed. Frank Jackson and Graham Priest, 173–80. Oxford: Oxford University Press.

Penrose, Roger. 2004. *The Road to Reality: A Complete Guide to the Laws of the Universe*. New York: Alfred A. Knopf.

Plantinga, Alvin. 2000. *Warranted Christian Belief*. Oxford: Oxford University Press.

Plato. 1961. 'Timaeus.' In *The Collected Dialogues of Plato*, ed. Edith Hamilton and Huntington Cairns, trans. Benjamin Jowett, 1151–1211. Princeton, NJ: Princeton University Press.

Plotinus. 1991. *The Enneads*, trans. Stephen MacKenna. New York: Penguin.

Proclus. 1987. *Commentary on Plato's Parmenides*, trans. Glenn R. Morrow and John M. Dillon. Princeton: Princeton University Press. ——. 2007. *Commentary on Plato's Timaeus: Volume 3, Book 3, Part 1, Proclus on the World's Body*, ed. and trans. Dirk Baltzly. Cambridge: Cambridge University Press.

Rea, Michael. 2001. 'How to Be an Eleatic Monist.' In *Philosophical Perspectives*. Vol.15, *Metaphysics*, ed. James E. Tomberlin, 129–51. Oxford: Basil Blackwell.

Ritchie, D. G. 1898. 'The One and the Many.' *Mind* 7: 449–76.

Rosen, Gideon. 2006. 'The Limits of Contingency.' In *Identity and Modality*, ed. Fraser MacBride, 13–39. Oxford: Oxford University Press.

Rosen, Gideon, and Cian Dorr. 2002. 'Composition as a Fiction.' In *The Blackwell Guide to Metaphysics*, ed. Richard Gale, 151–74. Oxford: Basil Blackwell.

Royce, Josiah. 1900. *The World and the Individual*. New York: Macmillan.

——. 1967. *The Spirit of Modern Philosophy*. New York: W. W. Norton.

Russell, Bertrand. 1985. 'The Philosophy of Logical Atomism.' In *The Philosophy of Logical Atomism*, ed. David Pears, 35–155. LaSalle, IL: Open Court.

——. 2003. 'Analytic Realism.' In *Russellon Metaphysics*, ed. Stephen Mumford, 91–96. London: Routledge.

Schaffer, Jonathan. 2003. 'Is There a Fundamental Level?' *Noûs* 37: 498–517.

——. 2007a. 'From Nihilism to Monism.' *Australasian Journal of Philosophy* 85: 175–91.

——. 2007b. 'Monism.' *Stanford Encyclopedia of Philosophy*, Spring 2007 edition, ed. Edward N. Zalta. http://plato.stanford.edu/archives/spr2007/ entries/monism/.

——. 2009. 'On What Grounds What.' In *Metametaphysics*, ed. David Chalmers, David Manley, and Ryan Wasserman, 347–83. Oxford: Oxford University Press.

——. Forthcoming. 'The Internal Relatedness of All Things.' *Mind*.

Schiller, F. C. S. 1897. 'Reply: Lotze's Monism.' *Philosophical Review* 6: 62–64.

Schrödinger, Erwin. 1935. 'Discussion of Probability Relations between Separated Systems.' *Proceedings of the Cambridge Philosophical Society* 31: 555–63.

Sedley, David. 1999. 'Parmenides and Melissus.' In *The Cambridge Companion to Early Greek Philosophy*, ed. A. A. Long, 113–33. Cambridge: Cambridge University Press.

Sider, Theodore. 2001. *Four-Dimensionalism: An Ontology of Persistence and Time*. Oxford: Oxford University Press.

——. 2007. 'Parthood.' *Philosophical Review* 116: 51–91.

Simons, Peter. 1987. *Parts: A Study in Ontology*. Oxford: Oxford University Press.

Spinoza, Benedict. 1994. *A Spinoza Reader: The Ethics and Other Works*, ed. and trans. Edwin Curley. Princeton, NJ: Princeton University Press.

Taylor, A. E. 1961. *Elements of Metaphysics*. New York: Barnes and Noble.

Teller, Paul. 1986. 'Relational Holism and Quantum Mechanics.' *British Journal for the Philosophy of Science* 37: 71–81.

Thomson, Judith Jarvis. 1999. 'Parthood and Identity across Time.' In *Metaphysics: An Anthology*, ed. Jaegwon Kim and Ernest Sosa, 301–11. Oxford: Basil Blackwell.

Toraldo di Francia, Giuliano. 1998. 'A World of Individual Objects?' In *Interpreting Bodies: Classical and Quantum Objects in Modern Physics*, ed. Elena Castellani, 21–29. Princeton: Princeton University Press.

Unger, Peter. 1980. 'The Problem of the Many.' *Midwest Studies in Philosophy* 5: 411–67.

Van Inwagen, Peter. 1990. *Material Beings*. Ithaca, NY: Cornell University Press.
——. 2002. *Metaphysics*. Boulder, CO: Westview.
Varzi, Achille. 2000. 'Mereological Commitments.' *Dialectica* 54: 283–305.
Weatherson, Brian. 2008. 'Intrinsic vs. Extrinsic Properties.' *Stanford Encyclopedia of Philosophy*, Fall 2008 edition, ed. Edward N. Zalta. http://plato.stanford .edu/archives/fall2008/entries/intrinsic-extrinsic/.
Williams, D. C. 1953. 'The Elements of Being.' *Review of Metaphysics* 7: 3–18; 171–92.
Wittgenstein, Ludwig. 1990. *Tractatus Logico-Philosophicus*, trans. C. K. Ogden. London: Routledge.
Zeh, H. D. 2003. 'There Is No 'First' Quantization.' *Physics Letters* A309: 329–34.
——. 2004. 'The Wave Function: It or Bit?' In *Science and Ultimate Reality: Quantum Theory, Cosmology and Complexity*, ed. John D. Barrow, Paul C. W. Davies, and Charles L. Harper, Jr., 103–20. Cambridge: Cambridge University Press.
Zimmerman, Dean. 1996. 'Could Extended Objects Be Made out of Simple Parts? An Argument for 'Atomless Gunk'.' *Philosophy and Phenomenological Research* 56: 1–29.

2

Existence Monism Trumps Priority Monism

Terry Horgan and Matjaž Potrč

Jonathan Schaffer has recently been defending a version of ontological monism concerning concrete objects that he calls 'priority monism' – the view that the whole cosmos is the only ontologically fundamental concrete object, and that although there are numerous concrete objects in the correct ontology that are proper parts of the whole, nevertheless the whole is ontologically prior to all these part-objects (Schaffer 2003, 2007 chapter 1, this volume). He contrasts this view with what he calls 'pluralism' – the view that the right ontology contains numerous concrete objects that are proper parts of the whole cosmos, and that these parts are ontologically prior to the whole. He also contrasts priority monism with what he calls 'existence monism' – the view that the whole cosmos is itself the only concrete object, and that the right ontology does not contain any concrete objects that are proper parts of the whole.

We ourselves have recently been defending a form of existence monism (Horgan and Potrč 2000, 2002, 2008). In the present chapter our principal goal is to argue that existence monism is theoretically preferable to priority monism. For present purposes, we will assume for argument's sake that Schaffer's arguments in favor of priority monism over pluralism are sound. We will harness those arguments, together with an argument of our own to the effect that ontological vagueness is impossible, to mount a case in favor of existence monism over priority monism.

Before proceeding, let us make some preliminary remarks by way of clarification. First, Schaffer does not classify spatiotemporal regions or spatiotemporal points as objects. Thus, for him a metaphysic can count as a version of existence monism even if it asserts that the right ontology contains spatiotemporal regions (perhaps including minimal ones – spatiotemporal points) that are proper parts of the whole cosmos – as long as the metaphysic does not posit concrete *objects* as proper parts. We ourselves have defended a version of existence monism we call *blobjectivism*, which asserts that the right ontology is not only free of the kinds of proper part-entities that Schaffer would count as objects, but also is free of regions or points that are proper parts of the whole. But in the present chapter our concern is to argue in favor of existence monism as a generic position, over against priority monism. So we will leave aside the question whether or not the right ontology includes regions or points as proper parts of the whole.

Second, it will be convenient for expository purposes to speak fairly freely both about the 'positing apparatus' of thoughts and statements, and also about 'posits,' i.e., putative entities that putatively answer to such positing apparatus. Positing apparatus includes, inter alia, singular referring expressions of natural language (e.g., names and definite descriptions), and thought-constituents expressible linguistically via such referring expressions. It also includes devices for affirmative existential quantification, in language and in thought. And when we mention posits of various kinds, this convenient material-mode manner of expression should not be construed as carrying ontological commitment to the relevant kinds of entities. Thus, although we say (for instance) that tables, chairs, and persons are 'posits' of everyday thought and discourse, as advocates of existence monism we also maintain that there are no such entities in the right ontology.

Third, our occasional deployment of the phrase 'in the right ontology', as in the last sentence of the previous paragraph, is intended to signal uses of singular-referential or quantificational language that convey ontological commitment or ontological denial. As will become clear below, we hold that there are numerous uses of singular referring terms, and of affirmative existential-quantificational claims, that do not actually carry ontological commitment to objects answering to the relevant singular terms or existential quantifiers. Likewise, numerous uses of predicates do not actually carry ontological commitment to properties or relations answering to those predicates. (We embrace a form of semantic contextualism that underwrites this position.) So we need a linguistic device for indicating, in a given context, that we are using such positing apparatus in a way that *is* intended to convey ontological commitment or ontological denial. (Are there tables, chairs, and cats? Of course! Are there tables, or chairs, or cats *in the right ontology*? No!)

2.1 Schaffer's arguments for priority monism and against pluralism

Schaffer offers two principal arguments in support of monism: the argument from emergence and the argument from gunk. He frames his argumentation in a way that effectively presupposes that the serious contenders in this metaphysical debate are priority monism and pluralism. He phrases the arguments in terms of whole, part, and priority. Here are his own summary formulations of the two arguments (see Schaffer 2007, p. 17 and p. 20):

The Argument from Emergence

a. The whole possesses emergent properties (due to quantum entanglement).

b. If the whole possesses emergent properties, then whole is prior to part.
c. Whole is prior to part.

The Argument from Gunk

a. Either the ultimate parts must be basic at all worlds, or the ultimate whole must be basic at all worlds.
b. There are gunky worlds without ultimate parts (and hence no ultimate parts are basic at those worlds).
c. The ultimate whole must be basic at all worlds.

He elaborates both arguments substantially, and argues in detail for each argument's premises. We will not repeat any of that elaboration or argumentation here.

Each of these arguments can be reformulated in a way that is conditional with respect to whether there are proper parts of the whole at all, thereby bracketing the presupposition that there are indeed proper parts. Doing that turns them into arguments for the generic version of monism, which has both existence monism and priority monism as species. (And as far as we can see, neither argument in its original formulation actually supports existence monism over against priority monism; rather, the original formulations simply *presuppose* that the right ontology includes objects that are proper parts of the whole.) Here are the reformulations:

The Conditional Argument from Emergence

a. The whole possesses emergent properties (due to quantum entanglement).
b. If the whole possesses emergent properties, and if the whole has proper parts, then whole is prior to part.
c. If the whole has proper parts, then whole is prior to part.

The Conditional Argument from Gunk

a. If the whole has proper parts, then either the ultimate parts must be basic at all worlds, or the ultimate whole must be basic at all worlds.
b. There are gunky worlds without ultimate parts (and hence no ultimate parts are basic at those worlds).
c. If the whole has proper parts, then the ultimate whole must be basic at all worlds.

We will assume in what follows that the conditional argument from emergence and the conditional argument from gunk are both sound. They establish the truth of generic monism, but are neutral between existence monism and priority monism.

2.2 A corollary: the whole does not require parts

The cosmos exhibits enormous structural variation and enormous non-homogeneity: it is nothing like the perfectly uniform, totally homogenous, One that supposedly was embraced by the ancient philosopher Parmenides. An initially plausible reason to be a pluralist, rather than being either an existence monist or a priority monist, is the thought that the structural complexity and non-homogeneity of the whole must be grounded in something more basic than the whole itself – viz., the various objects that are proper parts of the whole, and the relations that these objects bear to one another.

Assuming, however, that the conditional argument from emergence and the conditional argument from gunk are correct, then this thought about the nature of structural complexity and structural non-homogeneity is mistaken. Those features must be aspects of the whole qua whole, rather than being ontologically dependent on relations among proper parts that themselves are more basic than the whole they compose. (For one treatment of structural complexity seeking to implement this idea, see Horgan and Potrč 2008, sections 7.4.1 and 7.4.2.) So the conditional arguments from emergence and from gunk have the following corollary: the structural complexity and structural non-homogeneity of the whole are not ontologically grounded in relations among objects that are proper parts of the whole, but rather are sui generis aspects of the whole itself. This will play an important role in our case for the superiority of existence monism over priority monism.

2.3 Ontological vagueness is impossible

In this section we will briefly summarize some key aspects of the treatment of vagueness we call *transvaluationism*, which we elsewhere have articulated and defended at some length (see, e.g., Horgan 1995, 1998, 2010, Horgan and Potrč 2008, sections 7.4.1 and 7.4.2, Potrč 2002). We will also explain how this approach generates the conclusion that ontological vagueness is impossible.

Vagueness essentially involves *sorites-susceptibility*; i.e., for any vague item in language or thought, and for any putatively vague object or property, there is a sorites sequence directly involving that item – a progression of statements, or of states of affairs (actual or possible), that generates a sorites-paradoxical argument. A second essential feature is what Mark Sainsbury (1990) calls *boundarylessness* – which involves the simultaneous satisfaction by a sorites sequence of the following two conditions:

The Difference Condition: Initially in the sorites sequence there are items with a specific status, and every predecessor of an item with this

> status has the same status. Eventually in the sequence there are items with the polar-opposite status, and every successor of an item with this status has the same status. No item in the sequence has both the initial status and the polar-opposite status.
> **The Transition Condition:** There is no determinate fact of the matter about status-transitions in the sorites sequence.

The Transition Condition involves, essentially, two conceptual aspects or dimensions, one individualistic and the other collectivistic:

> **The Individualistic Same-Status Principle (ISS Principle):** Each item in the sorites sequence has the same status as its immediate neighbours.
> **The Collectivistic Status-Indeterminacy Principle (CSI Principle):** There is no correct overall distribution of statuses to the items in the sequence.

Vagueness thereby exhibits a certain specific kind of logical incoherence: viz., the mutual unsatisfiability of the operative principles (the Difference Condition, the ISS Principle, and the CSI Principle). The Difference Condition and the ISS Principle are pairwise incompatible; also, the CSI Principle and the ISS principle are pairwise incompatible if – as the Difference Condition requires – some items in the sorites sequence have a specific status.

These status-principles, despite being mutually unsatisfiable, exert normative governance over semantically correct affirmatory practice in language and thought. Such normative governance involves two key aspects. First, proper use of vague words and concepts must conform to the following two prohibitory practice-standards for semantically correct affirmations – standards that prohibit one from assigning statuses in ways that would *violate* the ISS Principle or the CSI Principle:

> **The Individualistic Status-Attribution Prohibition (ISA Prohibition):** Never attribute a specific status to an item in a sorites sequence and also attribute a different, incompatible status to its immediate neighbour.
> **The Collectivistic Status-Attribution Prohibition (CSA Prohibition):** Never affirm any determinate overall assignment of statuses to the items in a sorites sequence.

Second, the two prohibitory practice-standards are grounded not epistemologically, but rather semantically: not in ignorance of sharp boundaries (there are no sharp boundaries!), but rather in the ISS and CSI principles themselves. These status-principles are semantically 'in force,' even though they cannot be mutually satisfied by the respective items in a sorites sequence. They are in force in the sense that it would be *semantically* incorrect to engage in judgmental/affirmatory practice that violates them. Such status-assignment practice would be semantically incorrect *because* that assignment would be violation of the ISS Principle and/or the CSI Principle.

For vagueness to exist in thought or language, the Difference Condition and the Transition Condition both must be satisfied. However, satisfaction of the Transition Condition is not a matter of the ISS Principle and the CSI Principle both being satisfied themselves; for that is impossible (given that the Difference Condition must be satisfied). Rather, the Transition Condition is satisfied, by vagueness-exhibiting thought or language, provided that the ISS and CSI principles jointly exert *normative governance* over semantically correct affirmatory practice. Such normative governance is both possible and actual. And, indeed, vagueness in thought and language is itself both possible and actual – notwithstanding the fact that vagueness harbours an inherent form of logical incoherence, involving mutually unsatisfiable status-principles.[1]

But when one asks whether the right ontology could include vague objects, or vague properties and relations, the situation is very different. The world itself does not engage in norm-governed practice; thus, it would make no sense to appeal to practice standards that the world itself supposedly obeys. Rather, the only sense that can be made of satisfaction of the Transition Condition, insofar as putative ontological vagueness is concerned, is to construe it as a matter of outright satisfaction of the two constitutively involved status principles, the ISS Principle and the CSI principle. Each item in a sorites sequence would have to have the same status as its immediate neighbours (e.g., baldness, or non-baldness, or borderline-baldness), and collectively there would have to be no overall distribution of statuses exhibited by the items in a sorites sequence. But the ISS Principle and the CSI Principle *cannot* be mutually satisfied, along with the Difference Condition. Therefore, ontological vagueness is impossible: there cannot be vague objects, vague properties, or vague relations in the right ontology.

2.4 If ordinary objects are in the right ontology then they are vague

We will use the expression 'ordinary object' to apply to familiar posits of everyday thought and language – e.g., tables, chairs, rocks, mountains, buildings, persons – and also to apply to many posits of scientific theory – e.g., cells, multi-celled organisms, planets, galaxies. An ordinary object is one that (i) is in fact posited in true instances of everyday thought and language or in science, and (ii) is not conceived as fully determinate in all intrinsic respects. One way for a posit to fail to be conceived as fully determinate is this: it is not conceived as having fully determinate composition, i.e., it is not conceived in a way that sharply distinguishes between objects that are parts of the given object and objects that are located within the object without being parts of it. Another way is this: the object is not conceived as having fully determinate synchronic and diachronic spatiotemporal boundaries. Virtually all objects posited in everyday thought and language count as 'ordinary,' by these criteria – likewise for most objects posited by scientific theory, as well. (Fundamental particles posited in physics perhaps are an exception, or perhaps not.)

The following point bears emphasis. The claim that posited objects of a given kind *are not* conceived *as* fully determinate is logically weaker than the claim that such objects *are* conceived *as not* fully determinate. Thus, in principle there could be ordinary objects that in fact are fully determinate even though they are not normally conceived as having that feature – and such objects would not have natures that are *contrary* to how ordinary objects are normally conceived.

Nonetheless, it also bears emphasis that if someone wished to claim that ordinary objects of a given kind really are fully determinate despite not being conceived that way, then the advocate of this view would bear a strong burden of proof. That burden would be especially heavy because of Peter Unger's infamous 'problem of the many.' Once one posits at least one perfectly precise object that one claims is an eligible referent of a given ordinary-object-referring singular term (say, 'Tibbles', which purports to refer to a specific cat), shouldn't one also posit numerous (maybe even infinitely many) other perfectly precise objects that differ only slightly from one another (e.g., in their precise boundaries or their precise composition) and that therefore are equally eligible candidate-referents of that term? But, then, what could make it the case that the singular term denotes a given one of these precise candidate-referents, and fails to denote any of the others?

Moreover, if one were to try resisting the theoretical pressure to posit a multiplicity of fully determinate objects all of which are equally good candidates for being the referent of 'Tibbles', then one would thereby face a very similar, and very daunting-looking, burden anyway: viz., explaining why it should be the case that the right ontology includes a unique fully-determinate object that is the only eligible referent of 'Tibbles', rather than including a whole host of fully determinate objects that differ only slightly from one another and are all equally eligible candidate-referents.

In light of these considerations, it looks overwhelmingly likely that ordinary objects, if they belong to the right ontology at all, simply are not fully determinate. Given (i) that they are not *conceived* as fully determinate, and (ii) that it is very hard to see how an ontology containing determinate objects could yield a unique such object as a candidate for being identical to any given putative concrete object (such as the putative cat, Tibbles) rather than yielding a panoply of equally eligible candidates, an ontology that really does incorporate full-fledged ordinary objects – objects that are correctly countable the way people normally count them – would need to construe these putative entities as ontologically vague. Such an ontology would identify the unique cat Tibbles with a unique *vague* object, rather than identifying Tibbles with any of many slightly different, fully determinate, objects that are equally eligible Tibbles-candidates.

So we have the following argument for the claim that, if ordinary objects are in the right ontology then they are ontologically vague:

a. Every kind of ordinary object is such that: if there are objects of that kind in the right ontology, then they are indeterminate in certain ways – e.g., with respect to composition, and/or with respect to synchronic and diachronic boundaries.
b. To be indeterminate in one or more of these ways is to be ontologically vague.

Therefore,

c. Every kind of ordinary object is such that: if there are objects of that kind in the right ontology, then they are ontologically vague.

2.5 So ordinary objects are not included in the right ontology, and hence thought and talk about them cannot be accommodated via fully ontological vindication

The preceding two sections provide an argument for the conclusion that the right ontology, whatever exactly it is, does not include ordinary objects. The argument is this:

a. Ontological vagueness is impossible.
b. If any ordinary objects are in the right ontology, then they are ontologically vague.

Therefore,

c. There are no ordinary objects in the right ontology.

Does this argument establish the systematic falsity of all the numerous claims of ordinary thought and discourse, and of science, that posit ordinary objects? Not necessarily. It depends upon what is required to vindicate such claims, in light of the impossibility of ontological vagueness.

One potential form of vindication would rest upon a construal of truth, for thought and discourse about ordinary objects, as a quite direct form of correspondence between thought and language on one hand, and the world itself on the other hand. Claims that posit ordinary objects would count as true, under this direct-correspondence conception of truth, only if the right ontology contains objects and properties answering directly to the positing apparatus deployed in those claims. For example, the claim *Tibbles is hungry* is true, at a time t, just in case there is a unique object *o* in the right ontology that is denoted by 'Tibbles', and there is a unique property *P* in the right ontology that is expressed by the predicate 'is hungry', and *o* instantiates *P* (at t).

We will refer to this kind of vindication of ordinary-object claims – a form of vindication that is grounded in a conception of truth as direct correspondence between thought/language and world – as *fully ontological vindication*. Since ontological vagueness is impossible, fully ontological vindication of ordinary-object claims is not to be had. Metaphysicians must learn to live with this sobering conclusion.

2.6 Accommodating ordinary-object claims without fully ontological vindication: two alternative vindication programs

We will now describe two alternative programs for vindicating ordinary-object claims. Later in the chapter we will argue that the first of these is not viable, and that the second is the one to pursue. This subsidiary conclusion will then feed into our argument that existence monism is theoretically preferable to priority monism.

2.6.1 Partially ontological vindication

The first vindication program, which we will call *partially ontological* vindication, presupposes that the right ontology does not contain any ontologically vague items. It also claims that among the non-vague objects in the right ontology, some qualify as eligible referents for the vague positing apparatus that is deployed in ordinary-object claims. It handles the problem of the many by embracing the idea that typically there are many, slightly different, ontologically precise objects in the right ontology that each are equally eligible as candidate-referents for a given vague singular term; likewise, typically there are many, slightly different, ontologically precise properties or relations in the right ontology that each are equally eligible as candidate-referents for a given vague predicate.

We call this approach *partially* ontological because it does not actually posit, as items in the correct ontology, objects that answer uniquely to vague singular terms or vague singular thought-constituents – objects in the correct ontology that would underwrite *fully* ontological vindication. (Likewise, mutatis mutandis, for properties and relations in the right ontology, vis-à-vis vague predicates and vague predicative thought-constituents.) We call the approach partially *ontological* because it nonetheless requires the right ontology to include objects and properties that are *eligible* referents of the vague positing-apparatus of vague thought and vague language – despite also acknowledging that there is no object in the right ontology that is *uniquely* the referent of a vague singular term like 'Tibbles', and no property in the correct ontology that is uniquely the referent of a vague predicate like 'is hungry'.

The way that this approach proposes to vindicate ordinary-object claims is by construing truth for such claims, not as direct correspondence between thought/language and the world, but rather as an indirect form of correspondence. Specifically, the approach embraces a version of supervaluationist semantics, for ordinary-object claims. A 'permissible interpretation' of a thought or sentence containing vague positing-apparatus, on this view, assigns to each vague singular referring-constituent in the thought/statement a unique, ontologically precise, object in the right ontology; and it assigns to each vague predicative constituent in the thought/sentence an ontologically precise property or relation in the right ontology – a property or relation whose extension is a precise set of (ordered n-tuples of) ontologically precise objects in the right ontology. Under the proposed semantics, an ordinary-object claim is true simpliciter (i.e., super-true) just in case the claim comes out true under every permissible interpretation; it is false simpliciter (i.e., super-false) just in case it comes out false under every permissible interpretation; otherwise it is neither true simpliciter nor false simpliciter.

On this approach, the supervaluationist semantics for vagueness-involving claims is itself articulated in a metalanguage that is governed by direct-correspondence semantic standards, a metalanguage that therefore incurs ontological commitment to the items that it posits. The truth conditions for metalinguistic statements in this metalanguage conform to the construal of truth as direct correspondence because the items posited in the metalanguage – precise objects, precise properties, precise property-extensions with precise objects as elements – are all required by the truth conditions to be in the correct ontology. Thus, the claims made in the metalanguage are themselves subject to, and susceptible to, *full* ontological vindication. This means, inter alia, that the supervaluationist semantics set forth in the metalanguage are ontologically committed to a certain kind of reference relation, which we will call *ontological* reference (in order to signal that it is being posited as belonging to the right ontology). The semantics treat ontological reference as being one-to-many rather than one-to-one: a vague singular term like 'Tibbles' refers multiply to various precise objects that are Tibbles-candidates, a vague predicate like '...is a cat' refers multiply to various precise properties each of which has a determinate extension whose elements are all ontologically precise cat-candidates, etc. We will call this *multiple* ontological reference.[2]

Everyday counting-claims concerning ordinary objects are among the claims that get vindicated, on this approach. Suppose one says, for instance, 'There is exactly one cat present here now, viz., Tibbles.' Even though there are numerous (maybe infinitely many) ontologically precise objects present that largely overlap one another, and all are equally eligible to be referred to as 'Tibbles', the common-sense counting-claim counts as true anyway under the proposed supervaluationist semantics. That is, 'There is exactly one cat present here now, viz. Tibbles' comes out as true, by virtue of the fact that each permissible interpretation of this claim assigns to the singular term 'Tibbles' exactly one ontologically precise object from the correct ontology.

A natural add-on to this vindication program would be a contextualist construal of the concept of truth. The idea would be that this notion is governed by implicit contextual parameters. In some contexts – notably, the context of the 'ontology room,' and also the context in which one articulates semantics for ordinary-object claims – the parameters work in such a way that truth has a direct correspondence between thought/language and reality; under such a parameter-setting, one's uses of the positing apparatus of thought/language incur ontological commitments to the items posited. In most contexts, however (including numerous contexts of serious scientific inquiry), the parameters work in such a way that truth has an indirect correspondence – specifically, the kind of supervaluationist indirect correspondence lately described, in which the objects that figure in permissible interpretations are required to be items in the correct ontology, but a singular term that posits an ordinary object (e.g., the name 'Tibbles') does not uniquely denote any single item in the correct ontology. On this contextualist approach to truth, it would be far too crude to say that 'true' is ambiguous, or that there are multiple distinct concepts of truth. Rather, there is a single concept that involves implicit, contextually variable, parameters. Thus, 'true' is susceptible to fine-grained variations in meaning alongside coarse-grained commonality of meaning – where the coarse-grained commonality involves common implicit parameters, and the fine-grained variations involve different settings of those parameters.

The following question arises, concerning the ontologically precise objects that, according to the approach now being described, are items in the correct ontology and also are eligible candidates for being referred to as 'Tibbles'. Are these objects *cats*? More generally, as regards the ontologically precise objects in eligible interpretations of vague thoughts/statements, are these *ordinary* objects? In principle, an advocate of the program of partial ontological vindication could answer this question either affirmatively or negatively; and as far as we can see, very little hangs on how one answers it, as far as the viability of the program itself is concerned. However, there is a powerful-looking reason to answer negatively – viz., that ordinary counting practices seem to be constitutively built into the very notion of an ordinary object. If the right ontology really includes cats, then there is only *one* of these items present when you truly think or truly say, 'There is only one cat present, namely Tibbles.' So, if in fact there are numerous (maybe infinitely many) slightly different, ontologically precise, cat-candidates present, then none of them are cats; at best, they are highly numerous *quasi-cats*. Likewise, mutatis mutandis, for ordinary objects generally.

For our dialectical purposes in the present chapter, however, we do not need to insist on this point. Whether or not one embraces the extremely implausible claim that highly numerous, ontologically precise, objects are *ordinary* objects, the program of partially ontological vindication will come to ruin anyway (See section 2.7).

2.6.2 Non-ontological vindication

Above we emphasized that under the partially ontological vindication program, truth – for the forms of discourse to which the program applies – is an indirect form of correspondence between thought/language and the world. It is indirect because it invokes multiple ontological reference rather than unique ontological reference, and it treats full-fledged truth as 'supertruth' – i.e. truth under every permissible way of assigning, to each vague term or thought-constituent, a unique referent that is one of the various items to which the term or thought-constituent multiply refers. For example, the truth of the statement 'Tibbles is a cat' is not a direct correspondence, consisting of there being an object *o* in the right ontology that is uniquely referred to as 'Tibbles' and instantiates a property *P* in the right ontology that is uniquely ontologically referred to as 'cathood'. Rather, it is a form of indirect correspondence, consisting of a set of objects in the right ontology whose member objects are multiply ontologically referred to by 'Tibbles', and a set of properties in the right ontology whose member properties are multiply ontologically referred to as 'cathood', such that the statement 'Tibbles is a cat' comes out true under every permissible way of narrowing down the multiple references of 'Tibbles' and of 'cathood' to a unique reference.

We will call this form of truth *ontologically opulent* indirect correspondence, in order to signal that it involves truth conditions that carry full-fledged ontological commitment to the objects, properties, and property-extensions that it posits as the items to which vague terms and thought constituents bear the relation of ontological multiple reference. Ontologically opulent indirect correspondence requires the presence, in the right ontology, of items that are eligible candidate referents for ordinary-object-positing expressions; indirectness of correspondence comes in only because typically there are so many eligible candidates that one needs a semantics that supervaluates over all of them (rather than a direct-correspondence semantics that maps each vague singular term onto a unique object in the right ontology and maps each vague predicate onto a unique property in the right ontology).

Once one duly appreciates that the form of truth attributed to ordinary-object claims by the partially ontological vindication program is an indirect kind of correspondence, an important further possibility comes to light – viz., that there might well be certain types of thought/language for which truth is a kind of correspondence that is even more indirect than is the specific form of indirect correspondence envisioned in the vindication program. Consider, for example, the statement

(A) The politics of Arizona is much discussed in the American news media.

It is natural and plausible to construe the truth conditions for statement (A) as comprising a range of possible worlds – where a possible world is taken to be, say, a maximal property instantiable by the cosmos (i.e., a *way the world might be*). And it is plausible to claim both (i) that the maximal property actually instantiated by the cosmos is within this range of truth-making ways the world might be (and thus that statement (A) is true), and yet (ii) that there are no items in the right ontology that are even *eligible candidates* to be referred to by the various bits of sub-sentential positing apparatus in statement (A) such as 'Arizona', 'the politics of Arizona', and 'the American news media'.

This form of truth is what we call *ontologically austere* indirect correspondence. It arises when (i) the way the world actually is conspires with contextually operative semantic affirmability standards in such a way that a given thought/statement is correctly affirmable, and (ii) those semantic standards do not require the right ontology to include items that are eligible candidate-referents for the positing apparatus deployed in the thought/statement.

The contextualist approach to truth, as described late in section 2.6.1, can be naturally extended to encompass not only direct correspondence and ontologically opulent indirect correspondence, but also various types of ontologically austere indirect correspondence too. The concept of truth remains univocal, under such contextualism: truth is *semantically correct affirmability under contextually operative semantic affirmability standards*. But it also exhibits fine-grained variability, involving contextual variation in the implicit parameters that govern semantic correctness. Semantically correct affirmability is not in general reducible to an epistemic feature, such as warranted affirmability or 'ideal' warranted affirmability; for, in general it will be possible for a statement to be true (i.e., semantically correctly affirmable) without being well warranted, and it will be possible for a statement to be well warranted without being true. Nevertheless, normally the gap between what's required for epistemic warrant and what's required for semantic correctness will be a relatively small one – which means that positivists, and also neo-pragmatists such as Putnam (1981, 1983) and Rorty (1979, 1982), were onto something right and important, even though they were mistaken to think that truth is reducible to some epistemic feature like warranted affirmability. We all have a fairly good idea, for example, what would constitute good evidence for statement (A) above, and such evidence need not render likely the claim that the right ontology includes one or more items that are eligible candidate referents for, e.g., the expression 'the politics of Arizona'. So, since the gap between warranted affirmability and semantically correct affirmability is a small one, there is excellent reason to think that the semantic affirmability standards governing statement (A) are ontologically undemanding vis-a-vis the positing apparatus deployed in (A), and hence that what (A)'s truth consists of is ontologically austere indirect correspondence. (If the truth of (A) actually requires the right ontology to include some item(s) answering to the expression 'the politics of Arizona', then the epistemic-warrant criteria one would normally apply to (A) are far too lax; so, since such extreme and pervasive epistemic laxity is very unlikely, the truth of (A) is very probably a matter of ontologically austere indirect correspondence.)

So truth, for many kinds of claims made in typical real-life contexts, is plausibly construed as ontologically austere indirect correspondence. In light of this fact, there now arises the possibility that the same goes for numerous ordinary-object claims both in everyday thought/discourse and also in much serious science. There thus arises another vindication program regarding ordinary-object claims, distinct from both fully ontological vindication and partially ontological vindication – viz., the program of seeking to vindicate such claims by maintaining that *their* truth consists in ontologically austere indirect correspondence. We will call this the program of *non-ontological* vindication.

An advocate of this alternative vindication program need not necessarily deny that the right ontology contains ontologically precise objects. What does get denied, however, is the contention that the right ontology includes a relation of *ontological multiple reference* that links vague terms to such precise objects and to sets of such precise objects. Consider, for example, the name 'Tibbles'. According to the program of non-ontological vindication of ordinary-object claims, this name does not bear a relation of multiple ontological reference to any objects in the right ontology; likewise, the term 'cathood' does not bear a relation of multiple ontological reference to any properties in the right ontology. Rather, the kind of truth possessed by the statement 'Tibbles is a cat' is, like the kind of truth possessed by the statement (A) above, *ontologically austere* indirect correspondence.

Elsewhere we have articulated and defended at some length, under the rubric *contextual semantics*, a position maintaining (1) that truth is semantically correct affirmability under contextually operative semantic affirmability standards, (2) that affirmability standards for most kinds of thought/discourse, in most contexts, work in such a way that truth, for such thought/discourse, is ontologically austere indirect correspondence, and (3) that direct-correspondence semantic standards are sometimes, albeit rarely, contextually operative (e.g., in the venerable 'ontology room'). We have wedded this semantic position to a general ontological position claiming that numerous posits of everyday thought/discourse and of scientific thought/discourse – ordinary objects included – are not items in the correct ontology. We call this package-deal, ontological-cum-semantic, position *austere realism*. And we have defended a particular version of austere realism – viz., the form of existence monism we call *blobjectivism* (cf. the third paragraph of the present chapter). Inter alia, austere realism embraces, and seeks to make credible and plausible, the program of non-ontological vindication of ordinary-object claims.

2.7 Why partially ontological vindication is not viable

Our strategy in the present chapter is first to argue by elimination for the non-ontological vindication program by explaining why neither of the other alternative vindication programs (fully ontological and partially ontological) is viable, and then to argue, largely on the basis of the fact that the non-ontological vindication program is the only viable one remaining, that existence monism is theoretically preferable to priority monism. In section 2.5 we argued, by appeal to the impossibility of ontological vagueness, that the program of fully ontological vindication is not viable. In the present section we will argue that the impossibility of ontological vagueness also undermines the partially ontological vindication program.

As we stressed in section 2.3, essential to genuine vagueness is the feature of boundarylessness: there is no determinate fact of the matter about status-transitions in a sorites sequence. This means not just that there is no sharp transition between an initial status (e.g., truth) and the polar-opposite status (e.g., falsity), but also that there are no sharp status-transitions at all. Boundarylessness is therefore violated if one embraces what we call *standard supervaluationism* – the form of supervaluationism that is formulated in a non-vague metalanguage governed by classical logic and classical two-valued semantics. For, standard supervaluation is committed to two sharp boundaries in a sorites sequence of vague object-language statements: a sharp boundary between the status *true* and the status *neither true nor false*, and another sharp boundary between the status *neither true nor false* and the status *false*. Therefore, any version of supervaluationism that fully respects boundarylessness must be a form of what we call *iterated* supervaluationism: categories in the metalanguage – e.g., the category *permissible referent-object for 'Tibbles'*, or the category *permissible extension-assignment for the predicate '... is a cat'* – must be construed as vague themselves; and hence the metalanguage must itself have supervaluationist semantics expressible in a second-order metalanguage. By parallel reasoning, the second-order metalanguage must be vague and have supervaluationist semantics expressible in a third-order metalanguage; and so on, up iteratively through the whole infinite hierarchy of metalanguages.

According to the program of partially ontological vindication, however, claims about ordinary objects are to be vindicated via a version of supervaluationist semantics that is formulated in a metalanguage that is governed by direct-correspondence semantic standards and hence is ontologically committed to the items it posits. Given that ontological vagueness is impossible, such a metalanguage must eschew vague categories altogether. For instance, it must construe the category *permissible referent-object for 'Tibbles'* as applying to all and only the members of a unique, determinate, set of ontologically precise objects; it must construe the category *permissible extension-assignment for the predicate '...is a cat'* as applying to all and only the members of a unique, determinate, set of sets of ontologically precise objects; and so on, for all the semantic categories posited in the metalanguage.

This would be a version of standard supervaluationism, however. As such, it would not really acknowledge or accommodate the actual vagueness of actual human thought and actual human language, because genuine vagueness essentially involves boundarylessness. And of course, a semantics that fails even to accommodate genuine vagueness cannot provide a *vindication* of the claims expressed in vague discourse, or of the thoughts such claims express.

So the program of partially ontological vindication of ordinary-object claims comes to grief. The argument for this conclusion can be set forth as a dilemma, as follows. Supervaluationist semantics can be formulated either (1) in a metalanguage that is governed by direct-correspondence truth-conditions and therefore eschews vague categories, or (2) in a metalanguage that deploys vague categories and therefore is governed by indirect-correspondence semantic standards. Under option (1), genuine vagueness in language and thought is not accommodated, because genuine vagueness essentially involves boundarylessness. So, since ordinary-object claims do not get accommodated by the semantics, they do not get vindicated either. Under option (2), genuine vagueness in language and thought is evidently accommodated via the use of vague categories in the metalanguage, but now the vague claims in the metalanguage are themselves just as much in need of vindication as are the vague claims in the object language. So, since the claims in the metalanguage are as yet unvindicated themselves, these claims do not confer vindication upon the ordinary-object claims in the object language. Thus, under both option (1) and option (2), ordinary-object claims fail to get vindicated in the manner envisioned in section 2.6.1 – i.e., these claims fail to get vindicated by appeal to a supervaluationist semantics whose ur-elements are all ontologically precise items.

Another, closely related, way to argue for the non-viability of the program of partial ontological vindication of ordinary-object claims is to make use of this fact: when one is deploying language in a manner governed by direct-correspondence semantic standards, sorites arguments become powerful tools for reasoning via reductio ad absurdum. The argument goes as follows. Consider a sorites sequence of actual or possible ontologically precise objects with this feature: the successive objects in the sequence gradually 'morph' from ones that are extremely cat-like to ones that are extremely dog-like. Suppose, by way of reductio, that the right ontology includes the putative property *being an eligible cat-candidate*, and that some of the items early in the sequence instantiate this property. For any object in the sequence, if it is an eligible cat-candidate then so is its immediate successor; otherwise there would be a sharp transition in the sequence between the objects that instantiate the property *being an eligible cat-candidate* and the ones that do not – which in turn would yield a supervaluationist semantics that fails to honour the essential boundarylessness of vagueness. So every object in the sequence is an eligible cat-candidate. However, extremely dog-like objects late in the sequence surely are *not* eligible cat-candidates. Hence, there are objects late in the sequence that both are, and are not, eligible cat-candidates – which is impossible. So there is no such property in the right ontology as *being an eligible cat-candidate*, and hence there are no objects in the right ontology that are eligible cat-candidates. But if there are no such objects in the right ontology, then the project of partially ontological vindication of cat-discourse cannot even get started. Likewise, mutatis mutandis, for the project of partially ontological vindication of ordinary-object discourse in general. Therefore, that project is not viable.

At this juncture, it is important to maintain a clear-eyed view of the dialectical state of play. The reasoning in the previous paragraph was conducted under direct-correspondence semantic standards; it was reasoning of the kind that is appropriate when one is situated squarely within the proverbial 'ontology room.' But it's hard to breathe in there, because the air is so exquisitely thin. One can also stand in the doorway, so to speak, with one foot within the ontology room and one without. When so situated, one can coherently maintain, on one hand, that the right ontology does indeed contain ontologically precise objects, and on the other hand that some of these objects are rightly classified as eligible cat-candidates whereas others are not. But the crucial thing to appreciate about such a manner of thought/discourse is that it incorporates both direct-correspondence aspects and indirect-correspondence aspects, in a subtle and complex mixture. For, on one hand it carries genuine ontological commitment to ontologically precise objects. But on the other hand it does not, and cannot, carry genuine ontological commitment to a property *eligible cat-candidate-hood*, or to a set of ontologically determinate cat candidates, or to states of affairs consisting of an ontologically precise object being an eligible cat candidate. The category 'eligible cat candidate' is *vague* – as it must be within any form of supervaluationism that respects both the boundarylessness of vagueness and the fact that the category 'cat' is itself vague. So, since ontological vagueness is impossible, semantically correct affirmative uses of this category can only be indirect-correspondence uses. Thus, when one thinks or says, 'Some ontologically precise objects are eligible cat-candidates,' one's *overall* claim is being made under indirect-correspondence semantic standards – even though the claim really does carry ontological commitment to the items one is *calling* eligible cat candidates. It's fine to call them that, if you like – *but not in the ontology room!* (More on this theme in section 2.8.)

In a nutshell, here is the reason why the program of partially ontological vindication of ordinary-object claims is not viable: given the impossibility of ontological vagueness, and given that an adequate supervaluationist semantics must respect the boundarylessness of genuine vagueness, there cannot be items in the right ontology that simultaneously answer to the positing apparatus of one's proposed supervaluational semantics and also figure in a version of supervaluationism that respects boundarylessness. Rather, the only kind of supervaluationist semantics whose claims could be true in the ontology room – i.e., true under direct-correspondence semantic standards – is a version of *standard* supervaluationism. Standard supervaluationism deploys a non-vague notion of multiple reference, thereby steering clear of the impossibility of ontological vagueness. But for this very reason, standard supervaluationism blatantly fails to respect the boundarylessness of genuine vagueness.

Faced with these considerations, an advocate of partially ontological vindication of ordinary-object claims might try the following strategy: on one hand, concede that the program as originally conceived is not viable, but on the other hand, formulate and advocate a fallback version of the program. One potential fallback version goes as follows. First, one retains the idea of using supervaluationist semantics, with ontologically precise objects as ur-elements in the various sets of objects posited by the semantics. Second, one embraces iterated supervaluationism rather than standard supervaluationism, as a way to fully respect the boundarylessness of vagueness. Third, one acknowledges that the first-order metalanguage in which one's semantics for ordinary-object claims is being given deploys positing apparatus that is vague, and thus that this metalanguage is itself governed by indirect-correspondence semantic standards (so that the semantical notions should not be construed as invoking a relation of multiple *ontological* reference); likewise for the second-order metalanguage, and the third, and so on, ad infinitum. Fourth, one acknowledges that the vague claims in the first-order metalanguage are themselves in need of vindication; likewise for the second-order-metalanguage, and the third, and so on, ad infinitum. Fifth, one claims that the overall account yields the sought-for vindication, both for object-level discourse and for each level of metalinguistic discourse, in the following way: the claims of the object-level discourse are *conditionally* vindicated, relative to the claims of the first-order metalanguage; the claims of the first-order metalanguage are conditionally vindicated, relative to the claims in the second-order metalanguage; and so on, ad infinitum.

This fallback stance faces an obvious and fatal-looking problem, however: the extreme implausibility of the idea that an infinite series of sequentially-linked 'conditional vindications' somehow yields *unconditional* vindication for each item in the series. That idea is familiar from epistemology, in the specific form of an infinite chain of conditional epistemic-justification relations: belief b_1 is conditionally justified relative to belief$_2$; belief$_2$ is conditionally justified relative to belief$_3$; and so on, ad infinitum. Virtually nobody finds it credible that such an unending chain of epistemic dependence could confer *unconditional* justification on the respective beliefs in the chain. Likewise, it is thoroughly implausible – indeed, really not even intelligible – to claim that the strategy of infinite buck-passing of the request for a partially ontological vindication of vague discourse – from the object language to the first-order metalanguage, from the first-order metalanguage to the second-order metalanguage, and so on, ad infinitum – somehow actually *delivers* the sought-for vindication. It does not deliver it for the object language, or for any of the respective metalanguages either.

The upshot of our discussion in this subsection is as follows. The program of partially ontological, supervaluationism-based, vindication of ordinary-object discourse, conceived as being conducted within the ontology room under direct-correspondence semantic standards that confer ontological commitment upon one's metalinguistic claims, is not viable. For this program is limited to standard supervaluationism, which does not respect the boundarylessness of vagueness. The fallback version that appeals to iterated supervaluationism, and to an infinite chain of successive 'conditional' vindications, is not viable either. For this program fails to deliver unconditional vindication of vague thought and vague discourse, either for vague object-language claims or for any of the vague metalinguistic claims in the infinite sequence of vague metalanguages.

Is there some other kind of fallback variant of the partially ontological vindication program that is viable? Not that we can see, but we leave this as a challenge to those who would champion the idea of partially ontological vindication. It is very hard to envision how a viable fallback position could avoid relying, to some extent at least, upon *non-ontological* vindication. But once one takes steps in that direction, it will become a very serious question why one cannot just apply the strategy of non-ontological vindication directly to ordinary-object claims themselves – thereby eliminating the need to seek out a partially ontological form of vindication that requires claiming that the right ontology includes items that are eligible referent-candidates for vague categories.

2.8 Semantical theorizing outside the ontology room, and semantical theorizing in the doorway

Numerous interesting and important theoretical questions, both in science and in philosophy, arise and get addressed when one is deploying vague notions and one's thought/discourse is governed by austere indirect-correspondence semantic standards (for short, AIC semantic standards). It will be useful, as a complement to the preceding discussion, to focus briefly on a specific example: semantical theorizing concerning a version of Unger's 'problem of the many' in which none of the posited objects are ontologically precise. We will comment on David Lewis's treatment of such a version of the problem (Lewis 1999). Our main contention will be that Lewis can be read, and really should be read, in the following way: (1) the mode of discourse in which the theoretical question is posed, and in which it is addressed, is governed by AIC semantic standards; (2) because of this,

his discussion does not constitute an implementation of the program of partially ontological vindication of ordinary-object claims; and (3) the discussion nonetheless constitutes a plausible and credible semantical treatment of a theoretically important philosophical question.

Lewis begins his discussion with the following instance of the problem of the many (Lewis 1999, p. 167):

> Cat Tibbles is alone on the mat. Tibbles has hairs h_1, h_2, ... h_{1000}. Let c be Tibbles including all these hairs, let c_1 be Tibbles except for h_1; and similarly for c_2, ... c_{1000}. Each of these c's is a cat. So instead of one cat on the mat, Tibbles, we have at least 1001 cats – which is absurd.

The positing apparatus deployed in this passage is vague, as are the posited items. Tibbles is an ordinary cat, and therefore is vague in various respects – e.g., with respect to synchronic composition and with respect to diachronic duration of existence; and the posited objects c_1, ... c_n are each vague in the same way. So, since ontological vagueness is impossible, and since discourse deploying vague posits also does not exhibit an ontologically opulent kind of indirect language/world correspondence, the problem under discussion is being posed using language that is governed by AIC semantic standards.

Lewis offers two alternative ways of dealing with the conundrum of the 1001 cats. The first solution is to embrace a supervaluationist semantical treatment of everyday statements about cats (including statements about how many of them there are at specific locations):

> Super-truth, with respect to a language interpreted in an imperfectly decisive way, replaces truth *simpliciter* as the goal of a cooperative speaker attempting to impart information. We can put it another way: Whatever it is that we do to determine the 'intended' interpretation of our language determines not one interpretation but a range of interpretations. (The range depends on context, and is itself somewhat indeterminate.) .... Each intended interpretation of our language puts one of the cat-candidates on the mat into the extension of the word 'cat', and excludes all the rest. Likewise each intended interpretation picks out one cat-candidate, the same one, as the referent of 'Tibbles'. Therefore it is super-true that there is just one cat, Tibbles, on the mat. Because it is super-true, you are entitled to affirm it. (Lewis 1999, 172–3)

Note the parenthetical remark in this passage, about the range of interpretations being somewhat indeterminate itself. This effectively commits Lewis to the iterated kind of supervaluationism, since the metalinguistic category *range of eligible interpretations* is vague itself. Note too the fine-grained differences between (1) the contextually operative semantic standards that are at work in the metalanguage Lewis is employing and (2) the semantic standards governing the object-language discourse whose semantics is being described. In the metalanguage, the semantic standards permit the positing of those numerous cat-like objects $c_1 \ldots c_n$, all there on the mat; but in the object language, the semantic standards permit the positing of only one such object, viz., the unique cat Tibbles. (These fine-grained differences in the workings of contextually operative semantic standards both occur with the coarse-grained rubric of AIC semantic standards; neither the object-language claims or the metalinguistic claims are being made 'in the ontology room.')

Lewis's second proposed solution is to acknowledge all those cat-candidates, say they are all really cats, say they bear the relation 'almost identical' to one another, and repudiate the everyday counting-claims:

> [A]ny two of our cat-candidates overlap almost completely.... Assume our cat-candidates are genuine cats. (Set aside, for now, the supervaluationist solution.) Then, strictly speaking, the cats are many.... We have many cats, each one almost identical to all the rest.... [W]hat's true is that for some x, x is a cat on the mat, and every cat on the mat is almost identical to x. (Lewis 1999, 177–8)

This solution deploys a form of AIC discourse in which the positing apparatus is governed by fine-grained semantic standards rather similar to those at work in the metalanguage in which the supervaluationist solution was articulated, except that now the category *cathood* is being applied to all the cat-candidates themselves – and hence the usual contextual standards governing cat-counting are not in force.

Not surprisingly, given that Lewis is the author of the landmark paper about implicit contextual parameters 'Scorekeeping in a Language Game' (Lewis 1983), he goes contextualist about these two solutions, suggesting that sometimes the first solution is better and sometimes the second one is, depending on context:

> Sometimes, especially in our offhand and unphilosophical moments, ... the supervaluation rule ... will entitle us to say that there is only one cat. But sometimes, for instance when we have been explicitly attending to the many candidates and noting that they are equally cat-like, context will favor the ... many-cat sort of interpretation.... [W]e explicitly choose to say that the many are all cats, and we thereby make the supervaluation go away. (Lewis 1999, 179–80)

This passage should not be read, we suggest, as though it were written within the ontology room. That is, it should not be read as claiming that the right ontology includes the many cat-candidates and that they are all really cats. On the contrary, the cat-candidates-that-are-cats that Lewis is talking about are all *vague* posits, and ontological vagueness is impossible. (Moreover, the metalanguage employs a vague semantical notion too, viz., *range of eligible interpretations*. Since ontological vagueness is impossible, this notion cannot be construed as expressing a relation of ontological multiple reference.) The moments in which it is contextually appropriate to say, in a reflective and philosophical way, 'the many are all cats' are *not* moments when we mean to be doing serious ontology. Rather, they are moments in which we mean to be using cat-talk in a manner that is contextually most appropriate when, as Lewis puts it himself, 'we have been explicitly attending to the many candidates and noting that they are equally cat-like.' Not all serious philosophical questions are raised within the ontology room, and not all semantical proposals used to address serious philosophical questions are to be understood as coming from within the ontology room. Rather, a great deal of philosophical discourse, including semantical discourse within philosophy, is itself governed by AIC semantic standards. The ontology room is only a small part of the mansion of philosophy.

We have been urging that Lewis's discussion of the problem of the many is best construed as taking place entirely outside of the ontology room. (We take no stand on whether he himself intended this construal.[3]) But suppose now that one is standing in the doorway of that room, and one maintains that the right ontology contains numerous ontologically precise objects. Wouldn't it be contextually appropriate to say the following, using a mode of discourse that carries full-fledged ontological commitment to those objects?

> Some ontologically precise objects are cat-candidates and some are not, and the semantics of ordinary-object claims can be given via a version of supervaluationism in which the eligible interpretations are sets whose ur-elements are ontologically precise objects.

It would indeed be contextually appropriate to say this. And this would be quite a plausible thing to say, while standing in the door of the ontology room and ontologically committing oneself to a plethora of ontologically precise objects. (Whether it would be *true*, under the contextually operative semantic standards, depends on whether or not the correct ontology really does contain numerous ontologically precise objects. It doesn't – we're getting to that.) Lewis's remarks apply again here, mutatis mutandis – even though now, the many that are being explicitly attended to are ontologically precise posits, and are ones that the speaker explicitly thinks are in the right ontology.

But the crucial point to appreciate is this: even though the contextually operative semantic standards work in such a way that certain portions of one's current philosophical discourse are ontologically committing (viz., the portions involving the positing of ontologically precise objects), other portions are not like this. The category *cat-candidate* does not bear the relation of unique ontological reference to some specific set of ontologically precise objects, or the relation of multiple ontological reference to the members of some specific set of specific sets of ontologically precise objects. The term *cathood* does not bear the relation of unique ontological reference to some specific property in the right ontology, or the relation of multiple ontological reference to some specific set of such properties. And so forth. Thus, one's supervaluationist semantics for ordinary-object claims is being put forth within a form of discourse in which the contextually operative semantic standards are *very largely* of the AIC kind, even though a portion of the discourse is ontologically committal. One is incurring ontological commitment to precise objects, all right; but one is not incurring ontological commitment to a range of *cat-like* precise objects, because that posited range is vague. Thus, what one accomplishes with one's supervaluationism is like what Lewis accomplishes: squaring the positing of a vague range of eligible cat-candidates – in this case, a vague range of ontologically precise eligible cat-candidates – with ordinary ways of counting cats. That posited range of objects does not belong to the right ontology, even if ontologically precise objects themselves do belong to it.

What one does *not* accomplish with one's supervaluationism – not in this case any more than in a case where the posited many are vague objects themselves – is a successful implementation of the partially ontological vindication project. Standing in the doorway of the ontology room is crucially different from being fully inside. Go all the way in there if you like, closing the door behind you; but if you do then you will need to shift the score in the language game into direct-correspondence mode, and acknowledge that no ontologically precise objects are cats or even cat-candidates.

2.9 Existence monism is theoretically preferable to priority monism

Existence monism asserts that there is just one concrete object in the right ontology: the whole cosmos. There are no objects in the right ontology that are proper parts of the cosmos. Priority monism, by contrast, asserts that the right ontology does indeed include concrete objects that are proper parts of the cosmos; and it also asserts that the cosmos itself is ontologically fundamental, with the proper-part objects being ontologically dependent upon it (and not the other way around).

One can distinguish three broad types of priority monism. One type would claim that the right ontology includes ordinary objects that conform to the usual practices of counting and individuation, and that these objects are ontologically vague. It would embrace the program of full ontological vindication for ordinary-object claims. A second type would eschew ontological vagueness, would claim that the right ontology includes a plethora of ontologically precise objects, and would embrace the program of partial ontological vindication for ordinary-object claims. A third type would eschew ontological vagueness, would claim that the right ontology includes a plethora of ontologically precise objects, and would embrace the program of non-ontological vindication for ordinary-object claims.

In light of our arguments in preceding sections, neither the first type of priority monism nor the second is viable, because ordinary-object claims cannot be given either fully ontological vindication or partially ontological vindication. That leaves the third type. But this kind of priority monism faces the following awkward problem: there is no obvious theoretical role to be played, in ontology, by all those ontologically precise objects that are supposed to be proper parts of the whole cosmos. (One might have thought that their principal theoretical role is to figure in the vindication of ordinary-object claims, as per the partially ontological vindication program. But that program comes to grief, as we have argued.) Since these putative objects have no significant theoretical role to play in ontology, that is a strong reason to repudiate them. Better to embrace existence monism, on grounds of comparative theoretical simplicity.

This argument is further reinforced by the fact that eschewing all those putative concrete part-objects eliminates the need to introduce into one's ontology a relation of ontological priority among objects. Whether or not the notion of ontological priority among objects is problematically obscure (as some claim it is), it too evidently has no significant role to play in ontology, given the non-viability of both the fully ontological vindication program and the partially ontological vindication program. By embracing existence monism one eliminates from ontology two kinds of un-needed theoretical baggage: not only the putative, ontologically precise, objects that are proper parts of the whole cosmos, but also the putative relation of ontological priority between the cosmos and those putative proper parts. Yet more reason to embrace existence monism, on grounds of yet more comparative theoretical simplicity.

Now, one might think that there is still a vital ontological role to be played by ontologically precise objects that are proper parts of the whole cosmos. The cosmos is structurally complex and is highly non-homogeneous, after all. One might think that these features of the whole are only possible insofar as they are grounded ontologically in a plethora of concrete objects that are proper parts of the whole, and in the various relations that these concrete objects bear to one another. But we are assuming, remember, that the conditional versions of Schaffer's master arguments in favor of monism over pluralism are correct. A corollary of that assumption, as we stressed in section 2.2, is that the structural complexity and the non-homogeneity of the whole cosmos are not ontologically grounded in relations among proper parts. That corollary, together with the fact that neither the fully ontological vindication program nor the partially ontological vindication is viable, leaves one without any evident theoretical motivation to think that the right ontology includes either concrete objects that are parts of the whole, or a relation of ontological priority that the whole bears to such concrete objects.

But isn't it just lunatic to deny that there are tables, chairs, mountains, electrons, and persons? Well yes, of course. In most contexts of discourse and thought, including most contexts of serious scientific inquiry, such denials are indeed lunatic. But that is because in those contexts, the pertinent positing apparatus in language and in thought is governed by austere indirect-correspondence semantic standards – standards under which it is unproblematically true that there are tables, chairs, mountains, electrons, and persons. The context of serious ontological inquiry is another matter, however. When one steps into the ontology room, thereby shifting the language game into direct-correspondence semantic standards, what is true is this: There is exactly one concrete object, viz., the whole cosmos.

Notes

1. In Horgan and Potrč (2008) and Horgan (2010), it is argued that any approach to the logic and semantics of vagueness that thoroughly avoids any commitment to arbitrary sharp boundaries among semantic categories must really be, not an alternative to the transvaluationist conception of vagueness we have just been sketching, but rather an implementation of this conception. In particular, this is true of what we call 'iterated supervaluationism' – the kind of supervaluationism that treats its own metalinguistic categories as vague (and hence as themselves subject to supervaluationist semantics in a second-order metalanguage), and the semantic categories in the second-order metalanguage as vague, and so on *ad infinitum*, up through the metalinguistic hierarchy. The core idea behind the argument that approaches to vagueness like iterated supervaluationism are really implementations of transvaluationism – not alternatives to it – is this: an explanation is needed for the fact that that the entire infinite hierarchy fails to generate determinate sharp boundaries among semantic categories; and the only plausible (and therefore the best) explanation is that vagueness inherently involves the specific kind of logical incoherence that transvaluationism says it does.
2. One could hold a kind of supervaluationist picture according to which the various Tibbles-candidates are in the correct ontology, but there is no ontological reference-relation over these entities in the right ontology. But this picture would not conform to the program of partially ontological vindication of ordinary-object claims, because one's metalinguistic talk of multiple reference would itself stand in need of ontological vindication. (See also our remarks on semantical theorizing 'in the doorway of the ontology room,' in Section 2.8.)
3. In 1988, Lewis invited Horgan to Lewis's seminar at Princeton University on ontological commitment. On the syllabus for the week of Horgan's visit were several of Horgan's papers arguing that some existence claims, in context, are governed by AIC semantic standards (as we are now calling them) and do not carry ontological commitment to their posits. The syllabus also had the following title for that week's session and readings: 'Quantification with Crossed Fingers.' A year or two later, Horgan asked Lewis in conversation why he seemed reluctant to extend his own semantic contextualism to 'backwards-E' statements, and Lewis replied 'I

don't know, conservatism I guess.' In our view, he would have done well to firmly repudiate such conservatism.

References

Horgan, T., 1995. Transvaluationism: A Dionysian Approach to Vagueness, *Southern Journal of Philosophy* 33, Spindel Conference Supplement on Vagueness: 97–126.

Horgan, T., 1998. The Transvaluationist Conception of Vagueness, *The Monist* 81: 316–33.

Horgan, T., 2010. Transvaluationism about Vagueness: A Progress Report, *Southern Journal of Philosophy* 48: 67–94.

Horgan, T. and Potrč, M., 2000. Blobjectivism and Indirect Correspondence, *Facta Philosophica* 2: 249–70.

Horgan, T. and Potrč, M., 2002. Addressing Questions for Blobjectivism, *Facta Philosophica* 4: 311–21.

Horgan, T. and Potrč, M., 2008. *Austere Realism: Contextual Semantics Meets Minimal Ontology*. MIT Press.

Lewis, D., 1983. Scorekeeping in a Language Game. In his *Philosophical Papers, Volume 1*. Oxford University Press, 233–249.

Lewis, D., 1999. Many, But Almost One. In his *Papers in Metaphysics and Epistemology*. Cambridge University Press, 164–182.

Potrč, M., 2002. Transvaluationism, Common Sense and Indirect Correspondence, *Acta Analytica* 29, 101-119.Putnam, H., 1981. *Reason, Truth and History*. Cambridge University Press.

Putnam, H., 1983. *Realism and Reason: Philosophical Papers, Volume 3*. Cambridge University Press.

Rorty, R., 1979. *Philosophy and the Mirror of Nature*. Princeton University Press.

Rorty, R., 1982. *Consequences of Pragmatism*. University of Minnesota Press.

Sainsbury, M., 1990. *Concepts without Boundaries*. Inaugural Lecture, King's College London.Reprinted in R. Keefe and P. Smith (eds.), *Vagueness: A Reader* (MIT Press, 1996).

Schaffer, J., 2003. Is There a Fundamental Level? *Nous* 37: 498–517.

Schaffer, J., 2007. Monism, *Stanford Encyclopedia of Philosophy*.

3
Why the World Has Parts: Reply to Horgan and Potrč

Jonathan Schaffer

> [The parts] are not the whole reality but they are real in themselves, and it is only our imperfection as finites which conceals from us partially their true nature; how that is they are delimited against each other in Space-Time...The One is the system of the Many in which they are conserved not the vortex in which they are engulfed. (Alexander 1950: 347)

In 'Monism: The Priority of the Whole,' I proposed to revive the classical monistic tradition, in part by arguing that its dismissal was based on a misinterpretation. I argued that the classical monists were not defending the seemingly crazy view that only the one whole exists, but rather were defending the more sensible view that the one whole is ontologically prior to its many proper parts (which presupposes that the one whole and its many proper parts all exist). Taking it as obvious that many things exist (you and I, one hand and then another, etc.), I claimed that there remains an interesting question of what depends on what, with some plausible arguments for the monistic idea that the one whole is more fundamental, with its many proper parts existing as dependent fragments of an integrated substance.

In 'Existence Monism Trumps Priority Monism,' Terry Horgan and Matjaž Potrč aim to show that the view that only the one whole exists is neither so crazy nor so easy to dismiss. They argue that the view that only the one whole exists (*existence monism*) is actually preferable to the monistic view that I considered both more sensible and more historically accurate, on which the one whole is viewed as more fundamental than its many proper parts (*priority monism*).[1]

Horgan and Potrč prefer existence monism on grounds of *parsimony*, for doing without any of the many proper parts. But their main focus is on *vagueness*. For the main reason for regarding priority monism as more sensible is that it respects truisms such as Moore's (1993: 166): 'Here is one hand, and here is another.' Horgan and Potrč reply that considerations of vagueness preclude any 'ontological vindication' of such truisms, and would thus deny the advantage to priority monism. Instead they sketch an austere *contextual semantics*, on which truisms can come out true in contexts where the 'standards for correspondence to reality' are sufficiently lax, given only that the cosmos is suitable. They would thus deny that existence monism is crazy, on the grounds that it can still respect truisms, at least in lax enough contexts.

Overview: In §1 I will discuss vagueness and argue that priority monism remains the more sensible view. Given iterated supervaluationism (which Horgan and Potrč allow as viable) the many proper parts are needed to provide the extensions. Then in §2 I will discuss parsimony and argue that priority monism remains preferable. Horgan and Potrč require a more complicated and obscure semantics, without any compensating parsimony for primitive entities. While I admire Horgan and Potrč's bold attempt to revive existence monism, I must conclude that priority monism remains the more sensible (and historically accurate) form of monism.

My debate with Horgan and Potrč is primarily an internecine debate amongst monists. That said, it may be of interest to those who would oppose monism, if only to know the best form of what they would oppose. It may also have more general interest for connecting to the more general question of whether derivative entities are needed. This is a question that arises in a range of partially analogous debates, such as between the priority pluralist who thinks that mereological wholes exist as dependent entities and the 'conciliatory' mereological nihilist pluralist who would still respect truisms, and between the non-reductive physicalist who thinks that chemical compounds and biological organisms exist as dependent entities and the eliminative physicalist who would still try to sustain chemical and biological truths.

3.1 Vagueness and ontology

3.1.1 The Moorean argument for priority monism

Horgan and Potrč argue that considerations of vagueness preclude the priority monist from claiming the more sensible view. It will help to begin with a statement of the argument for priority monism being the more sensible view. Here is the argument I have in mind, which I will call *the Moorean argument for priority monism*:

1. Moore's claim ('Here is one hand, and here is another') is true
2. If Moore's claim is true, then there are proper parts to the cosmos
3. Thus there are proper parts to the cosmos

The argument is evidently valid, and its conclusion 3 conflicts with existence but not priority monism.

The existence monist could deny premise 1. She might then supply some paraphrase of Moore's claim which she accepts as true (perhaps: 'The cosmos is such that it seems as if here is one hand and here is another'), together with some error theory explaining why we confuse Moore's claim with the supplied paraphrase in judging what is true. But Horgan and Potrč's would accept 1. For they explicitly accept commonsensical truisms as true, and indeed they (2008: 3) render the third core semantic thesis of their austere realism as: 'Numerous statements and thought-contents involving common sense and science are true, even though the correct ontology does not include these posits.'

So, given that the inference to 3 is valid and that premise 1 is accepted, Horgan and Potrč must rebut 2 (or fail to address the argument). And so, if considerations of vagueness are to preclude the priority monist from claiming the more sensible view via the Moorean argument, they must do so by undermining 2.

3.1.2 Background assumption: iterated supervaluationism

What if any bearing considerations of vagueness have on 2 depends on how vagueness is understood. To this I now turn. Horgan and Potrč's (pp. 54–6) discussion of vagueness begins from Horgan's (1995, 2010) 'transvaluational' view, on which vagueness arises from the normative pull of logically incoherent principles governing the assignment of statuses across sorites sequences. This is said to entail that ontological vagueness is impossible, and also that views (including epistemicism and non-iterated versions of supervaluationism) are unacceptable for imputing sharp 'status transitions' to sorites sequences. I propose to accept all of this *arguendo*. Iterated supervaluationism is explicitly allowed as viable (p. 4; c.f. 2008: 83), so I propose to simply adopt iterated supervaluationism.

A brief and informal sketch of iterated supervaluationism may prove useful.[2] Iterated supervaluationism involves four core components. First, vagueness is understood as a particular sort of *semantic indecision*, in which certain object-language terms have only *partial extensions*. These terms admit of different 'admissible precisifications' in the meta-language (admissible for getting the clear cases right and preserving penumbral connections), which are different ways of making the further semantic decisions that would yield full extensions.

Secondly, the metalanguage itself is a vague language, since 'being an admissible precisification' is itself a vague phrase. So there will be admissible precisifications of 'being an admissible precisification,' which are themselves amenable to multiple admissible precisifications at the next level up, *ad infinitum*. So the iterated supervaluationist posits an infinite hierarchy of vague languages. (This is the sense in which the supervaluationism is 'iterated,' and the way in which higher-order vagueness is accommodated.) Thus if '*t*' is a vague phrase of the object-language, 'being an admissible precisification of '*t*'' will be a vague phrase of the meta-language, and 'being an admissible precisification of 'being an admissible precisification of '*t*''' will be a vague phrase of the meta-meta-language, *ad infinitum*. (This point will be stressed by Horgan and Potrč: there is vagueness all the way up.)

Thirdly, accompanying this infinite hierarchy of vague languages is an abundant background ontology of precise objects (e.g. various fusions of particles), which are what the various candidate extensions draw upon. If '*t*' is a vague phrase of a given *n*-level language, then '*t*' will be assigned a plurality of admissible precisifications in the *n*+1-level meta-language, which associate '*t*' with different extensions *over the many precise objects in the background ontology*. (This point will provide my reply: the many proper parts of the cosmos are still needed for the various candidate extensions to draw upon; the one cosmos alone would not provide the semantics with enough extensions.)

Fourthly, the iterated hierarchy of vague languages and the abundant background ontology can then be used to characterize various truth-like and reference-like notions including those of *super-truth* and *super-reference*. Super-truth is the notion of truth under all admissible precisifications one level up. Associated with the notion of super-truth is the operator 'Definitely,' which serves to express the *n*+1-level status of super-truth in the *n*-level language. Super-truth remains a vague notion: 'Definitely *s*' does not entail 'Definitely Definitely *s*.' The notion of super-truth is connected with the notion of *super-reference*, which holds one–many between a referring term and the plurality of its admissible referents one level up. A term '*t*' super-refers to the *Xs* if and only if the *Xs* are all and only the admissible referents for '*t*.' Super-reference likewise remains a vague notion: ''*t*' super-refers to the *Xs*' does not entail 'Definitely '*t*' super-refers to the *Xs*.'

With iterated supervaluationism adopted for the sake of the argument, the question thus becomes: does iterated supervaluationism undermine 2?

3.1.3 Horgan and Potrč's puzzling trilemma

Why might Horgan and Potrč think that iterated supervaluationism undermines 2, or makes any trouble for the priority monist's claim to provide the more sensible monism? Horgan and Potrč aim for a trilemma, with the following options described in their terminology (*warning*: I am about to complain that their terminology is misleading):

- Provide a 'fully ontological vindication' of Moore's claim
- Provide a 'partially ontological vindication' of Moore's claim
- Provide a 'non-ontological vindication' of Moore's claim

In this vein they (p. 65; c.f. pp. 73–4) describe their strategy as 'first to argue by elimination for the non-ontological vindication program by explaining why neither of the other alternative vindication programs (fully ontological or partially ontological) is viable,' and then to argue from the non-ontological vindication program to the preferability of existence monism.

By a 'fully ontological vindication' Horgan and Potrč (pp. 58–59) mean an ontology that posits exactly one entity per referring term, thereby positing a one–one correspondence between language and reality. (They (p. 58) also speak of this as a 'direct-correspondence' conception.) This would require, in the case of Moore's claim, that there be a one–one correspondence between, e.g., the term 'hand' and some unique ontological posit (the one real hand). They are right to rule this out: no supervaluationist will endorse such a fixed one–one correspondence between language and reality. Rather the supervaluationist will posit *many* admissible precisifications of the term 'hand.' And so the prospect of a 'fully ontological vindication' is said (p. 59) to be eliminated: 'Since ontological vagueness is impossible, fully ontological vindication of ordinary-object claims is not to be had. Metaphysicians must learn to live with this sobering conclusion.'

By a 'partially ontological vindication' Horgan and Potrč (p. 59) mean an ontology that posits many entities per referring term, thereby positing a one–many correspondence between language and reality. (They (p. 60) also speak of this as an 'indirect form of correspondence.') This would require, in the case of Moore's claim, that there be a one–many correspondence between, e.g., the term 'hand' and some plurality of ontological posits (the many apt hand candidates). They are perhaps right to rule this out as well: no *iterated* supervaluationalist will endorse any fixed one–many correspondence between language and reality. The iterated supervaluationist will posit many admissible precisifications of the term 'hand,' but will equally posit many admissible precisifications of 'admissible precisification of the term 'hand'', and so on up the hierarchy. This is just to say (as explained in §1.2) that for the iterated supervaluationist, super-truth and super-reference remain vague notions. It remains vague which are the apt hand candidates. And so Horgan and Potrč (p. 66) say: 'the program of partially ontological vindication of ordinary-object claims comes to grief,' since vagueness is never discharged but just pushed up the infinite hierarchy of languages:

> Under [iterated supervaluationism], genuine vagueness in language and thought is evidently accommodated via the use of vague categories in the metalanguage, but now the vague claims in the metalanguage are themselves just as much in need of vindication as are the vague claims in the object language. So, since the claims in the metalanguage are as yet unvindicated themselves, these claims do not confer vindication upon the ordinary-object claims in the object language.[3]

I propose to grant Horgan and Potrč the arguments against 'fully ontological' and 'partially ontological' vindication, but think it crucial to peel away their misleading jargon. All that I am granting, given iterated supervaluationism, is the following:

- There is no one–one correspondence between language and reality
- There is no one–many correspondence between language and reality

Phrased in this clearer way, it should be evident that there is a huge gap between these claims and the conclusion that ontological posits (e.g. the many proper parts of the cosmos) have no role whatsoever to play in vindicating Moore's claim. (I will explain the role they play in §1.4.) So I think that the trick must have come in the labelling: by calling these first two options 'fully ontological vindication' and 'partially ontological vindication,' a false suggestion was implanted to the effect that if there is neither 'full' nor 'partial' ontological vindication there must be none at all.

(I may be asked: am I granting that a 'non-ontological vindication' of Moore's claim is enough as per Horgan and Potrč's third remaining option, or am I maintaining that they have missed a fourth option intermediate between a 'partially ontological vindication' and a 'non-ontological vindication', perhaps that of a 'semi-partially ontological vindication'? I have no idea. This is not my terminology, and I find it confusing at best. I am about to explain why – given iterated supervaluationism – the proper parts play a crucial role in accounting for the truth of Moore's claim, without there being any one–one or one–many correspondence. By my lights Horgan and Potrč's terminology does not usefully characterize this role, and so is best abandoned.)

Returning to the crucial premise 2, and avoiding potentially misleading terminology, the question becomes: does the lack of either a one–one or a one–many correspondence between language and reality in any way undermine 2?

3.1.4 Key reply: the role of the many proper parts

As explained above (§1.2), the iterated supervaluationist invokes an abundant background ontology of precise objects (e.g. various fusions of particles), which are what the various candidate extensions draw upon. *The role of the proper parts of the cosmos is evident: they provide the needed extensions.* Without them some such further entities iterated supervaluationism would not have extensions enough to get the right truth values. Indeed this is a point that Horgan and Potrč (p. 62) explicitly acknowledge in describing iterated supervaluationism as 'ontologically opulent indirect correspondence' and explaining: 'Ontologically opulent indirect correspondence requires the presence, in the right ontology, of items that are eligible candidate-referents for ordinary-object positing expressions;...'

As such it should be clear why iterated supervaluationism supports rather than undermines 2 (despite implementing neither a one–one nor a one–many correspondence between language and reality). Recall that the contention of 2 is that *if Moore's claim is true, then there are proper parts to the cosmos*. Iterated supervaluationism – by requiring an abundant background ontology of precise objects to provide extensions – directly supports this contention. For if Moore's claim is true, then there must be various candidate extensions assigned to 'hand.' On the reasonable assumptions that the cosmos is not an admissible referent for this phrase, and that an admissible referent would need to be a proper part of the cosmos instead, proper parts of the cosmos are required. This should settle the status of the Moorean argument for priority monism, given that 1 is accepted and iterated supervaluationism assumed: *the argument is sound*.[4]

Indeed the following *iterated supervaluationist argument for priority monism* looks like a compelling argument, using premises that Horgan and Potrč allow:

4. Iterated supervaluationism is the right semantic treatment of vague discourse
5. Iterated supervaluationism requires many precise objects (to provide extensions)
6. Thus the right semantic treatment of vague discourse requires many precise objects

And so existence monism – which only posits the one whole – conflicts with what is required by the right semantic treatment of vague discourse. Thus I must conclude that iterated supervaluationism directly favours the priority form of monism. End of story.

Returning to Horgan and Potrč's discussion, it is worth looking further into what they say about 'non-ontological vindication' (the one remaining option they take to be open). Their (p. 74) objection to priority monism plus 'non-ontological vindication' runs as follows:

> [T]his kind of priority monism faces the following awkward problem: there is no obvious theoretical role to be played, in the ontology, by all those ontologically precise objects that are supposed to be proper parts of the whole cosmos...[5]

I hope my reply is clear. There is an obvious theoretical role to be played by the proper parts of the cosmos within iterated supervaluationism (a role Horgan and Potrč themselves acknowledge): *the proper parts are needed to provide extensions*.

The dispute between the existence monist and the priority monist concerns whether there are many proper parts of the cosmos, and hence the relevant question is simply: *must one recognize the many proper parts of the cosmos to vindicate ordinary truisms?* Given iterated supervaluationism, the answer to this question is an immediate *yes*, since with just the one whole one cannot construct the right extensions. Any question which receives a different answer (e.g. *is there is a partially ontological vindication of ordinary-object claims in the offing?*) must not be the relevant question.

3.1.5 Conclusions on vagueness and ontology

To summarize, the Moorean argument for priority monism (as given by 1–3) looks sound. Horgan and Potrč seem committed to denying premise 2, but the iterated supervaluationist approach which they allow supports rather than undermines 2. As such I do not see how Horgan and Potrč touch the argument. Horgan and Potrč should take this as an invitation to say what they think is wrong with the Moorean argument as stated.

Moreover, the iterated supervaluationist argument for priority monism (4–6) looks sound as well (given iterated supervaluationism). Horgan and Potrč's trilemma is an artifact of misleading labelling. They are right that neither a 'fully ontological vindication' nor a 'partially ontological vindication' is possible given iterated supervaluationism, but wrong to infer that no role for ontological posits remains. (I leave it open whether that means that they are wrong to infer that a 'non-ontological vindication' is all that remains, or wrong to infer that all forms of 'non-ontological vindication' deny a theoretical role for ontological posits.) Iterated supervaluationism requires the many proper parts of the cosmos to provide the right extensions, as per 5. Horgan and Potrč are invited to explain what they think is wrong with the iterated supervaluationist argument.

I have granted *arguendo* that iterated supervaluationism is the right treatment of vagueness, but it is worth peering beyond this assumption. For on ontological treatments of vagueness there would need to be entities in the ontology – hands and their ilk – to be what is vague. And on epistemic treatments of vagueness there would likewise need to be entities in the ontology to bear the precise but unknowable boundaries. So existence monism is not merely incompatible with iterated supervaluationism, it is incompatible with virtually every major alternative. (Indeed on both ontological and epistemic conceptions of vagueness, the priority monist could claim a precise one–one correspondence between language and reality: a 'fully ontological vindication.') The priority monist's success with vagueness is thus not a mere artifact of iterated supervaluationism, but extends to any standard treatment consonant with a *referential* view of language. For on any referential view of language, Moore's claim will require, e.g., some sort of referent(s) for 'hand.'

That said, there is one remaining view of vagueness that is consistent with existence monism: Horgan and Potrč's own preferred contextual semantics. They (pp. 62–4) advocate an austere program of 'non-ontological vindication' involving 'ontologically austere indirect correspondence,' which foregoes a referential view of language. Essentially they posit a many–one correspondence between language and reality, where reality contains just the one cosmos, but the truisms may still count as true given the way the cosmos is, relative to contexts permitting relatively indirect correspondence with reality. So they hold that Moore's claim about hands can still be true in lax enough contexts, provided only that the cosmos is suitable. With contextual semantics in hand, Horgan and Potrč would have an answer to the Moorean argument for priority monism (rejecting 2) and to the iterated supervaluationist argument (rejecting 4).

As such I see one last move open to Horgan and Potrč. They might leave considerations of vagueness aside, and grant (*pace* p. 74–75) that there is a stable package of priority monism plus iterated supervaluationism, with the many proper parts of the cosmos granted the theoretical role of providing extensions. But they can still try to argue that their package of existence monism plus contextual semantics is overall better than the package of priority monism plus iterated supervaluationism. Here they might appeal to *parsimony*, praising their package for doing without any of the many proper parts.

3.2 Parsimony and derivativeness

3.2.1 Horgan and Potrč's argument from ontological parsimony

Horgan and Potrč argue that considerations of ontological parsimony favor existence monism. Existence monism might be thought more parsimonious in at least three respects. First, existence monism involves a strictly leaner ontology, with a proper subset of the entities that priority monism involves. Existence monism does without any of the many proper parts. Second, the existence monist can also claim to do without any relation of ontological priority. As Horgan and Potrč (p. 74) explain:

> By embracing existence monism one eliminates from ontology two kinds of un-needed theoretical baggage: not only the putative, ontologically precise, objects that are proper parts of the whole cosmos, but also the putative relation of ontological priority between the cosmos and those putative proper parts. Yet more reason to embrace existence monism, on grounds of yet more comparative theoretical simplicity.

They might also have added, as a third respect of parsimony, that the existence monist (*qua* mereological nihilist) can also claim to do without any relation of proper parthood.

Horgan and Potrč could equally argue that these three respects of ontological parsimony favor the package of existence monism plus contextual semantics over the package of priority monism plus iterated supervaluationism. (This was the move I suggested on their behalf at the close of §1.) Thus *the parsimony argument for existence monism* might be phrased as per:

7. The package of existence monism plus contextual semantics is more ontologically parsimonious than the package of priority monism plus iterated supervaluationism
8. The more ontologically parsimonious package is (all else equal) the better package
9. Hence existence monism plus contextual semantics is (all else equal) the better package

The argument is evidently valid, and its conclusion 9 favours the package of existence monism plus contextual semantics, provided that all else is equal.

3.2.2 First reply: trading ontological for semantic complexity

I have two independent replies to offer to the parsimony argument for existence monism, the first of which is that *all else is not equal*: Horgan and Potrč pay for any ontological simplicity with a more complicated and obscure semantics. (This is to say that even if 9 is true, the package of existence monism plus contextual semantics is still not better overall.) Obviously a gain in ontological parsimony need not correspond to any overall gain in 'comparative theoretical simplicity' if it is paid for in ideological profligacy or other complexities. Ontological parsimony is not the only aspect of simplicity, and moreover simplicity is not the only methodological virtue.

Horgan and Potrč package their existence monism with an austere contextual semantics so as not to fall afoul of Moorean truisms (§1.5). But their contextual semantics is highly underdescribed. They provide nothing by way of semantic clauses. They (p. 63; c.f. 2006: 146) mention the idea that the truth-conditions for a given claim will be given by a range of possible worlds (or possible ways for the world to be), and that the way the cosmos is might or might not put it in this range. But no discussion of the *compositional determination* of these possible worlds truth-conditions is offered, which is where matters of reference to proper parts of the cosmos are standardly thought to arise. Thus they do not address how 'Here is one hand, and here is another' might have a possible worlds truth-condition without treating, e.g., 'hand' as a referring term.[6]

Horgan and Potrč do posit a parameter of context: the degree to which a given claim must correspond to reality. But no empirical motivation for this semantic posit is provided. Indeed I am not even sure I understand the idea of 'the degree' of correspondence with reality. Moreover, they provide virtually no rules for evaluating this parameter on a given occasion, and say virtually nothing about how to assess a proposition as against a given setting of this parameter. (They also introduce an error theory for 'scorekeeping confusions' to explain why people continue to think of tables and chairs as real in even the strictest context, without empirical support.)

At this point it should be evident that Horgan and Potrč pay for any ontological simplification with a more complex and obscure semantics. Indeed by my lights they have just swept all the complications under the semantic carpet. If they do not (and will not) articulate the clauses of their semantics, I do not see how *any* overall conclusions as to 'comparative theoretical simplicity' can be drawn. Indeed I do not think that the package of existence monism plus contextual semantics is sufficiently developed in its semantic aspect to even enter the competition.[7]

3.2.3 Second reply: ontological parsimony reconsidered

My second (independent) reply to the argument from parsimony is that I do not think that Horgan and Potrč have actually achieved any real gain in ontological parsimony, properly understood. That is to say, I independently think that 7 is false. Horgan and Potrč have not merely complicated and obscured the semantics (§2.2), they have done so for nothing. My views on parsimony are admittedly unorthodox. Occam's Razor tells us not to multiply entities without necessity, and that seems to speak in favor of doing without any of the many proper parts if possible. But I think that Occam's Razor needs revision to distinguish *fundamental* entities from *derivative* entities. On my view multiplication of derivative entities is no methodological sin (c.f. Schaffer 2007: 189; 2009: 361). What is to be avoided (*ceteris paribus*) is the multiplication of fundamental entities. It is only *primitives* that count against parsimony.

With respect to posited fundamental entities the existence monist and the priority monist have no disagreement at all: the one whole cosmos is the one and only fundamental entity. Hence I would say that both views are equally ontologically parsimonious, once the right measure of parsimony is employed. Thus what is at issue as to 7 is the right precept for ontological parsimony, as between:

- Do not multiply entities without necessity
- Do not multiply fundamental entities without necessity

How might one decide on the right measure of parsimony? The best recourse, it seems to me, is to look to the analogous notion of *conceptual simplicity*. Thus imagine that one has two theories to consider concerning a common domain. The first theory requires seven conceptual primitives, and uses these primitives to define an additional 43 derived concepts. The second theory gets by with just a single conceptual primitive, and uses this primitive to define all of the 50 concepts of the first theory plus an additional 49 useful concepts to boot. I take it as evident that – at least with respect to conceptual simplicity – it is the second theory that is vastly superior. The second theory – on the basis of a single conceptual primitive – has managed to define 100 concepts. This is an incredibly simple and strong theory. Its simplicity consists in its getting by with just a single primitive concept, and its strength consists in its ability to define 100 concepts on this slender basis. The first theory, by way of contrast, is neither as simple (requiring seven primitives rather than one) nor as strong (able to characterize only 50 concepts rather than 100).

In the case of conceptual simplicity, it should then be clear that we measure by the number of primitive undefined concepts, and not by the total number of (primitive or defined) concepts. For only that measure fits the evident truth that the second theory above is simpler than the first. Indeed if one did measure by the total number of (primitive or defined) concepts, one would reach the perverse conclusion that the first theory – with only 50 concepts – is 'simpler' than the second, with its 100 concepts.

Or – to take a case even more analogous to the current situation – imagine a first theory that employs a single conceptual primitive but refuses to define any further notions, and a second theory that employs the very same conceptual primitive but then puts this primitive to work in defining 100 further notions. It should be evident that these theories are equal in conceptual simplicity, insofar as they both posit exactly the same single conceptual primitive. The second theory though is clearly preferable, insofar as it is stronger. The second theory provides more 'bang for the buck' than the first theory. In this case the 'buck' is the same (the same primitive concept), but the 'bang' is greater on the second theory.[8]

It is true that in this special case just mooted the first theorist might claim the special 'virtue' of eliminating the relation of definability altogether. But that hardly seems to help the credibility of the first theory in any way. A conceptual system that lacks the power to define anything further should only be condemned. It would be perverse to make a virtue of eliminating the notion of definability, to defend such a weak proposal. Overall it seems to me that relations of definability form part of the fixed background against which conceptual simplicity is measured, and that a theory that refuses to see such relations gains no special credit by the lights of a measure that presupposes such relations.

Given that conceptual simplicity should be measured by the number of primitive concepts (and that overall virtuous methodology in the conceptual realm is governed by a 'bang for the buck' principle), it seems to me most reasonable to extend an analogous style of treatment to ontological parsimony, via a *bang for the buck* ontological precept:

> An ontological system should optimally balance simplicity and strength, positing as few fundamental entities as possible (simplicity), grounding as many derivative entities as possible (strength).

Priority monism is clearly more methodologically virtuous than existence monism by the lights of bang for the buck methodology, since both theories are equally parsimonious – both posit exactly the same single ontological fundament, namely the cosmos – but priority monism is stronger. The existence monist has perversely refused to put her fundament to work in deriving further entities. (Of course the existence monist also can claim the special 'virtues' of eliminating the relations of priority and parthood altogether. But this seems just as non-virtuous as the analogous claim to eliminate the notion of definability made on behalf of the theory that lacked the power to define anything.)

3.2.4 Conclusions on parsimony and derivativeness

To summarize, I have argued that Horgan and Potrč's preferred package of existence monism plus contextual semantics is methodologically inferior to the package of priority monism plus iterated supervaluationism, in two independent respects. First, their package merely trades ontological simplicity for semantic complexity and obscurity. So as to 'comparative theoretical simplicity,' I think that there is only one theory that is even eligible for comparison: the package of priority monism plus iterated supervaluationism should win by default. Horgan and Potrč should take this as an invitation to say *much more* about their contextual semantics, to the point where it may be properly compared with the elegant and well-articulated iterated supervaluationist semantics already on offer.

Second, their package does not even achieve a genuine gain in ontological parsimony (they have just complicated and obscured the semantics for nothing). They in no way minimize the number of *fundamental* entities posited. Moreover, their approach merely represents a *weakening* of the strength of the priority monistic approach: they get less bang for the same buck. They refuse to use their fundament to find the derivative entities (the many proper parts) that are there for the finding. Horgan and Potrč should take this as an invitation to discuss the right underlying measure of parsimony.

Bringing all of this together, I have argued that the package of priority monism plus iterated supervaluationism is preferable to the package of existence monism plus contextual semantics, for the following two reasons:

- The semantics of iterated supervaluationism is elegant and well-articulated, in contrast to contextual semantics which seems extremely complex and remains (at present) highly obscure
- The ontology of priority monism gets more bang for the same buck as does the ontology of existence monism

For whatever it is worth, priority monism packaged with well-articulated ontological or epistemic treatments of vagueness would equally enjoy these twin comparative advantages. As such I must conclude that priority monism remains the more sensible (and historically accurate) form of monism.[9]

Notes

1. Horgan and Potrč's defense of existence monism is a defense of one aspect of their (2000, 2008) *austere realism*. Existence monism corresponds to the first of their (2008: 3) 'Blobjectivist Ontological Theses,' which reads: 'There is really just one concrete particular, namely, the whole universe (the blobject).'
2. A more formal presentation would involve the notion of a partial model, and Fine's (1975) notion of a rooted specification space, characterizing possible extension paths for partial models.
3. In the main text I will grant this argument, but I am not certain it succeeds. Horgan and Potrč are right that, for the iterated supervaluationist, every level retains vague phrases. But it does not follow, from the fact that every level retains vague phrases, that vagueness is not discharged *at the limit*. The iterated supervaluationist might thus try to characterize notions of *omega-truth* and *omega-reference* that characterize admissibility all the way up the hierarchy (technically: at the edges of specification space, at which all semantic decisions have been made), perhaps via infinite blocks of 'Definitely' operators. Such 'omega' notions will not characterize any given level, but rather characterize a transcendent 'limit perspective' on the hierarchy at which point all vagueness is discharged (all semantic decisions are made). If so then the 'omega' notions might still back a 'partially ontological vindication,' should one be wanted. But I will not pursue this idea further.
4. Iterated supervaluationism requires many precise objects to provide admissible referents for terms like 'hand,' but does not require that these be proper parts of the cosmos. That is a further claim, albeit one which strikes me as independently reasonable. That said, there is room for intermediate views between existence monism and priority monism, which accept many precise entities (contra existence monism) but deny that they are proper parts of the cosmos (contra priority monism). Indeed, Guigon (this volume; c.f. Della Rocca 2008: ch. 2) provides impressive historical evidence for interpreting Spinoza as having held such an intermediate view, on which the many are the modes of the one substance, but modes are not parts of substances (Guigon details a fictionalist interpretation of Spinoza's talk of parts). Such a view, which Guigon labels substance monism, can accept both premise 1 of the Moorean argument and iterated supervaluationism, but still deny 2 by having the modes provide the extensions. Such a view is definitely worthy of further discussion, but falls beyond the scope of the present one.
5. Likewise in a first engagement with my views, Horgan and Potrč (2008: 188-9) write: '[T]here would be very little theoretical *need* for [the many parts] if 'the one whole'... is really ontologically basic. So if indeed the one whole is metaphysically basic, then it is also metaphysically exclusionary: the right ontology is blobjectivism.'
6. On this point I follow Korman (2008): '[Horgan and Potrč] lack the resources in their ontology to help themselves to any known compositional semantics in accounting for the truth of ordinary utterances about composite objects.'
7. The most I have seen elsewhere from Horgan and Potrč (2008: 37) is talk of 'contextually operative standards for semantic correctness' and (2008: 51) invocation of 'implicit, contextually variable, semantic parameters.' Indeed, elsewhere

Horgan and Potrč (2006: 157) invoke the view of 'quasi-particularist semantic normativity,' which rejects the burden of answering questions about the general semantics principles operative in a given context, or across contexts. Instead they (2006: 159) rest with semantic supervenience claims that 'are not systematizable in terms of compact, general, exceptionless, cognitively surveyable principles.'

8. Another way to put the point: it does not in any way count *against* the conceptual simplicity of certain primitives if one discovers that one can use these primitives to define a further concept. If anything such a discovery counts in favor of the strength (or fruitfulness) of such primitives.
9. Thanks to Philip Goff, Ghislain Guigon, Terry Horgan, Brian McLaughlin, Matjaž Potrč and the students in my Spring 2011 metaphysics seminar for helpful discussion.

References

Alexander, Samuel 1950. *Space, Time, and Deity: the Gifford Lectures at Glasgow 1916–1918, Vol. 1.* New York: The Humanities Press.

Della Rocca, Michael 2008. *Spinoza*. Routledge.

Fine, Kit 1975. Vagueness, Truth, and Logic. *Synthese* 30: 265–300.

Guigon, Ghislain *this volume*. Spinoza on Composition and Priority.

Horgan, Terry 1995. Transvaluationism: A Dionysian Approach to Vagueness. *Southern Journal of Philosophy* 33 (supp.): 97–126.

—— 2010. Transvaluationism about Vagueness: A Progress Report. *Southern Journal of Philosophy* 48: 67–94.

Horgan, Terry and Matjaž Potrč 2000. Blobjectivism and Indirect Correspondence. *Facta Philosophica* 2: 249–70.

—— 2006. Abundant Truth in an Austere World. *Truth and Realism: New Essays*, eds. Michael Lynch and Patrick Greenough: 137–67. Oxford University Press.

—— 2008. *Austere Realism: Contextual Semantics Meets Minimal Ontology*. MIT Press.

—— *this volume*. Existence Monism Trumps Priority Monism.

Korman, Daniel 2008. Review of *Austere Realism: Contextual Semantics Meets Minimal Ontology*. *Notre Dame Philosophical Reviews*: http://ndpr.nd.edu/review.cfm?id=14508.

Moore, G. E. 1993. Proof of an External World. *G. E. Moore: Selected Writings*, ed. Thomas Baldwin: 147–70. Routledge.

Schaffer, Jonathan 2007. From Nihilism to Monism. *Australasian Journal of Philosophy* 85: 175–91.

—— 2009. On What Grounds What. *Metametaphysics*, eds. David Chalmers, David Manley, and Ryan Wasserman: 347–83. Oxford University Press.

—— 2010 (also *this volume*). Monism: The Priority of the Whole. *Philosophical Review* 119: 31–76.

4
Against Monism

E. J. Lowe

In 'Monism: The Priority of the Whole', Jonathan Schaffer draws an important and often overlooked distinction between *priority* monism and *existence* monism, the former holding that, where concrete objects are concerned, *the whole cosmos* of which they are parts is ontologically prior to those parts, whereas the latter holds that the whole cosmos is the *only* concrete object. Thus, priority monism doesn't deny that the whole cosmos *has* parts, in the form of lesser concrete objects, only that any of these parts is ontologically prior, or even equal in respect of its ontological status, to the cosmos as a whole. Clearly, then, existence monism – defended by Terry Horgan and Matjaz Potrč in their 'Existence Monism Trumps Priority Monism' – is the more extreme doctrine and must fail if priority monism fails. However, important though Schaffer's distinction is, his arguments in favour of priority monism are, in my view, largely vitiated by unresolved ambiguities in his use of certain key terms – notably, 'object', 'concrete', 'part', and 'dependence'. When these ambiguities are resolved in appropriate ways, it is my belief that pluralism can be seen to be a highly plausible doctrine – both priority pluralism and so also, *a fortiori*, existence pluralism. As for Horgan and Potrč's arguments in favour of existence monism, which appeal largely to considerations concerning vagueness, I believe that these too fail, in virtue of making certain key assumptions which are, in my view, unwarranted. More generally, though, it is my opinion that arguments from vagueness are almost never to be trusted in metaphysics, particularly when, as so often happens, they lead to highly counterintuitive conclusions. In short, it is almost always preferable, when arguing for a position in metaphysics, to develop an argument which does not appeal to vagueness rather than to one that does. Apart from anything else, arguments appealing to vagueness almost never convince an opponent – they almost always lack persuasive power – because opponents always suspect them, generally rightly, of involving some sort of sleight of hand. In any case, there almost always turn out to be ways, whose ingenuity matches that of the arguments in question, of challenging those arguments, so that at best we are left with a stand-off.

In what follows, I shall begin with some criticisms of Schaffer's arguments and conclude with some criticisms of Horgan and Potrč's.

4.1 Schaffer on priority monism

I shall begin my critique of Schaffer's position by raising some queries concerning the meanings of certain key terms that he deploys. First, there is his use of the term 'the cosmos', which he takes to denote 'a maximal actual concrete object...of which all actual concrete objects are parts' (p. 11). He stresses that, when it comes to what the cosmos, as he understands it, consists of, '*possibilia, abstracta,* and actual concreta in categories other than object are not [his] concern' (p. 11). This immediately presents two problems. First, what are we to understand Schaffer to mean by 'concrete' and 'object'? Second, what *entitles* him to regard 'the cosmos' as *excluding* all such items as those just mentioned? Schaffer never really answers the first question and this, as we shall see, turns out to be quite a crucial failing. As for the second, one gathers that he supposes that the cosmos, as he characterizes it – 'the material cosmos and its planets, pebbles, particles, and other proper parts' (p. 11) – is just an obvious subject of both metaphysical and scientific concern. For he goes on to assert, as though it were uncontroversial, that 'Empirically, the cosmos is the object of empirical study...the primary subject matter of physical cosmology' (p. 11). However, this latter claim strikes me as rash. As I understand it, scientific cosmology is a branch of *physics* – one which specifically studies the large-scale structure of spacetime and the distribution of mass/energy across it. It does *not* concern a great many of the things that Schaffer would presumably include in *his* 'cosmos', such as living things and social entities – the subject matter of the special sciences of biology and sociology respectively. Furthermore, scientific cosmology clearly includes in its purview such items as the *fields of force* that pervade spacetime – above all, gravitational fields – and it seems clear that these do not belong to the category of 'concrete object', on any reasonable construal of the latter expression. It is very doubtful, indeed, that 'spacetime' denotes such an 'object' either. I begin to wonder, in fact, whether there is any good reason *at all* to believe in the existence of 'the cosmos', in Schaffer's sense.

Of course, if one believes that *some* concrete objects exist, and that every plurality of concrete objects has a unique mereological sum, then indeed one might reasonably suppose that a maximal sum of such objects exists which may be identified with Schaffer's 'cosmos'. However, this is to assume the correctness of classical mereology, which I for one am loath to do. In any case, my own view is that a mereological sum is always ontologically *posterior* to the items of which it is the sum, so that such a sum could never play the role that Schaffer's priority monism demands of it. Hence, it seems to me that Schaffer's assumption that there really *is* a 'maximal actual concrete object', apt to play the role that he wishes to assign to it, is an act of faith, unsupported by either good metaphysical or good scientific reasons. I should hasten to add that I *do* believe in the existence of composite concrete objects which are *not* mere mereological sums – objects such as living organisms – but also believe that in almost all such cases their *existence* and *principles of composition* are primarily matters for natural scientific inquiry. It is not the case, to my knowledge, that any science does, or even *could*, establish the existence and principle of composition of Schaffer's putative 'cosmos'.

The next thing I want to query is Schaffer's assumption that 'the priority relations among actual concrete objects form a well-founded partial ordering', where priority is treated as 'irreflexive, asymmetric, and transitive' and 'well-foundedness is imposed by requiring that all priority chains terminate' (p. 13). Part of the problem, as I see it, is that Schaffer thinks of 'priority' in terms of asymmetric ontological *dependence*, but offers no explication or analysis of the latter notion. He just operates with a brute and undefined relation on actual concrete objects expressed in the form '*x* depends on *y*', where '*x*' and '*y*' are variables taking actual concrete objects as their potential values. Indeed, he even seems to make a virtue of this, saying that although the notion of priority, cashed out by him in terms of dependence, may be 'amenable to further analysis', he himself is 'doubtful [and] will remain neutral on that question here' (p. 13). But, I suggest, a metaphysically serious and useful account of ontological dependence needs to be much more nuanced and informative than this. First of all, there are many different *species* of ontological dependence (see Lowe 1998: ch. 6 and Lowe 2010). To name just three: there is *rigid existential* dependence, *generic existential* dependence, and *identity* dependence. To borrow an example from set theory: a set all of whose members are concrete objects, such as the set of planets around the sun, is *rigidly existentially dependent* on those objects and also *identity dependent* on those objects. Similarly, an *aggregate* of concrete objects, such as a heap of rocks, is both rigidly existentially dependent on those objects and identity dependent on those objects. That is to say, of metaphysical necessity, *it* exists only if *they* exist, and *which* heap it is, is determined by *which* rocks it is a heap of. By contrast, a *living organism*, such as a cat, is neither rigidly existentially dependent nor identity dependent on, say, the molecules that compose it at any given time, since it may persist through a change of those molecules for different ones. Nonetheless, a cat is *generically* existentially dependent on molecules of suitable types, since a cat cannot exist unless it is composed of *some* suitable molecules, suitably arranged (the 'cannot' here being the 'cannot' of metaphysical impossibility).

Another thing to bear in mind is that even the three just-mentioned species of ontological dependence do not all have the same formal properties as relations. For instance, rigid existential dependence is *not* asymmetric (rather, it is non-symmetric), but identity dependence very plausibly *is* (at least, it is either asymmetric or else antisymmetric, my own preference being for the latter). Thus, a set is rigidly existentially dependent on its members, but they are likewise rigidly existentially dependent on it: *it* cannot exist unless *they* exist, but likewise *they* cannot exist unless *it* exists. Clearly, then, it cannot be *this* species of dependence that Schaffer has in mind as giving rise to the metaphysical or ontological *priority* of one concrete object to another. Indeed, he is quite explicit about this, saying that '{Socrates} exists *in virtue of* Socrates and not vice versa'. But that still leaves us very much in the dark as to what kind of dependence Schaffer *does* have in mind and even as to why he should suppose, as he clearly does, that there is just *one* kind of dependence that is relevant in the present context. He evidently *does* suppose this, for he tells us that he uses 'D' to 'express *the* relation of dependence' (p. 14, emphasis added). For my own part, I am happy to invoke the notion of *identity* dependence to account for the asymmetry between singleton Socrates, {Socrates}, and that unit set's sole member, Socrates: the singleton, like any other set (apart from the empty set), depends for its identity on its member(s), whereas Socrates does not depend for his identity on the singleton, or any other set, of which he is a member. *That's* why we can say that {Socrates} exists 'in virtue of' Socrates and not vice versa. But just saying the latter, without such an explanation, is not illuminating.

Moving on, I want to pick up again on Schaffer's lack of specificity concerning the expression 'concrete object'. He tells us that he uses 'C' to express the status of being a concrete object, defining this as follows: $Cx =_{df} Pxu$ – that is, by definition, x is a concrete object if and only if x is part of the cosmos (p. 14). Since he has so far told us only that 'the cosmos' is the 'maximal concrete object' (p. 11), this 'definition' is far from illuminating – indeed, it is implicitly circular. This defect is thus inherited by his use of 'B' to 'express the crucial status of being a basic actual concrete object', which he defines thus: $Bx =_{df} Cx \,\&\, \sim(\exists y)(Cy \,\&\, Dxy)$. Indeed, the latter definition is doubly defective, because it also appeals to the inadequately specified relation of *dependence*. Another problem touched on before arises soon after this, when Schaffer affirms his principle of *Covering*, formally stated thus: $\text{Sum}{:}x(Bx) = u$ – that is, the mereological sum or fusion of all the basic actual concrete objects is identical with the cosmos. As I've already indicated, I take the view, which is not uncommon, that a mereological sum of certain items, the *x*s, is *ontologically posterior* to those items. And I can now say more precisely why I believe this: it is because I believe that a mereological sum is not only rigidly existentially dependent on the items of which it is a sum – its 'summands' – but is also *identity* dependent on them. Accordingly, it exists *in virtue of* them, not vice versa, just as singleton Socrates, {Socrates}, exists *in virtue of* Socrates, not vice versa. In fact, it seems to me very peculiar that Schaffer accepts the standard view that a set's members have priority over the set, but apparently not the standard view that a sum's summands have priority over the sum. Really, I think, Schaffer would do better to take the view that 'the cosmos' stands to the concrete objects that are its parts somewhat as a living organism does to the molecules that compose it at any given time. But, unfortunately, the cost of doing so would be that this would make it much more difficult to establish that such a 'cosmos' really exists *at all*. If the 'cosmos' is merely something like a very big *aggregate* of lesser concrete objects, rather as a heap of rocks is an aggregate of those rocks, then it is perhaps quite plausible to say that it exists – but then it is no more plausible to say that it is *prior* to its parts than it is to say this about a heap of rocks.

I also have a problem with another fundamental principle of Schaffer's, which he calls *No Overlap*, this being 'the requirement that no two basic entities have a common part' (p. 15). More specifically, I have a problem with Schaffer's *reason* for demanding *No Overlap*, which he calls *the argument from recombinability*. He asserts that 'the fundamental actual concrete objects should be freely recombinable, serving as independent units of being (building blocks, as it were)' (p. 15). This claim, however, threatens to be in tension with some indisputable truths of fundamental particle physics, which tell us that such particles are *not* 'freely recombinable'. Only certain restricted combinations of elementary particles, such as electrons and quarks, can exist in nature, not just *any* combination. That being so, if Schaffer's claim is correct, he would seem to be in possession of a remarkable a priori argument demonstrating that such particles cannot *really* be 'basic' entities, whatever the physicists may think. Of course, some of the physicists *don't* think that these entities are basic, perhaps according that status instead to such items as superstrings. But, assuredly, they don't think this for *Schaffer's* reason, and no doubt do think, anyway, that superstrings themselves are not 'freely recombinable'.

But maybe I have misunderstood what Schaffer means by 'free recombinability'. What he *says* is that 'a plurality of entities is freely recombinable if and only if any combination of ways that each entity can be individually is a way that the plurality can be collectively' (p. 15). So consider, for instance, the two electrons orbiting a helium atom. *Each*, individually, can be either spin up or spin down, but – by Pauli's exclusion principle – *the pair* of them can't be such that either both are spin up or both are spin down. And so, indeed, it is for very many if not all pluralities of 'entangled' particles: there are restrictions of this kind on the members of the plurality. If this isn't contrary to Schaffer's principle of free recombinability, then I confess that I don't yet really understand what that principle is supposed to be. Presumably, however, Schaffer will just welcome this result with open arms, as confirming his conviction that quantum entities such as electrons can't be 'basic' concrete objects, thereby providing support for his contrary view that only 'the cosmos' has this status. The trouble is, though, that, far from providing grist to his mill, this result instead just calls into question the legitimacy of Schaffer's principle of free recombinability. If the principle makes it as easy as *this* to show that the elementary particles of quantum physics can't truly be 'basic concrete objects', then an impartial adjudicator can surely only say that the principle is blatantly question-begging.

In point of fact, though, Schaffer tells us that he doesn't strictly need anything quite as strong as *No Overlap* for his purposes and that the weaker *No Parthood* condition will suffice, this being the principle that 'no basics are related as part to whole' (p. 16). But I have a problem with this principle too. Recall that my own view is that it is the specific relation of *identity dependence* that needs to be invoked in order to cash out the idea of ontological or metaphysical priority. From this point of view, a 'basic' concrete object will be one which does not depend for its *identity* on anything (or, at least – if we take identity dependence to be antisymmetric – which does not depend for its identity on anything other than *itself*). Such an object will be 'identity independent', let us say. However, I would certainly want to allow that an object which is identity independent can have as *parts* other objects that are likewise identity independent. Why ever not? Undoubtedly, *some* composite objects do depend for their identity on their parts, and hence are not identity independent, aggregates such as heaps being a case in point. But, as I've also remarked, a composite object such as a living organism *doesn't* depend for its identity on, say, the molecules that compose it at any given time, since it can persist through a change of these. In fact, it doesn't appear to depend for its identity on *anything* that helps to compose it at any given time. But now take a highly complex organic molecule which helps to compose a living organism at a certain time, such as a strand of DNA in one of its cells. Or, indeed, take one of those cells. Neither the strand of DNA nor the cell is a mere *aggregate* of parts. Both are such that they could persist through a *change* of their parts, just as the whole living organism can. So they have no *less* a claim to being identity independent than the whole living organism does, despite the fact that they and the organism are 'related as part to whole'. (Note, in this connection, that it also seems clear that neither the strand of DNA nor the cell depends for its identity on the organism of which they are parts. After all, each of them could be 'transplanted' to become parts of a quite different organism.) Of course, I have so far only argued that the organism doesn't depend for its identity *on its parts* (and vice versa), which doesn't prove that it is entirely identity *independent*, since it might conceivably depend for its identity on some thing or things other than its parts. Likewise for the strand of DNA and the cell. However, I don't think this matters for present purposes, since the question at issue is whether the principle that 'no basics are related as part to whole' is credible: but the credibility of that principle can surely be thrown into doubt if we can find a plausible example of two things being related as part to whole despite the fact that each has *as good a claim as the other* to being an independent entity, in the relevant sense of 'independent': for then we can see that their *being related as part to whole* poses no threat to their 'basicness'. And my contention, of course, is that the relevant sense of 'independence' is *identity* independence: hence my chosen examples.

Now, however, if I am right in rejecting, or at least calling seriously into question, Schaffer's *No Parthood* principle, priority monism is thoroughly compromised. For it is now open to someone to *concede* that the cosmos is 'basic', without thereby having to concede that none of its proper parts is 'basic'. For my own part, however, I very much doubt whether the cosmos, in Schaffer's sense of the term, is 'basic', because I strongly suspect that the only 'concrete object' that could qualify as the cosmos in this sense would be a mere aggregate or mereological sum of its parts, which would accordingly have to be identity dependent on those parts and so *not* 'basic'. Indeed, as we have already seen, *Schaffer himself* identifies 'the cosmos' with just such a mereological sum, unwise though it is for him to do so, in view of the fairly evident identity dependence of mereological sums on their summands. Furthermore, we can now call into question too Schaffer's very definition of priority monism: *Monism* $=_{\mathrm{df}}$ B*x* & B*u* – there is a basic object and the cosmos is basic. As Schaffer explains, 'if the cosmos is basic, there can be no other basic actual concrete object since anything other would be a part of the cosmos' (p. 17) – which is ruled out by the *No Parthood* principle. But the *No Parthood* principle, as we have seen, is certainly questionable, thus rendering *Monism* equally questionable as a definition of priority monism. Rather, priority monism would be better defined explicitly as the doctrine that the cosmos, and *only* the cosmos, is a basic actual concrete object. I think it is a *false* doctrine, because in the only relevant sense of 'dependence' – which I take to be *identity* dependence – it seems evident, or at least extremely plausible, that there are *very many* actual concrete objects which are *not* dependent on the cosmos, even if there is any such thing as 'the cosmos'.

It is worth mentioning, in connection with Schaffer's *No Parthood* principle, that he himself assimilates it to the 'classical' doctrine that *no substance can have substantial proper parts* (footnote 17). This is interesting not least because it suggests that by a 'basic concrete object' Schaffer means what would traditionally have been called an *individual substance*. Now, it is true that many important substance ontologists of the past, including Aristotle and Leibniz, adhered to this classical doctrine, but, of course, it doesn't follow that the doctrine is correct. According to Schaffer, Aristotle held to the doctrine that 'no substance is composed of substances' because a substance must be a *unity*, and anything consisting of two substances must be 'actually two' and so 'never actually one'. That may indeed be so, but the reasoning here, even if it is Aristotle's, is fallacious. Certainly, anything which is 'actually two' is a *plurality* and so a fortiori not *one* thing and so not an individual substance. But it is false to claim that anything *consisting of* two substances must be 'actually two', because the *consists of* relation is not to be confused with *identity*. To say that *x* consists of *y* and *z* is just to say that *y* and *z* together wholly compose *x* – that is, compose *x* without remainder. For instance, a kitchen knife consists of its handle and its blade. What is 'actually two' here is the plurality of the handle and the blade. But that plurality doesn't (in the relevant sense) *consist of* – isn't *composed by* – the handle and blade. Rather, the plurality just *is* – that is, *is identical with* – the handle and the blade. *The knife*, however, is *one* and hence distinct from the plurality, which is *two*. Since the knife is one rather than two, it is certainly a *unity*. The only question remaining is whether it should be regarded as an *individual substance*. After all, even an *aggregate*, such as a heap of rocks, can in my view qualify as a unity – as being *one* thing – even though I would deny it the status of an individual substance because it is identity dependent on its parts, the rocks. For, what is crucial to the status of substancehood is *independence*, not mere *unity*, although the latter is certainly a *necessary* condition of substancehood. The upshot is that the 'Aristotelian' argument provides no support for the doctrine that a substance cannot be composed of other substances: it can be, provided that – as in the case of a living organism and the molecules that compose it – it does not *depend for its identity* on those other substances. (I say more about unity and plurality in Lowe 2009: ch. 4.)

I should not leave the foregoing point without commenting on something pertinent that Schaffer says later concerning the distinction between 'mere aggregates' and 'integrated wholes'. Schaffer remarks that 'Common sense probably does endorse the priority of the parts in cases of mere aggregation, such as with the heap... [but] probably endorses the priority of the whole in cases of integrated wholes' (p. 21). He further remarks, *a propos* of an organism and its organs, 'According to Aristotle, at least, the organism is prior, and the organs are defined by their functional integration within the organism' (p. 21). Now, the right thing to say here, I believe, is that Aristotle was correct on this point, but that this fact nonetheless does not really help Schaffer's position. This is because I think that there is a further unresolved ambiguity in Schaffer's discussion of these matters, this time concerning the term 'part'. In my view, a bodily organ, such as a heart or brain or liver, is a *functional* part of a living organism, but not a *component* part – not one of the things of which it is literally *composed*. By contrast, a *molecule*, and even a *cell*, is indeed a component part of an organism. As I see it, the heart or brain of a living organism is not to be identified with a *certain mass of organic tissue*, composed of very many individual cells. The crucial difference is this: a mass of organic tissue, or a cell helping to compose such a mass, can be identified as *the very thing that it is* independently of any role that it plays in the biological life of the organism, whereas this is not possible in the case of something like the organism's heart or brain. *Organs* like the latter are *identified* in terms of their functional role within the biological economy of the organism and hence are *identity dependent* on the organism.

The possibility of heart and even brain transplants does not compromise this claim. What is transplanted, literally, is just a mass of suitably specialized cells, not the donor organism's heart or brain itself, and the heart or brain that the recipient later possesses is *its own*, not literally *the donor's*. Thus, while I am happy to concede that individual substances such as living organisms possess certain 'parts' which are *not* prior to, but rather *dependent on*, those organisms – namely, various 'organs' – I do not regard such parts as *component* parts of those organisms. Moreover, most importantly, it seems clear that such organisms *do* have component parts – indeed are *wholly composed* of certain parts – which are *not* dependent on those organisms in the way that their 'organs' are. These component parts include, at different levels of composition, such things as subatomic particles, organic molecules, and cells.

Thus far, we have not yet actually reached Schaffer's arguments *in favour* of priority monism and, in fact, I do not have much to say about those arguments, because I consider so many of Schaffer's preliminary assumptions to be questionable. One thing, however, that I find particularly unconvincing is his claim that 'if anything, it is *Monism* that can claim the mantle of common sense' (p. 22). I find especially implausible his suggestion that 'According to common sense, the many proper parts [of the cosmos] are arbitrary portions of the cosmos' (p. 22). This claim might have at least some semblance of plausibility if one were to focus only on 'common objects like animals and artifacts' which are 'blurry at the edges' (p. 22). But common sense, I suggest, reaches a sticking point when it comes to *ourselves*. I am not at all inclined to regard *myself* as an 'arbitrary portion of the cosmos', even if I might take such an insouciant view of *my body*. Indeed, I cannot really even understand what it would *mean* to regard *myself* in such a way. I think that I have a perfectly determinate identity which distinguishes me objectively and unambiguously from anything else that exists. If I am mistaken about this, then I am subject to a very deep and intractable cognitive illusion, which might of course possibly be the case. What I cannot concede, however, is that 'common sense' suggests otherwise – that there is no determinately identifiable and non-arbitrary 'part of the cosmos' that is uniquely *me*.

However, much of this is not directly relevant to Schaffer's reasons for favouring priority monism, since he himself considers that, even if common sense is on the side of priority monism, 'this counts for little' (p. 23). Indeed, one of his main reasons for favouring priority monism, far from drawing on common sense, draws on quantum mechanical considerations which are vastly removed from common sense. The idea here is that the universe, according to quantum mechanics, will very likely turn out to be one enormous 'entangled' quantum system. Schaffer notes in passing that this claim will be undermined if 'there is ... some form of wave-function collapse ... that promotes disentanglement' (p. 25). However, this concession is by no means a minor one, since the majority view amongst quantum physicists still seems to be in favour of the occurrence of wave-function collapse whenever a quantum measurement is made. Indeed, no-collapse interpretations of quantum mechanics are highly speculative and intuitively very difficult to comprehend, since they imply that superposition – as in the notorious case of Schrödinger's cat, which is supposedly neither dead nor alive – is ubiquitous, even in the case of the macroscopic 'concrete objects' that Schaffer takes to be amongst the 'parts' of 'the cosmos'. If anything, such interpretations tend to suggest that a view of 'the cosmos' like Schaffer's is just an illusory product of pre-scientific ways of thinking and that physical reality is vastly stranger than anything that our human minds are equipped to comprehend. Thus, Schaffer's appeal to quantum mechanics is a dangerous one which threatens to backfire on him by consigning to the garbage bin of human thought the very idea of 'the cosmos' whose priority over its parts he seeks to establish. The dilemma that Schaffer faces is this: if wave-function collapse *does* occur, then entanglement is not ubiquitous and Schaffer's argument fails to go through; but if, on the other hand, wave-function collapse does *not* occur, then the whole idea of there being a 'cosmos' composed of 'concrete objects' threatens to be illusory, since the familiar notion of a 'concrete object' – even one with 'blurry edges' – is ostensibly incompatible with the idea of ubiquitous superposition.

I shall not comment here on Schaffer's other main argument in favour of priority monism – his argument from the possibility of atomless gunk – apart from remarking on his claim, which is crucial to that argument, that 'whichever doctrine [*Monism* or *Pluralism*] is true, is true with metaphysical necessity' (p. 28). He expands on this as follows: 'Just as the dispute as to whether properties are universals, tropes, or nominalistic constructions is thought to concern a metaphysical necessity, so the dispute over the priority of the whole seems to concern a comparable necessity' (p. 28). I entirely fail to see a parallel between the two cases. The question concerning properties is a question concerning the *categorial* structure of reality: what categories of being there are and how they are related. It is indeed reasonable to suppose that at least the *fundamental* categories of being are metaphysically necessary features of reality. By contrast, the question concerning monism versus pluralism is supposed to be one concerning how entities within a *single* category – the category of 'concrete object' – stand to one another in respect of their *dependence* relations when they are related as part to whole. The mere fact that both questions are *metaphysical* ones gives us no reason at all to suppose that their answers must hold with metaphysical necessity. *Some* 'metaphysical' features of a possible world may surely be contingent ones. Only if one thought that metaphysics is an entirely a priori discipline might one have cause to doubt this. For my own part, I am happy to allow that metaphysics includes some questions that are answerable a priori, including questions about the fundamental categorial structure of reality. But I think it also includes questions – such as the question of whether there are immaterial substances – which receive different answers with respect to different possible worlds, and whose answer with respect to the actual world rests at least in part on a posteriori evidence. Much of the a priori part of metaphysics, in my view, is concerned only to establish the metaphysical *possibility* of this or that feature of reality, leaving to empirical science the task of determining whether or not that possibility is actually realized (see Lowe 1998: ch. 1). It is quite wrong, I think, to suppose that metaphysics is confined to investigating only the metaphysically *necessary* features of reality. Anyway, I can see no reason at all why it would be incoherent to suppose that some possible worlds are *pluralist* worlds and others *monistic* ones.

In his Appendix, Schaffer turns to historical matters and, interesting though these are, I have space to discuss only one of them. Schaffer seems to want to recruit *Spinoza* as a priority monist, but I don't think that this can be correct. Recall that, according to Schaffer, priority monism is a doctrine concerning entities within a *single* category, that of 'concrete object', maintaining that one of these – the cosmos – has all of these as parts and is prior to all the rest, in that they all depend on it but not it on them. This might *sound* very much like Spinoza's metaphysical system, but it cannot be at all the same. For the parts of Spinoza's universal whole – *Deus sive Natura* – are *categorially* different from that whole. The whole is *the one substance*. The 'parts' are its *modes*: and *substance* and *mode* are different ontological categories for Spinoza, just as they are for any other traditional substance ontologist. It is true enough, as Schaffer points out, that Spinoza speaks of the universe as containing 'bodies'. And common sense regards bodies as being 'concrete objects' in Schaffer's sense. Nonetheless, it is abundantly clear that Spinoza does *not* conceive of 'bodies' as being items that belong to the same ontological category as the whole universe of which they are 'parts'. Hence, he cannot be a priority monist in Schaffer's sense. In fact, it seems that, for Schaffer's purposes, he can only qualify as an *existence* monist. This fact is perhaps disguised by Schaffer's unhappy characterization of existence monism as the view that 'denies that there is anything other than the cosmos' (p. 69). It does indeed deny that there is any *thing* – in the sense of 'concrete object' or (in more traditional terms) 'individual substance' – other than the cosmos, or the universe as a whole. But it doesn't necessarily deny that there is *anything* other than the cosmos, since it may well affirm, as Spinoza did, that there are entities belonging to ontological categories other than the category to which the cosmos belongs, such as *modes* (or, in modern parlance, *tropes*). Spinoza certainly believes that modes exist and that they are necessarily distinct from – not identical with – the substance of which they are modes, for it is one and they are many. He also believes, of course, that the modes are all *dependent* on the one substance, while it alone is *independent*. This makes him *sound* like a priority monist in Schaffer's sense. But, as we have seen, that cannot be the case, since Schaffer defines priority monism as an *intra*-categorial doctrine, not an *inter*-categorial one. It may well be, on reflection, that this was ultimately unhelpful and even confusing, especially when it comes to classifying past philosophers as either 'priority' or 'existence' monists. Maybe it is better to abandon such labels and just examine and evaluate different metaphysical systems on their own terms and on their own merits.

4.2 Horgan and Potrč on existence monism

I now turn to Horgan and Potrč's position. I find myself in much more fundamental disagreement with them than I do with Schaffer and can distil this disagreement into a smaller number of crucial points, although some of these will require fairly detailed discussion. First, I disagree with them that 'ontological vagueness is impossible' and will return to this shortly. Before we even get to that point, however, it strikes me that their entire enterprise is questionably coherent. A major aim of theirs, in challenging Schaffer, is to persuade us that 'the right ontology is ... free of the kinds of proper part entities that Schaffer would count as [concrete] objects' (p. 51). Directly at the outset, they draw a distinction between 'the 'positing apparatus' of thoughts and statements and 'posits', i.e., putative entities that putatively answer to such positing apparatus' (p. 52). They explain that the 'positing apparatus includes, inter alia, singular referring expressions of natural language (e.g., names and definite descriptions)', while '(for instance) tables, chairs, and persons are 'posits' of everyday thought and discourse'. Concerning the latter, they go on to say that 'as advocates of existence monism we ... maintain that there are no such entities in the right ontology' (p. 52).

Now, however, we are immediately faced with the following puzzle. Horgan and Potrč want to affirm that there are *really* no such things as tables, chairs, and persons, in the sense that there are no such things in 'the right ontology'. And yet their argument draws on a 'positing apparatus' which includes, inter alia, such items as *linguistic expressions* and *thoughts* – presumably, expressions used by people and thoughts had by people. (What else? Bits of language and thoughts don't just exist by themselves, unspoken and unthought by speakers and thinkers.) Now, Horgan and Potrč will probably retort that it would be naïve to suppose that they are caught here in self-contradiction, both affirming and denying that *persons* exist. But that is not going to be my point. They are far from being alone in denying the reality of persons, however counterintuitive the denial might be. My puzzlement runs much deeper than this. I just don't see where, on their view, the 'positing apparatus' *comes from* or how it relates to what supposedly *does* exist in 'the right ontology'. For the positing apparatus itself is described in thoroughly *object-laden terms*, of the very kind that Horgan and Potrč want us to regard as denoting *nothing* in 'the right ontology'. On their view, if it is to be consistent, there are no *names* or *definite descriptions* or *statements* or *thoughts* in 'the right ontology', whether or not there are *persons*. And yet their argument in favour of what they regard as 'the right ontology' unashamedly refers to just such entities and indeed cannot seemingly even get started without them. How exactly do they manage to pull *this* ladder up after them, once they deny the existence in 'the right ontology' of anything like the kind of 'object' that Schaffer – and almost everyone else – would say exists? I am loath to accuse them of making the mistake of supposing that a principled distinction can be drawn between *thought and language* on the one hand and 'the world' on the other – as though thought and language were not just *parts* of 'the world', if they are anything at all. I have no doubt that their position is supposed to be much more sophisticated than this and that we are supposed to think that, properly understood, it indulges in no such double-standard as it might appear to on first encounter. Unfortunately, however, I find nothing in their chapter to explain how this particular trick is brought off – the trick of *using* the 'positing apparatus' to motivate 'the right ontology' without engendering any tension with the implication that, in 'the right ontology', no such apparatus exists at all. If ever there was a case in philosophy in which the metaphors of painting oneself into a corner and cutting off the branch one is sitting on seemed apt, this one surely qualifies.

I come now to Horgan and Potrč's claim that ontological vagueness is impossible. For my own part, I don't believe this because I don't consider that the best-known and most compelling argument against the possibility of ontological vagueness – Gareth Evans's argument against the existence of vague objects – is valid (see Lowe 1994, Lowe 1998b: ch. 3, and Lowe 2005). But Horgan and Potrč's argument for the impossibility of ontological vagueness is different from Evans's and considerably more complex (which is also why it is much less immediately compelling). It appeals instead to two key claims, namely, that 'Vagueness essentially involves *sorites-susceptibility*' and that vagueness also essentially involves what they call, following Mark Sainsbury, 'boundarylessness'. I am not persuaded that either claim is correct, though I shall focus on the former. Putative cases of vague *identity* certainly do not always involve 'sorites-susceptibility'. For instance, as I have argued elsewhere, a plausible case can be made out for saying that vague identity can arise in cases of quantum superposition or entanglement, even though nothing like a sorites series has anything to do with such cases (see again Lowe 1994, Lowe 1998: ch. 3, and Lowe 2005). But let us set such cases aside here, controversial as they are. Another key claim of Horgan and Potrč's is that 'virtually all objects posited in everyday thought and language count as 'ordinary'' – an 'ordinary' object being one that 'is not conceived as fully determinate in all intrinsic respects' (p. 56). They then appeal to Peter Unger's notorious 'problem of the many' in an attempt to raise difficulties, turning on vagueness, for the legitimacy of including such objects in 'the right ontology'.

Of course, many other philosophers, not least Unger himself, have appealed to such considerations in order to cast doubt on the legitimacy of the ontology of 'ordinary objects'. It is interesting, then, to note that Horgan and Potrč, in their own argument from vagueness against ordinary objects, make an assumption which is commonplace in this context, but certainly open to question. This assumption manifests itself in the following passage from their chapter:

> Once one posits at least one perfectly precise object that one claims is an eligible referent of a given ordinary-object-referring singular term (say, 'Tibbles', which purports to refer to a specific cat), shouldn't one also posit numerous (maybe infinitely many) other perfectly precise objects that differ only slightly from one another (e.g., in their precise boundaries or their precise composition) and that therefore are equally eligible candidate-referents of that term? But, then, what could make it the case that the singular term denotes a given one of these precise candidate-referents, and fails to denote any of the others? (p. 57)

The questions raised here are clearly intended to be purely rhetorical and Horgan and Potrč evidently consider that the correct answers to them are 'Yes' and 'Nothing' respectively. We are then supposed to accept what they take to be the consequences of these answers, namely, that 'ordinary objects, if they belong to the right ontology at all, simply are not fully determinate' (p. 57) and that 'Such an ontology would [have to] identify the unique cat Tibbles with a unique *vague* object, rather than identifying Tibbles with any of many slightly different, fully determinate, objects that are equally eligible Tibbles-candidates' (pp. 57–8). This, then, is supposed to set us up for the conclusion that 'There are no ordinary objects in the right ontology' (p. 58), because such objects would be ontologically vague and 'Ontological vagueness is impossible' (p. 58).

What is crucially questionable in the passage quoted earlier is the assumption that the defender of ordinary objects, such as Tibbles, is under any pressure to regard the many slightly different 'precise' objects in Tibbles's vicinity as being eligible candidates for being *the referent of the name 'Tibbles'*. Indeed, quite to the contrary, the defender of ordinary objects is really obliged *not* to regard them as such candidates. This is because it is integral to the very concept of an ordinary object, such as a cat, that objects of this type cannot extensively *overlap* with many other such objects of the same kind. Thus, it is perfectly possible to maintain that there is, quite unambiguously, just *one* legitimate candidate for the referent of the name 'Tibbles', while also acknowledging that it is to some degree indeterminate where Tibbles's boundaries lie. For we need not attribute that indeterminacy to an indeterminacy as to which of many supposedly equally eligible, but very largely overlapping, candidates for *being Tibbles* is the referent of the name 'Tibbles'. Instead, by distinguishing, as we need to in any case, between *Tibbles the cat* – a certain living organism – and *the mass of feline tissue* that *constitutes* Tibbles at any given time, we can attribute the vagueness of Tibbles's boundaries to vagueness as to which of many very largely overlapping masses of feline tissue *constitutes* Tibbles at any given time (see Lowe 1995). As I have just indicated, a leading thought here is that cats are just not the sort of thing that can significantly *overlap* – they can only do so to the extent, say, that might be involved in a case of conjoined twins – whereas masses of feline tissue, like masses of matter of any other kind, are eminently suited to such overlap. Only a category mistake could lead one to confuse *a cat* with a mass of animal tissue fit to *constitute* a cat. The upshot is that there need be no indeterminacy or vagueness about the *referent* of the name 'Tibbles', for which there can *be* only one eligible candidate, albeit a candidate whose *boundaries* are vague because it inherits its boundaries from those of the mass of feline tissue constituting it, and it is to a degree indeterminate *which* of many such overlapping masses constitutes Tibbles.

However, it may now seem that in saying this I am just playing into Horgan and Potrč's hands. For am I not now *agreeing* that, in their words, 'Such an ontology would [have to] identify the unique cat Tibbles with a unique *vague* object, rather than identifying Tibbles with any of many slightly different, fully determinate, objects that are equally eligible Tibbles-candidates' (p. 57–8)? (Agree, that is, apart from conceding that the many objects in question are *Tibbles*-candidates.) Well, yes, up to a point. I agree that, by my account, Tibbles is a unique object, which is vague in the sense that its *boundaries* are vague – although, at the same time, I have now *explained* why this should be the case and thereby, I would say, rendered it entirely unmysterious. Tibbles has vague boundaries simply because it is to a degree undetermined *which* precise mass of feline tissue constitutes Tibbles at any given time. But Tibbles, by this account, isn't a 'vague' object in the sense that there is any vagueness as to Tibbles's *identity*, that is, as to *which* object in the ontology is Tibbles. However, Horgan and Potrč will no doubt urge that I have already conceded enough to condemn the ontology of ordinary objects, because even admitting to vagueness concerning Tibbles's *boundaries* is enough to condemn Tibbles to non-existence in 'the right ontology'.

In order to proceed further, however, we need to understand exactly why Horgan and Potrč believe that 'ontological vagueness is impossible', including vagueness of the sort that I have just admitted concerning Tibbles's boundaries. This brings us back to their key claim that vagueness essentially involves *sorites-susceptibility*. Only if what I have said concerning Tibbles's boundaries is *sorites-susceptible* am I even in any danger of falling prey to their strictures. Now, what I have said concerning Tibbles's boundaries is that they are indeterminate only because it is to a degree undetermined *which* of many very largely overlapping masses of feline tissue constitutes Tibbles at any given time, since Tibbles inherits his boundaries from the mass of feline tissue that constitutes him. Consequently, it appears that the vagueness of Tibbles's boundaries is sorites-susceptible only if the vagueness of Tibbles's *constitution*, which generates the vagueness of his boundaries, is likewise sorites-susceptible. I shall argue that it is *not*, or at least not obviously so.

Now, if one thought of these masses of feline tissue as consisting of so-called *atomless gunk*, then there would be infinitely many of them and some sort of sorites sequence could presumably be envisaged, starting with masses which are definitely contained within Tibbles as proper parts of him and ending with masses which are definitely not parts of him. However, that is not consistent with the physics of the actual world. Each mass of feline tissue which is a candidate for constituting Tibbles at any given time consists of a determinate and finite, albeit very large, number of molecules. Each of these molecules has a determinate structure and composition, consisting as it does of various atoms in a certain arrangement, bonded by certain fundamental forces. It would be wrong, of course, to think of these atoms on the model of tiny solar systems, in which there can be indeterminacy as to whether a distant object really belongs to a given solar system because the gravitational force between that system's sun and the distant object is so weak. In the case of a solar system, it may indeed be the case that a sorites sequence can be envisaged, starting with objects which definitely qualify as planets of the system and ending with ones which definitely do not qualify. But atoms aren't like that, according to modern quantum physics. Nucleons are either definitely bonded together by the strong nuclear force or definitely not so bonded. Likewise, an electron either definitely occupies an orbit in one of an atom's electron shells or it definitely does not, and transitions between energy levels in the shells are always discrete, not continuous. In short, while classical, Newtonian physics might be susceptible to sorites sequences, quantum physics is apparently not, precisely because of the ubiquitous feature of *quantization* which renders it discrete rather than continuous. There seems to be no reason, then, to suppose that the physical world at the fundamental level, as it is 'posited' by modern quantum physics, harbours any basis for generating sorites sequences. Perhaps this is why Horgan and Potrč say only that '*Virtually all* objects posited in everyday thought and language count as 'ordinary' ... and *most* objects posited by scientific theory, as well' (p. 57, emphases added) – though even this concession seems enough to undermine their attempt to motivate their version of existence monism, since *some* 'objects' that are smaller than the universe as a whole seem fit to escape their strictures.

Thus, it seems, the defender of ordinary objects can actually recruit quantum physics as an ally against those philosophers, including Horgan and Potrč, who seek to make trouble for such objects on grounds of vagueness. However, there is an obvious objection to this line of thought, namely, that it is wrong to suppose that sorites sequences need to exhibit *continuity* (although they *may* of course do so, as in the case of the colour spectrum between red and orange). Indeed, the very example from which we get the term 'sorites' – the example of the heap – involves a discrete and finite series of steps, beginning with one pebble, which cannot make a heap, and ending with many pebbles, which can. Am I not, then, committed to acknowledging that a *finite* sorites sequence can be set up amongst masses of feline tissue in Tibbles's vicinity, beginning with some mass that is *definitely* a (proper) part of Tibbles and ending with one which is definitely *not* a part (either proper or improper) of Tibbles? Well, *perhaps* so – and this is a matter that we shall return to shortly – but that is not really the question immediately at issue. The immediate question is whether one can set up a sorites sequence amongst masses of feline tissue in Tibbles's vicinity in respect of their possessing or not possessing the property of *constituting* Tibbles. Each of these masses will be a certain *precise* mass of feline tissue, consisting of a certain precise number of molecules. (And note that here we already have a *macroscopic* object which is 'posited' by science and yet which apparently escapes Horgan and Potrč's strictures, for the reasons set out in my preceding paragraph: for if individual *atoms* and *molecules* escape those strictures, then so too do *masses* consisting of precise numbers of molecules.) But observe that we can't say that one of these masses, at one end of a putative sorites sequence, *definitely* constitutes Tibbles, while another, at the other end, definitely does *not* constitute Tibbles. We can't, because *no* mass of feline matter in Tibbles's vicinity is such that it *definitely* constitutes Tibbles, even if some are such that they definitely do *not* constitute Tibbles. All that is definite as to Tibbles's constitution is that *some* mass of feline matter in Tibbles's vicinity constitutes Tibbles. So it seems that there is no prospect of setting up a sorites sequence amongst masses of feline tissue in Tibbles's vicinity in respect of their possessing or not possessing the property of *constituting Tibbles*. And this, if correct, is already enough to show that sorites-susceptibility is not, as Horgan and Potrč claim, an essential feature of vagueness. For, if I am right, there is vagueness concerning which mass of feline tissue in Tibbles's vicinity constitutes Tibbles, but no prospect of setting up a sorites sequence in respect of this vagueness.

But what, now, about the possibility of setting up a sorites sequence in respect of certain items possessing or not possessing the property of *being a (proper) part of Tibbles*? Well, consider a spatial path beginning near Tibbles's centre and extending two metres outward from there, bearing in mind that no *cat* is spatially extended by anything near as much as two metres in any direction. At the beginning of that path there will be a molecule which is *definitely* a part of Tibbles and at the end there will be a molecule (quite possibly a molecule of air, though it might be a molecule in *another* cat) which is *definitely not* a part of Tibbles. Somewhere in between there will be molecules on the path which are *neither* definitely parts of Tibbles *nor* definitely *not* parts of Tibbles. So this might appear to constitute a sorites sequence. But on closer examination it seems clear that it does *not*. The molecules which are neither definitely parts of Tibbles nor definitely not parts of Tibbles will all be ones that are included in *some but not all* of the masses of feline tissue in Tibbles's vicinity which are eligible candidates for being the mass that constitutes Tibbles. The molecules which are *definitely* parts of Tibbles will be all those on the path that are included in *all* of the masses of feline tissue that are eligible candidates, while those which are *definitely not* parts of Tibbles will be all those on the path that are *not* included in *any* of the masses of feline tissue that are eligible candidates. Hence, all the molecules on the path will be partitioned unambiguously into three mutually disjoint sets. This is quite unlike the case of a finite sorites sequence, such as the one arising in the case of heaps, where we have a sequence of items apparently exhibiting a *gradual change* from one condition to its polar opposite condition, with an indeterminate borderline region which does not have an unambiguous first or last member. In the case of heaps, we have at one end, say, 100 pebbles, which definitely *can* make a heap, and at the other end just one pebble, which definitely *cannot* make a heap, and *somewhere* in between – though we can't say *precisely* where – we have numbers of pebbles concerning which we can only say that they neither definitely *can* make a heap nor definitely *cannot* make a heap. In the case of the molecules on the path beginning near Tibbles's centre and extending outward two metres from there, there is no *gradual change* discernible anywhere along the path in respect of the property of *being a part of Tibbles*. After all, it is not as though a molecule near the tip of one of Tibbles's firmly attached and still growing whiskers is somehow less evidently a *part* of Tibbles than one inside Tibbles's heart, purely because it is further from Tibbles's centre. Nor is it as though a molecule in a feline hair from another cat that is loosely attached to Tibbles's fur is somehow less evidently *not* a part of Tibbles than one in a hair that is firmly attached and still growing on a cat that is a metre away from Tibbles.

At this point, it might be contended that a sorites sequence is still constructable in the case of Tibbles and moreover one involving *constitution*, albeit one involving *higher-order* vagueness. This sequence would have at one end some mass of feline matter in Tibbles's vicinity which *definitely* has the property of definitely not constituting Tibbles and at the other end some mass of feline matter in Tibbles's vicinity which definitely does *not* have the property of definitely not constituting Tibbles. In between, there would be borderline cases of masses of matter in Tibbles's vicinity which neither definitely *have* nor definitely *do not have* the property of definitely not constituting Tibbles. But can we really identify such a putative borderline case? It is not clear to me that we can. If a mass of matter in Tibbles's vicinity does *not* definitely have the property of definitely not constituting Tibbles, then I think it definitely does *not* have the property of definitely not constituting Tibbles. For in this case it seems that the mass is definitely one that *could* constitute Tibbles – it is definitely an eligible candidate for the role of being *the* mass that constitutes Tibbles – and this requires that it definitely does *not* have a property which would render it incapable of occupying that role, namely, the property of definitely not constituting Tibbles. It really is very hard, I think, to model vagueness of constitution on any kind of vagueness that is typically to be found in sorites sequences. All we can do in Tibbles's case, I think, is to identify various different masses of feline matter in Tibbles's vicinity which definitely *do not* constitute Tibbles – for instance, a mass including a loosely attached hair picked up from another cat, or a mass omitting one of Tibbles's firmly attached and still growing whiskers – and *all the rest*, which are the eligible candidates for being *the* mass that constitutes Tibbles, every one of which is such that it does *not* definitely constitute Tibbles (for *no* mass definitely constitutes Tibbles). If a mass is not definitely *excluded* from constituting Tibbles, then it automatically qualifies as an eligible candidate for constituting Tibbles. What we cannot do, I believe, is to arrange any number of these masses into a sorites sequence involving the constitution relation. So, once again, I think that we have here a case of vagueness which is not 'sorites-susceptible', contrary to one of Horgan and Potrč's key claims.

Of course, I haven't so far discussed at all Horgan and Potrč's reasons for supposing that, where we *do* have a case of vagueness involving some kind of sorites sequence, we cannot take the vagueness in question to be 'ontological'. There are certainly queries that could be raised concerning their argument on this matter, although it is not vital for me to raise them since I have argued that vagueness of constitution does not involve sorites-susceptibility. For instance, although they contend that sorites-susceptible vagueness exhibits a certain kind of 'logical incoherence' which, they suggest, 'the world itself' (as opposed to language and thought) could not be guilty of, they don't consider the possibility that 'the world itself' conforms to a logic that is *dialetheist* in character. (This possibility is relevant, since it seems clear that the 'logical incoherence' of which they speak is supposed to involve logical *contradiction*.) For my own part, given a choice between renouncing the existence of all 'ordinary objects', including persons such as ourselves, and embracing dialetheism, I would readily chose the latter. Indeed, if I thought that Horgan and Potrč's argument in favour of existence monism actually *worked*, on its own terms, I would be very inclined to conclude that we had a strong reason to take dialetheism seriously. Metaphysics, I believe, trumps logic in a case like this. This isn't to endorse any kind of irrationalism, since I am not suggesting that metaphysics should ever lead us simply to abandon logic altogether. The point is just that there are many alternative logics, between which it is sometimes very difficult to decide – much more difficult to decide than it sometimes is to decide between alternative metaphysical systems. For logic is *technical*, in a way that basic metaphysics is not. Basic metaphysics is a matter of making sense of the world and our place in it, and that is a concern that everyone has, independent of any special disciplinary expertise. Our metaphysics ought not to be made a slave to the technicalities of any particular system of logic. In any case, I am not persuaded that Horgan and Potrč's conception of 'the right ontology' helps us at all to make sense of the world and our place in it.

I shall conclude with a brief discussion of Horgan and Potrč's positive suggestions concerning the truth conditions of statements in everyday language. They take as an example the statement (A), 'The politics of Arizona is much discussed in the American news media' and claim that it is 'natural and plausible to construe the truth conditions for statement (A) as comprising a range of possible worlds – where a possible world is taken to be ... a maximal property instantiable by the cosmos' (p. 63). They go on: 'We all have a fairly good idea ... what would constitute good evidence for statement (A) ... and such evidence need not render likely the claim that the right ontology includes one or more items that are eligible candidate-referents for, e.g., the expression 'the politics of Arizona'' (p. 63). Now, as I see it, there is a mixture of the plausible and the most *im*plausible in what Horgan and Potrč say here. Most philosophers would readily agree that there is little reason to suppose that the expression 'the politics of Arizona' refers to some unique, real entity, any more than the expression 'the average American citizen' does. But it is a big stretch from saying that to saying that what makes statement (A) true is some 'maximal property instantiable by the cosmos', which involves the existence of no objects other than the cosmos as a whole. For most philosophers would want to say that what makes statement (A) true is some very complex disjunctive fact involving quantification over many objects which are much smaller than the cosmos as a whole and various properties of those objects – objects that would include, for instance, individual American politicians and individual American news journalists. It is thus breathtaking for Horgan and Potrč to conclude as blithely as they do that 'truth, for many kinds of claims made in typical real-life contexts, is plausibly construed as ontologically austere indirect correspondence' (p. 64). Indeed, I would suggest that, barring some sort of explication in terms of quantification over ordinary objects and their properties, no one has *the slightest idea* as to what kind of 'maximal property instantiable by the cosmos' could serve to make statement (A) true. It seems that such a property, as conceived by Horgan and Potrč, would be one that God alone would have an ample enough mind to comprehend. Certainly, the move from saying that an expression like 'the politics of Arizona' plausibly does not denote an object in 'the right ontology' to suggesting that no names or definite descriptions for ordinary objects plausibly do so either is far too quick. If we can defend the ontology of ordinary objects, as I certainly believe we can, we can certainly resist Horgan and Potrč's highly implausible – indeed, doubtfully comprehensible – account of the truth conditions of statements in everyday and scientific language.

References

Lowe, E. J. 1994. Vague Identity and Quantum Indeterminacy. *Analysis* 54: 110–114.

Lowe, E. J. 1995. The Problem of the Many and the Vagueness of Constitution. *Analysis* 55: 179–182.

Lowe, E. J. 1998. *The Possibility of Metaphysics: Substance, Identity, and Time*. Oxford: Clarendon Press.

Lowe, E. J. 2005. Identity, Vagueness, and Modality. *Thought, Reference, and Experience: Themes from the Philosophy of Gareth Evans*, ed. J. L. Bermúdez. Oxford: Oxford University Press.

Lowe, E. J. 2009. *More Kinds of Being: A Further Study of Individuation, Identity, and the Logic of Sortal Terms*. Malden, MA and Oxford: Wiley-Blackwell.

Lowe, E. J. 2010. Ontological Dependence. *The Stanford Encyclopedia of Philosophy (Spring 2010 Edition)*, ed. E. N. Zalta. http://plato.stanford.edu/entries/dependence-ontological/

5
There Is More Than One Thing

Philip Goff

For those with a taste for desert landscapes, the existence monism of Horgan and Potrč[1] is the ultimate thrill. No tables, no chairs, not even particles in the void. Just the One jelly-like blobject, wobbling away – or to put it more precisely: instantiating various properties in spatiotemporally local manners. Unfortunately, this beautifully minimalist view cannot possibly be true, for it is inconsistent with certain things we know to be true.

At this moment, I am experiencing no pleasure, but I do feel a terrible pain in my knee. I know that there is something that feels pain but no pleasure. Even if it turns out that I am in The Matrix, this is something the evil computers cannot be deceiving me about. Sitting across from me is Dave, who is eating an ice cream. He tells me he is currently enjoying a pain free existence, and is in fact extracting great pleasure from his ice cream. If common sense is to have any sway in my metaphysical speculation, then I must set aside scepticism about other minds when compiling the data a theory must explain. I therefore take it that Dave, in his own case, has certainty that there is something that currently feels pleasure but no pain, akin to the certainty I have that there is currently something that feels pain but no pleasure. It follows that there are currently at least two things in existence: one that feels pain but no pleasure, and another that feels pleasure but no pain. Therefore, existence monism is false.

Of course, this is too quick. Horgan and Potrč accept the truth of all kinds of *sentences* which quantify over a plurality of objects, but deny that the truth of such sentences is a matter of a direct correspondence between the quantificational posits of the sentence and the items of the world. Rather, such sentences are made true by an indirect correspondence between the sentence and the one blobject instantiating properties in spatiotemporally local manners. The sentence T: 'There are two tables in regions 1 and 2 of my front room' is true in virtue of an indirect correspondence between T and the state of affairs of the blobject instantiating certain physical properties R1-ly and R2-ly.

Given their respect for common sense, I take it that Horgan and Potrč will accept that sentence S: 'There currently exists something that feels pain but no pleasure, and something that feels pleasure but no pain' is true, but will hold that the truth of S is a matter of an indirect correspondence between S and a state of affairs involving the blobject having properties in spatiotemporally local ways, rather than a direct correspondence to a state of affairs involving two distinct things.

There seem to be two ways in which this might be done. Firstly, a physicalist proposal, according to which S is made true by the blobject instantiating physical properties in spatiotemporally local ways. Secondly, a non-physicalist proposal, according to which S is made true by the universe instantiating irreducible phenomenal properties in spatiotemporally local ways. I shall consider and reject both of these proposals in turn.

The physicalist proposal

> S is made true by the fact that the blobject instantiates c-fibres firing R1-ly but not R2-ly, and instantiates p-fibres firing R2-ly but not R1-ly (where c-fibres firing is the physical property which underlies pain, p-fibres firing is the physical property that underlies pleasure, and R1 and R2 are spatiotemporally local manners of instantiation).

A sentence (in a context) makes demands on reality, such that if those demands are satisfied the sentence is true. In order for the physicalist proposal to be true, S must make demands on the world such that those demands are satisfied by the universe instantiating physical properties in spatiotemporally local manners.

In order to assess the physicalist proposal, we must first answer the following question: are the demands S makes on the world a priori accessible (for someone who understands S, and in virtue of understanding S)?[2] Let us say that a sentence is 'transparent' iff it is a priori – for someone who understands the sentence and has sufficient rational powers – what that sentence requires of the world for its truth: 'There is a Euclidean sphere', 'There is an omnipotent being', seem plausible examples of transparent sentences. The sentences, 'The Earth is getting hotter', 'Everything is made of Gold' seem plausible examples of non-transparent sentences.[3]

I will assess the physicalist proposal first under the assumption that S is transparent, and secondly under the assumption that S is non-transparent.

S as transparent

It is not plausible that it is a priori that pain is c-fibres firing and pleasure p-fibres firing; one can competently use the terms 'pleasure' and 'pain' without knowing any brain science. But if (i) S is transparent, and (ii) the physicalist proposal is true, then there must be a priori accessible demands of S which are satisfied by facts about the blobject's instantiation of c-fibres and p-fibres.

Therefore, for the physicalist/transparency combo to possess a modicum of plausibility it must involve a commitment to some kind of analytic functionalism, which will provide a conceptual middle man between the mental and the physical. The claim must be that we know a priori that to 'feel pleasure' is to be in the state of having some state that is playing the pleasure role, and to 'feel pain' is to be in the state of having some state that is playing the pain role, together with the claim that, as it happens, p-fibres firing and c-fibres firing respectively play these roles.[4] It is only by taking this detour through functional facts that we can make it at all plausible that I can know a priori what S demands of reality, such that those demands are satisfied by physical facts about the blobject.

Unfortunately this reductionist proposal is demonstrably false, not in the sense that premises can be produced that are inconsistent with it, but in the sense that you can make apparent to yourself its falsity by sticking a pin in your finger and then taking Cartesian doubt to its natural end. I can doubt that I have causal powers, but I cannot doubt that I am currently in pain. By supposing that I have no causal powers, whilst at the same time supposing that I am in pain, I find I am conceiving of myself as something that feels pain but has no causal powers. If it were an analytic truth that to 'feel pain' is to be in the state of having some state that is playing that pain role, this would not be conceivable. Therefore, it cannot be analytic that to 'feel pain' is to be in the state of having some state that is playing the pain role.[5]

Note that this is not a repeat of Descartes' argument for dualism, and hence is not subject to well-known critiques. There is no dodgy move here from epistemic premises to a metaphysical conclusion. Rather the move is from an epistemic premise – that I can conceive of myself as a thing that feels pain but has no causal powers – to an epistemic conclusion – it cannot be part of the concept of 'feeling pain' that to feel pain is to be in the state of having some state that plays a certain causal role.

We are currently trying to make sense of the view that the demands of S are both a priori accessible and satisfied by the physical facts. A commitment to a certain view about our mental concepts – namely analytic functionalism – is required to make sense of the demands of S having both these features, and that view about mental concepts is inconsistent with certain evident facts about what is conceivable.[6]

S as non-transparent

I turn now to assessing the physicalist proposal on the assumption that S is non-transparent. In the last twenty years, many physicalists wrestling with the 'hard problem of consciousness' have been drawn to semantic externalism about phenomenal concepts (by 'phenomenal concept' I mean the kind of concept employed when one thinks about one's own conscious states in terms of what it is like to have them).[7] Such semantic externalism seems to offer hope of reconciling the conceptual gulf between the phenomenal and the physical with the metaphysical intimacy that these two realms are supposed to enjoy according to physicalism. If the content of the phenomenal concept <pain> is determined by facts outside of what is a priori accessible to the concept user, then this explains why the physical nature of pain is not a priori accessible to the concept user, and consequently why it is conceptually coherent to suppose that pain is not a physical state.

Semantic externalism about phenomenal concepts offers hope of making sense of physicalism without relying on analytic functionalism. If Horgan and Potrč could make sense of S being non-transparent, then they could perhaps pursue a similar strategy for making sense of the physicalist proposal currently under consideration. They could simply claim that, as a matter of a posteriori fact, S demands that the there be two spatially local manners of instantiation, Rx and Ry, such that the blobject currently instantiates c-fibres firing Rx-ly but not Ry-ly, and instantiates p-fibres firing Ry-ly but not Rx-ly.

This version of the physicalist proposal cannot be defeated by considerations of conceivability; if it is a posteriori that S demands that P, then 'S but not P' is conceivably true. Compare: it is a posteriori that 'There is water in the glass' demands that there be H_2O in the glass, and hence 'There is water in the glass, but there is no H_2O in the glass' is conceivably true.

But is it plausible to hold that S is non-transparent? I will argue that it is not, by first arguing against the plausibility of semantic externalist accounts of phenomenal concepts.

It will be useful to sketch a bit more of a framework to help in thinking about the issues here. Let us distinguish between three kinds of property concept as follows:

Transparent property concept: A property concept is transparent iff everything of what it is for the property denoted to be instantiated is a priori accessible (to someone possessing the concept, and in virtue of possessing the concept).

Translucent property concept: A property concept is translucent iff something but not everything of what it is for the property denoted to be instantiated is a priori accessible (to someone possessing the concept, and in virtue of possessing the concept).

Opaque property concept: A property concept is opaque iff nothing of what it is for the property to be denoted is a priori accessible (for someone possessing the concept, and in virtue of possessing the concept).[8]

A plausible example of a transparent concept is the concept <Euclidean sphericity>. For something to be spherical in Euclidean geometry is for it to have all points on its surface equidistant from its centre. For someone possessing the concept <Euclidean sphericity>, this information concerning what it is for something to possess Euclidean sphericity is a priori accessible.

A plausible example of a translucent property concept is <being a Euclidean sphere roughly the same size as the Earth>. The property denoted here has two aspects: being a Euclidean sphere, and being roughly the same size as the Earth. The concept reveals what it is for the former aspect to be instantiated, but empirical investigation is required to know what it is for the latter aspect to be instantiated. The concept denoting the property formed of those two aspects, therefore, is translucent.

If there are concepts which are such that reference is determined wholly by facts outside of what is a priori accessible to the concept user – for example, by causal relations between concept and referent, by sub-personal recognitional capacities of the concept user, or by the evolutionary history of the concept – then such concepts will be opaque.

Clearly, then, semantic externalism about phenomenal concepts is committed to the opacity of phenomenal concepts. There are a couple of reasons why this view is implausible.

Firstly, supposing that the phenomenal concept of pain is opaque makes it difficult to see how many of those normative judgements we generally take to be well-grounded could indeed be well-grounded. I believe that the fact that someone is in severe, unnecessary pain, is of great normative significance. I come to this conclusion not by doing experiments, but by reflecting on what it's like to feel pain. But for a judgement of the normative significance of a certain descriptive property to be well-grounded, I must surely have some understanding of the nature of that descriptive property, of what it is for it to be instantiated. Therefore, if my phenomenal concept of pain provides me with no understanding of what it is for something to feel pain, then the judgement of the normative significance of pain that I form when employing that concept must be ill-grounded.

Secondly, supposing that phenomenal concepts in general are opaque makes it difficult to make sense of the fact that we have a priori knowledge concerning internal relations phenomenal qualities bear to each other. What it's like to see red is similar to what it's like to see orange. This is an internal relation these qualities bear to each other, that is, it's a relation which is entailed by the intrinsic nature of the relata. The mere existence of phenomenal red and phenomenal orange is sufficient for it to be the case that these two qualities resemble each other. If I have no a priori access to the nature of these qualities, it is hard to see how I could have a priori access to the fact that they have a nature such that they essentially resemble each other.[9]

These considerations make the thesis that phenomenal concepts are opaque overwhelmingly implausible. What about the thesis that phenomenal concepts are translucent? Making sense of this thesis requires dividing between the aspect of, say, how pain feels, that we transparently understand, and the aspect of how pain feels that we can denote but don't have a transparent grasp of. The trouble is that the conception of my pain I have when I reflect on it and think about it in terms of how it feels seems too simple to be divided up in this way.

To my knowledge, there has been only one proposal according to which phenomenal concepts are translucent, and that is Robert Schroer's proposal that phenomenal concepts have descriptive and demonstrative elements.[10] According to Schroer, <phenomenal red> picks out phenomenal red under the description 'that property which is such and such a combination of phenomenal hue, phenomenal saturation and phenomenal lightness', where reference to these more basic elements of phenomenology is determined by facts outside of what is a priori accessible.

Schroer's proposal is hopeless for a number of reasons which I have laid out in detail elsewhere.[11] Here's a very simple but very serious difficulty with the view. In paradigmatic deployments of phenomenal concepts, we pick out phenomenal qualities in virtue of instantiating them in experience. I am looking at a red ball, and I turn my attention to how the red looks, and think about it as such. But this fact – that I pick out phenomenal red in virtue of its presence in my current experience – seems inconsistent with the thesis that I pick out phenomenal red descriptively as 'that property, whatever it is, that is composed of such and such a combination of certain elements.' It is very hard to see how this fact and this thesis could be merged into a single account of the reference fixing of phenomenal concepts.

If we know that phenomenal concepts reveal something of the nature of phenomenal qualities, and we cannot make sense of their being translucent, then we must suppose that they are transparent. But if we know a priori what it is for something to feel pain, and we know a priori what it is for something to feel pleasure, then we surely know a priori what the sentence 'There currently exists something that feels pain but no pleasure, and something that feels pleasure but no pain' demands for its truth. All that has added to the terms expressing transparent concepts, in order to form this sentence, is some quantifications structure.[12]

In summary of the argument so far:

1. If S is transparent, then either analytic functionalism is true or the physicalist proposal is false.
2. S is transparent.
3. Analytic functionalism is false.
4. Therefore, the physicalist proposal is false.

The non-physicalist proposal

> The demands of S are satisfied by the fact that the blobject feels pain R1-ly but not R2-ly, and feels pleasure R2-ly but not R1-ly.

If a competent speaker of English inspected a world and found that there existed one thing that felt both pleasure and pain, she would not describe that world as one where 'There exists two things, one of which feels pleasure but no pain, and another of which feels pain but no pleasure'. Rather she would describe it as a world where 'There exists one thing that feels both pleasure and pain.'

Of course, the proposal under consideration is that the blobject experiences pain in one spatiotemporally local manner, and pleasure in another, quite distinct, spatiotemporally local manner. It's not easy to make sense of what it would be for a phenomenal quality to be instantiated in a spatiotemporally local manner, but let us suppose that this reflects our cognitive limitations rather than of an absence of possibility. Still, once we know about a world that it contains one thing that feels both pleasure and pain, we know enough about that world to know that it would not be appropriate to describe it as a world where S is true.

I am not simply supposing here that truth must always consist in direct correspondence, that each of the objects quantified over in a true sentence must exist in reality. I am inclined to agree with Horgan and Potrč that there are numerous cases in which a state of affairs can make true a given sentence, despite the fact that the quantificational structure of the state of affairs does not mirror the quantificational structure of the sentence. Consider a world where there are no composite objects, but in which there are particles arranged yellow-sofa-wise and brown-table-wise[13] in my front room. I would be inclined to describe this world as one where the ordinary English sentence, 'There is a yellow sofa and a brown table in my front room' is true. Ordinary English sentences are not used to convey information about the metaphysical structure of reality, and therefore an absence of direct correspondence should not be taken to entail falsity.

Nor am I denying that the single blobject is capable of serving as truthmaker for many ordinary English sentences which quantify over numerous distinct objects. Consider a blobjectivist world where the blobject instantiates yellowness and solidity sofa-shaped-region-in-my-front-room-right-now-ly but not table-shaped-region-in-my-front-room-right-now-ly, and brownness and solidity table-shaped-region-in-my-front-room-ly but not sofa-shaped-region-of-my-front-room-ly. I would be inclined to describe this as another world where the ordinary sentence of English 'There is a sofa in my front room which is yellow but not brown, and a table in my front room which is brown but not yellow.' Appreciation of the everyday purposes to which such a sentence is put, e.g. getting round the room, achieving certain goals such as sitting down,[14] makes it implausible that the sentence demands a direct correspondence with reality for its truth.

But the purposes of mental ascriptions are different. When I'm relaxing in front of the TV on a Sunday, I don't care whether my front room contains a sofa, or whether my front room contains particles arranged sofa-wise, or whether the blobject instantiates solidity sofa-shaped-region-of-my-front-room-ly. So long as it feels comfortable when I sit down, I'm happy. This is why, metaphysically speaking, sentences about tables and chairs are so easily pleased.

But my interest in mental properties of others is not so metaphysically neutral. When, whilst watching TV in my front room, I worry about how many are suffering in Syria right now, I have a concern that goes beyond practicalities. I am concerned with how the world is in and of itself. I am worried because I take it to be inherently bad that there are many things in the world – 'thing' in the sense of something that has properties – instantiating the property of feeling pained. Interest in mentality is interest in the world.

This is a crucial difference between talk of tables and chairs and talk of mental properties, which accounts for the fact that, when assessing whether a given state of affairs is sufficient truthmaker for a given mental ascription, we are much less inclined to say 'Oh that'll do', than we are when assessing whether a given state of affairs is sufficient truthmaker for some sentence about furniture arrangement. But the ultimate reason the non-physicalist blobjectivist proposal fails is simply that nobody who understands the sentence 'There is a something which feels pleasure but no pain and something which feels pain but no pleasure', upon considering an irreducible state of affairs of a single object feeling both pleasure and pain (albeit in distinct spatiotemporally local manners) would describe that world using that sentence. Rather they would describe it using the following sentence, 'There is one thing which feels both pleasure and pain'.

Conclusion

I hope to have shown that a world where there is only one thing could not be truly described as a world where 'There currently exists something that feels pain but no pleasure, and something that feels pleasure but no pain.' I am inclined to think that I can know with Cartesian certainty that the thing that feels my pain is not identical to the thing that feels Dave's pleasure; even the evil computers couldn't be deceiving me into thinking I'm not feeling the pleasure of eating ice cream right now when in fact I am. If I'm right about this, then either blobjectivism is false, or Dave and his ice cream joy is a figment of my imagination. Of course, the same would go for all the other conscious states I ordinarily suppose to currently exist, but am certain that I am not currently instantiating. Blobjectivism would entail solipsism, which would make the view very implausible indeed. Maybe you believe it yourself, but why bother telling me about it?

But suppose I am wrong in thinking that I can rule out with certainty that the thing that instantiates my conscious states also instantiates Dave's and everyone else's. Still, the view of Horgan and Potrč is not supposed to involve the denial of commonsense truths, and to deny truth to sentences such as S concerning the existence of distinct subjects of experience would clearly be a mortal sin against common sense. I hope to have shown that Blobjectivism cannot account for the truth of such sentences, and hence cannot be reconciled with common sense.

Notes

1. Horgan and Potrč 2008; this volume.
2. More precisely: sentence S makes P a priori accessible iff there is a possible world where someone comes to know that P a priori, in virtue of understanding S.
3. It may be that *something* of what a non-transparent sentence demands from the world is a priori accessible. For a sentence to be transparent it must reveal *everything* that it demands from the world.
4. I will charitably assume that Horgan and Potrč can give an account of the blobject having a state that plays the pain role, in terms of its instantiation of physical properties in spatiotemporally local manners.
5. I give this argument from Cartesian doubt to the falsity of analytic functionalism in more detail in Goff forthcoming. The materialism of Lewis (1994) and Armstrong (1968) does not count as a view according to which S is transparent, although according to it we have a transparent understanding of the functional states we use to pick out mental states. The consideration I advance in favour of the transparency of S below, therefore, would not count against the Lewis/Armstrong view. In Goff forthcoming, however, I argue that Cartesian doubt can also be used to demonstrate the falsity of the Lewis/Armstrong view.
6. There are of course a number of other well known arguments against analytic functionalism, such as the zombie-conceivability argument and the knowledge argument (these arguments are intended as arguments against physicalism as such, but work best as arguments against forms of physicalism according to which the mental facts are a priori entailed by the physical facts).
7. Levine [1983]; Loar [1990; 2003]; Papineau [1993a; 2002]; Tye [1995]; Lycan [1996]; Hill [1997]; Hill and McLaughlin [1998]; Block and Stalnaker [1999]; Perry [2001].
8. See footnote 2 for an analysis of a priori accessibility.
9. I have defended these arguments against semantic externalism about phenomenal concepts in more detail in Goff 2011.
10. Schroer 2010.
11. Goff MS.
12. This is not quite correct: we have also added reference to the present moment. Even if our temporal concepts are not transparent, it is difficult to see how this could help Horgan and Potrč make sense of the physicalist proposal.
13. I use 'yellow-sofa-wise' as shorthand for 'whatever arrangements of particles would be sufficient for the existence of yellow sofas, if there were yellow sofas.' This kind of phrasing originates in van Inwagan 1990.

14. Of course if blobjectivism is true there is not really a room to get around, nor a person which might sit down, but I will assume for the sake of discussion that Horgan and Potrč could come up with some appropriate paraphrases of these goals.

References

Armstrong, D. M. 1968. *A Materialist Theory of Mind*, Routledge.
Block, N. and R. Stalnaker, 1999. Conceptual Analysis, Dualism and the Explanatory Gap, *Philosophical Review* 108/1: 1–46.
Goff, P. 2011. 'A posteriori physicalists get our phenomenal concepts wrong,' *Australasian Journal of Philosophy*, 89: 2,191–209.
Goff, P. Forthcoming. 'A priori physicalism, lonely ghosts and Cartesian doubt,' *Consciousness and Cognition*.
Goff, P. MS. 'Do physicalists finally have a plausible theory of phenomenal concepts?'
Hill, C. 1997. Imaginability, Conceivability, Possibility and the Mind–Body Problem, *Philosophical Studies*, 87/1: 61–85.
Hill, C. and B. McLaughlin 1999. There are Fewer Things in Reality than are Dreamt of in Chalmers's Philosophy, *Philosophy and Phenomenological Research*, 59/2: 445–54.
Horgan, T. and Potrč, M. 2008. *Austere Realism: Contextual Semantic Meets Minimal Ontology*, Cambridge, Massachusetts, London, England: MIT Press.
Horgan, T. And Potrč, M. This volume. 'Existence monism trumps priority monism.'
Levine, J. 1983. Materialism and Qualia: the Explanatory Gap, *Pacific Philosophical Quarterly*, 64/9: 354–61.
Lewis, D. 1994. 'Reduction of Mind,' in S. Guttenplan, *Companion to the Philosophy of Mind*, Blackwell, 412–31.
Loar, B. 1990. Phenomenal States, in Philosophical Perspectives 4, (ed.) James Tomberlin, Northridge: Ridgeview, 81–108.
Loar, B. 1997. Phenomenal States, in The Nature of Consciousness, in *Consciousness and Philosophical Debates*, (eds.) N. Block, F. Flanagan and G. Güzeldere 1997, Cambridge, MA: MIT Press, 597–616.
Loar, B. 2003. Qualia, Properties, Modality, *Philosophical Issues*, 13/1: 113–129.
Lycan, W.G. 1996. *Consciousness and Experience*, Cambridge, Mass: MIT Press.
Papineau, D. 1993. Physicalism, Consciousness, and the Antipathetic Fallacy, *Australasian Journal of Philosophy*, 71/2: 169–83.
Papineau, D. 2002. *Thinking about Consciousness*, Clarendon Press: Oxford.
Perry, J. 2001. *Knowledge, Possibility and Consciousness*, Cambridge, Mass: MIT Press.
Schroer, R.2010. Where's the Beef? Phenomenal Concepts as Both Demonstrative and Substantial, *Australasian Journal of Philosophy*, 88/3: 505–22.
Tye, M. 1995. *Ten Problems of Consciousness: A Representational Theory of the Phenomenal Mind*, Cambridge, Mass: MIT Press.
van Inwagan, P. *Material Beings, Ithaca and London*, Cornell University Press.

6
The World as We Know It

Richard Healey

6.1 Introduction

In his fourth lecture on pragmatism, William James asked his audience to bear with him while he tried to inspire them with his interest in what he considered the most central of all philosophical problems – the ancient problem of the one and the many. More than a century after the rise of analytic philosophy, few are likely to endorse James's positioning of this problem. From their vantage point in the thick of one contemporary debate or another, many philosophers may well view the present collection of essays on monism as an expedition into a musty intellectual attic of abandoned doctrines, a quixotic attempt by analytic metaphysicians to justify the existence of their discipline by attempting to revive a dead dispute, or both. A due respect for science would seem to require a pluralist ontology that at least includes such fundamental entities as electrons and quarks – not to mention atoms, molecules, neurons and stem cells. Even instrumentalists and constructive empiricists are committed to a plurality of eyes, ears, brains, bodies, microscopes and (so-called!) particle accelerators. As he points out, simply acknowledging with Moore that one has two hands already appears to establish what Schaffer (2007) calls existence pluralism – the view that there is more than one concrete object.

Nevertheless, one can trace a line of thought from Einstein back to Spinoza and forward to our currently best fundamental physics that provides the materials for a scientifically-based argument for existence monism. If this argument were to succeed, it might be taken to supplement Horgan and Potrč's (2008) semantic argument for that thesis. Though fascinating, I believe the argument fails. Moreover, the reasons for its failure cast doubt on Horgan and Potrč's semantic argument. In the end, contemporary physics does not furnish us with a good argument for existence monism. In an ironic twist, it rather furnishes us with an argument for a Jamesian pluralism.

After this brief introduction, the chapter begins by locating Einstein's thought in relation to Spinoza's philosophy as well as the history of twentieth century physics. It is well known that in his later years, Einstein often alluded to Spinoza when expressing his attitude to life and work. What is less often appreciated is that the (unsuccessful) research into a unified field theory on which Einstein was then engaged could be seen as an attempt to create a theory of nature that would have accorded well with Spinoza's metaphysics – at least as interpreted by one recent commentator (Jonathan Bennett). What increasingly set Einstein apart from the mainstream of physics was his unorthodox view of quantum theory and unwillingness to acknowledge its fundamental status within physics. Years after Einstein's death, progress in physics led to the development of what is known as the Standard Model. Because of its successful unification of fields responsible for fundamental forces, this has sometimes been touted as at least the partial realization of Einstein's dream of a unified field theory. But these are not classical but *quantum* fields – a crucial difference for the issue of monism (or so I shall argue).

In section 3 I explain alternative ways of understanding the ontology of a classical field. On one understanding, a unified *classical* field theory of the kind Einstein unsuccessfully sought would have provided a scientific basis for an argument for existence monism.

But the partial unification of fundamental interactions in the Standard Model has been achieved not by classical but by quantum field theories, whose features are sufficiently different as to rule out any simple extension or analog of this argument. Section 4 explains why it is so hard to provide *any* ontology for a quantum field theory – any account of what such a theory might be taken to describe or represent.

Section 5 explores the idea of a radically monist ontology for the interacting quantum fields of the Standard Model and a possibly more unified successor theory. At first sight this may seem to provide the basis for an argument from fundamental physics to a monism like that advocated on very different grounds by Horgan and Potrč. But on closer examination this argument fails because it rests on an equivocal use of the term 'fundamental'.

Clarifying the usage of this term reveals a tension between this scientifically-based argument and the semantics underlying Horgan and Potrč's argument for monism. Section 6 argues that replacing their contextual but still representationally based semantics by an inferentialist alternative makes it possible to combine a non-pluralist ontology *for fundamental physical theory* with a whole-hearted acceptance of a plurality of quarks, electrons and other scientific as well as ordinary objects. I think the resulting resolution of this dispute between monism and pluralism would gladden the heart of a reconciliatory pragmatist like James.

6.2 Historical background

Einstein read and was influenced by the work of several philosophers, including Hume, Kant and Mach. But it was only Spinoza whom he regarded with reverence, referring to him in correspondence as 'our master Spinoza, who was the first' and even writing a poem entitled 'For Spinoza's *Ethics*' which begins 'How much do I love that noble man, more than I could tell with words'. Such reverence stems more from Einstein's identification with the life and ideals of Spinoza than from endorsement of his philosophy, of whose details Einstein repeatedly claimed ignorance. As Paty (1986) says

> If we want to give meaning to such a question as *to what extent is Einstein's thought Spinozistic?* we must understand 'Spinozistic' not as a model, a system, or even a tradition, but as a way of being, as a thinker, in the world. (270)

But Einstein had good reasons to think he shared some of his deepest beliefs with Spinoza, as when he famously said

> I believe in Spinoza's God, who reveals Himself in the orderly harmony of what exists, not in a God who concerns Himself with fates and actions of human beings.[1]

Einstein wrote of this same God in the letter to Max Born which included the famous passage

> Quantum mechanics is certainly imposing. But an inner voice tells me that it is not yet the real thing. The theory says a lot, but does not really bring us closer to the secret of the 'old one'. I, at any rate, am convinced that *He* is not playing at dice.[2]

Here Einstein gives voice to a commitment to determinism that he also shared with Spinoza, and which he viewed not as a limitation on human freedom and creativity, but rather as a way of reconciling oneself to the apparent evil and stupidity of human actions. He made that shared commitment explicit in a letter answering a question of a Brooklyn Rabbi:

> I share exactly Spinoza's opinion and ... as a convinced determinist, I have no sympathy at all for the monotheist conceptions.[3]

Einstein recognized Spinoza as a fellow spirit because he shared his intense desire to understand the unity of what the latter referred to as *Deus sive*

Natura as a way of transcending the merely personal and attaining the 'Joy in looking and comprehending [that] is nature's most beautiful gift'.[4] That is what motivated him to say to a young student (Esther Salaman)

> I want to know how God created this world. I'm not interested in this or that phenomenon, in the spectrum of this or that element. I want to know His thoughts, the rest are details.[5]

Of course, Einstein's fame rests on his scientific achievements and not on the opinions on non-scientific subjects solicited from him in consequence. In turning now to Einstein's work as a physicist, it is important not to over-interpret the influence of these opinions on his physics. Nevertheless, the search for unity in nature, and at least a preference for seeking such unity in a deterministic physics, did characterize Einstein's approach to research in physics, successful as well as unsuccessful. His theory of special relativity enabled us to see space and time as different aspects of a single spacetime, while electric and magnetic fields are different aspects of a single electromagnetic field. The general theory of relativity subsequently knitted geometry to gravity, now understood both as spacetime curvature and as a four-dimensional gravitational field. But in its original formulation it could not be considered a unified theory of all physical phenomena, for several reasons. One reason stemmed from the need separately to postulate a geodesic law of motion for material particles. Einstein himself took the first step to remove this element of disunity by deriving this law from the field equations themselves, treating a material particle as a singularity of the gravitational field. A second reason stemmed from the fact that the field equations include a schematic term (the stress-energy tensor) associated with non-gravitational matter of a kind that must be independently specified.[6] A more unified theory would replace this schema by a tensor associated with some specific matter field – if not the electromagnetic field tensor, then some suitably unified generalization representing *all* non-gravitational matter. Einstein (1949, 89–94) explained how he hoped to remedy this defect in the unified field theory on which he worked without success for many years toward the end of his life, effectively isolating himself from the mainstream of research in physics. But the most important barrier to Einstein's quest for the unification of physics came from developments in that mainstream itself.

On the one hand, experiments had revealed new short-range fundamental forces associated with nuclear and sub-nuclear phenomena (corresponding to the so-called weak and strong interactions) that would also somehow need to be incorporated into a unified physics. On the other hand, the quantum theory to whose development Einstein had made significant early contributions (notably including the 1905 paper cited in the award of his Nobel prize) came to be applied with great success to an increasingly wide range of phenomena. Einstein certainly recognized this as an enormous advance, and did not reject the quantum theory that made it possible. But he viewed quantum theory from an unorthodox perspective from which it could not be seen as the kind of fundamental theory he continued to seek. Since his view is still widely misunderstood, it may be worth spending some time to explain Einstein's attitude toward quantum theory.

This is based on his conception of the task of physics, which he states as follows:

> Physics is an attempt conceptually to grasp reality as it is thought independently of its being observed. In this sense one speaks of 'physical reality'. In pre-quantum physics there was no doubt as to how this was to be understood. ... In quantum mechanics it is not so easily seen. If one asks: does a ψ-function of the quantum theory represent a real factual situation in the same sense in which this is the case of a material system of points or of an electromagnetic field, one hesitates to reply with a simple 'yes' or 'no'. (Einstein (1949), 82–3)

Einstein (here as elsewhere) went on to argue that the ψ-function does *not* constitute a complete description of a real factual situation, and continued (p. 87):

> The statistical character of the present theory would then have to be a necessary consequence of the incompleteness of the description of the systems in quantum mechanics, and there would no longer exist any ground for the supposition that a future basis of physics must be based on statistics.
>
> It is my opinion that the contemporary quantum theory by means of certain definitely laid down basic concepts, which on the whole have been taken over from classical mechanics, constitutes an optimum formulation of the connections. I believe, however, that this theory offers no useful point of departure for future development.

He further elaborates in his 'Reply to Criticisms' in the same work (p. 672):

> Assuming the success of efforts to accomplish a complete physical description, the statistical quantum theory would, within the framework of future physics, take an approximately analogous position to the statistical mechanics within the framework of classical mechanics. I am rather firmly convinced that the development of theoretical physics will be of this type; but the path will be lengthy and difficult.

Einstein did not reject quantum theory because of his commitment to determinism ('God does not play dice'). He simply denied that it could be a fundamental theory, because he insisted that physics provided a description of reality, and he thought he had arguments proving that quantum theory cannot completely describe a physical situation. The unified field theory he sought would have provided the complete description required of any fundamental theory, and might (but perhaps need not) have done so in such a way as to restore determinism. In the light of this theory, quantum probabilities could then be seen to be merely epistemic, just like those of classical statistical mechanics.

Theoretical physics has not progressed along the path Einstein foretold in 1949, but along a different path. While his theory of general relativity remains our best theory of gravity, having withstood severe observational tests, this theory stubbornly resists attempts to unify it with other fundamental interactions – electromagnetic, weak and nuclear. These attempts are now understood to require a quantum theory of gravity, largely because our best theories of fundamental non-gravitational interactions are quantum theories, and since the 1970's these *have* been to a large extent unified in the so-called Standard Model. Contrary to Einstein's conviction, and despite his scruples, there is a widespread belief today that any plausible candidate for a unified fundamental theory (a 'Theory of Everything') would be a quantum theory.

The experimentally successful Standard Model incorporates quantum field theories characterizing two ways in which matter can interact: quantum chromodynamics (for the strong interaction) and unified electro-weak theory (for the electromagnetic and weak interactions). Attempts to further unify these interactions into a so-called grand unified theory (GUT) have so far not proved experimentally successful. Many physicists believe that superstring theory (or its generalization, *M*-theory) hold the best prospects for a successful unified theory, of not only strong and electro-weak interactions, but also gravity. But in so far as any such theory is a quantum theory, it would not constitute a unified field theory of a kind that Einstein could have considered fundamental: he would have taken it to offer us, at best, a pointer along the path to such a theory.

Now while Einstein was firmly convinced that theoretical physics would follow the path on which he himself set out, he stressed that this path would be lengthy and difficult. Perhaps centuries hence physicists will look upon our present infatuation with quantum theory as a temporary detour from that path – necessary, perhaps, to reach a vantage point from which to get a better view of the way ahead? Even if Einstein's conviction proves unfounded, it is interesting to ask how well a classical, unified field theory of the kind Einstein sought would have squared with Spinoza's metaphysics. If one follows Bennett's (1984; 1991) interpretation of his metaphysics, I think the answer is 'remarkably well'.

Bennett takes Spinoza to adopt a field metaphysics in his *Ethics*. This enables him to reconcile his claim that there is only one substance (*Deus sive Natura*) with the plurality of concrete objects we take ourselves to experience in the world (each other, sticks, tables, planets, ...). Bennett typically refers to this one substance as space – God/Nature under the attribute of extension. His Spinoza takes a planet (for example) to consist in a complex feature (a 'mode') of space, so that its 'existence' consists of space's exhibiting a continuous sequence of closely related physical properties *planetary-trajectory-wise* (as it were, on a spatio-temporally continuous sequence of spacetime points strung along its trajectory – except that, since there are no such spacetime points, the italicized phrase must be understood as an adverbial modification of each property). It is but a little stretch to take the one substance to be spacetime rather than space. Indeed, that modification would give Spinoza a deep reason to explain why God is eternal and unchanging – it makes no sense to suppose that *spacetime* changes.

So modified, one can take Einstein's search for a unified field theory as an attempt to realize Spinoza's metaphysics of Nature. Einstein (1954) himself likened the spacetime of general relativity to Descartes' space:

> There is no such thing as an empty space, i.e. a space without a field. Spacetime does not claim existence on its own, but only as a structural quality of the field.
>
> Thus Descartes was not so far from the truth when he believed he must exclude the existence of an empty space. The notion indeed appears absurd, as long as physical reality is seen exclusively in ponderable bodies. It requires the idea of the field as the representative of reality, in combination with the general principle of relativity, to show the true kernel of Descartes' idea; there exists no space 'empty of field.' (155–6)

An Einsteinian unified field would be a remarkably unified Spinozan *Natura*, at least in its attribute of extension. Not only spacetime, but every concrete 'thing' would emerge as 'a structural quality of the field' – the one true substance. Given Einstein's awe of nature and denial of a personal God, one can even see Einstein as thinking of the unified field as a Spinozan *Deus*, under the attribute of thought!

6.3 Classical field theory and existence monism

Quite apart from the historical context, one can raise the question as to whether an Einsteinian unified field theory would have vindicated existence monism – the view that there is exactly one concrete object. Is there a good argument for existence monism based on such a classical field theory? To address this question it is first necessary to clarify the notion, and especially the ontology, of a classical field theory.

What is a classical field? A particular classical field configuration represents an assignment of a numerical value to each of one or more related field magnitudes at every spacetime point. A classical field theory includes field equations that specify the physically possible field configurations as those in which the values assigned at different points are appropriately related to one another.

Classical electro-statistics provides a simple example of a field theory. The electric potential $\varphi(\boldsymbol{r},t)$ is a function that assigns a real number (a so-called scalar) to each point $\boldsymbol{r}$ of space at each instant t (indeed, the same number for every instant – which is why it's called electro-statics!) The electric field $\boldsymbol{E}(\boldsymbol{r},t)$ then equals the gradient of φ – it is a vector field that determines the rate of change of the electric potential in any arbitrary direction in space. A charged particle with charge q placed at $\boldsymbol{r}$ will experience a force $\boldsymbol{F}=q\boldsymbol{E}$, whose effects on its motion can be directly observed, thereby indirectly manifesting the electric field that is responsible for this force. Both $\boldsymbol{E}$ and φ count as classical fields, as I have explained that notion.

What can we conclude about the ontology of a classical field theory? First consider a scalar field f. Here is one possible ontological analysis. Corresponding to each real number x in the range of f there is a property P_x: to say that $f(\boldsymbol{r},t) = x$ is just to say that spacetime point $\boldsymbol{r},t$ has property P_x. Taken at face value, this analysis commits one to an ontology of spacetime points (labeled by) $\boldsymbol{r},t$ and an ideology (in Quine's sense) of determinate properties of the form P_x associated with the determinable magnitude $f(\boldsymbol{r},t)$.[7] An ontology of spacetime points is acceptable to a spacetime substantivalist, and Hartry Field (1986) for one took this analysis of fields as presenting a challenge to a relationist opponent.

The analysis of vector fields like $\boldsymbol{E}$ is trickier, because these involve spatial directions as well as scalar magnitudes. But the underlying ontology is still one of spacetime points. Even if the analysis of vector magnitudes requires the attribution of relations between them, the points concerned will be arbitrarily close together, in conformity to the guiding intuition that everything supervenes on local matters of fact. Moreover, if a vector field like $\boldsymbol{E}$ were itself to supervene on an underlying scalar field like φ, then no modification would be needed.

But here an interesting issue arises. According to the theory of electrostatics, all observable effects of φ are 'filtered through' the action of $\boldsymbol{E}$ on charged particles. Distinct scalar potentials φ_1,φ_2 correspond to the same electric field $\boldsymbol{E}$ if they differ by a constant: $\varphi_1=\varphi_2+C$. It follows from the theory that no observation or measurement can distinguish between electric potentials that differ in just this way. It is not just verificationists who will take this fact to warrant scepticism about the ontological credentials of the scalar field φ.

The magnetic field $\boldsymbol{B}$ of classical electromagnetic theory is similarly related to a vector potential $\boldsymbol{A}$, but in this case the range of distinct magnetic potentials $\boldsymbol{A}$ corresponding to a single magnetic field $\boldsymbol{B}$ is far greater: a transformation from one to another is called a gauge transformation.

The full theory of classical electromagnetism portrays electric and magnetic fields as just different aspects of a single electromagnetic field F. This field is associated with an electromagnetic potential A: each of φ, $\boldsymbol{A}$ represents a different aspect of A. Again, a transformation between distinct electromagnetic potentials A_1, A_2 corresponding to the same electromagnetic field F is called a gauge transformation, and potentials related in this way are said to be gauge-equivalent. In purely classical physics, gauge-equivalent potentials are generally regarded as merely alternative ways of representing the same physical situation, which may be represented more directly by the one electromagnetic field F to which they correspond.

But when classical electromagnetism is married to quantum particle mechanics, phenomena arise which have prompted physicists to re-examine this instrumentalist attitude toward electromagnetic potentials. Effects are observed that seem to show that there is more to classical electromagnetism than can be represented by the F field alone. And yet the gauge symmetry of this combined gauge theory implies that these phenomena still provide no way for measurements to discriminate among distinct electromagnetic potentials A_1, A_2 related by a gauge transformation!

There is a way of resolving this puzzling situation, and it has some interesting metaphysical implications. To each smooth closed loop in spacetime there corresponds a magnitude called the holonomy of that loop. Like the values of the electromagnetic field F, the values of all holonomies are independent of which of a gauge-equivalent class of potentials A is chosen to compute them. But the holonomies of all closed curves in a region do not supervene on the values of the electromagnetic field F at points in that region. It is natural to take the value of the holonomy of a loop to represent a physical property of that loop. For such properties provide the basis for a unified and predictively accurate account of otherwise puzzling electromagnetic phenomena. Detailed observations of such phenomena would provide a way to measure the values of holonomies of loops in regions where the phenomena occur. But the potential A remains unmeasurable, and the same ontological scruples continue to favour an instrumentalist attitude toward it.[8]

The success of this application of classical electromagnetism when married to the quantum mechanics of particles provides a strong reason to countenance holistic properties – specifically, properties of closed loops in spacetime that do not supervene on properties of their constituent spacetime points. Moreover, some of these loops must be macroscopic to explain observed phenomena. Although acceptance of holistic properties remains consistent with an ontology of spacetime points, the resultant ideology is in radical contradiction to Humean supervenience.

Before moving on to consider the ontology of quantum field theories, let me suggest an alternative analysis of purely classical fields whose acceptance would threaten an ontology of spacetime points. I think that we can arrive at it by a somewhat surprising extension of a familiar metaphysical view.

This is the view that objects persist by enduring rather than perduring (to adopt David Lewis's terminology). While a perduring object persists in virtue of the relations obtaining among its various temporal parts, an enduring object persists even though it has no temporal parts, since it is wholly present at each moment of its existence.

To extend this view to fields, consider a field as something that is wholly present at each moment and at each place of its existence. A fundamental field like gravity or electromagnetism is something which is wholly present everywhere and at all times, or better, wholly present at every spacetime point. In accordance with Einstein's (1954) view, by such omnipresence a classical field constitutes spacetime. On this view, a field is an ontologically primitive entity. But spacetime points and regions need not be accepted as objects at all. On an adverbial version of the view along the lines of Bennett's Spinoza, one can regard them rather as spatio-temporal ways for a field to possess properties such as a particular electromagnetic field strength.

On this understanding of the ontology of classical fields, a successful Einsteinian fundamental physics would require only a single concrete object – the unified field itself. This would then ground the following argument for existence monism.[9]

1. The unified field is the only concrete object needed to understand the structure and evolution of the world.
2. If the unified field is the only concrete object needed to understand the structure and evolution of the world, then any other concrete objects would be explanatorily redundant or epiphenomenal entities.
3. There are no explanatorily redundant or epiphenomenal entities.
4. The unified field – the world – is the only concrete object.

Premise (1) is based on the assumed explanatory success of a classical, Einsteinian unified field theory. The understanding is provided by the (hypothetical) field equations, whose solution governs how the properties of the field are spatio-temporally distributed – or rather what are the spatio-temporally modified properties of the unified field (since spatio-temporality is now to be understood in terms of adverbial modifications of a property of the field, not in terms of field properties of or at spacetime locations). This argument may be criticized on various grounds (cf. Schaffer (2007)), but I think it will hold a powerful appeal for one who shares Einstein's vision of a harmonious and unified Nature whose details, though present, have no grounding in features of a miscellany of independently existing concrete objects.

6.4 The problematic ontology of quantum field theories

In a typical formulation, a quantum field is represented by an assignment of one or more related *operators* to every spacetime point. A quantum field theory includes field equations that specify how the operators assigned at different points are appropriately related to one another. A field operator is a mathematical object that maps vectors in an abstract vector space onto one another. The state of a system is specified by a vector from this space, and not by a particular assignment of field operators to spacetime points. Neither the quantum field nor the state vector assigns numerical values to magnitudes defined at each spacetime point. Rather, in combination they specify the expected value of each observable magnitude – the average value one would expect to get if one were to perform repeated measurements of that magnitude in that state. (Given the probabilistic nature of the theory, such measurements would generally not be expected to give the same result on every occasion.) Some of these magnitudes are local – they pertain to restricted spacetime regions: others are global – they concern the field as a whole, without reference to any spacetime region.

It follows that an assignment of expectation values to local magnitudes in a quantum field theory is quite different from an assignment of a numerical value at every spacetime point to each independent magnitude of a classical field theory. But suppose that the state of a quantum field is represented by a vector for which the theory predicts that a measurement of magnitude M will give result m with probability 1. It is tempting to claim that M has value m in that state, which is then called an eigenstate of M with eigenvalue m. This claim is called the eigenvalue-eigenstate link, and it plays a role in attempts to interpret quantum field theory as describing the behaviour of particles.

One can construct a quantum theory of an electron field aimed at describing the behaviour of hypothetical free electrons – electrons assumed not to be subject to electromagnetic or other interactions. The space of state vectors in this theory may be constructed by taking all linear combinations of certain basis vectors. Each of these basis vectors is an eigenstate of so-called number operators $\hat{N}_k$, themselves constructed from the basic quantum field operator. Each $\hat{N}_k$ has integer eigenvalues, so a basis state | , may be labeled by the set of these values $|n_1, n_2, \ldots$,: this is called the occupation number representation. The state of the field in which all these numbers are zero is called the vacuum state: it is the lowest energy state of the field. Applying the eigenvalue-eigenstate link, an excited eigenstate of $\hat{N}_k$ with eigenvalue n_k is taken to contain n_k field quanta of kind k. ($n_k = 0,1$ in this case, since electrons are represented by a fermionic field. This is how the theory represents the famous Pauli exclusion principle, which applies also to other fermions, including quarks. $n_k = 0,1,2,\ldots$ for photons or other bosons represented by a bosonic field.) The total number of quanta in a basis state is then the sum $n = n_1+n_2+\ldots$ of all the n_k.

By identifying these quanta with particles (e.g. electrons), one can try to interpret $|n_1, n_2, \ldots,$ as a state in which there are n_1 electrons with feature 1, n_2 electrons with feature 2, etc. (where the feature has, for example, a certain momentum). In favour of this interpretation, the total momentum and energy of the field each arises naturally as the sum or integral of the corresponding values for the individual quanta. But the interpretation faces serious problems.

First, these quanta cannot be localized in space – there is no well-behaved position operator whose eigenstates could be interpreted as states in which a single particle is present at a specific location.

Second, two distinct quanta with the same features in a basis state seem indiscernible and cannot be distinguished by their properties, apparently making it hard to reconcile their individual existence with empirically confirmed statistics of states supposedly containing large numbers of particles.

Third, the particle interpretation does not extend easily to an interpretation of states other than the basis states of the occupation number representation. A generic linear combination of basis states is a state that resists any natural particle interpretation – for example, how many particles are present in a superposition of a 3-particle basis state and a 17-particle basis state? Interpreting superpositions is always problematic in quantum mechanics, but here the problem strikes at the heart of a particle interpretation.

Fourth, there are situations in which the state of a quantum field may be represented in two quite different ways, leading to two completely different interpretations of its particle content. For example, a situation in which no particles are present in the standard representation (the Minkowski vacuum) may have a non-standard representation in which an indefinitely large number of particles are present (the so-called Rindler particles, which would indeed be detected by a uniformly accelerated observer).

These four problems already afflict a particle interpretation of a quantum field theory supposedly describing the behaviour of hypothetical free electrons. But real electrons are never free. Because of their electric charge, they are subject to electromagnetic interactions.

Taking stable atomic matter to be composed of fermions – electrons and the quark constituents of the nucleus – fermionic fields are regarded as matter fields. But ordinary matter is held together by interactions ('forces' – though this term now functions more as a metaphor than a literal description of these interactions). While electrons are bound to the nucleus by the electromagnetic interaction, it is the strong interaction between quarks that holds the nucleus together despite electrical repulsions among its constituents. A free bosonic field represents bosons such as the photons associated with electromagnetic radiation.

There is a prescription for combining free fermionic and bosonic fields in the Standard Model, and their combination is taken to represent the interactions between fermions. These interactions are often said to be mediated by exchange of bosons of the corresponding bosonic field. Photons mediate the electromagnetic interaction, while gluons mediate the strong interaction.

Extending the already problematic particle interpretation of a free quantum field to cover interacting fields raises yet more problems! As Fraser (2008) explains, the mathematics of interaction blocks even the initial interpretative moves that gave plausibility to a particle interpretation of free quantum fields. Suffice it to say that no description of how properties of particles like electrons or *W* and *Z* bosons change during an interaction is forthcoming from quantum field theory.

We have seen that quantum field theory appears incompatible with a field ontology that requires assignment of numerical values to physical magnitudes at spacetime points: rather, a quantum field assigns *operators* at spacetime points. An alternative way to connect quantum to classical fields focuses instead on the elements of the space on which such operators act. The idea is to take elements of this space to be neither abstract vectors nor wave-functions (as in quantum mechanics) but wave-function*als*, i.e. functions of classical field configurations over spacetime. But Baker (2009) shows how the arguments of Fraser (2008) against particle interpretations of quantum field theory may be extended so as to exclude this kind of field interpretation of quantum field theory. Is there some other ontological account of a quantum field theory? I will briefly mention four proposals, only to dismiss them and pass on.

In her interesting book *How Is Quantum Field Theory Possible?* Auyang (1995) proposes an event ontology for a system of interacting quantum fields. These are supposedly spatio-temporally local events constituted by local field operators at each spacetime point. The spacetime points are not ontologically basic, but are rather themselves abstracted from the events, as their qualities or modes of occurrence. Unfortunately, the character of these supposed events remains quite unclear, and she offers no account of our epistemic access to them. Dennis Dieks (2000) has proposed an alternative event ontology which is problematic for other reasons.

Andrew Wayne (2002) has suggested that a quantum field should be understood as an ascription of a hierarchy of external relations to spacetime points: unary, binary, ternary, n-ary, for all n. He relies on a theorem of Wightman which states that a quantum field is completely characterized by the vacuum expectation values (VEVs) of all n-fold products of field operators, each pertaining to a spacetime point (making n possibly distinct points in all). At first sight, this appears to yield an ontology radically at variance with Humean supervenience, since it would involve non-spatiotemporal external relations among arbitrarily many spacetime points, no matter how far apart. But on closer inspection it is not clear that the VEV interpretation has given us an ontology for a quantum field theory. For an expectation value merely represents the expected average of a sequence of measurements, none of which can be thought merely to reveal the pre-existing value of a magnitude defined at (one or more) spacetime points.

A fourth proposal for an ontology for quantum field theory deserves more extended consideration. It has been made by those following David Bohm in his attempt to extend his famous 'hidden variable theory' of quantum mechanics to quantum field theory.

One way of realizing the state vector of a system is by a wave-function $\psi(\boldsymbol{r}_1, \boldsymbol{r}_2, .. \boldsymbol{r}_n, t)$. Bohmian particle mechanics supplements the wave-function representing the state of a system of particles by ascribing a position $\boldsymbol{r}_i$ to the *i*th particle that varies continuously in a way that depends on that wave-function. Similarly, Bohmian field mechanics supplements the wave-function representing the state of a quantum field by the assignment of a particular classical field configuration that varies continuously in a way that depends on the wave-function. The wave-function then represents (a probability distribution over) all possible field configurations, while the actual state of the quantum field is represented by one particular classical field configuration.

According to Bohm's own interpretation of the theory of the quantized electromagnetic field, the state of a free field at each moment is given by a particular classical vector potential $\boldsymbol{A}(\boldsymbol{r},t)$, whose evolution is specified by a wave-function $\Psi[\boldsymbol{A}(\boldsymbol{r},t)]$. This potential gives rise to a corresponding classical electromagnetic field *F*, but it is also responsible for effects even in regions where that field is everywhere zero.

The same reasoning that motivated associating holistic properties with classical electromagnetism also favours taking the holonomies of $\boldsymbol{A}$, instead of $\boldsymbol{A}$ itself, to represent holistic properties on a Bohmian interpretation of the quantized electromagnetic field. A similar Bohmian interpretation may also be offered for the other free bosonic gauge fields of the Standard Model.

But this is only half the story: the empirical success of the theory stems from its application to interactions between these gauge fields and the electron and other fermion fields. A complete Bohmian ontology has to apply to those fermion fields also. But here problems arise. For a classical Bohmian fermion field is represented by functions that assign Grassman numbers rather than ordinary numbers to spacetime points. (A non-zero Grassman number η may satisfy the equation $\eta^2 = 0$!) I don't know how to make sense of such a field, either on a local property or on a global substance conception of fields. Even if one could make sense of a Grassman electron field, its basic ontology would not include electrons. We are a long way here from any kind of basic atomistic ontology!

One idea (of Struyve and Westman (2007)) is to treat fermionic fields as ontologically parasitic on bosonic gauge fields – as representing uninterpreted additional degrees of freedom of those fields. The idea is that fermions, and fermionic fields, don't contribute to ontology – in a sense electrons and the electron field have no independent existence. But they are not exactly fictions either. Rather, they represent additional 'hidden' structures of a fundamentally bosonic world. This would invert the usual ontological priority of matter (made of fermions) over force (mediated by bosons). It would also represent a novel twist on Berkeley's doctrine of *esse est percipi*, in so far as it portrays the world as constituted by the very bosonic fields (primarily the electromagnetic field) that mediate all our sensory contact with it.

6.5 A monist physical ontology?

The problem of giving *any* coherent ontological interpretation of quantum field theory may seem so intractable as to tempt a retreat into instrumentalism. An instrumentalist is content to regard quantum field theory as merely a remarkably successful tool for accurately predicting and organizing information about observable results in a wide variety of experimental situations. This attitude was recommended by Davies (1984) in his provocatively titled 'Particles do not Exist':

> There are quantum states and there are particle detectors. Quantum field theory enables us to predict probabilistically how a particular detector will respond to that state. That is all. That is all there can ever be in physics, because physics is about the observations and measurements that we can make in the world. We can't talk meaningfully about whether such-and-such a state contains particles except in the context of a specified particle detector measurement. (69)

But one non-instrumentalist option is always available for the ontology of any physical theory – namely the World!

Here's the idea. What is there in a world described by the theories of the Standard Model? Ultimately, there is only one object – the world itself. It has no parts – neither elementary particles, nor spacetime points, nor particle-detectors, nor people, nor planets nor galaxies. It neither perdures nor endures: like spacetime (if there were such a thing!), it exists atemporally. But it has an enormously rich *structure* – so rich, in fact, that everything we think of as an ordinary or extraordinary object emerges as an aspect of this structure. The quantum field theories of the Standard Model give us ways of modelling details of this structure that are not available to us in any other way. Other scientific theories, as well as everyday beliefs, model other aspects of world-structure. But none of these systems of thought and experience ultimately refer to any objects except the world itself.

A classical field theory like general relativity is capable of modelling the structure of the world as a whole; which is to say that it permits structural ascriptions relating properties every spacetime-point-wise. A quantum field theory offers only more limited models, though these can capture more details of world-structure within their limits.

From this point of view, a composition relation itself emerges as higher-order structure. All nontrivial claims of composition are literally false, since the World has no parts. But aspects of world-structure themselves display a structure that warrants us in making compositional claims on whose truth-value we can come to agree – for example, the claim that a proton is composed of two up quarks and one down quark, or the claim that your nose is part of your face.

Turning this idea into an argument for existence monism requires appeal to the fundamental status of the Standard Model within contemporary physics. We do not believe that the interacting quantum field theories of the Standard Model will be physics's last word on the fundamental structure of the world. But the success of those theories, as the present cutting edge of a progressive research tradition in quantum field theory that began with quantum electrodynamics, may be thought to warrant the following claim:

(5) We have reason to believe that a completely successful fundamental theory of physics will be a quantum field theory.

Success would include explanatory power as well as predictive accuracy. Complete success would require that the theory provide a unified account of the world. What is it for a theory to be fundamental? Here is one plausible way to cash out this condition:

(6) A theory of physics is fundamental if and only if its description of the world suffices to account for every other feature of the world.

Of course this leaves open the question as to just what *are* those features, and what it takes to account for them. But it will not be necessary to provide a complete answer to this question to use (6) together with (5) in the following argument for existence monism:

(5) We have reason to believe that a completely successful fundamental theory of physics will be a quantum field theory.
(6) A theory of physics is fundamental if and only if its description of the world suffices to account for every other feature of the world.
(7) A quantum field theory does not describe any proper parts of the world.

Therefore

(8) We have reason to believe that any account of the world that describes its proper parts is either false or else incorporates explanatorily redundant or epiphenomenal entities.

But

(9) There are no explanatorily redundant or epiphenomenal entities.

Hence

(10) We have reason to believe that the world is the only concrete object.

How good is this argument? There are several weak points. (9) may be challenged on various grounds, but since (9) and (3) are identical these challenges apply equally to section 3's argument for existence monism based on a unified *classical* field theory. The inference to (8) implicitly assumes (we have reason to believe that) some fundamental theory of physics *will be* completely successful – an assumption that is at most a regulative ideal for physics. In so far as the justification for (1) also rested on a similar, but (given the present state of physics) much less plausible, version of this same implicit assumption, the present argument represents an improvement. Section 4 provided arguments in support of (7). The important difference between section 3's argument for existence monism and the present argument based on a unified *quantum* field theory concerns premise (6).

I believe that objections to (6) fatally undermine this revised physics-based argument for existence monism. As I have argued elsewhere (2010; forthcoming), the success of quantum theory shows us that a physical theory – even a fundamental theory – may be completely successful in all its applications without offering a representation of reality at all. The quantum field theories of the Standard Model serve as examples of highly successful fundamental theories that do not themselves purport to represent or describe the world: rather, they provide us with mathematical objects (including quantum fields and quantum states) that we can use as reliable guides in making descriptive claims in various circumstances. This does not amount to adopting an instrumentalist interpretation of these theories. Such licensed descriptive claims concern matters that are certainly unobservable through unaided human senses: indeed, many can be checked only by using extremely sophisticated instruments whose design and operation cannot be understood without a great deal of theory, often including some form of quantum theory.

The claim of Standard Model theories to be fundamental rests on their position within contemporary physics, and in particular their predictive and explanatory relations to experiment as well as to other physical theories. A wide variety of descriptive claims licensed (but *not* implied) by these theories have been tested and confirmed in high energy accelerators. The theory of quantum electrodynamics (QED) that results from the unified electroweak theory of the Standard Model by spontaneous symmetry breaking has led to some of the most precise and accurate predictions in all of science. While the explanatory relations of Standard Model theories to the rest of physics are complex and interesting, few would wish to take issue with Weinberg's (1992) claim that in some sense:

> ... any questions about the physical and chemical properties of calcium carbonate [common chalk] lead us in much the same way through a chain of whys down to the same point of convergence: to our present quantum-mechanical theory of elementary particles, the standard model (31)

although his further claim that:

> no one doubts that with a large enough computer we could in principle explain all the properties of DNA by solving the equations of quantum mechanics for electrons and the nuclei of a few common elements, whose properties are explained in turn by the standard model (32)

is likely to raise a few eyebrows among biochemists! The quantum field theories of the Standard Model are fundamental not because they *describe* the world in more detail than any other theories in physics or the rest of science, but because they have the widest (potential) application, because we can use them to predict and explain phenomena that no other theory is capable of predicting and/or explaining, and because they help to unify the rest of physics, if not the rest of science.

Where does the failure of this section's argument from the success of the quantum field theories of the Standard Model leave the doctrine of monism? While the argument fails to support existence monism, the reasons for this failure do nothing to undermine premises (5) and (7). A convinced monist can continue to maintain that the best, and perhaps the only, ontology for a completely successful fundamental theory of physics will be the World, since any such theory would be a quantum field theory and no quantum field theory describes any proper part of the World. But what kind of description of the World could such a theory provide? The motivating idea behind the argument was that the World has an enormously rich *structure* – so rich, in fact, that everything we think of as an ordinary or extraordinary object emerges as an aspect of this structure.

But if no quantum field theory implies any descriptive or representational claims, then a quantum field theory cannot *itself* model any details of World-structure, even if using it helps *us* to do so. If the World *does* have an enormously rich structure, then quantum field theory is silent on what that structure is. I think this renders vacuous both the claim that a quantum field theory describes the World, and the associated claim that the World provides the best, or the only, ontology for a quantum field theory. Unlike a (hypothetical) unified *classical* field theory, a unified *quantum* field theory would have not a monist but a nihilist ontology. Rather than supporting an argument for existence monism, the success of contemporary quantum field theories undercuts an essential premise of an argument similar to one that might have been based on a unified theory of the kind sought by Einstein – if only such a classical field theory had proved successful.

6.6 A pragmatist alternative

Horgan and Potrč (2008, this volume) have offered a very different argument for existence monism that is independent of details of contemporary science, including fundamental physics. They argue that ordinary language as well as at least a large part of scientific language is vague, whereas neither objects nor properties in the world can be vague. They conclude that, if evaluated in accordance with a semantics requiring direct word–world correspondence, a vast number of familiar claims made in ordinary and scientific language will turn out to be false. In large part to avoid this sceptical consequence they advocate an alternative semantic analysis intended to vindicate these claims by showing that, under contextually operative semantic standards, they come out true when evaluated on the basis of ontologically Austere Indirect Correspondence (AIC). Such correspondence is austere in so far as the only concrete *object* appealed to is the World (which, with tongue firmly in cheek, they call 'the blobject').

So now we have three different arguments for existence monism: Horgan and Potrč's semantic argument; and the arguments of sections 3 and 5 of this chapter, both of which were analyzed and seen to be flawed. If arguments appealing to unified field theories of fundamental physics don't establish existence monism, does Horgan and Potrč's apparently independent semantic argument? I will argue that, contrary to appearances, these arguments are *not* independent. The critique of the previous section's argument did nothing to undermine premises (5) and (7): but these premises can now be seen to represent a serious challenge to Horgan and Potrč's AIC-based semantics.

Horgan and Potrč (this volume) argue that truth for many kinds of claims made in real-life contexts is plausibly construed as ontologically austere indirect correspondence, so such truth may be non-ontologically vindicated. Ontologically austere indirect correspondence arises:

> when (i) the way the world actually is conspires with contextually operative semantic affirmability standards in such a way that a given thought/statement is correctly affirmable, and (ii) those semantic standards do not require the right ontology to include items that are eligible candidate-referents for the positing apparatus deployed in the thought/statement.

Now suppose that a completely successful fundamental theory of physics will be a quantum field theory, as (5) says we have reason to believe it will be, but (in accordance with (7)) a quantum field theory does not describe any proper parts of the world. Then nothing in a completely successful theory of physics will describe any proper part of the world. Moreover, as we saw in section 5, this is not because fundamental physics will give us an enormously rich description/representation of *global properties* of the world, but because a completely successful theory of physics will not describe the world at all. If the World *does* have an enormously rich structure, then even a completely successful fundamental physical theory will, then, be silent on what that structure is. But that would render the way the world actually is epistemically inaccessible to us, along with its ability to conspire with contextually operative semantic affirmability standards.

Now it may well be that certain aspects of world structure will remain forever beyond the ken of cognitively, practically and spatio-temporally limited humankind (or even some future extension of our epistemic community to include non-human inquirers). But nothing can function as a contextually operative semantic affirmability standard unless it can influence affirmations. We make claims and evaluate them (fallibly) for truth or falsity. It is a precondition of the possibility of this practice that we have adequate understanding of the content of a claim (including the context in which it is made) and sufficient epistemic access to evidence relevant to its evaluation. If we accept that a completely successful fundamental physics fails to describe the structure of the world then we have no epistemic access to the way the world is at a fundamental level and so no way of stating or holding ourselves to the contextually operative semantic affirmability standards out of which ontologically austere indirect correspondence supposedly arises.

In response to this objection one might argue that there is no need to resort to a fundamental physical theory to say how the world is and to apply contextually operative semantic affirmability standards to the evaluation of a claim such as:

(A) The politics of Arizona is much discussed in the American news media.

All one has to do is to sketch ways the world might be in broad-brush strokes to establish that the way our world actually is suffices to render it semantically correct to affirm (A) under contextually operative semantic affirmability standards. But how would this sketching go? Suppose one appealed to a characterization of worlds in terms of their distributions of ordinary physical properties (shapes, sizes, colours, etc.) of macroscopic physical objects (landmasses with geographical boundaries; human bodies, buildings, TV sets, broadcast antennae, electrical and cable connections, newspapers, etc.). Such a characterization would be vague, and so would itself have to be evaluated under AIC standards, requiring a more fine-grained description of worlds in microscopic physical terms (atomic constitution of deserts, TV sets and human bodies; wavelengths of broadcast radiation, etc). This is still vague, necessitating a characterization in terms of 'elementary particles' such as electrons, quarks and photons. But now we have reached the level of fundamental physics, and section 4 queried the ontological credentials of such 'objects' within a quantum field theory. The program of non-ontological vindication supposedly 'bottoms out' in a direct correspondence account of truth connecting statements in some hypothetical non-vague scientific language of fundamental physics to enormously complex structural properties of a single object, the blobject. With no such direct correspondence foundation, the whole structure collapses. Acceptance of (5) and (7) removes the foundation.

And yet we *do* succeed in affirming claims like (A) and evaluating them for truth and falsity, despite their undoubted vagueness. Moreover, scientists confidently affirm their beliefs about elementary particles, even if quantum field theory itself describes no such objects. Here are three examples:

> Here, right now, in a little cylindrical domain ... in the center of our Penning trap resides positron (or anti-electron) Priscilla, who has been giving spontaneous and command performances of her quantum jump ballets for the last three months.

Wick (1995, 137) quotes this from the press release reporting the results of experiments conducted in Hans Dehmelt's laboratory in 1984 with a Penning trap – a device whose name indicates its alleged function of confining charged particles by means of electromagnetic fields. Dehmelt was awarded a Nobel prize in 1989 for his research on Priscilla and other isolated charged particles. The most expensive and elaborate experimental device ever built (the Large Hadron Collider – a proton accelerator) is currently in operation in Geneva with the declared aim of putting the finishing touches to the Standard Model by producing and detecting the elusive Higgs boson. Recently a group at CERN claimed success in a different experiment. By producing and trapping large numbers of positrons and antiprotons (the antiparticles of protons) they were able to combine some of them into atoms of antimatter – specifically, anti-hydrogen – which they were able to store for a short period before they annihilated with matter in their container.

Why are scientists correct to affirm that Priscilla resided in the center of Dehmelt's Penning trap for three months in 1984, and that 38 atoms of anti-hydrogen formed from positrons and antiprotons created at CERN were recently trapped for about 1/6 of a second? What would make them correct to affirm that the LHC has discovered the Higgs boson? Such affirmations may be *justified* by the evidence adduced in their support. But of course such evidence does not entail the *truth* of what is affirmed. Claims based on strong evidence may be retracted subsequently on the basis of additional evidence, in science as in daily life. For it to be *correct* to affirm that the Higgs boson has been discovered at the LHC two conditions must be satisfied:

(a) The situation to which the claim pertains must be one in which the relevant quantum field theory *licenses* the claim that a Higgs particle is present, and
(b) The experimental evidence provided by analyzing the data produced by the detectors must *warrant* that claim.

Condition (b) is a matter of evidence, but condition (a) is not. As I (forthcoming) have argued elsewhere, no quantum theory itself implies any descriptive claim concerning a system such as a particle or field. In particular, a quantum field theory never implies the *existence* of any particle or field: in that sense, the ontology of a quantum field theory contains neither fields nor particles nor any other physical system. That is why I called it a nihilist ontology in section 5.

But a quantum theory may be applied in a situation in which it licenses a user of the theory to make various descriptive claims about one or more physical systems. Such a license may be more or less restricted in scope: the wider the license, the more material inferences from that claim are permitted. Since the *content* of such a claim is a function of the web of material inferences in which it is embedded, (a) is a semantic rather than an epistemic condition. So, correctness of an affirmation of existence based on a quantum field theory has a semantic component. But this is neither grounded in nor grounds any correspondence notion of *truth*, indirect, direct or AIC.

So what would it take for statement (H) to be true?

(H) The Higgs boson is discovered at CERN during the 21st century.

As Tarski insisted,

(H) is true if and only if the Higgs boson is discovered at CERN during the 21st century.

But surely, if (H) is true then at least one Higgs boson exists at some time during the 21st century?

Yes, indeed. If conditions (a) and (b) are satisfied, then the claim

(E) A Higgs boson exists at some time during the 21st century.

is both licensed and warranted, because (H) is. If (H) is true, so is (E). But what would then *make* (H) and (E) true is not a relation of direct or indirect correspondence between these claims and the world somehow set up by physicists and other language-users that involves a highly selective referential mechanism (causal or otherwise) between the term 'Higgs boson' and physical objects or properties (Higgs bosons, *is a Higgs boson*, the World, *manifests Higgs-boson-ness-CERN-21st century-wise*). In answer to a demand for a truth-maker for statements such as (H) and (E), the best thing one can do is to simply (re)assert that very claim, backed up (if this is found unsatisfying) by as complete as possible an account of the evidential grounds on which it rests. There is nothing more to be said in response to a demand for truth-makers for (H) and (E) than one would find in the published paper reporting and justifying the claim, amplified by the collective knowledge and wisdom of its authors as well as the whole community of physicists involved, including their abilities as users of the various natural (and technical) languages in which they communicate.

More generally, there is not much more to be said about truth, and nothing more should be said in the attempt to cash out the metaphor of truth as correspondence – to Reality, to the Facts or to anything else. It is not necessary to vindicate true claims (including (A)) by showing how they may be seen to correspond to the world. The important questions are how a claim gets its content, and how it is evaluated on the basis of the evidence. The concept of truth is best avoided while addressing these questions. Any residual questions about truth concern the role that concept plays in the social practice of communicative discourse, among scientists just as among the rest of us.

6.7 Conclusion

Existence monism is the thesis that there is exactly one concrete object – the World, or the blobject. One kind of argument for this thesis appeals to considerations drawn from science, and specifically to aspects of fundamental physics. In Einstein's view, a fundamental theory of physics would permit a complete description of the world at the deepest level – a description sufficient (in principle) to determine exactly how the world is. His own attempts to create a fundamental unified field theory did not succeed. Had they succeeded, a classical unified field theory could have provided the basis for a serious argument for existence monism – an argument that would certainly have appealed to a Spinozistic thinker like Einstein himself.

But fundamental physics took a different path, which has so far led to the interacting quantum field theories of the Standard Model. Though highly successful, these theories do not themselves constitute a fully unified fundamental quantum field theory. But their success does provide some reason to believe that a completely successful fundamental physics would take the form of a quantum field theory. However, convincing objections have been raised against interpretations of a quantum field theory that portray this as describing elementary particles, fields, or any other physical system, including the world as a whole. This does not show that no quantum field theory can be fundamental, if what is required of a fundamental theory of physics is that we can use it successfully to predict and completely to account for all physical phenomena in a unified way. But it does mean that such a unified *quantum* field theory would provide no basis for an analogous argument for existence monism.

A different kind of argument for that thesis appeals to the semantics of our language, ordinary as well as scientific. This argument (due to Horgan and Potrč) employs an account of truth as AIC correspondence. For AIC correspondence to hold between a statement *S* and the world, there must be some relation of direct correspondence between statements or thought-contents and the world as a whole that makes *S* true. The ability to apply contextually operative semantic standards so as to evaluate the truth of a statement *S* in terms of AIC correspondence ultimately rests on the possibility of epistemic access to this relation of direct correspondence. But we have reason to believe that even if we had a completely successful fundamental physical theory we would still not have such access. While this does not settle the question as to whether the world *has* some determinate structure at a fundamental level (or the prior question as to what this could mean), it does show that we have reason to believe that our ability correctly to make and justify claims about the world does not depend on the assumption that the world has some determinate structure at a fundamental level.

Physicists use quantum theories, including the quantum field theories of the Standard Model, to guide them in determining both the correct affirmability and the content of claims about particles, fields and other physical items. They have developed the instrumental, mathematical and conceptual resources to permit sensitive evaluation of the evidence for or against such claims. They are often in a position authoritatively to judge some such claims true and others false on the basis of such evidence, though any particular judgment remains fallible. The judgment that an elementary particle (such as an electron or the Higgs boson) exists with certain properties may authoritatively be judged as true even though no completely successful fundamental physical theory ascribes these properties to this particle or includes the particle in its ontology.

Truth does not rest on direct correspondence even at the level of fundamental physics. Tarski *T*-sentences express an insubstantial kind of word–world correspondence at any level of science or daily life. Armed with such insubstantial correspondence, one can cheerfully adopt a pluralist ontology of electrons, photons, classical electromagnetic as well as gravitational fields, acids, mitochondria, and slime molds within science; states, media and politics in the social sphere; and the blobject for philosophers who want it. Each such ontology works well within its own limits, and each underwrites truth claims. But as James and Carnap told us, there is no single right ontology.

Notes

1. *The New York Times*, April 25th, 1929, p. 60, col.4.
2. In *The Born-Einstein Letters* (Born (1971), 91).
3. Letter to Rabbi A. Geller, September 4th, 1930, Einstein Archives, unpublished.
4. Einstein (1954a), 28.
5. E. Salaman, 'A Talk with Einstein,' *The Listener 54* (1955), 370–371.
6. Einstein(1936, 370) likened the stress-energy tensor associated with non-gravitational matter on the right-hand side of his field equations to low grade wood, in contrast to the 'fine marble' of the Einstein tensor associated with the gravitational field on their left-hand side.
7. Carnap (1956;1966) did not take such an analysis at face value. As Friedman (forthcoming) explains, he proposed to dissolve the dispute between realist and instrumentalist about the reference of theoretical terms such as those purportedly denoting classical fields. Roughly, his proposal was to regard a scalar field f as a purely mathematical function from quadruples of real numbers $\mathbf{r},t$ (*not* 'concrete' spacetime points these label!) into the real numbers. The ontological question was then to be replaced by the question as to whether or not to use a language including such a theoretical term for the purposes of physics – a question to be answered on purely pragmatic grounds.
8. For further details, see Healey (2007).
9. This is a suitably modified version of a similar argument of Schaffer (2007).

References

Auyang, S. (1995). *How is Quantum Field Theory Possible?* New York: Oxford University Press.

Baker, D. J. (2009). 'Against field interpretations of quantum field theory', *British Journal for the Philosophy of Science, 60*, 585–609.

Bennett, J. (1984). *A Study of Spinoza's Ethics*. Indianapolis: Hackett.

Bennett, J. (1991). 'Spinoza's Monism: a Reply to Curley', in *God and Nature: Spinoza's Metaphysics*, ed. Yirmiyahu Yovel. Leiden: E. J. Brill, 53–9.

Born, M. (1971). *The Born–Einstein Letters*. Translated by Irene Born. London: Macmillan.

Carnap, R. (1956). 'The methodological character of theoretical concepts', In H. Feigl and M. Scriven (eds.), *Minnesota studies in the philosophy of science, vol. I: The foundations of science and the concepts of psychology and psychoanalysis*. Minneapolis: University of Minnesota Press, 38–76.

Carnap, R. (1966). *Philosophical Foundations of Physics: an Introduction to the Philosophy of Science*. New York: Basic Books.
Davies, P. C. W. (1984). 'Particles do not Exist', in S.M. Christensen, ed. *Quantum Theory of Gravity*. Bristol: Adam Hilger Ltd, 66–77.
Dieks, D. (2000). 'Consistent histories and relativistic invariance in the modal interpretation of quantum mechanics', *Physics Letters A, 265*, 317–25.
Einstein, A. (1936). 'Physics and reality', *Journal of the Franklin Institute 221*, 349–382. Reprinted in Einstein, A. (1954a), 290–323.
Einstein, A. (1949). 'Autobiographical Notes', 'Reply to Criticisms', in Schilpp, P.A. (ed.) *Albert Einstein: Philosopher–Scientist*. La Salle, Illinois: Open Court, 3–94; 665–88.
Einstein, A. (1954). *Relativity: the Special and the General Theory (15th edition)*. London: Methuen.
Einstein, A. (1954a). *Ideas and Opinions*. New York: Bonanza.
Field, H. (1986). 'Can we Dispense with Space-Time?', in P. D. Asquith and P. Kitcher (eds.), *PSA 1984, Volume 2, Proceedings of the 1984 Biennial Meeting of the Philosophy of Science Association*. East Lansing, Michigan: Philosophy of Science Association, 33–90.
Fraser, D. (2008). 'The fate of 'particles' in quantum field theories with interactions', *Studies in History and Philosophy of Modern Physics*, 39, 841–859.
Friedman, M. (forthcoming). 'Carnap on Theoretical Terms: Structuralism without Metaphysics'.
Healey, R. (2007) *Gauging What's Real*. Oxford: Oxford University Press.
Healey, R. (2010). 'Science without Representation', *Analysis Reviews 70*, 536–547.
Healey, R. (forthcoming). 'Quantum Theory: a Pragmatist Approach'.
Horgan, T. and Potrč, M. (2008). *Austere Realism: Contextual Semantics meets Minimal Ontology*. Cambridge, Mass.: MIT Press.
Horgan, T. and Potrč, M. (2011). 'Existence Monism Trumps Priority Monism', this volume.
James, W. (1907). *Pragmatism: a New Name for some Old Ways of Thinking*. New York: Longmans, Green.
Paty, M. (1986). 'Einstein and Spinoza', in *Spinoza and the Sciences*, eds. Marjorie Grene and Debra Nails. Dordrecht: Reidel, 267–302.
Schaffer, J. (2007). 'Monism'. *Stanford Electronic Encyclopedia of Philosophy*.
Struyve, W. and Westman, H. (2007). 'A minimalist pilot-wave model for quantum electrodynamics', *Proceedings of the Royal Society A*, 463, 3115–3129.
Wayne, A. (2002). 'A Naive View of the Quantum Field', in Kuhlmann, M., Lyre, H. and Wayne, A., (eds.) *Ontological. Aspects of Quantum Field Theory*, Singapore: World Scientific.
Weinberg S. (1992). *Dreams of a Final Theory*. New York: Pantheon.
Wick, D. (1995). *The Infamous Boundary*. Boston: Birkhäuser.

7
On the Common Sense Argument for Monism

Donnchadh O'Conaill and Tuomas E. Tahko

Priority monism is the claim that there is one fundamental entity, upon which all other entities are ontologically dependent (by 'entity', we mean any portion of the universe which can be distinguished from other portions by its identity conditions). The priority monism we shall address in this chapter regards the entire spatiotemporal cosmos as the fundamental entity. Shoes, ships, sealing-wax and any other spatiotemporal entities are all parts of, and exist in virtue of, this entity.[1]

One argument against monism goes back at least to Russell, who claimed that pluralism is favoured by common sense: 'I share the common-sense belief that there are many separate things; I do not regard the apparent multiplicity of the world as consisting merely in phases and unreal divisions of a single indivisible Reality' (1985, 36; quoted in Schaffer this volume, 20). In response to this argument, Schaffer first points out that it does not contradict priority monism. The priority monist allows that there is a plurality of different things; they just insist that one of these things (the cosmos) is fundamental, and that everything else is a part of it (Schaffer this volume, 20).

Second, Schaffer argues that common sense favours priority monism over any pluralist position. To this end, he appeals to a distinction in mereology, between mere aggregates and integrated wholes. A *mere aggregate* is a collection of entities such that the parts (the entities in the collection) are ontologically prior to the whole (the collection itself). For example, the grains of sand in the heap would seem to be prior to the heap. But in an *integrated whole*, the whole itself is prior to its parts. Consider the relation between a circle and any semicircles one could carve from it. If we start with the integrated circle, then any semicircle carved from it will be merely an arbitrary portion of the circle. Hence, common sense would seem to suggest that the circle must be prior.

Accordingly, Schaffer (21–22) provides a common sense argument for priority monism:

> P1: according to common sense, integrated wholes are prior to their arbitrary portions.

P2: according to common sense, the cosmos is an integrated whole.

P3: according to common sense, the many proper parts of the cosmos are arbitrary portions.

C: according to common sense, the cosmos is prior to its many proper parts.

We wish to challenge this argument. We are not concerned to establish the truth of pluralism, nor to give reasons for thinking that monism cannot be correct. We merely want to establish that Schaffer's argument does not give one reason to think that priority monism is correct.[2] To do this, we shall challenge P3.[3] In response to this premise, we wish to argue that there are at least some spatiotemporal entities which are not arbitrary portions of the cosmos. So what is at issue in this chapter is a certain line of thought which is conducive to monism; the suggestion that the different entities in the universe are arbitrarily carved portions. It is this arbitrariness claim which shall be our direct target in what follows.[4]

In section I, we shall outline an argument Schaffer offers in defence of P3, and briefly sketch the position we shall defend. Sections II and III shall each present an argument in defence of our position, on ontological and semantic grounds respectively. Lastly, in section IV we shall consider and reply to a possible response which is available to Schaffer.

I

To get a handle on what precisely is at issue in this chapter, consider a line of thought Schaffer offers in defence of his premise 3: 'Common sense appreciates that there are many ways to carve the world. Consider all the ways that one may slice a pie, or all the ways of drawing lines on a map. There seems no objective ground for carving things in just one way' (this volume, 22).[5] We accept that this line of thought tells against a certain type of metaphysical position. Positions of this type can be characterised by the positing of what we shall term a *Complete Scheme (CS)*, a way of carving up the universe such that:

1. every portion so carved is carved on objective grounds; and
2. every entity in the universe is a portion so carved.

The term *'objective ground'* is Schaffer's own. We understand him to mean by this that such grounds would be the way the world is itself, regardless of all and any interests of any persons. The notion of objective grounds for carving things in one way or another allows us to clarify the notion of an arbitrary portion. An arbitrary portion is not a fictional entity; rather, it is a proper part of the world, but one whose identity and distinction from other parts depends on its being identified and differentiated by some observer, according to the interests of that observer. To say that there are objective grounds for carving the world into certain portions is to say that these portions have identity and existence conditions which are not dependent on their being recognized by any observer as those very portions.

We accept that there are reasons to believe that no scheme can possibly meet both (i) and (ii). First, it is possible to carve the world in different ways. Such reasons may be found in the reactions of some philosophers to debates about whether points on a Euclidean plane are real parts of the plane or idealized constructions from it (Putnam 1990, 97), and whether any of the various conceptions of biological species carve reality at its joints or should be understood in terms of so called 'species pluralism' according to which there is no one correct conception of biological species (e.g. Dupré 1993). One is not being *ipso facto* untrue to the way the world is by choosing to carve it in one of these ways as opposed to another. Furthermore, there are many objects whose specifications are dependent on the particular interests of the persons doing the carving (e.g., interest rates, moral patients, music). It seems impossible to capture these objects in any scheme which satisfies (i).

For these reasons, we accept that a CS is impossible. But the notion of a CS does point to something important. We propose to capture this point by refining the notion of a CS, into what we shall call a *Near-Complete Scheme (NCS)*. This is a way of carving up the universe such that:

1. every portion so carved is carved on objective grounds; and
2. every entity in the universe is either a portion so carved, or is ontologically dependent on some such portion or combination of portions.[6]

An NCS keeps the first condition for a CS, but adjusts the second, while nonetheless holding to an important asymmetry between the objects it picks out and all other objects. It captures the sense we have that interest rates, music, moral patients and so on all depend for their existence on the existence of things which do not require the existence of interest rates, etc., in order to themselves exist; things which, unlike interest rates, etc., are not dependent for their existence on the interests of any persons.

In what follows, we shall defend the necessity of an NCS. We shall not, in this chapter, be defending any particular NCS, though we will gesture towards where we think the best such scheme might be found. Rather, we will present reasons for thinking that such a scheme is necessary, given certain assumptions about the world and how we understand it.[7]

II

In this section and the next, we shall develop two arguments in favour of an NCS, the first on semantic grounds, the second based on ontological considerations. The semantic argument supports the claim that priority monism cannot account for the truth of certain judgements about parts of the world. The ontological argument supports the claim that priority monism cannot account for the ontological grounds of certain parts of the world (macrophysical objects).

The semantic argument begins with two assumptions: first, that we can make judgements about the parts of the universe which can be true or false (e.g., judgements about what parts exist, about the properties of particular parts, about the relations of parts to each other, etc.); and second, that some of these judgements will be true or false partly in virtue of the way the world is (in virtue of what items exist in the world, what their properties are, etc.). Given these two assumptions, we argue that it follows that one must think of the world as having a nature (as being the way it is) independently of whatever judgements can be made of it. This independent nature would constitute the objective grounds required for an NCS.

The first of these assumptions we take to be uncontentious, but the second must be spelled out more carefully. We think that it cannot be made consistent with Schaffer's denial that there are objective grounds for carving the world in any particular way. To explain the relation between our second assumption and Schaffer's denial of objective grounds, we shall consider a position which tries to balance both of these demands. This is the position which has been developed (and modified) by Hilary Putnam over the past three decades.

Putnam's starting point is that questions such as 'what is the nature of reality?' make sense only in the context of a particular theory or conceptual scheme (1981, 49). In order to frame a question of this sort, we must do so against an agreed background, within which our terms are defined. The example of a mini-world with three individuals, A, B and C, is meant to illustrate this point. On Carnapian logic, which takes each object to be an individual, this world contains three objects. But on a Lezniewskian logic, which incorporates objects made of composites of individuals, this world has seven objects: A, B, C, and the mereological sums [A+B], [A+C], [B+C] and [A+B+C]. The question 'How many objects are in this mini-world?' will receive different answers depending on which logic (and therefore, which use of the term 'object') one chooses to employ. More importantly in the present context, this question only makes sense given *some* standard or other as to what counts as an object. There is no sense to the question 'How many objects does the mini-world *really* have, independently of any particular logical scheme?' (Putnam 1990, 98).

The standard realist response to this is to accept that there are many ways of thinking about reality, but that the world itself exists independently of how we choose to think about it. But Putnam points out that the realist cannot provide a description of reality which is neutral between the various possible standards we can apply. All one can do is choose a particular set of standards and interpret reality using these (1990, 97). Even concepts such as 'object' or 'exist' are relative to some conceptual scheme or other (1990, 97; 2004, 37; 43). The world itself does not decide which set of standards we ought to use (2004, 51). This claim we take to be equivalent to Schaffer's denial of objective grounds for carving reality in any particular way.

However, Putnam acknowledges that given particular standards, what makes one's judgements true or false are the facts about the world. In the case of the mini-world, 'If I choose Carnap's language, I must say there are three objects because that is how many there are' (1987, 33; see also 2004, 45). This acknowledgement we take to be equivalent to our second assumption, that some of our judgements will be true or false partly in virtue of the way the world is. What we wish to stress is that this imposes a necessary limit to the degree to which one's carving up of the world can be arbitrary. In order to think of one's judgements as being made true or false by the way the world is, one must have some conception of the way the world is. This conception must be relatively determinate, and it must involve the idea that the way the world is (the nature of the world) is independent of what anyone judges to be the case. We suggest that this independent nature constitutes precisely the objective grounds which Schaffer denies can dictate which way the world should be carved up.

To illustrate the claim that one must have a conception of the way the world is, and that it must include the idea that the world is independent of one's judgements, consider again the mini-world. We hold (as Putnam does) that the way the mini-world is makes an independent contribution to deciding the truth or falsity of judgements about it. Given this, we suggest that one must have a conception of the mini-world as having a nature which is not itself determined by the standards of counting one chooses to use. For let us say the reverse were true: that the nature of the mini-world was entirely determined by one's standards. In that case, once one had chosen one's standards, the truth or falsity of one's judgements would thereby have been decided, because those standards would, *ex hypothesi*, have determined the nature of the world which is supposed to decide the truth or falsity of the judgements. On this understanding, the nature of the world could not make any contribution in addition to that made by the standards one chooses. This would be problematic in two ways. First, it would render otiose the claim that given a particular set of standards, it is the nature of the mini-world itself which decides the truth or falsity of the judgements. Second, it would make unclear how one could possibly make false judgements about the mini-world when one correctly understands and applies one's own standards. But this does seem possible.[8]

What holds in the case of the mini-world holds for the actual world as well. One chooses the standards to apply to it, but for the world itself to make a separate contribution to deciding the truth or falsity of one's judgements, it must be the way that it is independently of one's standards. This independent nature would constitute objective grounds for carving at least certain parts of the world in one way rather than another; these grounds being objective in that they are the way the world is itself, regardless of all and any interests of any persons. This independent nature thus constitutes the objective grounds which an NCS requires.

We suggest that this conception of the world must be 'determinate'. By this, we mean that it cannot be exhausted by ideas such as 'whatever is the case' or 'however it is that things are'. It must be a conception of the world which allows one to think that it is the way the world is which makes one's judgements true or false. If the content of this conception was something like 'whatever is the case', then the thought that it is the way the world is which makes one's judgements true or false becomes vacuous (something like 'this judgement is rendered true or false by the way that whatever all these judgements are about actually is'). One way of putting this point is that one can slice a pie in as many different ways as one likes, but in order to be aware that what one is doing is slicing a pie which can be sliced in many other ways, your conception of the pie cannot be just 'whatever I have when I put these slices together'. This description, while correct, fails to capture the independence of the pie from any particular way of slicing it. If the pie is characterised in this way, one's awareness of what one is doing will be empty (it will be an awareness that one is slicing whatever it is that these ways of slicing are in fact slicing). We would lose the notion that what we are doing in slicing (or judging) is constrained by a reality external to our activity.[9]

In saying that this conception of reality must be relatively determinate, we are happy to admit that it will probably contain gaps. There may well always be aspects of reality which are not fully known or understood. For these, a hand-waving gesture such as 'whatever is the case' may be appropriate. But this cannot be the case with one's understanding of the entire world, on pain of losing any sense of one's judgements being made true or false by how things are.[10]

This conception of the world does not exhaust our understanding of what there is. In a wide variety of cases, what exists and its properties are in fact determined by our local standards (those particular to a culture, a society or a language). For example, actions or persons cannot be chivalrous except in certain social contexts; likewise, the world will not contain any banknotes unless a certain number of people believe it to. These are examples of properties and entities which are not independent parts of the world. Because we can make true or false judgements about these properties and entities, it follows that the conception of the world as independent does not exhaust all of our true thought. For this reason, the conception of the world we are defending is an NCS rather than a full-blown CS. However, we suggest that any properties or entities which are dependent on our judgements or standards are also dependent on other entities which are themselves independent of our judgements and standards. That is, entities and properties such as chivalry, banknotes, and anything else which depends for its existence on particular standards or judgements will also depend on the existence of an objective nature.

We have two reasons in support of this suggestion. First, any judgements and standards will be dependent on subjects who make or use them. These subjects will themselves be dependent on other entities, but these other entities cannot all be dependent on the judgements or standards, on pain of vicious circularity.[11] Second, the most plausible account of the ontology of entities and properties which depend on judgements characterises them as resulting from subjects taking independent features of reality to be a certain way.[12] For example, while the type 'banknote' is functionally defined rather than being a natural kind, all actual banknotes will be constituted by or identical to physical items whose existence does not depend on judgements about them.[13] Similarly, the property of being chivalrous will attach to persons whose existence is not dependent on any judgements or standards (or it will attach to modes of behaviour of such persons; these modes of behaviour may be dependent on judgements, but not the persons behaving in these ways).

This first criticism of Schaffer has the form of a transcendental argument: given that we can make true judgements about the world, and given that these judgements are made true or false by the way the world is, we must conceive of the world as having a nature which is independent of our judgements regarding it. A standard rejoinder to transcendental arguments of this sort is that they only demonstrate what one must think to be the case, not that anything actually is the case. Therefore, the rejoinder might be continued, we have not shown that there are any objective grounds for carving up reality in one way rather than another. At best, we have only shown that one must think that there are such grounds, in order to make sense of one's judgements about reality being true or false.

We accept that this rejoinder is correct as far as it goes, but we do not think that it shows that our transcendental argument is irrelevant to Schaffer's position. Our argument does give one reason to think that there must be an objective order to the world. If one has reason to think that one's judgements about the world can be made true or false by the way the world is, then one has reason to think that this state of affairs (one's judgements about the world being made true or false by the way the world is) is possible only if the universe has a nature which is independent both of one's judgements and one's standards. And this gives one reason to think that the universe has a nature which is independent of either judgements or standards.

III

In this section we will develop an ontological argument which supports the idea of an NCS. This argument begins with the basic idea that, since there are macrophysical objects in the cosmos, the microphysical structure of the cosmos must be such that it enables the possibility of macrophysical objects. Importantly for the purposes of challenging Schaffer's argument, this is a form of asymmetrical existential dependence: macrophysical objects depend for their existence on microphysical objects, but the latter could exist without the former. It is easy to illustrate this asymmetry by considering an alternative history of the cosmos where one of the fundamental physical forces, such as the strong nuclear force which binds the nuclei of atoms together, had been significantly weaker: the cosmos would still have a microphysical structure, but there would be no 'clumps' of matter, no macrophysical objects.

So, what are the necessary microphysical requirements for the existence of macrophysical phenomena? The key here seems to be the ability of the proper parts of macrophysical objects to bind together, specifically, the ability of subatomic particles to form atoms, atoms to form molecules, and molecules to form macrophysical objects. We suggest that this binding ability requires non-arbitrariness in the microphysical structure of the cosmos; if this structure were to be arbitrary, the stability required to form macrophysical objects could not be achieved.

Physics tells us that the binding of molecules and atoms is dependent on the electron configuration of individual atoms, which in turn depends on the energy levels of specific electrons and is moderated by the Pauli Exclusion Principle.[14] Similarly, the manner in which subatomic particles form atoms is dependent on the individual charges of subatomic particles – the negative charges of the electrons and the positive charges of the protons, where each proton consists of three quarks which make up the total charge of the proton.

Charge is one of the most important properties when considering the requirements for the possibility of bond forming and the stability of macrophysical objects. In fact, the *elementary charge*, namely $1.6021892 \times 10^{-19}$ coulombs, is one of the fundamental physical constants. This is the charge of protons, whereas electrons have a negative charge of equal strength. Interestingly, the charge of all other freely existing subatomic particles that have a charge is either equal to or an integer multiple of the elementary charge. Quarks have charges that are integer multiples of one third of the elementary charge, but they are not freely existing – quarks occur only as parts of other subatomic particles. The total charge of the atom is of course neutral. What is most important for our purposes is that even if we were unable to accurately state the charges of each subatomic particle which together form an atom, we do know that their sum has to be zero, as otherwise the atom would not be stable. The upshot of this is that certain entities, namely electrons and quarks, must possess an exact charge. The requirement of *exactness* imposes a crucial constraint for the microphysical structure of the cosmos. Given that our cosmos includes macrophysical phenomena, the microphysical phenomena must have certain exact properties (such as the exact elementary charge). These properties cannot be arbitrary; nor can they vary according to our particular interests.

This is not quite sufficient for our conclusion though, since it seems that arbitrarily carved portions of the cosmos also have exact properties. Consider the city of London, a rather arbitrarily carved portion of the cosmos: it has a number of exact properties at any given time, such as the number of underground stations, annual budget and the number of citizens. There is, however, a fine difference between the exact properties that the city of London or any other arbitrarily carved portion of the cosmos may have and the exact properties that, for instance, electrons have. The latter are *necessary* properties, whereas the former are only contingent. Accordingly, only non-arbitrary proper parts of the cosmos could possess the kind of exact, necessary properties that are required for the stability of macrophysical objects.

Consider the property 'number of citizens'. We could circle any area of land and count the people living there, giving the property of the number of citizens in that area, and this may be the basis of all sorts of things, such as taxation. However, it seems arbitrary which area of land we decide to circle; there are no constraints for this. The property 'number of citizens' is, we might say, an arbitrary property: although it is exact at any given time, it has no fixed requirements. It can change as our interests alter, and we could even have decided not to introduce it at all. In contrast, if the charges of electrons and protons were not identical, then the microphysical structure required for the existence of macroscopic objects would not have existed. That is, it is *necessary* for the emergence of macroscopic objects that the sum of the charges of subatomic particles adds up to zero, whereas the population of London is thoroughly contingent.

It could be objected here that, for instance, the arbitrarily carved portion of the cosmos that consists of two electrons in my left hand surely has certain necessary properties, e.g., the sum of the charges of these electrons. This will hardly undermine the argument though, for the necessity involved here is based on the necessary properties of the individual electrons, so the portion of the cosmos in question will not have necessary properties in its own right.

Another possible objection concerns systematic changes in the microphysical structure of the cosmos. For instance, if the charge of the electron changes, an equal change in the charge of the proton would presumably maintain stability (as well as other changes in fundamental physical constants). This is a fair point, but it misses the target: variation over time in certain fundamental physical constants *may* be possible, but what is important for the stability of matter is that their relative values remain the same. In fact, there are very specific constraints for the possible changes in fundamental physical constants which would still enable the emergence of macrophysical objects (cf. Barrow 2001). Accordingly, the necessity of exact properties appears to be a good indicator of the non-arbitrariness of the microphysical structure of the cosmos.

If what has been said so far is correct, then we have a strong case not just for the non-arbitrariness of the microphysical, but for the necessity of this non-arbitrary microphysical structure for all macrophysical phenomena. For it is easy to see that even interest rates and music require stability on the microphysical level; in fact, they require much more than that, namely the existence of rational beings who are able to set up a stock market and play music. In other words, the existence of these macrophysical phenomena is ontologically dependent on the existence of rational beings, whose existence is dependent on the ability of their constituent molecules to form bonds, and so on. It is important to note that this argument does not commit us to the claim that microphysical particles are ontologically fundamental or basic. That is, we adopt a fallibilist position about what the basic objects in fact are; we only insist that there must be some basic objects, which are non-arbitrary and upon which the non-arbitrary portions of the universe depends. Thus, in contrast with Schaffer's view that only the cosmos as a whole can be basic and non-arbitrary, we are prepared to allow for a whole range of basic, non-arbitrary objects.

IV

Consider again Schaffer's common sense argument in favour of priority monism. If an NCS is necessary, then premise P3 of this argument must be amended. At most, all we can assume is that some of the proper parts of the cosmos are arbitrary portions. But some of its proper parts must also be non-arbitrary; these are the parts which would be picked out in an NCS. If this is the case, Schaffer's common sense argument can no longer go through.

It might be suggested in response to our arguments that P3 could be derived from P1 and P2, and that the three premises together could then be used to establish the conclusion. But this would require an extra premise, along the lines of:

> P1a: according to common sense, integrated wholes can have no parts other than their arbitrary portions.

If P1a is accepted, then P3 would indeed follow from P1, P1a and P2. It might be possible to take issue with P1a, but more importantly in the present context, the arguments we have given in sections II and III would count against P2, given the claim about integrated wholes expressed in P1a. That is, our arguments give reason to believe that the cosmos is not an integrated whole, on this understanding of such wholes. And if P2 cannot be accepted, then P3 loses its support. So unless our arguments can be refuted, neither P3 nor Schaffer's common sense argument can be rescued.

There is a way in which Schaffer could respond to both the arguments we have given. He could grant that these arguments each show that there must be more to the universe than a collection of arbitrary portions, but argue that this does not entail the conclusion that the universe must contain non-arbitrary parts. Instead of appealing to non-arbitrary parts, the suggestion would be that we can appeal to the whole itself, the entire spatiotemporal cosmos. The cosmos consists of a whole whose parts are all arbitrary portions, but which is not itself an arbitrary portion.

Given this, it might seem that Schaffer can answer each of the arguments outlined above, by accepting the premises of each but denying that in either case the conclusion that the world has non-arbitrary parts actually follows. The argument in section II starts with the premise that our judgements about the world are made true or false by the way the world is itself, and moves to the conclusion that the world is the way it is independently of how we judge it to be. But Schaffer could argue that the cosmos as a whole may have its own nature, without that nature involving or depending on any non-arbitrary parts.

Similarly, the argument given in section III moves from the premise that some necessary (i.e., non-arbitrary) basis is required for any arbitrary portions to exist, to the conclusion that the universe must contain some non-arbitrary parts. Yet it seems that Schaffer can accept this premise, but argue that the non-arbitrary basis for the existence of the arbitrary portions is provided, not by any parts of the universe, but by the cosmos as a whole. This is a line of thought which emerges from a further argument for monism which Schaffer entertains. Specifically, Schaffer wishes to dismiss the view that empirical considerations – input from physics – would support pluralism:

> [...] it is one thing to assume that physics is fundamental, and another to assume that fundamental physics will deal in particles [...]. The monist can and should allow that physics will tell the complete causal story of the world. The monist will maintain that this physical story is best told in terms of fields pervading the whole cosmos, rather than in terms of local particles. (Schaffer this volume, 24)

This passage highlights the typical pluralist's commitment to mereological atomism, but Schaffer claims that physics does not support this commitment. He argues that physics suggests that the cosmos is in an entangled state and hence particles do not feature in it in the sense that atomism suggests.[15]

In response to this possible reply, we first concede that it is possible that the cosmos could have been such that it had an independent nature which neither involved nor depended upon having any proper parts (that is, there are possible worlds in which priority monism is correct). For example, the cosmos might have been a simple entity, without any proper parts but nonetheless having a nature independent of any judgements about it. However, we suggest that one cannot accept the premises of either of the arguments we have developed (the semantic argument in section II, or the ontological argument in section III) and hold that the cosmos is actually such that it has no non-arbitrary parts.[16]

Let us start with the semantic argument. Its premises were that we can make judgements about the world, and that these judgements are made true or false by the way the world is. From this, we argued that the way the world is, which makes our judgements true or false, is independent of these judgements. The issue is whether this independent nature must involve proper parts.

The judgements we make need not be about the world as a whole; typically, they are about particular parts of it (particular entities, states of affairs, etc.). We suggest that the world as a whole cannot be that which makes certain judgements about its parts true and others false. The judgements we have in mind are those which meet two conditions: they are made true by an independent reality; and the features of reality which make different judgements true are themselves different from each other, independently of our judgements about them. It would not help here to appeal to arbitrary portions, parts which are different from each other only insofar as we regard them as being different. The identity and existence of these portions depend on our applying certain standards to the world. Therefore, they could not make a contribution to the truth or falsity of our judgements independently of our standards.

Schaffer is aware of the problem of how the priority monist can explain the fact that the world is heterogeneous (though as we shall see, this problem is in fact different to the one we are raising). He mentions three possible responses the monist can make to the problem of heterogeneity. One response would be to regionalise properties: to say that seemingly monadic properties have an extra argument place for a region of space-time. So instead of simply predicating a property such as roundness, one might predicate 'roundness here' of a particular region of spacetime (Schaffer this volume, 31). A second response would be to build regions, not into the properties themselves, but into their instantiations: roundness is not just instantiated, but instantiated-here.[17]

We think that neither of these suggestions can answer the problem we are raising. The appeal to regionalised instantiations would seem to meet our first condition for putative truth-makers, in that the properties instantiated presumably could exist independently of our judgements about them. However, properties which are instantiated in this relativistic way do not meet the second condition. It seems clear that regions of the cosmos are arbitrary portions. In Schaffer's own examples they are distinguished indexically. Even if they were not (if they could be distinguished by references on a grid of spacetime points), regions would be differentiated from each other only insofar as we distinguish them.[18] Therefore, they cannot serve as truth-makers in a way which meets the requirements of the semantic argument. The same point holds, *mutatis mutandis*, for the appeal to regionalized properties.

Schaffer's other response, which he himself favours, is to appeal to distributional properties (this volume, 31). This involves no appeal to different regions. Rather, the whole cosmos itself bears a heterogeneous property (Schaffer's example of such a property is 'being polka-dotted'). The necessary variation between truth-makers would thus be found, not in differences between properties, nor in differences between property bearers, but in the heterogeneous nature of the property itself. Specifically, the fact that the world is heterogeneous is to be explained by the entire cosmos bearing the property of 'being heterogeneous'. This is a determinable property, which is determined by the path the cosmos traces through a multidimensional 'physical configuration space' (this volume, 31).

We accept that if the cosmos as a whole has a distributional property or properties, this would suffice to make it heterogeneous. However, this brings us to the afore-mentioned difference between the problem we are raising and the issue of heterogeneity. What our account requires is not just heterogeneity, but a particular distribution of different properties to different portions of the cosmos. Schaffer might reply that this distribution is provided by the particular determination of the heterogeneity of the universe. That is, as the universe moves through physical configuration space, the specific way it is heterogeneous will change. But we think that this too is insufficient. Take a true judgement such as 'the ball is red'. What, on Schaffer's account, could the truth-maker for this judgement be? It seems it must either be the state of the entire cosmos at the moment the judgement is true, or the state of that particular (spatial) region of the cosmos at that moment. But neither of these accounts seems adequate. The appeal to regions we have already dealt with. If the truth-maker is the state of the entire universe at that time, then we seem faced with the original problem of the whole cosmos being the truth-maker for a large array of truths.[19] Furthermore, we doubt that such an account would be able to handle certain changes. For example, we don't see how the cosmos' movements through physical configuration space could explain the difference between the following two scenarios: a ball changes colour; a ball of one colour disappears and a different ball with a different colour appears in the same spot. Note that we are not saying that these two cases could not be distinguished; rather, we are saying that on Schaffer's account, there would appear to be no metaphysical difference between the two cases.

Turning to the argument developed in section III, we need to keep in mind that we are only interested in a world which contains macrophysical objects. The argument developed in section III concerns the non-self-sufficiency of macrophysical objects, their dependence on the proper parts that make them up. It was suggested that this requires stability on the microphysical level, and that such stability can only be produced by a non-arbitrary microphysical structure. This should already be enough to block Schaffer's possible reply. According to current physics, the stability of matter depends on a fine-tuned microphysical organisation. As we observed, one of these fine-tuned properties is the elementary charge, which must be identical in strength and of a different polarity in electrons and protons; otherwise atoms would not hold together. Hence, the stability of all macrophysical objects depends on this non-arbitrary microphysical organisation.

A further objection may be derived from the idea that the cosmos is in an entangled state, which Schaffer uses to construct another argument for monism (Schaffer this volume, 25 ff). The argument suggests that the phenomenon of quantum entanglement can be applied to the whole cosmos and hence the cosmos must be viewed as an entangled system itself.[20] This line can be further augmented with the formalism of relativistic quantum field theory, which effectively removes any reference to particles as objective components of the cosmos and replaces them with fields. The upshot is that the cosmos can be viewed as an entangled system which is a fundamental whole and has emergent properties.

Since our aim was only to address Schaffer's common sense argument, we will not engage with his quantum mechanical argument in detail. However, the quantum mechanical argument does not refute our arguments. The idea we are defending, of a Near-Complete Scheme, does not commit us to the claim that the cosmos as a whole cannot be independent of its proper parts (rather, it is a claim that those parts are either non-arbitrary or depend on some non-arbitrary parts). It is specifically worth noting that this ontological claim does not need to assume mereological atomism.

We have demonstrated that Schaffer's common sense argument in favour of priority monism cannot work, for both semantic and ontological reasons. In the process of criticising this argument we have made some suggestions as to what a NCS could look like. We remain neutral as to the details of this scheme, but we believe that there are good reasons to think that one must exist.[21]

Notes

1. In this chapter, we shall be considering only spatiotemporal entities. We shall thus ignore the relation between the cosmos and abstract entities such as numbers or sets.
2. Schaffer's premises and conclusion are presented in terms of the deliveries of common sense, but in what follows we shall drop any reference to the origin of these claims. The point of our argument is that there is good reason to think that not all the proper parts of the cosmos are arbitrary portions. To support this claim, we shall appeal both to semantic reasons which resonate with common sense, and to scientific reasons which certainly go beyond it.

3. We shall not question P1 or P2, but see Schaffer (2010, 48–49) for some discussion about the source of these premises.
4. Schaffer's priority monism, although related to Spinoza's monism, differs from it: both share the idea that the cosmos as a whole is independent and all entities are dependent on that whole, but there seems to be no suggestion in Spinoza that the many proper parts of the cosmos are arbitrary (cf. Spinoza E1p14).
5. Schaffer links this claim both to Spinoza's monism and to Dummett's amorphous lump view (this volume, n. 26). It is an interesting question whether, in doing so, Schaffer takes a step towards existence monism, the view that the cosmos is the only existing concrete entity. At the very least, we see a tension between Schaffer's professed acceptance that the cosmos has parts and any appeal to the amorphous lump view, which explicitly rules this out (cf. Dummett 1973, 577).
6. The sense of ontological dependence which we will use is asymmetrical existential dependence, which can be defined as follows: an entity x depends for its existence on the existence of another entity y if and only if, necessarily, if x exists, then so does y, and y may exist without x existing. See Correia (2008) for further specifications concerning the notion of ontological dependence.
7. Schaffer also develops a second line of thought in support of premise 3. He suggests that common sense recognises that many objects have arbitrary boundaries; that their edges are not clearly defined, and so they cannot be precisely distinguished from each other in a non-arbitrary way (this volume, 22). In response to this line of thought, note first that it is in fact compatible with there being objective grounds for carving reality, as Schaffer himself accepts (this volume, 22). Second, there are grounds for treating this vagueness as an epistemic or conceptual matter, rather than a metaphysical one. Many concepts are by their very nature imprecise, allowing distinctions to be drawn only in a particular context (e.g., 'tall', 'rich', 'bald'). Other concepts are precise at one level of discourse, but not at another. If someone tells you 'that table is a metre long', they have given you what might be a very precise measurement at one level of discourse, but imprecise at another (e.g., if you were asking how many millimetres the length of the table was). These basically pragmatic considerations can account for many of the kinds of cases Schaffer mentions. For example, we suggest the concept 'mountain' has a degree of precision, but only at a certain level of discourse. The crucial point here is that we are committed to saying that not everything in the cosmos can be vague in this way. We shall argue in favor of this claim in section III below.
8. The point here does not concern which standards one chooses. Rather, what is at issue is whether or not the standards one chooses can themselves decide the nature of the world. If they do, and if one correctly understands and applies them, the question is what the error of one's judgements might then consist in. The position we are defending provides a clear answer: the world has an independent nature, which one's judgement might fail to match. It is not clear that any answer to this question is available if one denies that the world has an independent nature.
9. The key point here is the constraint (which is suggested by McDowell – e.g., 1996, 25). Schaffer's monism may be consistent with there being an external reality, but it is not a reality which could constrain our judgements in the way required, by helping to make them true or false. We develop this point further in section IV.

10. It is worth pointing out that this conception of reality is not intended to serve as an *epistemic* constraint; for instance, as a constraint on when one is *justified* in asserting something of reality. Rather, it is a constraint on being able to think of one's empirical judgements as being made true or false by reality. This issue is prior to that of deciding whether or not one is justified in making any particular judgement.
11. It is possible that this point (the dependence of arbitrary portions on our standards or interests, and the dependence of these standards or interests on the subjects who apply or have them) could be developed into an independent argument against premise 3. The suggestion would be that in order for there to be arbitrary portions as we have defined them, it is necessary that there exist subjects with interests; but these subjects cannot themselves be arbitrary portions, on pain of either circularity or infinite regress (we owe this suggestion to Olley Pearson).
12. For more on this approach to the ontology of social entities and properties, see Searle 1995.
13. The claim that banknotes are constituted by the bits of paper is developed by Baker (2000). The claim that they are identical with the bits of paper is argued by, for example, Van Inwagen 2002, 141.
14. The Pauli Exclusion Principle states that no two identical fermions can have the same quantum number at the same time.
15. Note also the reference to 'fields' here. Schaffer briefly discusses quantum field theory, but on some level Spinoza may have been a proponent of a 'field metaphysic' (cf. Viljanen 2007).
16. Therefore, we reject claim 15 in Schaffer 2008, the claim that either the ultimate parts must be basic in all worlds or the ultimate whole must be basic in all worlds (§3.2.4). We agree that the direction of priority must be a necessary truth, but we suggest that it can be *contingently necessary*. That is, given certain features of the universe which may not themselves be necessary, then necessarily priority monism is false. Therefore, we deny that it could be possible to have worlds which are otherwise indiscernible save for differences in the direction of priority. But we do not think this possibility must be assumed in order to deny Schaffer's claim 15. Similar remarks have been made about the gunk/atomism debate (Sider 1993). Both atomistic and gunky worlds seem possible, but if it were the case that, for instance, living beings are not possible in a gunky world, then we would know that the actual world could not turn out to be gunky.
17. A related approach is the monistic semantics developed by Horgan and Potrč (2000). On this account, the truthmakers of statements about particular parts of the cosmos are variations at different spatiotemporal locations of properties belonging to the cosmos as a whole. (Note that Horgan and Potrč, unlike Schaffer, are existence monists, and thus deny there are any entities other than the cosmos itself.) We think that this monistic semantics cannot accommodate the premises of our semantic argument, for reasons similar to those we shall outline against any appeal to regionalized properties and regionalized instantiations of properties.
18. The extent of any region through space and time would be a matter of stipulation or convention. An alternative approach might be to identify regions by appealing to properties or to the instantiations of properties. This would threaten to make any predications of properties circular. Furthermore, it would struggle to accommodate cases where an object changes one of its properties, or where an

object simultaneously has more than one determinate property from the same determinable (e.g., a ball which is multicoloured).

19. Schaffer denies that this is a problem at all (2010b). However, he does not address the most obvious problem with the suggestion that the only truth-maker is the entire cosmos: the problem of coarseness. It is correct that different judgements can be made true by the same state of affairs (e.g., 'The ball is red' and 'The ball is coloured'). However, the total condition of the ball is not appropriate to serve as the truth-maker, since it includes features which are irrelevant to either of the judgements under consideration. This objection to coarseness applies, only far more strongly, to any appeal to the cosmos as the truth-maker of either of these judgements. Such appeals to relevance are common in the literature (e.g., Rodriguez-Pereyra 2009, 230–234). This point does not show that Schaffer's truth-maker monism is wrong, but motivates the claim that it is a problematic view.
20. Schaffer notes that, following Teller (1986), one could attempt to maintain that particles are fundamental by introducing external *entanglement relations*. Teller himself develops a type of quantum holism from this idea, the intention of which is that we have *non-supervenience* between entangled systems and their separate components; that is, an entangled system can have emergent properties (cf. Morganti 2009). We wish to make no commitments regarding such speculative accounts of quantum mechanics. In any case Schaffer is suspicious of Teller's account and suggests, on the basis of quantum field theory, that this line may not help in retaining particles in the fundamental theory (this volume, 26–7).
21. We would like to thank Matteo Morganti, Olley Pearson and Valtteri Viljanen for comments on earlier drafts of this chapter. Drafts of this chapter were presented at the Durham departmental seminar and the Durham metaphysics reading group – we would like to thank all those who offered criticism and suggestions at these events. One of the authors (Tahko), would also like to acknowledge the financial support of the Academy of Finland during the writing of this chapter.

References

Baker, L. R. (2000) *Persons and Bodies: A Constitution View*. Cambridge: Cambridge University Press

Barrow, J. D. (2001) 'Cosmology, Life, and the Anthropic Principle', *Annals of the New York Academy of Sciences* 950: 139–53.

Correia, F. (2008) 'Ontological Dependence', *Philosophy Compass* 3: 1013–32.

Dummett, M. (1973) *Frege: Philosophy of Language*. Cambridge MA/London: Harvard University Press.

Dupré, J., (1993) *The Disorder of Things: Metaphysical Foundations of the Disunity of Science*. Cambridge MA/London: Harvard University Press.

Horgan, T. & Potrč, M. (2000) 'Blobjectivism and Indirect Correspondence', *Facta Philosophica* 2: 249–270.

Lewis, P. J. (2006) 'GRW: A Case Study in Quantum Ontology', *Philosophy Compass* 1/2: 224–44.

McDowell, J. (1996) *Mind and World (second edition)*. Cambridge MA/London: Harvard University Press.

Morganti, M. (2009) 'A New Look at Relational Holism in Quantum Mechanics', *Philosophy of Science* 76: 1027–1038.

Putnam, H. (1981) *Reason, Truth & History*. Cambridge: Cambridge University Press.

Putnam, H. (1990) *Realism with a Human Face*. Cambridge MA/London: Harvard University Press.

Putnam, H. (2004) *Ethics without Ontology*. Cambridge MA/London: Harvard University Press.

Rodriguez–Pereyra, G. (2009) 'Why Truth–Makers', in Lowe, E. J. & Rami, A. (eds.) *Truth and Truth–Making*. Stocksfield: Acumen.

Schaffer, J. (2003) 'Is There a Fundamental Level?', *Noûs* 37: 498–517.

Schaffer, J. (2008) 'Monism', *The Stanford Encyclopedia of Philosophy (Fall 2008 Edition)*, E. N. Zalta (ed.), URL = <http://plato.stanford.edu/archives/fall2008/entries/monism/>.

Schaffer, J. This volume. 'Monism: the Priority of the Whole'.

Schaffer, J. (2010b) 'The Least Discerning and Most Promiscuous Truthmaker', *The Philosophical Quarterly* 60 (239): 307–324.

Searle, J. (1995) *The Construction of Social Reality*. London: Penguin.

Sider, T. (1993) 'Van Inwagen and the Possibility of Gunk', *Analysis* 53: 285–89.

Spinoza, B. (1985) *Ethics*, in E. Curley, translator, *The Collected Writings of Spinoza*, volume 1. Princeton: Princeton University Press.

Teller, P. (1986) 'Relational Holism and Quantum Mechanics', *British Journal for the Philosophy of Science* 37: 71–81.

Van Inwagen, P. (2002) 'Review of Baker, *Persons and Bodies: A Constitution View*', *The Philosophical Review* 111: 1 (pp. 138–141).

Viljanen, V. (2007) 'Field Metaphysic, Power, and Individuation in Spinoza', *Canadian Journal of Philosophy* 37 (3): 393–418.

8
Substances Stressed

John Heil

> The infinite turns out to be the contrary of what it is said to be. It is not what has nothing outside it that is infinite, but what always has something outside it.... A quantity is infinite if it is such that we can always take a part outside what has already been taken.
>
> (Aristotle, Physics III, 206b 33–207a 11)

> We have...been compelled to dismiss the idea that...a particle is an individual entity which retains its 'sameness' forever. Quite the contrary, we are now obliged to assert that the ultimate constituents of matter have no 'sameness' at all.
>
> (Schrödinger 1996, 121)

> I think it is safe to say that no one understands Quantum Mechanics.
>
> (Attributed to Richard Feynman)

Ontological dependence

On one traditional conception, a substance is a bearer of properties: substances are property bearers. On such a conception, substance and property are complementary categories. Properties are ways substances are and every substance is some way or other. Another tradition begins with a notion of independence: a substance is a non-dependent entity, one the existence of which does not require the existence of any other distinct entity (see, e.g., Campbell 1976; Robb 2009). Substances are basic entities, basic particulars. Properties, in contrast, are dependent. Properties depend on the substances that bear them.[1]

One result of characterizing substances in this second way is that complex objects – objects with substantial parts, parts that are themselves substances – will not be substances. At least they will not be substances if wholes depend ontologically on their parts. Complex wholes are *made up of* their parts. A whole – or some wholes – could be thought to survive gradual *replacement* of its parts, perhaps, but not their elimination. Your automobile could survive your gradually replacing each of its parts, but removal of parts without replacement results in the automobile's demise.

Arguably, a conception of substances as property bearers leads to the same conclusion. If properties are ways substances are, if a substance's possessing a property is a matter of that substance's being a particular way, then the sense in which an *arrangement* of substances might possess a property differs dramatically from the sense in which a *substance* possesses a property. What we regard as properties of complexes – ways those complexes are – are nothing more than the constituent substances duly propertied and duly arranged. If complexes are substances-by-courtesy, properties of complexes are properties-by-courtesy.

I do not expect many readers to accept my word for this. I mean only to point out that whether you begin with a characterization of substances as property bearers or as non-dependent entities, it might be thought to follow that substances could not be made up of other substances, substances could not be mereologically complex.

In this context it is crucial to bear in mind a distinction between *substantial* parts, on the one hand, and, on the other hand, *spatial* – or *temporal*, a possibility I shall leave aside here – parts. A substantial part of a complex object is a part that is itself a substance. Although a spatial part could coincide with a substantial part, a simple substance could be spatially extended, a simple could have endless spatial parts. In fact, anything that has spatial parts, must it seems have an infinity of spatial parts.[2] In asking whether an object is divisible, then, it is important to make it clear whether the divisibility in question is substantial or spatial.

Spatial and substantial parts exhibit an important asymmetry. Although it seems right to think of a complex object as depending ontologically on its substantial parts, the opposite is so for an object's spatial parts. An object is not *made up* of its spatial parts: spatial parts are regions *of some object*.

Consider, now, the possibility that *every* apparent substance is infinitely complex. The substance has parts, and each part has parts. These parts are substantial parts – but not really. A substantial part is itself a substance. But if a part *itself* has substantial parts, it is not a substance. Were *everything* divisible this way, were everything endlessly divisible, there would, it seems, be no substances, no simple, non-dependent entities. The world would be, in David Lewis's memorable phrase, 'atomless gunk' (Lewis 1991, 20–1).

The world's being infinitely divisible would seem to be a live possibility. But a commitment to substances – in the sense of ontologically non-dependent entities – is apparently at odds with this possibility. If wholes depend upon their parts, *everything* could not be a whole made up of parts. Ontological dependence of wholes upon parts apparently requires non-dependent entities, in this case substances, simples.[3]

Although the notion that wholes depend upon their parts, coupled with the idea that dependence of this kind must 'bottom out', implies the existence of simple substances, you might regard this as objectionable if you thought that an infinitely divisible world were a genuine possibility. Jonathan Schaffer (2010) argues that the possibility that the world is 'gunky' supports 'priority monism', the view that the world is a whole on which its parts depend, thereby reversing the order of dependency. If substances are characterized as non-dependent entities, then there is just one substance, the world as a whole, the One. In that case, 'parts' of this substance would not be substantial parts.

This might or might not be what Schaffer has in mind, but it *is* Spinoza's view. What we ordinarily consider to be parts of the world (electrons, pebbles, trees, galaxies) are, in fact, not substances, but modes, ways the world is. This is how Descartes thinks of extended bodies: there is but one extended substance, space itself. What we regard as material substances are, in reality, modes, ways space itself is. This is how you might think of 'gunky' worlds. Such worlds are not infinitely divisible into substantial or quasi-substantial parts themselves infinitely divisible. 'Gunky' worlds are seamless. 'Gunky' worlds are themselves simple substances. Their complexity is 'non-mereological', their parts are not genuine parts, not *substantial* parts, any more than the left and right halves of a tomato are parts of the tomato. A tomato's left and right half might *coincide* with substantial parts of the tomato, but that is another matter.

If you begin with the idea that substances are non-dependent entities, you seem to be faced with a choice between (a) a denial of the possibility that the world could be 'gunky'; and (b) regarding 'gunky' worlds as simples.[4] What if you begin with a characterization of substances as simple property bearers? A 'gunky' world might seem to be a world with no substances, hence no properties. Now the problem would be to find truthmakers for truths holding in such a world. If there are simple substances, then we can have truthmakers for 'The tomato is red and spherical', namely a particular arrangement of simple substances, or, if there is but one substance, a particular way that substance is.

What is emerging here is the idea that it is a mistake to think of a 'gunky' world as a world with literally endless parts. The parts of such a world would not be substantial parts. They would resemble spatial parts. A 'gunky' world would be an extended simple substance, a One.

You might be suspicious of this line of reasoning on the grounds that it apparently assumes without warrant that the world is finite. Consider a world containing simple substances, the fundamental particles, say, but an infinite number of these. Such a world would be a world with an infinite number of parts!

I take up this possibility below. Meanwhile, it is important to see that 'gunky' worlds are not just worlds with an endless number of parts. Rather, a 'gunky' world is a world with *no* simple parts, no parts themselves lacking parts. The suggestion is that it would be a mistake to regard such a world as being made up of, hence dependent on, its parts.

Infinite divisibility

Consider again the possibility that the world is 'infinitely divisible', where the divisibility in question is substantial divisibility, not spatial divisibility. It is tempting to think of such a world as one in which every object has parts that are themselves objects with objects as parts. Such a world would contain no simples, hence, it would appear, no substances – and no properties! But is such a world genuinely conceivable? Parts of an object make up the object. But it is hard to see how anything could be made up of parts that are themselves made up of parts, that are themselves made up of parts that are.... The difficulty here is not simply a failure of imagination, however.

Talk of 'infinite divisibility' is cheap. A line of whatever length is infinitely divisible in the sense that any of its segments, however small, could be regarded as having further spatial divisions. But the segments do not *make up* the line in the way pearls make up a necklace. A necklace depends on individual pearls that make it up. In an important sense, however, a line's segments depend on the line rather than it on them.

Consider infinity.[5] An infinite number is not merely a very large number. An infinite series is not a very, very long series. An infinite series is a series that has no end, no last member. Infinite numbers differ qualitatively, not quantitatively, from finite numbers, however large. For this reason, it is at least misleading to think of an 'infinitely divisible' world as one made up of an inordinately large number of parts. 'Infinite divisibility' is not just divisibility into very small parts, it is divisibility without end.

Our world might be made up of a finite number of simple substances or it might be a continuous 'gunky' world lacking parts – substantial parts – altogether. Thus the world might contain a very large number of simples (the fundamental particles, the electrons and quarks, for instance), or only a handful (the fundamental fields), or the world might turn out to be a single unity (spacetime itself, or the One). This is an empirical question concerning which the ontological picture on the table is officially neutral. Whatever conception of the world we find in fundamental physics, however, that conception will include simple, propertied substances. We look to science to fill in the blanks, to tell us what the fundamental substances and properties are.

These issues are frustratingly elusive. Philosophers have grown accustomed to talk of infinite numbers and sets. Infinity is mathematically indispensable. Infinity has earned its keep. The difficulty is to understand possible applications of the concept of infinity to the world, to understand the *ontology* of infinity. With this in mind, it might be useful to approach these matters from a slightly different direction.

An infinity of substances

Might the world contain an infinite number of substances? Could there be an infinite number of electrons, for instance? You might regard this as an obvious possibility: why on earth *not*?

Consider, first, how this question is related to the possibility discussed earlier, the possibility that everything might be infinitely complex: everything might have an infinite number of proper substantial parts. Start with any object, this tomato, say. The tomato has parts – stem, seeds, pulp, skin – and each of these parts has parts – living cells. Eventually you reach the atomic level. But atoms too have parts: electrons protons, neutrons. And we know that protons and neutrons have nucleons and quarks as parts. Suppose there were no end to this kind of division, suppose every object could be decomposed into parts, and these parts into parts, and so on to infinity.

As noted already, a sensible discussion of this topic requires distinguishing spatial (or temporal) parts from substantial parts. Geometry tells us that any finite line comprises an infinite number of line segments. But these segments do not make up the line, they are not elements you assemble to create a line. Any actual line is made up of physical constituents, which are not to be confused with purely spatial magnitudes.

The Greeks distinguished two kinds of infinity: what was infinite by addition and what was infinite by division. A Euclidean line is infinitely divisible, but it does not follow that any actual line could be made up from the addition of an infinity of elements. How, exactly, would that work? A line with infinite divisions is one in which every division could be further divided. Such divisions are, quite literally, endless. Although you might be sanguine about infinite spatial divisibility, there is something deeply puzzling about the prospect of a finite object's being made up of an infinite number of substantial parts. True, if you thought that a given line were infinitely divisible, you could think of it as including all of the infinite segments into which it is divided. But this is not to regard the line as being made up of an infinite number of parts.

One difficulty about such cases stems from apparent constraints on composition. Wholes 'metaphysically depend' on the parts that make them up. Complex wholes (tomatoes, for instance) are made up of other complex wholes (seeds, pulp, skin) that are made up in turn of other complex wholes (cells, molecules), and so on. I have assumed for purposes of discussion an ontology of substance and property, noting that substances must be simple, substances lack parts that are themselves substances. Substances are the fundamental building blocks. Characteristics of complex objects result from arrangements of substances possessing various properties. If you take away the substances, you take away the properties and the arrangements, you take away the world.

It goes without saying that there is no knock-down argument for any of this. If you reject it, however, you are under obligation to provide an account of the resulting ontology: the ball is in your court. And in these cases, formal hand-waving is not to the point.

Before moving on, let me make one matter clear. Nothing I have said here implies that the world is corpuscular, that the world *is* made up of a very large number of proper parts that are themselves simple substances. This is important, because I believe that the idea that the world might be infinitely divisible makes perfect sense provided we are prepared to regard the world as itself a simple substance. In that case, the divisions do not mark off substances, the world is not made up of, does not depend on, proper substantial parts: the parts depend on the whole (see Schaffer 2009).

An appeal to proprietary notions of substance and property – albeit ones that I believe stem naturally from reflection on the nature of things – might arouse suspicion about these conclusions. Consider, however, an independent line of reasoning that supports the idea that there is something deeply puzzling about wholes made up of an infinity of substantial parts.

First, return to a question posed earlier. Might there be an infinite number of electrons? Suppose there were. Suppose, further, that the electrons were arranged so as to form a cosmic sphere. We know that electrons have finite masses. We know, as well, that it is in the nature of an infinite set to have a proper subset, members of which can be put into one–one correspondence with members of the whole set. In the case of integers, for instance, the even numbers can be paired one–one with all the integers: the odds plus the evens. This feature of infinite sets makes it clear why it is a mistake to think of an infinite number as a very large number. Infinite numbers differ *qualitatively*, from finite numbers.

The mass of all the electrons is what you get by combining the masses of individual electrons. Now consider all the even numbered electrons. These might be the electrons making up the left hemisphere of the electron sphere. These electrons, a proper subset of all the electrons, stand in a one–one correspondence to all the electrons. But then it would seem that the mass of one of the hemispheres would have to equal the mass of the sphere itself, the whole that includes each hemisphere as a proper part. But wait! How could the mass of a whole be the same as the mass of one of its proper parts?

Imagine God extracting the even-numbered electrons and arranging them so as to form a second sphere. This sphere will have the same mass as the original sphere. But now God, merely by rearranging the electrons, will have doubled their mass![6]

Does it help that both masses are infinite? I don't see how. You still have a hemisphere with the same mass as the whole sphere that includes that hemisphere as a proper part. You still have a second sphere constructed from a proper part of the original sphere that has the same mass as the original. Have I muddied the water in supposing that a one–one correspondence yields this result? The question might be turned around: why *shouldn't* this result follow from a definitive characteristic of infinite numbers?

The weirdness of actual infinities

Perhaps, given the nature of infinity, the result is neither puzzling nor in any way objectionable. The result is not puzzling in one respect: it is just what you would expect under the circumstances. What it calls into question is whether we can muster a coherent conception of composition that covers cases in which wholes are taken to be *made up of* an infinite number of proper substantial parts. Ordinary tenets of composition suggest that objects that lose proper parts suffer diminution, and that collections of an object's proper parts cannot be put into correspondence with all of the object's parts. In attempting to imagine objects with an infinity of proper substantial parts, we have, I think, lost a grip on the thought that complex objects have parts, that complex objects are made up of their substantial parts.

Some readers will dismiss such concerns. Maybe the normal rules of composition apply only to finite collections. Maybe infinite collections differ compositionally from finite collections in a way analogous to the way infinite numbers differ from finite numbers.

Such a response betrays a lack of sensitivity to the manifest weirdness of actual infinities. One way to desensitize yourself is to start with a notion of the infinite-by-division. It is relatively easy to regard a line or a surface as being infinitely divisible into spatial segments or regions. So we have infinity on the table. That would seem to be the hard part. Now we imagine an infinity by addition. We start with an electron and we imagine adding electrons until we cross the threshold and have an infinite number of electrons. But, as noted earlier, an infinite number of electrons is not just a very large number of electrons, it is a literally *endless* number of electrons. Just as there is no greatest integer, if the electrons are infinite in number, there would be no definite number of them. But how could that be? In a universe containing an infinite number of electrons would mass-energy be conserved? In a world comprising an infinite number of electrons, electrons could come and go without affecting the total mass. Under the circumstances, it is difficult to know what to say.

My recommendation is that we take all this to heart and reject the possibility that the world could be made up of an infinite number of substances. We can allow an infinite number of spatial or temporal divisions, perhaps, but it would be a mistake to move from these possibilities to the possibility that the world could be infinitely complex, the possibility that the world could contain an infinite number of distinct substances.

If this is a constraint on scientific theorizing, it is not much of a constraint. It allows for the possibility that there could be many, many particles. These particles could have many, many parts, and the parts could have many, many parts. But these possibilities do not take us down a road to an infinity of substances or to objects with an infinite number of proper parts. That would require a leap for which it is hard to imagine empirical warrant.

From the weirdness of infinity to quantum weirdness

In a world made up of multitudinous distinct substances, truths about the world are made true by the substances, their properties, and their arrangements. What we regard as complex objects – tables, trees, planets, atoms, are not substances, but complexes made up of substances. What we regard as properties of complexes are just what you get when you arrange substances of these kinds in these ways. Just as complex objects are no addition of being but simply the substances duly propertied and duly arranged, so characteristics – 'properties' – of complex objects are no addition of being. The truthmakers for all the truths concerning complex objects are particular arrangements of simples.

This conception of substances and properties is compatible with, but does not imply, corpuscularism, the doctrine that the post-Big-Bang world is made up of arrangements of particles.[7] The conception is compatible with the possibility that the fundamental substances, the fundamental property-bearers, are fields and with the possibility that there is just one substance, space or space–time, the One, the World Whole. These are matters to be settled by fundamental physics.

A number of philosophers have argued that quantum theory as it now stands is sharply at odds with corpuscularism. The phenomena of 'entanglement' and 'nonsesparability' force us to accept the idea that quantum systems are 'holistic' (see Teller 1986, 1995; Healey 1991). Such systems appear to possess properties not founded on properties of their constituents. If it turns out that the world is best seen as a single entangled system, then we have something like the world of Spinoza: the One.

Before discussing why physicists or philosophers might be attracted to such a position, let me say something about how it bears on the conception of substance and property in play here.

Suppose quantum systems are genuinely 'holistic', suppose their characteristics really do outstrip characteristics of their ingredients. In that case, it would be at least misleading to describe such systems as being *made up of* their parts – electrons, photons, quarks. The 'parts' of such systems would resemble modes or spatial parts: the wholes of which they are parts do not depend on the parts, the parts depend on the wholes.[8] On a 'classical' model, complex systems are invariably made up of, hence dependent on, the elementary parts that make them up: electrons, protons, and the like. These parts are simple substances. Truths about such wholes are made true by particular arrangements of these substantial parts.

Quantum physics affords a different picture. Although it is convenient to speak of electrons, for instance, as particles or elementary substances, when electrons enter into relations, they 'lose their individuality' (see the Schrödinger quotation at the outset of this chapter). An electron becomes, on this conception, a kind of abstract particular, a mode, a way a given system is. The system must be various ways, but the ways do not *make up* the system.

The situation is sometimes described, as Schrödinger describes it, with the suggestion that, in entering into a relation with another electron, an electron 'loses its identity'. This suggests that, left to themselves, electrons are well-behaved simple substances possessing definite identities. When they enter into various relations with other particles, however, their individuality is compromised. Here is how E. J. Lowe puts it:

> Suppose ... that in an ionization chamber a free electron *a* is captured by a certain atom to form a negative ion which, a short time later, reverts to a neutral state by releasing an electron *b* ... [A]ccording to currently accepted quantum-mechanical principles there may simply be no objective fact of the matter as to whether or not *a* is identical with *b* ... [W]hat is being proposed here is *not* merely that we may well have no way of telling whether or not *a* and *b* are identical, which would imply only an epistemic indeterminacy. It is well known that the sort of indeterminacy presupposed by orthodox interpretations of quantum theory is more than merely epistemic – it is *ontic*. The key feature of the example is that in such an interaction electron *a* and other electrons in the outer shell of the relevant atom enter an 'entangled' or 'superposed' state in which the *number* of electrons present is determinate but the identity of any one of them with *a* is not, thus rendering likewise indeterminate the identity of *a* with the released electron *b*. (Lowe 1994, 110)

The idea that an electron could 'lose its identity' – and perhaps later regain a definite identity – can be avoided if you take electrons – and the particles, generally – to exist *only* in entangled states. In this regard, the particles are more naturally regarded as waves, the position towards which Schrödinger himself was inclined.[9] Waves do not exhibit identity crises of the kind associated with entangled particles. On such a conception, fundamental 'particles' are not like water droplets that cease to exist as definite individuals when they combine to make up a puddle. Rather, they are abstractions, the nature and identity of which is dependent on the systems to which they belong.

I have followed other authors who have written on this topic and spoken of 'holism' and holistic systems. But what is holism? Explicating holism is subject to the same sorts of difficulty associated with explications of 'emergence'. In fact the ideas are related. A holistic system is one in which a property emerges, a property of the *system*, a property not founded on properties of the system's components. This, by my lights, requires the emergence of a substance, the bearer of the emergent property. Emergent substances, like any substances, are simple; emergent substances lack substantial parts. What might be thought of as the system's parts are abstractions, ways the substance is. Particles would be abstractions in the sense that a Cartesian billiard ball would be an abstraction, a way space is configured.

With all this in mind, I propose to consider very briefly one aspect of quantum physics that has led its interpreters to abandon the classical picture and embrace some form of holism. My discussion ignores a host of technical distinctions, and disagreements in interpretation that fill the literature. My aim, however, is merely to depict the kinds of consideration that might be thought to undermine corpuscularism, the idea that the world and objects in it are made up of myriad fundamental simple substances.

Quantum statistics

Consider two coins, *a* and *b*, and two 'states' of the coins, *H* and *T*, heads and tails. Let *Ha* and *Ta*, indicate that *a* is in the *H* state and *a* is in the *T* state, respectively. When we toss the coins we expect four possible outcomes:

(1) *Ha* and *Hb*
(2) *Ha* and *Tb*
(3) *Ta* and *Hb*
(4) *Ta* and *Tb*

Assume that the coins are 'fair': the probability of *Ha* is ½ and the probability of *Ta* is ½; similarly, the probability of *Hb* is ½ and the probability of *Tb* is ½. Each of these paired outcomes, (1)–(4) is equally probable, each has a probability of ¼. This means that the probability that the coins are in state (2) or state (3), a state in which one coin is *H* and the other *T*, is ½. Sure enough, when we observe many sequences of tosses, this is what we find.

$$\text{Prob}(Ha) = \tfrac{1}{2} \qquad\qquad \text{Prob}(Ta) = \tfrac{1}{2}$$

$$\text{Prob}(Hb) = \tfrac{1}{2} \qquad\qquad \text{Prob}(Tb) = \tfrac{1}{2}$$

$$\text{Prob}(Ha + Hb) = \text{Prob}(Ha) \times \text{Prob}(Hb/Ha) = \tfrac{1}{4}$$

$$\text{Prob}(Ta + Tb) = \text{Prob}(Ta) \times \text{Prob}(Tb/Ta) = \tfrac{1}{4}$$

$$\text{Prob}((Ta + Hb) \text{ or } (Ha + Tb)) = \tfrac{1}{2}$$

Classical Statistics

When we look at paired quantum particles, matters are different. Pretend that *a* and *b* are, not coins, but pairs of electrons and that *H* and *T* are states of these electrons. Stunningly, the theory predicts, and observation confirms, that the probability that both electrons will be in the *H*-state is 1/3, the probability that both will be in the *T*-state is 1/3, and the probability that one electron will be in the *H*-state, the other in the *T*-state is 1/3. This encourages the thought that we must treat (2) and (3) above as a *single* state.

Prob(*Ha*) = ½	Prob(*Ta*) = ½
Prob(*Hb*) = ½	Prob(*Tb*) = ½

Prob(*Ha* + *Hb*) = Prob(*Ha*) × Prob(*Hb*/*Ha*) = 1/3

Prob(*Ta* + *Tb*) = Prob(*Ta*) × Prob(*Tb*/*Ta*) = 1/3

Prob((*Ta* + *Hb*) or (*Ha* + *Tb*)) = 1/3

Nonclassical Statistics

This is what leads to talk of a 'loss of identity'. Considered together, the particles 'shed their identity'. There continue to be two of them, two particles, but there is no 'fact of the matter' as to which is which.

> In quantum physics a permutation of indistinguishable objects between states is typically not regarded as leading to a new arrangement. Hence, it was concluded, such objects should not be regarded as individuals, or at least in the sense that they are not taken to be in [classical] statistics. (French and Krause 2006, 84)

True, there are other ways of construing such cases. Return to the original example of tossed coins. We might expect to obtain the 1/3, 1/3, 1/3 probability distribution if the tosses were not in fact independent, if outcomes causally influenced other outcomes. The difficulty of supposing that this is what is going on in the quantum case is that entangled particles can be widely dispersed. Particles would need to influence one another at a distance. As Reichenbach notes, 'these causal relationships would represent action at a distance, since the particles could be far apart; that is the dependence relations would constitute causal anomalies' (Reichenbach 1956, 234).

Another possibility, one suggested by Einstein and discussed already, is that the particles in question are, not particles after all, but *waves* (French and Krause 2006, 88–9). In this case, what we have called particles, would be modes, not substances, not substantial constituents, of systems. Systems would take on the role of substances. Such systems would not be made up of particles. Particles would be abstractions, dependent on the systems to which they belonged. Were quantum 'entanglement' universal, the world would amount to a single, dynamic substance. What we regard as objects – commonsense substances, including the particles – would be modifications of the one substance, modes. Paul Teller puts this in terms of 'inherent relations':

> The world is a more deeply intermeshed web than we had thought. Indeed, according to quantum mechanics, the extent of entanglement through inherent relations is all pervasive. (Teller 1986, 80–81)

I prefer to leave open the ontological lessons to be extracted from quantum physics. Quantum physics supplies us with equations that physicists regard as indispensable. The difficulty is to understand what these equations tell us about the world. Attempts to bridge the gap between theory and ontology abound in the form of multiple 'interpretations' of quantum theory. However, there is scant agreement among physicists as to the correct, or best interpretation. Nevertheless, it would seem that, whatever ontology we draw out of fundamental physics, it will be an ontology of substance and property. The scientific question is, what are the substances? Are they the particles? The fields? The World Whole? And, what are the properties? Mass, charge, spin? The electrons and quarks themselves?

Taking stock

The emerging picture is that the world – any world – must include substances and properties. Substance and property are reciprocal, complementary categories. Substances are the bearers of properties, and properties are ways substances are. Substances and properties alike are 'abstractions': you can consider a substance as a property bearer or you can consider its properties, but substances and properties could not exist apart. Substances are not compound entities made up of 'bare particulars' clothed in properties.

Substances must be simple, lacking substantial proper parts, although a simple substance can bear many properties and have endless spatial (and perhaps temporal) parts or divisions. Substances are *mereologically* simple. Complex entities, if there are any, could not be bearers of properties. If simple substances are genuine atoms, you might put this by saying that atomism is true of necessity. The question is, what are the atoms, and this is an empirical question. There might be many atoms, as Locke and Leibniz thought, or one big atom (Descartes, Spinoza), or there might be a handful of atoms (the fundamental fields). A complex object consisting of propertied substances standing in particular relations can serve as a truthmaker for a range of truths. This tomato is apparently a complex entity, not a substance. We can say truly that the tomato is red, that it is spherical, that it has a particular mass. But the truthmakers for such claims are the constituent substances, with their properties, arranged and interacting as they are. Only in the case of simples are judgments of the form '*a* is *F*', made true by a substance *a* bearing a property *F*.

What the substances are, what the properties are is an empirical question, one we turn to fundamental physics to answer. Thus, although we need the categories of substance and property, this does not imply that corpuscularism is true. The substances could be fields, space or space–time, or Spinoza's *Deus sive Natura*, the world as a whole. Were that so, what we might ordinarily regard as paradigmatic substances would turn out to be properties: ways the substance or substances are. Trees, electrons, planets, then, could turn out to be particular fluctuations in the quantum field or thickenings in space–time. The central idea here is that, whatever story we tell, it will be one featuring substances and properties.

Notes

1. If, like me, you regard properties as modes, every property would depend on its bearer: Socrates' whiteness depends on Socrates. This is what E. J. Lowe calls 'rigid existential dependence'. If you think of properties as universals and you hold, with Armstrong and Lowe, that universals must be instantiated, then a property depends, not on a particular substance, but on some substance or other. This is Lowe's 'non-rigid existential dependence'. (Lowe 2006 § 3.1)
2. Unless space is 'granular': some spatial parts lack spatial parts. Although this could be a real possibility, I shall ignore it here in the interests of simplifying the discussion.
3. The dependence problem does not stem from infinite divisibility alone, but from the lack of a 'ground floor' of non-dependent simples. Ross Cameron (2008) disagrees.
4. Cameron (2008) argues that, although an infinitely divisible world is possible, there are good reasons to think that the actual world includes simples.
5. A. W. Moore (2001) offers a trenchant account of the concept of infinity and its troubled history.
6. This possibility was suggested to me by Roy Sorensen.
7. I distinguish atomism from corpuscularism, a species of atomism. Atomism is the view that the world is made up of simple substances. This is compatible with the possibility that the world is made up of many simple substances, the corpuscles, but also with the possibility that the world is a single simple substance, and with the possibility that there is some small number of simple substances, the fields.
8. This point is made forcefully by Schaffer (2010) in his defense of 'priority monism'.
9. See French and Krause 2006, § 3.6. This is also close to what Schaffer has in mind.

References

Campbell, K. (1976) *Metaphysics: An Introduction*. Encino: Dickenson Publishing Co.

French, S. and D. Krause (2006) *Identity in Physics: A Historical, Philosophical, and Formal Analysis*. Oxford: Clarendon Press.

Healey, R. A. (1991) 'Holism and Nonseparability. *Journal of Philosophy* 88: 393–421.
Lowe, E. J. (1994) 'Vague Identity and Quantum Indeterminacy'. *Analysis* 54: 110–14.
Moore, A. W. (2001) *The Infinite*, 2d ed. London: Routledge.
Reichenbach, H. (1956) *The Direction of Time*. Berkeley: University of California Press.
Robb, D. M. (2009) 'Substance'. In Le Poidevin et al (2009): 256–64.
Schaffer, J. (2010) 'Monism: The Priority of the Whole'. *Philosophical Review* 119: 31–76, reprinted in this volume.
Teller, P. (1986) 'Relational Holism and Quantum Mechanics'. *British Journal for the Philosophy of Science* 37: 71-81
Teller, P. (1995) *An Interpretive Introduction to Quantum Field Theory*. Princeton: Princeton University Press.
Robb, D. M. (2009) 'Substance'. In Le Poidevin et al (2009): 256–64.

Part II

Monism in Spinoza

9
Spinoza on Composition and Priority

Ghislain Guigon

Spinoza held that there is only one possible substance, God or Nature, and that this unique substance is an extended one. By doing so he departed from the Cartesian doctrine according to which God is not extended because God is simple and indivisible, while no extended thing is mereologically simple.[1] Spinoza was aware that his Cartesian fellows would challenge his attributing extension to God. So he addressed this challenge by arguing, in the demonstrations and *scholia* that immediately precede and follow his affirmation of *Substance Monism*, that no substance is divisible and that the extended substance, in particular, is mereologically simple.[2]

But scholars have found Spinoza's answer to the Cartesian challenge to Substance Monism inconsistent with passages wherein Spinoza talks of Nature as if it were composed of parts. In this chapter, I shall argue that Spinoza has a consistent view on composition. Given the importance Spinoza attached to the Cartesian challenge to Substance Monism, my interpretation of Spinoza's discourse on composition should shed some new light on Substance Monism itself.

Working out what view on composition Spinoza held is not just a matter of interest for historians of philosophy. In a series of articles,[3] Jonathan Schaffer has defended *Priority Monism* – the thesis that the most comprehensive concrete thing (the cosmos) is more basic than any of its proper parts – against *Existence Monism* – the thesis that there is exactly one concrete thing – and *Priority Pluralism* – the thesis that the cosmos's proper parts are more basic than the cosmos itself. In these articles, Schaffer argues that authors in the monistic tradition are better interpreted as Priority than as Existence Monists. In this chapter, I shall give evidence that Spinoza's Monism is neither an Existence nor a Priority Monism. For, according to Spinoza's Monism, (i) there is exactly one basic concrete thing, (ii) there are many less basic concrete things, and (iii) parts are more basic than the whole they compose. If the conjunction of (i) and (ii) is incompatible with both Existence Monism and Priority Pluralism, the conjunction of (ii) and (iii) is incompatible with Priority Monism. So the insight of this chapter goes beyond history of philosophy. For it shows that the contemporary debate among monists in fundamental metaphysics is not exhausted by the debate between Existence and Priority Monists. There is room for a third kind of Monism, which is a Substance Monism.

In section 9.1 I argue that Spinoza agrees that there are many concrete things though there is only one fundamental concrete thing. In section 9.2 I argue that Spinoza's view is that the fundamental concrete thing, the extended substance, is mereologically simple. However, this interpretation of Spinoza faces two challenges that I shall explore: a puzzle about the occurrence of composition in extended reality, and a puzzle about substantial simplicity. Sections 9.3 and 9.4 provide conceptual tools that will allow me to address these two challenges in sections 9.5 and 9.6: section 9.3 introduces Spinoza's threefold distinction between kinds of composition and section 9.4 is a study of Spinoza's doctrine about *beings of reason*.

9.1 Preliminaries

I start with an introduction to various Monist and Pluralist theses; then I will display fundamental claims of Spinoza's prime philosophy. These claims will allow me to settle precisely the disagreements between Substance Monism and other forms of Monism. In particular, they shall allow me to contend that what Substance and Priority Monists disagree about is the mereology of the concrete world. The remainder of this article, which develops an original interpretation of Spinoza's discourse on composition, can be understood as a defence of this contention.

9.1.1 Monisms and pluralisms

Existence Monism (EM) is the thesis that there is exactly one concrete thing, the *cosmos* or *Nature* (Schaffer Chapter 1, this volume). Existence Monism is opposed to Existence Pluralism (EP) according to which there are many concrete things. So what Existence Monists and Existence Pluralists disagree about is the cardinality of the concrete world.

We should distinguish between two forms of Priority Monism, a weak and a strong one, which are both distinct from EM. Weak Priority Monism (WPM), on the one hand, is the thesis that there is exactly one basic, fundamental, concrete thing (where, for any x, x is a basic concrete thing if and only if no concrete thing is ontologically prior to x). WPM is opposed to Weak Priority Pluralism (WPP), which is the claim that there are several basic concrete things. So what Weak Priority Monists and Weak Priority Pluralists disagree about is the cardinality of the *basic* concrete world. If there is exactly one concrete thing, there is exactly one basic concrete thing. So EM entails WPM. However, WPM is consistent with EP.

On the other hand, Strong Priority Monism (SPM) is the thesis that (i) every concrete thing distinct from the cosmos or Nature is a proper part of it and (ii) the whole is prior to each of its proper parts. Since SPM is not committed to the existence of several concrete things, it is compatible with EM. Moreover, SPM entails that there is exactly one basic concrete thing, namely the cosmos or Nature. So SPM entails WPM. However, WPM does not entail SPM since a Weak Priority Monist might deny that Nature is a composite whole whose parts are the less basic concrete things.

SPM is opposed to Strong Priority Pluralism (SPP), namely the view that (i) every concrete thing distinct from the cosmos or Nature is a proper part of it and (ii) proper parts are prior to the whole they compose. SPP entails WPP only on the further assumption that EP is true. For SPP is compatible with EM which entails WPM. So what Strong Priority Monists and Strong Priority Pluralists disagree about is the direction of the priority relation among parts and whole.

So far I have distinguished three forms of Monism. Which of these three corresponds to Schaffer's Priority Monism? Schaffer's (Chapter 1, this volume) definition of Priority Monism is the following (where the quantifier is restricted to actual concrete things):

(PM) $(\exists!x)\ \mathrm{B}x\ \&\ \mathrm{B}u$

which means that there is exactly one basic concrete object, *u*, which is defined as *the* thing all actual concrete objects are parts of. Schaffer's Priority Monism is a Strong Priority Monism about the actual world. So, given that Schaffer does not distinguish between the strong and the weak forms of Monism that I introduced, I shall reserve the label 'Priority Monism' (and cognates) for the strong version of Priority Monism.

Schaffer suggests that Spinoza is better interpreted as a Priority Monist than as an Existence Monist because of his apparent commitment to concrete parts of Nature in his letter *Ep.* 15(32) to Oldenburg:

> A third main thread in the monistic tradition is that of *the world as an integrated system*. Arguably the seed of this idea can be found in what Spinoza wrote to Oldenburg: 'Concerning whole and parts, I consider things as parts of some whole insofar as the nature of the one so adapts itself to the nature of the other that so far as possible they are in harmony with one another' (1994, 82-3). And thus: '[E]ach body, in so far as it exists modified in a certain way, must be considered as a part of the whole universe, must agree with the whole to which it belongs, and must cohere with the remaining bodies' (1994, 84) [...] The idea of the cosmos as an integrated system is incompatible with *Existence Monism*. For *Existence Monism* denies that there is anything other than the cosmos. Hence it denies that there are any things to be integrated into the cosmos. Thus any historical monist who claims that the cosmos is an integrated system

> is committed to the existence of the parts, as what are integrated in the whole. (Schaffer Chapter 1, this volume: 38).

I agree with Schaffer that Spinoza is not an Existence Monist since he maintains that there are several bodies. However, Spinoza's discourse of bodies as being parts of the universe in this passage is a mere figure of speech and does not commit him to Priority Monism, or so I shall argue in this chapter. Considering the varieties of Monism and Pluralism I have introduced so far, I shall interpret Spinoza as agreeing with EP and WPM but as denying both SPM and SPP. This is a coherent view if according to it the many concrete things stand in *substance-mode* relations but one denies that modes of substances are component parts of substances. This view is Spinoza's Substance Monism.

In the next preliminary I shall explain why I believe that Spinoza agrees with both EP and WPM. My argument for the claim that Spinoza rejects both SPM and SPP is the core of this chapter.

9.1.2 Substance and modes

According to Spinoza, there are two categories of *extended* beings: extended substances and modes of extension. Likewise, there are two categories of *thinking* beings: thinking substances and modes of thinking. A substance is defined as 'what is in itself and is conceived through itself, i.e. that whose concept does not require the concept of another thing, from which it must be formed' (*E* Id3). Substances have attributes, which are defined as 'what the intellect perceives of a substance, as constituting its essence' (*E* Id4). Thus, extension is an attribute of extended substances and thought is an attribute of thinking substances. Finally, modes are understood as 'the affections of a substance, *or* that which is in another through which it is also conceived' (*E* Id5).

Modes of extension are of two kinds. First, there are *bodies* (*E* IId1), which are extended in space and time – and thus are concrete, according to our contemporary use of 'concrete'. Bodies are finite, have a determinate existence, and are regularly called 'individuals' by Spinoza (*E* IId7, *E* IIp13a2). Second, there are affections of bodies (*E* IIId3) that should be understood as extended modes of extended modes of extended substances, *i.e.* second-order modes of extension.

Modes of thinking are of various kinds: *ideas of objects*, affections of minds that are ideas of affections of bodies (*E* IIId3), but also *beings of reason* and mere fictitious beings. Ideas of objects are the basic modes of thinking because any further mode of thinking depends on an idea of an object (*E* IIa3). The networks of modes of extension and of *these* modes of thinking that are ideas are causally isomorphic (*E* IIp7d).[4] Modes that stand in correspondence in parallel networks are identical to one another (*E* IIp7s).

So there are various ways substances are affected. But while there are many modes, there is only one substance, God or Nature, which is an extended and thinking substance (*E* Ip14). Every mode, then, is either a mode of the unique substance or a mode of a mode of the substance conceived through a certain attribute. The main thesis about the relationship between substances and modes is introduced as the first proposition of the *Ethics*: substances are prior in nature to their modes (*E* Ip1). This proposition, which, Spinoza claims, directly follows from his definitions of substance and mode, plays a central role in Spinoza's account of the mereology of the concrete world that I will display in the next section.

Therefore, admitting that extended individuals are concrete, there are many concrete things in Spinoza's system: Nature – the unique extended substance – and bodies – first-order modes of Nature. Hence Spinoza agrees with EP and denies EM. Since only one of these concrete things is a substance and since any other concrete thing is a mode of this extended substance, it directly follows from *E* Ip1 that there is exactly one basic concrete thing: Nature. So Spinoza agrees with WPM. But is Spinoza a Priority Monist? If there is exactly one basic concrete thing and if bodies are concrete things distinct from the basic concrete thing, then the further assumption that bodies are parts of Nature yields Schaffer's Priority Monism. However, we shall see that Spinoza denies that Nature has any component parts.

9.2 A simple substance

The Cartesian challenge to Substance Monism is the following valid argument (reconstructed from Descartes' *Principles* I: 23 and Spinoza's *KV* I: 2[18][5] and *E* Ip15s):

1. God, being perfect, is indivisible and does not consist of parts.
2. The extended substance is divisible and consists of parts.
3. Therefore, God and the extended substance are numerically distinct.

The conclusion of this argument clearly conflicts with the main thesis of Substance Monism, according to which there is exactly one substance. So Spinoza addresses this challenge in many places by rejecting the second premise, *i.e.* by arguing that no substance is divisible and that Nature, the extended substance, is simple.

Spinoza argues that no substance is divisible into parts in the demonstrations and *scholia* (*E* Ip12d, *E* Ip13d, and *E* Ip13s) that immediately precede the affirmation of Substance Monism in *E* Ip14.[6] These demonstrations appeal to the following claims:

1. Wholes could neither be nor be conceived without their parts;[7]
2. Each substance is infinite (demonstrated in E Ip8d, and E Ip8s);
3. Each substance is its own cause (demonstrated in E Ip7d);

4. No two substances can have an attribute in common (demonstrated in E Ip5d);
5. Each substance is eternal (demonstrated in E Ip7d).

In *E* Ip15s[IV], Spinoza maintains that his demonstrations of substantial indivisibility (in *E* Ip12d and *E* Ip13d) establish that the 'supposition that corporeal substance is composed of parts [...] [is] absurd'. In other terms, these demonstrations, if sound, establish not only that Nature is *indivisible* but also that Nature is mereologically simple.[8] Indeed, the claim that wholes could neither be nor be conceived without their parts, together with the definition of a substance as an independent and independently conceived being, entails that no substance is composed of substances and, together with the definition of a mode and *E* Ip1, entails that no substance is composed of modes.

Spinoza offers further arguments in favour of the simplicity of God (*CM* II: 5, *Ep.* 40(35)), or of the extended substance (*KV* I: 2[19]-[20]).[9] The first argument of *KV* I: 2[19] appeals to the assumption that wholes could neither be nor be conceived without their parts. Moreover, Spinoza's demonstrations of God's simplicity in *CM* II: 5 and *Ep.* 40(35) essentially appeal to the equivalent claim that component parts are (*CM* II: 5), or must be (Ep. 40(35)), prior in nature and knowledge to the whole they compose.[10] However, despite his systematic and essential use of the assumption that wholes could neither be nor be conceived without their parts, Spinoza offers no justification in favour of this assumption. Indeed, he declares it 'clear through itself' (*CM* II: 5) and its negation 'absurd as no one will be able to doubt' (*E* Ip12d). Why does Spinoza judge so? Plausibly, his reason for thinking this is that this assumption is in line with the Aristotelian tradition he is familiar with.

Aristotle himself seems to be arguing in chapters 10 and 11 of *Metaphysics Z* that concrete substances (made of matter and form) perish into material parts from which they are constituted as *principles*, that parts of concrete substances are *anterior* to their composites, and that the *definitions* of material parts of concrete substances will occur in the *definition* of their composite (Heinaman 1997). Boethius (1998: especially 879c) also claims that the whole is posterior to its parts, a claim assumed by medieval thinkers in their demonstrations of God's simplicity (e.g., Anselm *Proslogion* 18; Aquinas *Summa Theologiae* I, q. 3, a. 7). Likewise, late medieval thinkers, including William of Ockham (1967–1986: *Quaestiones in Librum Quartum Sententiarum*, q. 13), John Buridan (2010: 1.13), and Albert of Saxony (1999: in particular *Quaestiones in Phys.* 1.8), share the view that objects like rivers, houses, and cats are dependent upon their parts.[11] So Spinoza's insistent appeal to the claim that parts are, or must be, prior in nature and knowledge to the whole they compose in his demonstrations of substantial simplicity is in line with the Tradition.

Given Spinoza's definition of a substance (*E* Id3), it is impossible that a substance depends on another substance (or is conceived through it). So, Spinoza concludes, parts of a substance cannot be substances themselves since composites can neither exist nor be conceived without their parts. But parts of a substance cannot be modes either. For by *E* Ip1 substances are prior in nature to their modes, whereas parts are prior to the whole they compose. So neither modes nor substances can be parts of substances, and we must conclude from Spinoza's agreement with the Aristotelian doctrine of the priority of the parts that substances are mereologically simple.

Therefore, we have abundant evidence that Spinoza holds the view (i) that parts are or must be prior to the whole they compose[12] and (ii) that there is exactly one basic concrete thing, Nature, which is mereologically simple.[13] This view conflicts with Schaffer's Priority Monism according to which the basic concrete thing is the thing all actual concrete objects are parts of. For suppose for *reductio* that there is a thing all actual concrete objects are parts of in Spinoza's Monism. Then, given Spinoza's commitment to the priority of the parts, this composite thing is not a substance and so is not basic. In other terms, Spinoza's Nature is not Schaffer's cosmos and there is nothing like Schaffer's cosmos in the ontology of Substance Monism since there is no composite whole that is also basic. Nevertheless, since Spinoza's Substance Monism entails both EP and WPM, Spinoza is neither an Existence Monist nor a Priority Pluralist.

But puzzling passages in Spinoza's writings threaten this interpretation. These passages give rise to two challenges that I shall explore. First, Spinoza's commitment to the view that Nature is mereologically simple motivates his claim that, 'part and whole are not true or actual beings but only beings of reason; consequently in Nature there are neither whole nor parts' (*KV* I: 2[19]).[14] This suggests that Spinoza denies that composition occurs in extended, mind-independent, reality. However, on some occasions Spinoza talks *as if* composition takes place between extended modes. Thus he writes in *E* IIp13pos1 that, 'the human Body is composed of a great many individuals of different natures, each of which is highly composite.' But how could the human body be composed of parts if part and whole are beings of reason?

Second, although Spinoza holds that the extended substance is mereologically simple in several writings, we find him talking of God or Nature as being composed of parts on three separate occasions. First, Spinoza writes in *KV* II: 22[7] that, '[the effect] is so united with [its cause] that together they form a whole' where God is the freest cause of all to which Spinoza is referring here. Then, in Part II of the *Ethics* Spinoza writes:

> And if we proceed in this way to infinity, we shall easily conceive that the whole of nature is one Individual, whose parts, i.e., all bodies, vary in infinite ways, without any change of the whole Individual. (*E* IIp13l7s)

Finally, in a letter he writes to Oldenburg:

> Hence it follows that each body, in so far as it exists as modified in a particular manner, must be considered as a part of the whole universe, as agreeing with the whole, and associated with the remaining parts. [...] But, in respect to substance, I conceive that each part has a more close union with its whole. (*Ep.* 15(32))

It is even more puzzling that in this letter Spinoza seems to deny what he vigorously affirms elsewhere, namely that parts are prior to the whole they compose:

> For, as I said in my first letter [...], substance being infinite in its nature, it follows, as I endeavoured to show, that each part belongs to the nature of substance, and, without it, can neither be nor be conceived. (*Ep.* 15(32))

On the balance of evidence, these texts should not induce us to doubt that Spinoza's official doctrine is that Nature is mereologically simple and that parts are prior to the whole they compose. Still, interpreters of Spinoza's discourse about parthood have to address these challenges. In order to do so, I shall first introduce Spinoza's threefold distinction of kinds of composition and his doctrine of beings of reason.

9.3 Three kinds of composition

Chapter 5 of part II of Spinoza's *Metaphysical Thoughts* is devoted to the demonstration of God's simplicity. There, Spinoza introduces and distinguishes three kinds of composition. I shall introduce labels for these three kinds of composition. Then, paying attention to which kind of composition is involved in which context, I will be able to solve the difficulties met at the end of the last section.

First, some preliminary remarks about the interpretation of *CM* II: 5 are required. *CM* is the appendix of Spinoza's *Exposition in the geometrical manner of Descartes' Principles of Philosophy*. Spinoza offers in *PP* an axiomatic presentation of theses that are demonstrated by Descartes in the first and second parts of his masterpiece, whereas he offers in *CM* original demonstrations of theses that are endorsed without demonstration by Descartes. The result is that in *CM* Spinoza often asserts statements he disagrees with in order to demonstrate Cartesian theses.

There is little doubt that Spinoza sees the threefold distinction between kinds of composition that is displayed in *CM* II: 5 as presupposed by Descartes' metaphysics. For he claims there that this distinction directly follows from Descartes' three kinds of distinction: *real, modal,* and *of reason*. However, that Spinoza conceives of the threefold distinction of kinds of composition as being presupposed by Descartes' philosophy does not mean that he would deny this distinction. And while there is no textual evidence that Spinoza disagrees with it, there are good reasons to believe that Spinoza endorses it. For Spinoza agrees with Descartes that beings are divided into substance and mode and he thinks that admitting this division of beings yields Descartes' three kinds of distinction. So by transitivity the threefold distinction between kinds of composition is derived from the division of beings into substance and modes Spinoza is committed to. Moreover, assuming that Spinoza agrees with the threefold distinction between kinds of composition provides an adequate account of his discourse about composition in his more original works, as I shall argue in subsequent sections.

Spinoza begins his demonstration of God's simplicity in *CM* II: 5 by reminding us of Descartes' *three distinctions*:

> We proceed to the simplicity of God. In order to understand this attribute of God rightly, we need to recall what Descartes has taught (*Principles* I, 48, 49), viz. that there is nothing in nature but substances and their modes. From this a threefold distinction of things is deduced (I, 60-62), viz. *real*, *modal*, and *of reason*.

The *real distinction* is the distinction by which two substances are distinguished from one another (*Principles* I: 60). The *modal distinction* is the one by which different modes of a same substance, on the one hand, and a substance and its modes, on the other hand, are distinguished from one another (*Principles* I: 61). The third distinction, called *distinction of reason*, is in Descartes the one by which a substance and its principal attribute are distinguished (*Principles* I: 62).

Spinoza writes that, 'From [Descartes'] distinctions, all composition arises' (*CM* II: 5). Then he distinguishes three kinds of composition on this basis. The first kind of composition, which I shall call *substantial composition*, is introduced thus:

> The first sort of composition is that which comes from two or more substances which have the same attribute (e.g., all composition which arises from two or more bodies) or which have different attributes (e.g., man). (*CM* II: 5)

He then claims that 'the second [sort of composition]', which I shall call *modal composition*, 'comes from the union of different modes'. Finally, about the third kind of composition, which I shall label *composition of reason*, Spinoza writes that it 'does not occur, but is only conceived by the reason as if it occurred, so that the thing may be the more easily understood'. So composition is either substantial, modal, or of reason. Spinoza concludes by affirming that, 'whatever is not composed in these first two ways should be called simple' (*ibid.*).

Thus, according to this threefold distinction of kinds of composition, only two of them are genuine kinds of composition: substantial composition and modal composition. It should be noticed that as Spinoza is, in *CM*, demonstrating theses held by Descartes, it is not surprising to find him asserting in this context that substantial composition occurs. For Descartes agrees that composition does occur between *bodies*, which are substances in his system. However, Spinoza denies that bodies are substances[15] and that substantial composition occurs. Indeed, if there is only one substance, if Substance Monism is true, then no substance can be composed of several substances! So, despite the fact that Spinoza describes substantial composition as occurring in the Cartesian context of *CM* II: 5, it is clear that his own view is that, necessarily, substantial composition never occurs.

The distinction of reason is not a distinction that occurs in reality but is merely a product of the mind thinking of two ways of conceiving a single entity as if they were two entities. Likewise, composition of reason does not occur but is merely conceived by reason as if it occurred. For things that are merely conceived by reason as if they were wholes composed of parts are, strictly speaking, mereologically simple. And just as it is literally false to say of things that are only distinguished by reason that they are numerically distinct, it is literally false to say of a thing that is merely composed by reason that it is a composite. Nevertheless, according to Spinoza, composition of reason might play some useful theoretical role: it can help us to understand things more easily. So we can talk of simple things as if they had component parts if it helps us, for instance, to understand more easily a difficult philosophical thesis.

In contemporary debates between realists and anti-realists, we say that someone is a *fictionalist* about a region of discourse if she takes all positive statements about this region of discourse to be literally false but nevertheless worth using for some theoretical purpose.[16] In this sense, it is not inappropriate to regard Spinoza as a fictionalist about mereology when, *and only when,* the mereological vocabulary is to be interpreted in terms of composition of reason. If so, careful examination might reveal that, in some contexts at least, Spinoza asserts statements of the form '*x* is a part of *y*' because they are useful but without being committed to the truth of these statements. What is at stake there is composition of reason.

So, according to Spinoza's distinction between three kinds of composition and given his commitment to Substance Monism, positive mereological claims are literally false when the mereological vocabulary they contain ('part', 'whole', and cognates) is interpreted either in terms of substantial composition or in terms of composition of reason. In the latter case, positive mereological claims can be worth using to play theoretic roles despite their falsity. It remains to be considered whether positive mereological claims can be true when the mereological vocabulary they contain is interpreted in terms of modal composition. But first I have to introduce Spinoza's doctrine about beings of reason.

9.4 Spinoza's doctrine of beings of reason

Spinoza's doctrine of beings of reason is displayed in the first chapter of *CM*.[17] Spinoza's starting point is a definition of a *being* as '*whatever, when it is clearly and distinctly perceived, we find to exist necessarily, or at least to be able to exist*' (*CM* I: 1 '*The definition of Being*'). It follows from this definition, Spinoza claims, that beings of reason are not beings but 'mere modes of thinking' (*ibid*. '*Chimeras, Fictitious Beings, and Beings of reason are not beings*').

Mere modes of thinking are modes of thinking that are not ideas. Thus beings of reason are not ideas but are wrongly taken to be ideas because they directly follow from ideas (*CM* I: 1 '*Why beings of reason are not Ideas of things and are nevertheless taken to be ideas*'). Since beings of reason are not ideas, 'they also have no object that exists necessarily, or can exist' (*ibid*.). In other words, beings of reason represent neither the extended substance nor any of its modes in the way expressed by the thesis of *parallelism* (*E* IIp7). In a slogan: modes of extension are *sparse*, modes of thinking are *abundant*. Only ideas correspond to modes of extension. And since beings of reason 'cannot be called ideas', they cannot 'be said to be true or false, just as love cannot be called true or false, but [only] good or bad' (*CM* I: 1 '*In what sense Beings of reason can be called a mere nothing, and in what sense they can be called real Beings*').

The relevant consequence of Spinoza's claim that beings of reason are not ideas is that beings of reason have no real definition but only have stipulative ones. In his letter *Ep*. 9(27) to Simon De Vries, Spinoza explains that there are two kinds of definition. Definitions of the first kind, which I call *real*, 'ought to be true' and explain things as they are outside the intellect in that these definitions are 'concerned solely with the essences of things or their affections'. Definitions of the second kind, which I call *stipulative*, explain things as we conceive, or can conceive, them and 'need not [...] be conceived as true' but only need to be conceived. Then Spinoza explains to De Vries that a good definition need not be a real one:

> If I say that each substance has only one attribute, that is only a proposition and requires a demonstration. But if I say 'By substance I understand what consists of one attribute only,' that will be a good definition, provided that afterwards beings consisting of more attributes than one are designed by a word other than substance. (*Ep*. 9(27))[18]

Spinoza accounts for truth in terms of correspondence: a truth is an affirmation or a denial about something that corresponds to the thing itself, whereas a falsity is an affirmation or denial about something that does not correspond to this thing.[19] So, if beings of reason are modes of thinking that have no object they can represent, their definitions are not *truth-apt* because there is nothing to which these definitions can correspond. *A fortiori* then, if part and whole are beings of reason, then definitions we can offer for 'part' and 'whole' must be stipulative: definitions that are neither true nor false but can still be good definitions if we regiment our discourse accordingly.

If beings of reason are not ideas, what kind of modes of thinking are they? Here is Spinoza's answer:

> Finally, a *Being of reason* is nothing but a mode of thinking, which helps us to more easily *retain, explain, and imagine* the things we have understood. (*CM* I: 1 '*Chimeras, Fictitious Beings, and Beings of reason are no beings*')

Distinct beings of reason can play distinct cognitive roles. Some beings of reason help us to keep present to our memory what we have understood. Among these we find the modes of genus and species (*ibid. 'By what modes of thinking we retain things'*). Some beings of reason 'serve to *explain* a thing by determining it through comparison to another' (*ibid. 'By what modes of thinking we explain things'*). As examples of these beings of reason whose purpose is explanation Spinoza offers time, number, and measure. Finally, some beings of reason help us 'to depict in our fantasy images of whatever we understand' and to 'imagine nonentities positively, as beings' (*ibid. 'By what modes of thinking we imagine things'*). So it happens, Spinoza claims, that we imagine, as if they were beings, modes that are used by the mind for negating things: blindness, extremity or limit, term, darkness, etc. (*ibid*).[20]

Assuming that part and whole are beings of reason, what is their cognitive purpose? Much evidence indicates that, according to Spinoza, part and whole are beings of reason whose purpose is to help us to more easily imagine things we have understood. First, Spinoza accounts for wholes and composition in terms of agreement in his letter *Ep.* 15(32) to Oldenburg. But in *CM* I: 5 he claims that agreement is a 'mode of thinking by which we retain or imagine the things themselves more easily'. Second, in *KV* I: 2nd dialogue [9], Spinoza accounts for the claim that part and whole are beings of reason by exhibiting the close similarity between wholes and universals. Yet Spinoza contends that universals are products of our imagination (*E* IIp40s). But the main evidence is perhaps what Spinoza says in *E* Ip15s[V]. There, Spinoza claims that the reason why we tend to think of matter as being divisible and composed of parts is because we conceive of it 'as it is in the imagination'.

Therefore, when Spinoza claims that part and whole are beings of reason, his aim is to emphasise that part and whole are not ideas. They are modes of thinking that do not correspond to any mode of extension. For this reason, definitions of mereological vocabulary are stipulative instead of real ones.

Nevertheless, mereological discourse may play an important cognitive role, which is to help us imagine things.

9.5 Modal composition and beings of reason

Spinoza claims that part and whole are beings of reason. His reason appears to be his belief that Nature is mereologically simple. We have been puzzled by the fact that Spinoza's claim that part and whole are not true beings but only beings of reason seems *prima facie* incompatible with passages in which Spinoza seems to assert that composition occurs in extended beings. However, the displayed elucidation of Spinoza's notion of a being of reason shows that there is no inconsistency in maintaining both that part and whole are beings of reason and that composition can occur in extended reality. In particular, *modes* of extension can compose further modes of extension.

Consider blindness. According to Spinoza, who follows Suárez on this point, blindness is like every negative mode of thinking a mere being of reason. Obviously, this does not mean that Spinoza, a specialist of optics, denies that there are blind people. So what does it mean? Spinoza would probably admit the following definition of a blind person: a blind person is a person who lacks visual perception due to physiological factors. We can regard this as a good definition of a blind person according to which *there are* blind people. Nevertheless, for Spinoza this definition of a blind person is stipulative. For blindness being a being of reason definitions of 'blindness' cannot be truth-apt. In other words, the offered definition is stipulative because no mode of extension parallels the mode of thinking that is *absence* of visual perception due to physiological factors. There is no such mode of extension because every mode of extension is positive. This is what Spinoza means when saying that blindness, and in general negative modes of thinking, are beings of reason. By contrast, the positive mode of having visual perception is an extended mode of human bodies: a second-order mode of extension. So, according to the stipulative definition of blindness, blindness occurs in human bodies whenever people *fail to have*, for physiological reasons, the extended mode of having visual perception. Since it is an objective and determinate fact that some people fail to have this mode of extension, it is literally and objectively true that some people are blind. Therefore, according to the displayed account of Spinoza's doctrine about beings of reason, there is no inconsistency between the claim that blindness occurs in bodies, which are modes of extension, and the claim that blindness is a being of reason.[21]

Now Spinoza's view is that blindness, part, and whole are modes of thinking of the very same category: they are beings of reason whose purpose is to help us to more easily imagine things we have understood. So if propositions of the form '*x* is blind' can be literally true even though blindness is such a being of reason, *a fortiori* propositions of the forms '*x* and *y* compose a whole' and '*y* is a composite whole' can be literally true even if part and whole are beings of reason. So suppose that one stipulates that, for any extended *x* and *y*, *x* and *y* compose a whole if and only if *x* and *y* are *affected* in a particular given way. Then it turns out to be literally true that *x* and *y* compose a whole if they are affected in this particular given way. So, as for blindness, there is no inconsistency between the claim that composition occurs in modes of extension and the claim that part and whole are beings of reason. Modal composition is the kind of composition that occurs between modes. Hence, the claim that part and whole are beings of reason is consistent with the claim that modal composition occurs in extension. And so is solved the first puzzle about parthood that I introduced at the end of section 9.2: Spinoza's postulate that 'the human Body is composed of a great many individuals of different natures, each of which is highly composite' does not conflict with the claim that part and whole are mere beings of reason.

We have abundant evidence that Spinoza believes both that modal composition occurs and that part and whole are beings of reason. In chapter 2 of part I of *KV*, Spinoza both claims that part and whole are not true or actual beings but beings of reason (*KV* I: 2[19]) and that composition never occurs in the substance but always and only in the modes (*KV* I: 2[21]–[22]). This suggests that Spinoza does not take these two claims to be contradictory and that he believes that modal composition occurs. The content of the fifth *scholium* following *E* Ip15 also indicates that, according to Spinoza, composition occurs between modes of extension. There Spinoza distinguishes two ways of conceiving of matter. We can, he says, 'conceive of it as it is *in the imagination'*, and in this case it will be found finite, divisible, and composed of parts. But we can also conceive of matter as it is in the intellect, in which case matter is found to be infinite, indivisible, and simple. Then Spinoza illustrates this claim by adding the following:

> Parts are distinguished in [matter] only insofar as we conceive matter to be affected in different ways, so that its parts are distinguished only modally, but not really. For example, we conceive that water is divided and its parts separated from one another – insofar as it is water, but not insofar as it is corporeal substance. For, insofar as it is substance, it is neither separated nor divided. (*E* Ip15s[V])

Spinoza's appeal to the *modal distinction* in relation to imagination in this passage makes it clear that he relates modal composition to our faculty of imagination.

But the main evidence that Spinoza agrees that modal composition occurs in extended modes is his definition of a composite body in the *Ethics*:

> Definition: *When a number of bodies, whether of the same or of different size, are so constrained by other bodies that they lie upon another, or if they so move, whether with the same degree or different degrees of speed, that they*

> *communicate their motions to each other in a certain fixed manner, we shall say that those bodies are united with one another and that they all together compose one body or Individual, which is distinguished from the others by this union of bodies.* (*E* IIp13a2′)

This definition provides meaning to the postulate that, 'the human Body is composed of a great many individuals of different natures, each of which is highly composite' (*E* IIp13pos1). If my understanding of Spinoza's doctrine of beings of reason is correct, then this definition of a composite body must be stipulative. Indeed, what Spinoza does in this definition is to introduce new theoretical terms. For he is explaining how he will thereafter use the phrases 'union of bodies' and 'individual composed of parts'. Now Spinoza believes that, sometimes, bodies lie upon one another or move in such a way that they communicate their motions in the relevant fixed manner. So, given Spinoza's definition of a composite body, the concrete world is such that, sometimes, bodies unite so as to form a composite body. And so for Spinoza some propositions of the forms '*x* is a part of *y*' and '*y* is a composite whole' are literally and objectively true. Such propositions are literally true when *being a part of* and *being a composite whole* are understood in terms of modal composition and when bodies satisfy the stipulative definition of an individual composed of parts.

Spinoza's definitions of the union of modes and of a composite individual in *E* IIp13a2 are similar to the definitions he couched in less precise terms in his letter to Oldenburg:

> By the association of parts, then, I merely mean that the laws or nature of one part adapt themselves to the laws or nature of another part, so as to cause the least possible inconsistency. As to the whole and the parts, I mean that a given number of things are parts of a whole, in so far as the nature of each of them is adapted to the nature of the rest, so that they all, as far as possible, agree together. On the other hand, in so far as they do not agree, each of them forms, in our mind, a separate idea, and is to that extent considered as a whole, not as a part. (*Ep.* 15(32))

It is plausible to think that what Spinoza describes here as the adaptation of the laws of parts to the laws of other parts is what he described in the *Ethics* as bodies communicating their motions to each other in a certain fixed manner. And so it is plausible to think that what Spinoza calls 'the association of parts' is what he calls the 'union of bodies' in the *Ethics*. It should be noticed that *immediately* before he defines the association of parts in *Ep.* 15(32), Spinoza writes:

> I will premise that I do not attribute to nature either beauty or deformity, order or confusion. Only in relation to our imagination can things be called beautiful or deformed, ordered or confused.

Yet, in *CM* I: 5, Spinoza claims that *order* is a mode of thinking by which we either retain or imagine things we have understood. Likewise, in the Appendix [III.] of *E* I, Spinoza argues that order is a *mode of imagining*. Plausibly, there cannot be any *adaptation* between the laws of bodies, if the extended world is devoid of order. So Spinoza's premise to his definition of the association of parts shows that he is assuming in his letter to Oldenburg that part and whole are beings of reason by which we imagine things.

Therefore, Spinoza agrees that modal composition occurs between bodies, which are modes of extension, despite his commitment to the view that part and whole are beings of reason, and it is consistent for him to do so.

9.6 The challenge to substantial simplicity

Spinoza has been busy arguing that Nature is mereologically simple on the basis of the principle that parts are or must be prior to the whole they compose. Yet on two occasions he claims that Nature is composed of parts that are bodies (in *E* IIp13l7 and *Ep.* 15(32)). And on one of these occasions (*Ep.* 15(32)) he also claims that parts of the substance can neither be nor be conceived without the whole they compose. Does Spinoza contradict himself about substantial simplicity and the priority of the parts? I shall argue on the basis of his threefold distinction between kinds of composition that Spinoza's discourse about composition and priority is thoroughly consistent.

So far I have argued that Spinoza's claim that part and whole are beings of reason is consistent with the view that composition occurs in the modes of the extended substance. Also I have argued that Spinoza makes use of mereological discourse to describe affections of extended modes: for instance, in his definitions of the union of modes and of a composite individual in *E* IIp13a2. This does not mean, however, that each time Spinoza makes use of mereological discourse he should be taken at face value.

The correct understanding of Spinoza is, I think, the following. Whether the definition of the union of bodies (*E* IIp13a2), or of the association of parts (*Ep.* 15(32)), captures a kind of composition that occurs in concrete reality depends on the domain of individuals on which we apply this definition. If we apply it on a domain of finite individuals, the definition captures the modal kind of composition that comes from the union of bodies. But if our imagination keeps applying this definition to an infinite being, then what we do is merely conceive of a simple being *as if* it were a composite one. In other words, when applied to an infinite entity, our stipulative definition of the union of bodies no longer captures the kind of composition I called modal, but only captures *composition of reason*. For infinite beings are incapable of being divided and composed of parts as Spinoza repeatedly argues in *KV* I: 2[19]–[20], *E* Ip12d, *E* Ip13d, and the whole *scholium* of *E* Ip15.

There is no direct textual evidence that Spinoza is talking of composition of reason in passages where he claims that God forms a whole with its effects (*KV* I: 2nd dialogue [3]), that 'if we proceed to infinity, we shall easily conceive that the whole of nature is an Individual' having parts (*E* IIp13l7), and that we ought to conceive each body as a part of the extended substance without which they can neither be nor be conceived (*Ep.* 15(32)). Nevertheless, there are some clues, and Spinoza's demonstrations of Nature's simplicity and his distinction between three kinds of composition show that we can, and I think that we ought to, interpret him as talking of composition of reason in these puzzling passages.

According to Spinoza, a substance is prior in nature and knowledge to its modes (*E* Ip1). So Nature, the extended substance, is prior in nature and knowledge to bodies, which are first-order modes of extension. Thus bodies can neither be nor be conceived without Nature. If so it is not surprising that, when Spinoza allows himself to describe the substance–mode relation between Nature and bodies in mereological terms in *Ep.* 15(32), he maintains that Nature – described as 'the whole' – is prior in nature and knowledge to bodies – described as 'parts'. The question is: Is the kind of composition that arises between Nature and bodies a kind of composition that occurs? The answer must be negative. We have seen that Spinoza denies that substantial composition occurs.[22] And we have seen him affirming that no mode can be a component part of a substance.[23] Therefore, whenever modes compose anything, the thing they compose must itself be a mode. So the kind of composition that arises between Nature and bodies is neither substantial nor modal composition. In other words, the composition of Nature by bodies must be a composition of reason.

Furthermore, we have seen that when Spinoza argues that Nature or God is simple and not divisible, he does so by appealing with insistence both to the infinity of Nature and to the principle that parts are prior to the whole they compose. So it would be absurd for Spinoza to maintain thereafter that Nature is not simple even though it is infinite and prior to its modes. If Spinoza had changed his mind regarding the simplicity of Nature, he should also, given his arguments for substantial simplicity and indivisibility, have changed his mind regarding the infinity of the substance and the priority of the substance. But *Ep.* 15(32) shows that Spinoza did not change his mind on the latter issues. So there is no good reason to think that he changed his mind on Nature's simplicity.[24]

However, if it is true that Spinoza's talk of Nature *as if* composed of bodies is to be interpreted in terms of composition of reason, then Spinoza must have some theoretical reason to talk of a simple thing as if it were a composite one. For we have seen (section 9.3) that the purpose of composition of reason is merely to help us to understand things more easily. So what is it that Spinoza wants us to understand more easily when he talks of Nature *as if* it were a composite? Of course, we can only speculate as to what Spinoza's intentions were; still there are some clues.

When he claims in *KV* that God forms a whole with its effects, Spinoza's purpose is to help us to understand that God is an immanent cause instead of a transitive one. For in this text Spinoza always uses this metaphor in addition to arguments for the view that causation is immanent.[25] And indeed the image of God forming a whole with its effects provides a powerful means to illustrate the idea of an immanent cause. But it is a mere figure.

What is Spinoza's purpose when he claims, in the *Ethics*, that if we proceed in this way to infinity, then we shall easily conceive that the whole of nature is one individual having parts that are affected in many ways without any change in its form? I think that his purpose here is to help us to understand more easily the iterative character of his definition of a composite individual. For, immediately before making this claim in *E* IIp13l7, he writes that if we take two arbitrary individuals and form from them a third one according to his definition of a composite individual, we should see that the composite individual has the characteristic feature of being affected in many ways without any change in its form. So the phrase 'if we proceed in this way to infinity' plays the role of an 'and so on to infinity': no matter how complex individuals are, any composite individual has this characteristic feature of being affected in many ways without any change in its form. In any case, Spinoza does not contend in *E* IIp13l7 that we *have to* proceed in this way to infinity. So, in the *Ethics*, Spinoza never affirms that the substance is composed of parts.

It is for the same purpose that Spinoza allows himself to talk as if Nature were composed of bodies in his letter to Oldenburg. For he begins there to illustrate his definition of the association of parts to the composition of the blood and goes on to more and more complex individuals so as to emphasise the iterative character of his definition. However, in this text Spinoza contends that we *ought to* conceive each body as being a part of the infinite substance. Why does he claim this? Here is my attempt at an explanation. The opening paragraph of *Ep.* 15(32) shows that Spinoza's remarks on composition in this letter are introduced to answer a question asked by Oldenburg:

> You ask me my opinion on the question raised concerning our knowledge of the means, whereby each part of nature agrees with its whole, and the manner in which it is associated with the remaining parts. (*Ep.* 15(32))

The view that Nature is composed of parts is common among the founders of the Royal Society. Therefore it is not surprising that Oldenburg, secretary of the Royal Society, asks his question in mereological terms. So presumably Spinoza talks of the extended substance *as if* it were composed of parts in this letter simply because Oldenburg's question is formulated in these terms.

Strictly speaking, bodies are modes, not parts, of Nature since there is only one substance and since modes of a substance are not parts of a substance. So when Spinoza claims that each body ought to be conceived as a part of the infinite substance, he aims to claim that each body ought to be conceived as a mode of the infinite substance. But Spinoza might have thought, with reason, that talking of bodies in terms of modes of Nature would make his answer to Oldenburg's question more difficult to understand and perhaps less convincing.[26] So he allowed himself to answer it without entering into irrelevant peculiarities of his monistic doctrine. In other words, he allowed himself to talk of bodies as if they were parts of Nature *so as to make his answer more easily understandable* to his reader. This is the purpose and nature of composition of reason.

If I am right that Spinoza's talk of the substance as if it were composed of bodies is to be interpreted in terms of composition of reason, then there is no inconsistency between his commitment to the view that Nature is mereologically simple and his sparse talk of Nature as having bodies for parts. For use of composition of reason is non-committal. It allows us to talk of a simple entity as if it were composed of parts, if we need to, for cognitive or theoretical purposes.

9.7 Conclusion

Spinoza holds that Nature is mereologically simple because it is absolutely infinite and prior to any other concrete being. Since he denies mereological complexity to Nature, he maintains that parts and whole are beings of reason, so that neither 'part' nor 'whole' has a real definition. Still he allows himself to introduce stipulative definitions of composite individuals in such a way that, according to his doctrine, composition occurs in the concrete modes of Nature. However, applying these stipulative definitions to an infinite being results in a kind of composition that is merely of reason: a kind of composition that does not occur but that we can conceive of *as if* it occurred for theoretical reasons, *i.e.* to help us to understand more easily difficult issues.

According to the interpretation of Spinoza I have displayed in this article, Spinoza is not a Priority Monist, nor is he an Existence Monist or a Priority Pluralist. He is not an Existence Monist because he agrees that there are many concrete, extended, individuals: Nature and bodies, which are modes of Nature. Of course, Spinoza is committed to the thesis that I called Weak Priority Monism given that, according to him, there is exactly one basic concrete thing, namely Nature. But Spinoza's Nature is not Schaffer's cosmos as the former is mereologically simple while the latter is composed of parts. Since Spinoza commits himself to the Aristotelian principle that parts must be prior to the whole they compose, he would have been a Priority Pluralist if he had endorsed the view that each body is a component part of Nature. But since Spinoza denies that Nature has any component part, he is neither a Priority Pluralist nor a Priority Monist. Therefore, Spinoza's Monism is neither an Existence nor a Priority Monism. It is a Substance Monism, a Monism according to which there is a unique simple substance modified in an infinite variety of ways.

Notes

I would like to thank Jonathan Schaffer whose work and encouragement motivated this chapter. This work also benefited greatly from comments by Andrew Arlig, Richard Glauser, Philip Goff, Jessica Leech, Christiaan Remmelzwaal, and Gonzalo Rodriguez-Pereyra; I thank them all.

1. *Principles* I: 23. '*Principles* I: 23' refers to article 23 of part I of Descartes's *Principles of Philosophy*.
2. Substance Monism is affirmed in *E* Ip14d. Spinoza's reply to the Cartesian challenge to Substance Monism is displayed in *E* Ip15s and relies on his demonstrations of the indivisibility of substances offered in *E* Ip12d, *E* Ip13d, and *E* Ip13s. Thus I agree with Curley (1985: 422) and others that Descartes is the opponent Spinoza is targeting at in *E* Ip15s and that Wolfson's (1962: 262-295) argument to the contrary is unconvincing.

   Unless otherwise marked, all references to the *Ethics* [*E*] and the early works of Spinoza are to Curley 1985. In reference to letters of Spinoza, I have used the Unabridged R.H.M. Elwes Translation. The arrangement of letters is as found in the *Opera Posthuma* while numbers in parenthesis are as arranged in Van Vloten's edition. I use the following standard abbreviations for Spinoza's works:
   KV = *Short Treatise on God, Man, and His Well-Being* = *Short Treatise*;
   Ep. = *Letters;*
   PP = *Parts I and II of Descartes' Principles of Philosophy;*
   CM = *Appendix Containing Metaphysical Thoughts* = *Metaphysical Thoughts*;
   E = *Ethics.*

   Passages from the *Ethics* will be referred to by means of the following standard abbreviations: initial Latin numerals stand for part numbers; 'a' for 'axiom'; 'c' for 'corollary'; 'p' for 'proposition'; 's' for '*scholium*'; 'd' stands for either 'definition' (when it appears immediately to the right of the part of the book), or 'demonstration' (in all other cases); 'pos' stands for 'postulate', and 'l' for lemma. Hence, '*E* Ip14d' refers to the demonstration of proposition 14 of part I of the *Ethics*, and '*E* Ip15s' refers to the *scholium* of proposition 15 of part I of the *Ethics*.
3. See in particular Schaffer 2008 and Schaffer Chapter 1, this volume.
4. This is the so-called *thesis of parallelism*; see, for instance, Della Rocca 1996, Chapter 2.
5. '*KV* I: 2[18]' stands for paragraph 18 of chapter 2 of Part I of the *Short Treatise*.
6. Spinoza also argues that God is indivisible in *Ep.* 40(35), IV. This argument is a summary of the arguments of *E* 1p12d, *E* Ip13d, and *E* Ip13s.
7. *E* Ip12d: 'Furthermore, [if the parts of the divided substance will retain the nature of the substance] [...] the whole (by d4 and p10) could both be and be conceived without its parts, which is absurd, as no one will be able to doubt.'
8. Notice that, for Spinoza, division, unlike composition, is a process. By dividing a whole into parts, the whole ceases to exist. Division being thus conceived, it is logically possible that some whole is composed of parts and yet indivisible.

I am grateful to Jonathan Schaffer for pointing out this possibility. However, Spinoza's view is that substances are both indivisible and simple.

9. In *KV* I: 2[19]-[20], Spinoza offers no less than three arguments to the conclusion that the extended substance is simple.
10. *CM* II: 5: 'It must be shown, therefore, that God is not something composite [...]. For since it is clear through itself that component parts are prior in nature at least to the thing composed, those substances by whose coalition and union God is composed will necessarily be prior in nature to God himself [...]. But since nothing more absurd than this can be said we conclude that God is not composed of a coalition and union of substances.'

    Ep. 40(35): 'II. It [God] must be simple, not made up of parts. For parts must in nature and knowledge be prior to the whole they compose: this could not be the case with regard to that which is eternal.'
11. On medieval views about composition and priority I have benefited greatly from Andrew Arlig's forthcoming works 'Nothing other than the parts' and 'Medieval Mereology'.
12. See *KV* I: 2[19], *CM* II: 5, *E* Ip12d, *Ep. 40(35)*.
13. See *KV* I: 2[19]–[20], *CM* II: 5, *E* Ip12 and *E* Ip12d, *E* Ip13 and *E* Ip13d, *E* Ip13c, *E* Ip13s, *E* Ip15s, and *Ep. 40(35)*.
14. This is clear from the argumentative structure of *KV* I: 2[18]–[19]. The Cartesian challenge to Substance Monism is displayed in *KV* I: 2[18]. *KV* I: 2[19] is Spinoza's reply to this objection and begins as follows: 'To this we reply: 1. That parts and whole are not true or actual beings, but only beings of reason; consequently in Nature there are neither whole nor parts'. In a note, Spinoza makes it clear that by 'Nature' here he means substantial extension. The remaining of *KV* I: 2[19] consists in Spinoza's first and second arguments for the simplicity of extension, making clear that these arguments are intended to support the thesis that part and whole are beings of reason.
15. See section 9.1.2.
16. In this sense Hartry Field (1989) is a fictionalist about mathematics since he holds that statements committed to the existence of mathematical entities are all false although many of them are very useful.
17. So one may wonder whether the doctrine that is displayed in *CM* I: 1 is Descartes' or Spinoza's view. The account of beings of reason which is displayed in this text is largely that of Suárez (1994). But Freudenthal (1887: 108) argues that Suárez is the target of Spinoza when he argues in *CM* I: 1 that, 'many wrongly confound beings of reason with fictitious beings'. Since no such attack is to be found in Descartes' writings and since the distinction between beings of reason and fictitious beings is not relevant to the content of Descartes' *Principles I* and *II*, there seems to be no reason why Spinoza would ascribe this attack to Descartes. Moreover, the Cartesian Heereboord (1680: 222 and 225) seems to be the target of Spinoza's criticism that, 'those who say that a being of reason is not a mere nothing speak improperly'. All this indicates that the doctrine of beings of reason that is displayed in *CM* I: 1 is not Descartes' but Spinoza's doctrine.
18. Notice that Spinoza denies the *proposition* that it is impossible for a substance to have more than one attribute; see *E* Ip9.
19. See *KV* II: 15[1], *CM* I: 6, and Spinoza's argument against ghosts in *Ep.* 60(56).
20. Spinoza is in line with the Aristotelian tradition when he denies that nature is negatively affected and claims that negative affections are mere beings of reason. See Suárez 1994, section 9.5.

21. This view should be compared with the treatment of negative predications in sparse theories of properties. For instance, Armstrong (1978: 23–9) endorses a sparse view of properties according to which there are no negative properties. But there are true negative predications, of course. So things truly can truly satisfy a negative predicate to which no property corresponds when they lack the corresponding property.
22. See section 9.2 and section 9.3.
23. See section 9.2.
24. Notice also that *Ep.* 40(35), in which Spinoza asserts that God is simple *because* parts must in nature and knowledge be prior to the whole they compose, is posterior to *Ep.* 15(32). So if Spinoza has changed his mind on this issue, it is in favor of the simplicity of the substance.
25. In *KV* I: 2nd dialogue [3], and in *KV* II: 22[7].
26. It should be noticed that Spinoza concludes his answer to Oldenburg's question by writing, 'I am afraid that I may have mistaken your meaning, and given an answer to a different question from that which you asked' (*Ep.* 15(32)).

References

Albert of Saxony. 1999. *Expositio et quaestiones in Aristotelis Physicam ad Albertum de Saxonia attributae,* volume II: *Quaestiones,* books I–III, ed. Benoît Patar. Louvain-Paris: Éditions Peeters.

Arlig, Andrew. 'Nothing other than the parts', forthcoming in John Marenbon (ed.) *The Oxford Handbook of Medieval Philosophy.* Oxford University Press.

Arlig, Andrew. 'Medieval mereology', forthcoming in Hans Burkhardt, Johanna Seift, and Guido Imagure (eds.) *The Handbook of Mereology.* Philosophia Verlag.

Armstrong, David M. 1978. *Universals & Scientific Realism II.* Cambridge: Cambridge University Press.

Boethius. 1998. *De Divisione liber,* ed. and trans. J. Magee. Leiden: E. J. Brill.

Buridan, John. 2010. *Quaestiones super libro De generatione et corruptione Aristotelis,* edited by M. Steijger, P. J. J. M. Bakker, and J. M. M. H. Thijssen, History of Science and Medicine Library vol. 17. Leiden: E. J. Brill.

Curley, Edwin M. 1985. *The Collected Works of Spinoza,* vol. 1. Princeton: Princeton University Press.

Della Rocca, Michael. 1996. *Representation and the Mind-Body Problem in Spinoza.* New York: Oxford University Press.

Descartes, René. 1984. *Principles of Philosophy,* translation by R. P. Miller. Springer.

Field, Hartry. 1989. *Realism, Mathematics and Modality.* New York: Blackwell.

Freudenthal, Jacob. 1887. 'Spinoza und die Scholastik', in *Philosophische Aufsätze E. Zeller gewidmet.* Leibniz.

Heereboord, Adrian. 1680. *Meletamata philosophica.* Amsterdam.

Heinaman, Robert. 1997. 'Frede and Patzig on Definition in *Metaphysics* Z.10 and 11', in *Phronesis* XLII, pp. 283–97.

Ockham, William. 1967-1986. *Opera Theologica,* vol. 7, numerous editors. St. Bonaventure, NY: Franciscan Institute of St. Bonaventure University.

Schaffer, Jonathan. 2008. 'Monism', in *The Stanford Encyclopedia of Philosophy (Fall 2008 Edition)*, E. N. Zalta (ed.).
URL = http://plato.stanford.edu/archives/fall2008/entries/monism/.
Suárez, Francisco. 1994. *On Beings of Reason, Metaphysical Disputation LIV*, translation by John P. Doyle. Marquette University Press.
Wolfson, H., *The Philosophy of Spinoza*. Cambridge MA: Harvard University Press.

10
Why Spinoza is not an Eleatic Monist (Or Why Diversity Exists)

Yitzhak Y. Melamed

> Eternal Master, who reigned supreme
> Before all of creation was drawn
>
> (Attributed to Salomon Ibn-Gabirol)

Introduction[1]

'Why did God create the World?' is one of the traditional questions of theology. In the twentieth century this question was rephrased in a secularized manner as 'Why is there something rather than nothing?'[2] While creation – at least in its traditional, temporal, sense[3] – has little place in Spinoza's system, a variant of the same questions puts Spinoza's system under significant pressure. According to Spinoza, God, or the substance, has infinitely many modes. This infinity of modes follow from the essence of God. If we ask: 'Why must God have modes?', we seem to be trapped in a real catch. On the one hand, Spinoza's commitment to thoroughgoing rationalism demands that there must be a reason for the existence of the radical plurality of modes.[4] On the other hand, the asymmetric dependence of modes on the substance seems to imply that the substance does not *need* the modes, and that it can exist without the modes. But if the substance does not need the modes, then why are there modes at all? Furthermore, Spinoza cannot explain the existence of modes as an arbitrary act of grace on God's side since Spinoza's God does not act arbitrarily. Surprisingly, this problem has hardly been addressed in the existing literature on Spinoza's metaphysics, and it is my primary aim here to draw attention to this problem.[5]

In the first part of the chapter I will present and explain the problem of justifying the existence of infinite plurality modes in Spinoza's system. In the second part of the chapter I consider the radical solution to the problem according to which modes do not really exist, and show that this solution must be rejected upon consideration. In the third and final part of the chapter I will suggest my own solution according to which the essence of God is *active* and it is this feature of God's essence which requires the flow of modes from God's essence. I also suggest that Spinoza considered radical infinity and radical unity to be roughly the same, and that the absolute infinity of what follow from God's essence is grounded in the absolute infinity of God's essence itself.

10.1 The problem

Spinoza defines a mode at the very opening of the *Ethics.*

> E1d5: By mode I understand the affections of a substance, or that which is in another through which it is also conceived [*Per modum intelligo substantiae affectiones, sive id, quod in alio est, per quod etiam concipitur*].

A mode is an affection, i.e. a quality which depends on its substance both for its existence (it is 'in another') and for its conception (it is 'conceived through another'). In contrast to the mode, a substance is defined as being 'in itself' and 'conceived through itself.'

> E1d3: By substance I understand what is in itself and is conceived through itself, i.e., that whose concept does not require the concept of another thing, from which it must be formed [*Per substantiam intelligo id quod in se est et per se concipitur; hoc est id cuius conceptus non indiget conceptu alterius rei, a quo formari debeat*].[6]

A mode depends on its substance in order to be and be conceived while the substance does not depend on another thing. The first proposition of part one of the *Ethics* relies on the two definitions above in order to state that the substance is *prior* to its modes.

> E1p1: A substance is prior in nature to its affections [*Substantia prior est natura suis affectionibus*].

Spinoza's understanding of the substance–mode relation as exhibiting an asymmetric dependence of the modes on the substance is in line with the standard view of this relation among early modern philosophers.[7]

From the two definitions and the proposition above one could conclude that a state of affairs in which the substance exists without having any modes is possible. However, Spinoza is also committed to strict necessitarianism, i.e., the view that whatever is possible is actual and in fact, necessary, and that whatever is not necessary is not possible.[8] Spinoza also thinks that God, the unique and infinite substance, has modes. In one of the most central propositions of the *Ethics*, Spinoza proves that modes must follow from the essence of God.

> E1p16: From the necessity of the divine nature there must follow infinitely many things in infinitely many modes (i.e., everything which can fall under an infinite intellect) [*Ex necessitate divinae naturae infinita infinitis modis (hoc est, omnia, quae sub intellectum infinitum cadere possunt) sequi debent*].

Thus, given E1p16 it seems that a state of affairs in which God exists without its modes is strictly impossible since the flow of the modes from God's essence or nature is necessary. Indeed, Spinoza stresses this point toward the end of Part One of the *Ethics*. In E1p33, Spinoza argues that

> Things could have been produced by God in no other way, and in no other order than they have been produced [*Res nullo alio modo, neque alio ordine a Deo produci potuerunt, quam productae sunt*].

And in the second scholium to this proposition he claims,

> God can never decree anything different, and never could have, *or* that God was not before his decrees, and cannot be without them [*Deum ante sua decreta non fuisse, nec sine ipsis esse posse*] (II/75/15).

God's decrees are the effects, i.e., the modes which follow from God's essence, and according to the scholium above God cannot be without his effects, or modes.[9]

One way of putting the problem in sharp relief is by considering the relation between the realms[10] Spinoza terms '*natura naturans*' and '*natura naturata*.' Spinoza explains this important distinction in E1p29s:

> Before I proceed further, I wish to explain here – or rather to advise [the reader] what we must understand by *Natura naturans* and *Natura naturata*. For from the preceding I think it is already established that by *Natura naturans* we must understand what is in itself and is conceived through itself, *or* such attributes of substance as express an eternal and infinite essence, i.e. (by P14C1 and P17C2), God, insofar as he is considered as a free cause.
>
> But by *Natura naturata* I understand whatever follows from the necessity of God's nature, *or* from any of God's attributes, i.e., all the modes of God's attributes insofar as they are considered as things which are in God, and can neither be nor be conceived without God.

Natura naturans is the realm of God's essence, i.e., substance and its attributes. Spinoza provides three characterizations of this realm. It is 'in itself', 'conceived through itself', and constitutes God as a free cause, as cause that is determined to act by itself alone (see E1d7 and E1p17). *Natura naturata* is the realm of modes, i.e., of what follows from God's essence (E1p16). In E1p29s

Spinoza stresses that *Natura naturata* cannot be or be conceived without *natura naturans*. In contrast, *natura naturans* does not depend on the existence of *natura naturata*, hence it is not the case that *natura naturans* needs *natura naturata* in order to be or be conceived. Why then does *natura naturata* exist and not only *natura naturans*? Or in other words, why are there modes at all? The question seems to be perfectly clear and legitimate, and therefore Spinoza's rationalism commits him to provide an answer to this question. Yet, it is not clear where one should turn in order to find the answer. *Natura naturata* is caused by *natura naturans* and therefore it should be explained by *natura naturans* (E1a4). Yet, *natura naturans* is defined as ontologically and conceptually self-sufficient, and therefore it seems that the self-sufficiency of *natura naturans* should allow for (rather than ban) the existence of *natura naturans* without *natura naturata*.[11]

So far we discussed the question of the reason for the existence of any modes at all. A closely related, yet distinct, problem is how to explain the flow of the radical diversity of *natura naturata* from the indivisible unity of *natura naturans*. In proposition 12 and 13 of part 1 of the *Ethics* Spinoza argues that both the substance and attributes are strictly indivisible.

> E1p12: No attribute of a substance can be truly conceived from which it follows that the substance can be divided [*Nullum substantiae attributum potest vere concipi, ex quo sequatur, substantiam posse dividi*].
>
> E1p13: A substance which is absolutely infinite is indivisible [*Substantia absolute infinita est indivisibilis].*

The infinitely many attributes of Spinoza's God are not parts of God (or of God's essence), since this would conflict with E1p12. Rather they are infinitely many adequate conceptions of one and the same substance.[12] According to E1p16, from the unity and indivisibility of *natura naturans* follow *infinita infinitis modis* (which could be translated as either 'infinitely many things in infinitely many modes' or alternatively 'an infinity in infinite ways'). From E1p16 Spinoza derives the corollary that 'God is the efficient cause of all things which can fall under an infinite intellect' (E1p16c1). For Spinoza, the intellect – and even more so, the infinite intellect – cannot err.[13] Thus, E1p16c1 clearly implies that God is the cause of all things. The plentitude of *infinita infinitis modis* of *natura naturata* seems to outstrip any diversity that we may find in *natura naturans*. Even if we consider the infinity of attributes as constituting real diversity (rather than diversity of conceptions of one and the same *res*), it seems that when *natura naturans* flow into *natura naturata* it refracts further into another infinity which Spinoza stresses in the double infinity of the expression '*infinita infinitis modis*'.[14] It seems that within each attribute the flow from *natura naturans* into *natura naturata* involves refraction from unity and indivisibility into a plentitude of radical plurality and divisibility.[15] But what is the reason for this further refraction? If in the realm of *natura naturans* each attribute is strictly indivisible, why does the flow to *natura naturata* bring about any further diversity? What justifies the emergence of the many from the indivisible one?[16]

10.2 First attempt at a solution: acosmism

One radical solution to the problems we have discussed in the previous section is simply to deny that Spinoza ascribes any reality to *natura naturata*. This view of Spinoza was widely advocated among the German and British Idealists.[17] Shortly after Spinoza's death, several writers were already suggesting that Spinoza's philosophy was a revival of ancient Eleatic monism, which rejects the reality of change and diversification. Bayle makes this association quite explicitly in several passages in his dictionary,[18] while Leibniz argues (against Malebranche) that to claim that 'all things are only some evanescent or flowing modifications and phantasms, so to speak, of the one permanent divine substance' is to endorse 'that doctrine of most evil repute, which a certain subtle and profane writer recently introduced into the world, or *revived* [*pessimae notae doctrinam nuper scriptor quidem subtilis, at profanus, orbi invexit vel renovavit*] – that the very nature or substance of all things is God'.[19] There is little doubt that the 'subtle but indeed irreligious' writer in question is Spinoza, and it is quite plausible that the revived doctrines are those of the Eleatics.

Almost a century later, with the emergence of German Idealism, the identification of Spinoza with Eleatic monism became the standard view.[20] Hegel, for example, announces:

> Taken as a whole this constitutes the Idea of Spinoza, and it is just what was '*tò ón*' to the Eleatics [Dies ist im ganzen die Spinozistische Idee. Es ist dasselbe, was bei den Eleaten das *ón*']…. Spinoza is far from having proved this unity as convincingly as was done by the ancients; but what constitutes the grandeur of Spinoza's manner of thought is that he is able to renounce all that is determinate and particular, and restrict himself to the One, giving heed to this alone.[21]

A crucial impetus to the propagation of this view was the new understanding of Spinoza as a radical religious thinker, whose position was the complete opposite of atheism. According to this understanding – first suggested by Salomon Maimon in 1792[22] – Spinoza does not deny the reality of God, but rather the reality of the world ('cosmos') of finite things and diversification.[23]

> In Spinoza's system the unity is real while the diversity is merely ideal. In the atheistic system it is just the other way around. *The diversity is*

> *real* and grounded in the very nature of things, while the unity, which one observes in the order and regularity of nature, is consequently only coincidental; through this unity we determine our arbitrary system for the sake of our knowledge.
>
> *It is inconceivable how one could turn the Spinozistic system into atheism since these two systems are the exact opposites of each other* [my emphases]. Atheism denies the existence of *God*, Spinozism denies the existence of the *world*. Rather, Spinozism should be called 'acosmism'.[24]

Interestingly, Maimon contrasts Spinoza's position not only with atheism but also with Leibniz's view. The latter is taken to be a mere compromise between Spinozism and atheism, one which asserts the reality of both God and the diversified world.[25] (Doubtless few Leibnizians would be happy to find themselves described as *more* atheistic than Spinoza). These claims of Maimon initiated a radical change in the perception of Spinoza and in the next four decades we find them echoed time and again.[26] The person who throughout the eighteenth century was unquestionably taken as a damned atheist became a 'God intoxicated man',[27] in whose system there is 'too much God [*zu viel Gott*]'.[28] Hegel's endorsement of the acosmist interpretation of Spinoza had an enormous and lasting impact on nineteenth and early twentieth century perceptions of Spinoza both on the continent and in England.[29]

One of the main elements of the acosmist reading of Spinoza was the view of the plurality of modes and attributes as a mere illusion. Thus, Hegel writes:

> Parmenides has to reckon with illusion and opinion, the opposites of being and truth; *Spinoza likewise, with attributes, modes,* extension, movement, understanding, will, and so on.[30]

Hegel stresses the unreality of modes in several other crucial places in his discussions of Spinoza.[31] If modes are merely illusory then the question of the reason for their flow from the substance becomes far less urgent.[32] Hegel's response to our question is indeed quite radical. It simply rejects our very assumption that there *are* modes.

Despite the boldness and charm of the acosmist reading, I believe it must be ultimately rejected.[33] In the following, I summarize very briefly some of the main problems with this reading. (1). *Third Kind of Knowledge* – the third kind of knowledge 'proceeds from an adequate idea of the formal essence of certain attributes to the adequate knowledge of the essence of things' (E2p40s2). Spinoza's discussion of the third kind of knowledge in part five of the *Ethics* makes clear that it pertains to the knowledge of *finite* modes – such as our bodies, and minds as well (see, for example, E5p22 and E5p31). But were the finite modes mere illusions, why would they be the objects of the (adequate) third kind of knowledge? (2). *E1p36* – we have seen that in E1p16 Spinoza claims that the modes are just what follow necessarily from God's nature or essence. In E1p36 ('Nothing exists from whose nature some effect does not follow'[34]) Spinoza argues that everything, including God's nature, *must* have some effects. But, if the modes (i.e. the effects of God's nature) were illusory, then God's nature would not really have any effects.[35] (3) *The Parallelism among the Attributes* – in E2p7s Spinoza argues that the order and connection of causes in all attributes is the same.[36] This doctrine bluntly contradicts the acosmist reading of Spinoza, insofar as it clearly asserts the existence of a plurality of entities. Simply put, were Spinoza's substance a singular, undifferentiated, entity, it would be pointless to speak of any 'order' or 'connection' among things, since no plurality would obtain in such a world. (4) *Knowledge of God via Knowledge of Finite Nature* – in the fourth chapter of the TTP, Spinoza claims that 'we acquire a greater and more perfect knowledge of God as we gain more knowledge of natural things [*res naturales*]' (III/60).[37] Were finite things ('natural things') merely illusory, it would make little sense that by engaging with such illusions we could promote our knowledge of God. Spinoza continues by making the point even more explicit: 'To put it another way, since the knowledge of an effect through its cause is nothing other than the knowledge of the property of that cause [*causae proprietatem aliquam cognoscere*], the greater our knowledge of natural things, the more perfect is our knowledge of God's essence, which is the cause of all things' (III/60/11–12). Knowledge of finite things increases our knowledge of God, since these finite things are nothing but God's properties (or rather, *propria*), which follow from God's essence.[38] Clearly, granting such an elevated status to finite things (i.e., being properties of God) is hardly consistent with viewing them as illusions. (5) *'Falls under the Intellect'* – in E1p16 Spinoza equates the *infinita infinitis modis* which follow from God's essence with 'everything which can fall under an infinite intellect [*omnia, quae sub intellectum infinitum cadere possunt*].' For Spinoza, the only cause of error is the imagination, while the perceptions of the intellect are always adequate (E2p41). Thus, what 'falls under' the intellect cannot be an illusion.[39] (6) *Only Nothingness has no Properties* – Spinoza subscribes to the view that reality comes in degrees and like Descartes he accepts that only nothingness has no properties;[40] the more reality or being [*esse*] a thing has the more properties or attributes belong to it (E1p10s and E1p16d). Since God is real, it must have properties. In fact, since God is absolutely infinite and most real, it must have infinitely many attributes.[41]

Interestingly, Spinoza uses the last consideration not only in order to argue that God must have infinitely many attributes (E1p10s), but also to justify the infinite abundance of modes that follow from God's essence (E1p16d). Thus, the last consideration not only helps refute the acosmist interpretation, but also provides some motivation for the existence of modes: the flow of the modes from God's essence must result from the definition of God as an absolutely infinite being. We can thus conclude that the acosmist interpretation – which cuts the problem of explaining the flow of modes at its roots – cannot be right. I turn now to suggesting an alternative solution to our problem.

10.3 The suggested solution: modes as necessitated by God's activity and absolute infinity

We have already seen Spinoza's claim in E1p33s2 that 'God cannot be without his decrees.' Spinoza makes a closely related claim in E2p3s. E2p3 itself states:

> In God there is necessarily an idea, both of his essence and of everything that necessarily follows from his essence.

In the scholium to this proposition Spinoza criticizes the vulgar and anthropomorphic conception of God's power that ascribes to God free will. God's actions, claims Spinoza, are just as necessary as the flow of ideas in God's understanding. Then, he makes the following statement:

> We have shown in IP34 that God's power is nothing except God's active essence. And so *it is as impossible for us to conceive that God does not act* as it is to conceive that he does not exist [*Deinde Propositione 34. partis 1. ostendimus, Dei potentiam nihil esse, praeterquam Dei actuosam essentiam; adeoque tam nobis impossibile est concipere, Deum non agere, quam Deum non esse*].

E1p34 reads:

> God's power is his essence itself [*Dei potentia est ipsa ipsius essentia*].
>
> Dem.: For from the necessity alone of God's essence it follows that God is the cause of himself (by P11) and (by P16 and P16C) of all things.

The above passages from E2p3s and E1p34 seem to show that for Spinoza God's essence (i.e. *natura naturans*) must be active, and that it is just as impossible for *natura naturans* not to be active as it is impossible for it not to exist. This insight might advance us significantly toward an answer to our question. Consider now a state of affairs (which, as we have just seen, is strictly impossible for Spinoza) in which *natura naturans* presumably exists without *natura naturata*. Can *natura naturans* still have any causal efficacy? Well, it could still cause *itself*, and thus would have causal efficacy. But would it be proper to describe such a state of affairs as active? I do not think so.

In a hypothetical world in which only *natura naturans* exists, and in which *natura naturans* is just causing itself, *natura naturans* would be *just as active as it is passive*. The same causal relation that supports ascription of activity to *natura naturans* (insofar as *natura naturans* is the cause or agent of the action) would equally support ascription of passivity to *natura naturans* (insofar as *natura naturans* is also the effect or patient of the same act). In other words, in the absence of *natura naturata*, the self-causing activity of *natura naturans* would make it 'beyond action and passion,' and this I think Spinoza is not willing to allow since the activity of *natura naturans* is essential to it.

Thus, it would seem that *natura naturans* generates *natura naturata* by virtue of its own character as an *active* entity. In other words, the reason for the existence of *natura naturata* lies in the nature of *natura naturans*. In the same way that it is essential for *natura naturans* to be infinite (see E1d6), it is equally essential that *natura naturans* be active. But in order for *natura naturans* to be active it must cause *natura naturata*.

As far as I can see, this explanation provides a prima facie good and deep explanation for the generation of *natura naturans*, but we still have to address our other question. Why does the unity and divisibility of *natura naturans* turn into, or flow into, the radical plurality of the *infinita infinitis modis* of *natura naturata*? The answer to this question appears to be even more surprising.

Spinoza defines God as an 'absolutely infinite being':

> E1d6: By God I understand a being absolutely infinite, that is, a substance consisting of an infinity of attributes, of which each one expresses an eternal and infinite essence [*Per Deum intelligo ens absolute infinitum, hoc est, substantiam constantem infinitis attributis, quorum unumquodque aeternam, et infinitam essentiam exprimit*].

He then turns to explain why God must be defined as *absolutely* infinite:

> E1d6e: I say absolutely infinite, not infinite in its own kind; for if something is only infinite in its own kind, we can deny infinite attributes of it but if something is absolutely infinite, whatever expresses essence and involves no negation pertains to its essence.

For Spinoza, a proper definition expresses the essence of the thing defined.[42] Hence, absolute infinity must belong to God's essence. Indeed, on several occasions Spinoza ascribes absolute infinity to *natura naturans*. Thus, for example, in E1p16d he speaks about the 'divine nature that has absolutely infinite attributes [*natura divina infinita absolute attributa habeat*]' (II/60/27). Thus, God's absolute infinity does not emerge only at the realm of *natura naturata*, but is already present in the realm constituting God's essence: *natura naturans*. Hence, the absolute infinity of *infinita infinitis modis* which flows from God's essence has its ground in the absolute infinity of God's essence. Yet, one could and should press the question further. How can *natura naturans* be on the one hand absolutely infinite, yet, on the other hand, unified to the extent that it is indivisible? It is true that for Spinoza both infinity and uniqueness are *not* numerical. On several occasions Spinoza stresses that it is improper to call God 'one [*unum*]', since number, including the number one, doesn't pertain to God's essence.[43] Instead, Spinoza claims, we can only say that God is 'unique [*unicum*]' (E1p14c1). Relying on this claim one could perhaps argue that for Spinoza radical unity and infinity are not only not opposed but perhaps even identical (under this reading, both infinity and uniqueness are opposed to number and finite quantity). This is, I think, an interesting suggestion that demands a close study of Spinoza's understanding of number and infinity.[44] Yet, even if this last, speculative, claim turns out to be right, we could and should ask ourselves two further questions. First, does *natura naturata* have any feature that distinguishes it from *natura naturans*? In E1p4, Spinoza makes a claim that seems to be his own formulation of the Identity of Indiscernibles that rules out brute difference.[45] Thus, if *natura naturata* is to be in any sense distinct from *natura naturans* there must be some qualitative feature that distinguishes the two. This qualitative feature could have been the mere activity of *natura naturans* as opposed to the fact that *natura naturata* is being acted on. But, as has been noted before, Spinoza seems to suggest another crucial difference between *natura naturans* and *natura naturata*: the former, but not latter, is indivisible. Thus, our original question may now come and haunt us again: Why does the indivisibility of *natura naturans* flow into the divisibility of *natura naturata*? Since *natura naturans* is the cause of *natura naturata*, how can we explain the appearance of divisibility in the effect which was never present in the cause?

Summary

In the current chapter I have attempted to draw attention to an important problem in Spinoza's philosophy that so far has hardly been addressed. I argued that Spinoza must provide an explanation for the existence of the diversity of things that follows from the unity of God's essence, and that providing such an explanation is not a trivial task. In the second part, I have considered the acosmist interpretation of Spinoza suggested by the German Idealists which solves the problem simply by ascribing to Spinoza the rejection of the reality of finite things and diversity. I have pointed out several considerations that tell strongly against this reading of Spinoza. In the third part of this chapter I have argued that *natura naturans* must generate *natura naturata* not because it lacks anything but rather because activity is an essential feature of *natura naturans* itself which requires causation that is not merely reflexive. Finally, I have attempted to explain the emergence of radical diversity from God's indivisible essence. While some crucial questions still remain, I hope this chapter made significant progress in addressing most aspects of the question originally posed.

Notes

Is Spinoza an existence, or priority, monist? Oddly enough in his excellent, influential, *Stanford Encyclopedia of Philosophy* entry on 'Monism', Jonathan Schaffer lists Spinoza under *both* headings. As far as I can see, the source of this confusion is that Schaffer's definition of *priority monism* is not precise enough and lumps together a variety of priority relations. Thus, it would seem that according to Schaffer's rather loose understanding of priority, even a view which (i) grants priority to the cause over the effect, and (ii) affirms the existence of an ultimate cause for anything that is, should qualify as *bona fide* 'priority monism.' While I find Schaffer's distinction between existence and priority monism very helpful, I believe it needs more fine tuning in order to avoid confusing priority monism with existence monism on the one hand (as in the case specifying Spinoza's kind of monism), with pluralist views (e.g., monotheism) on the other hand.

1. Unless otherwise marked, all references to the *Ethics,* the early works of Spinoza, and Letters 1–29 are to Curley's translations. In references to the other letters of Spinoza I have used Shirley's translation (henceforward, **S**). I use the following standard abbreviations for Spinoza's works: **TIE** – *Treatise on the Emendation of the Intellect* [*Tractatus de Intellectus Emendatione*], **TTP** –*Theological-Political Treatise* [*Tractatus Theologico-Politicus*], **DPP** – *Descartes' Principles of Philosophy* [*Renati des Cartes Principiorum Philosophiae Parts I & II],* **CM** – *Metaphysical Thoughts* [*Cogitata Metaphysica*], **KV** – *Short Treatise on God, Man, and his Well-Being* [*Korte Verhandeling van God de Mesch en deszelfs Welstand*], **Ep.** – *Letters.* Passages in the *Ethics* will be referred to by means of the following abbreviations: a(-xiom), c(-orollary), p(-roposition), s(-cholium) and app(-endix); 'd' stands for either 'definition' (when it appears immediately to the right of the part of the book), or 'demonstration' (in all other cases). Hence, E1d3 is the third definition of part 1 and E1p16d is the demonstration of proposition 16 of part 1. I am indebted to Steven Nadler, Mike LeBuffe, and Philip Goff for helpful comments on an earlier version of this chapter.
2. See Heidegger, *Einführung in die Metaphysik,* 1. For two insightful analytic discussions of this questions, see Nozick, *Philosophical Explanations,* 115–164, and Rundle, *Why There Is Something Rather Than Nothing.*
3. In the early *Cogitata Metaphysica* Spinoza frequently refers to creation and 'created things' though it is not clear that even at this stage he takes creation as a process occurring in time (see CM II x).
4. On Spinoza's strict commitment to the Principle of Sufficient Reason (i.e., the claims that everything must be explainable), see Della Rocca, Spinoza, Ch. 1, and Melamed and Lin, 'The Principle of Sufficient Reason.'
5. For a notable exception see Steven Nadler's essay in this volume. Our chapters pursue different strategies to address this question.
6. On the development of Spinoza's definitions of substance and mode in the early drafts of the *Ethics*, see my article, 'The Building Blocks of Spinoza's Metaphysics.'
7. Scholarly debates about the relation: Curley and Della Rocca do not challenge the asymmetric nature of the dependence.
8. For a statement of Spinoza's necessitarianism, see E1p33. For an excellent discussion of this issue, see Garrett's, 'Spinoza's Necessitarianism.'

9. This does not necessarily mean that God *depends* on the modes, since, as I will shortly argue, God must generate the modes by virtue of a feature that belongs to his essence.
10. I call *natura naturans* and *natura naturata* 'realms' since both are populated by *res* (though at least in the case of *natura naturans* there is only one *res* at stake. I take the distinction between Spinoza's substance and the attributes as a distinction of reason. For a detailed discussion of this issue, see my 'The Building Blocks of Spinoza's Metaphysics,' Part II.).
11. The question of the reason for the existence of modes in Spinoza continues another traditional problem in metaphysics (in addition to the question about the reasons for God's creation). Traditionally, accidents were considered to depend *asymmetrically* on their substance, yet some medieval writers held that substances cannot be without their accidents. See Normore. 'Accidents and Modes,' 674–5. Similarly in the *Mondaology* (§ 21) Leibniz argues that the Monad (which is prior to its states) cannot subsist without some property [*affection*].
12. For a discussion of the relation between the substance and its attributes, see Della Rocca, *Representation and the Mind-Body Problem*, 157–71, and Melamed 'The Building Blocks of Spinoza's Metaphysics', Part II.
13. 'Knowledge of the first kind is the only cause of falsity, whereas knowledge of the second and third kind is necessarily true' (E2p41). Knowledge of the first kind is 'opinion or imagination' (E2p40s2).
14. For a more detailed discussion, see my 'Spinoza's Metaphysics of Thought.'
15. Indeed, Spinoza stresses explicitly that modes and only modes are divisible. See KV I/26/8–16.
16. This question has a long history as well. If the created world contains a plurality of things and God is simple, it seems that the effect of a simple being can be diverse. However, many medieval philosophers adhered to the view that the effect of a simple being must be simple itself too (since otherwise, the diversity would be brute). See Maimonides, *Guide* II 22 (P II 317).
17. For a discussion of the German Idealist interpretation of Spinoza as an 'acosmist', see my 'Salomon Maimon and the Rise of Spinozism,' and 'Acosmism or Weak Individuals?' For the British Idealists' reading of Spinoza, see Parkinson, 'Spinoza and British Idealism.' Parts of the current section of this chapter are adopted from my 'Acosmism or Weak Individuals?'.
18. See the entries 'Xenophanes' and 'Zeno of Elea' (remark K). Spinoza's own claim in Letter 73 that he sides 'with all the ancient philosophers [*cum omnibus antiquis Philosophis*]' in asserting that all things are in God might tempt the reader to think that Spinoza himself associated his views with the Eleatics. However, Spinoza's discussion of Zeno's argument against the reality of motion is highly critical (DPP IIp6s| I/192–6) and clearly defends the reality of movement and change.
19. Italics mine. 'On Nature Itself, or On the Inherent Force and Actions of Created Things' (1698) (Gerhardt IV, 508–9| Loemker, 502). Cf. Adams, *Leibniz*, 132. For further texts in which Leibniz associates Spinoza with Eleatic philosophy, see his annotations to Oldenburg's Letter from October 1676 (A VI–3, 370), and §21 of the *Discours sur la théologie naturelle des Chinois* (1716). I am indebted to Mogens Laerke for the latter reference.
20. See for example Maimon's *Streifereien*, 40–1 (*Gesammelte Werke* IV 62–3): 'Spinoza behauptet nach dem Parmenides 'nur das Reelle, vom Verstande begriffene existiert, was mit dem Reellen in einem endlichen Wesen verknüpft ist, ist bloß

die Einschränkung des Reellen, eine Negation, der keine Existenz beigelegt werden kann". Similarly, Schopenhauer repeatedly claims that 'Spinoza was a mere reviver of the Eleatics' (*Parerga and Paralipomena*, vol. 1, 71, 76–77). An interesting work in this context is *Natur und Gott nach Spinoza* by Karl Heinrich Heydenreich (1789. Reprinted in the *Aetas Kantiana* series (Num. 98), Brussels 1973). The book discusses at length Spinoza's philosophy and its contemporary interpretation in the form of a dialogue between Parmenides and Xenophanes. I am unaware of any major discussion of Spinoza in this period (roughly 1790 to 1840) which fails to make this association.

21. Hegel, *Lectures on the History of Philosophy*, vol. 3 pp. 257–8, cf. the same lectures, vol. 1 p. 244, and Hegel's *Lectures on the Philosophy of Religion*, vol.1, 376.
22. The view of Spinoza as annihilating individual things is already mentioned in Jacobi's *Über der Lehre der Spinoza* (1785, 1789). While there is no doubt, to my mind, that Maimon read Jacobi's discussion of Spinoza (and clearly Hegel was strongly influenced by Jacobi's writing on Spinoza), it is not at all clear that Jacobi ascribed to Spinoza the same acosmistic position as Maimon and Hegel did. Jacobi suggests that for Spinoza finite things are not real (i.e., are *non-entia*) in very few passages (Jacobi, *Main Philosophical Writings*, 220–1 (§§. Xii and xix)| *Werke*, 1,1, 100 and 102), and the issue was far less central to his reading of Spinoza in comparison with those of Maimon and Hegel. Furthermore, Jacobi thought that Spinoza's strict and consistent rationalism led to the annihilation of the infinite as well as the finite, i.e., it led to nihilism and atheism. Maimon may have had this view of Jacobi in mind, but gave it a different twist, far removed from Jacobi's original contention, by arguing that Spinoza was a radical *religious* thinker who denied the reality of anything but God. For a very helpful discussion of Jacobi's view on the reality of finite things in Spinoza, see Franks, *All or Nothing*, 10, 95 and 170.
23. Maimon himself endorsed the very same view (i.e., 'acosmism') in his early Hebrew manuscript, written (mostly) in 1778, before his migration to Germany and his first encounter with Spinoza's writings: 'It is impossible to conceive any other existence but His, may he be blessed, no matter whether it is a substantial or an accidental existence. And this is the secret of the aforementioned unity [that God is the cause of world in all four respects: formally, materially, efficiently and finally], namely, *that only God, may he be blessed, exists, and that nothing but him has any existence at all'*. (*Hesheq Shelomo* (Hebrew: Solomon's Desire), 139. My translation and emphasis) Cf. my article, 'Salomon Maimon and the Rise of Spinozism in German Idealism', 79–80.
24. 'Es ist unbegreiflich, wie man das spinozistische System zum atheistischen machen konnte, da sie doch einander gerade entgegengesetzt sind. In diesem wird das Dasein *Gottes*, in jenem aber das Dasein der *Welt* geleugnet. Es müßte also eher das akosmische System heißen.' (*Lebensgeschichte*, 217. This passage, like many other theoretical passages, is omitted in Murray's translation. The present translation is mine).
25. Maimon, *Lebensgeschichte*, 217.
26. 'For Spinoza the absolute is substance, and no being is ascribed to the finite; his position is therefore monotheism and acosmism. So strictly is there only God, that there is no world at all; in this [position] the finite has no genuine actuality' (Hegel, *Lectures on the Philosophy of Religion*, vol. 1, 432). For similar claims by Hegel, see the same work, page 377, *Lectures on the History of Philosophy*, vol. 3, page 281, and *The Encyclopedia Logic*, pages 10, 97 and 226–7. For Hegel's criticism of the 'popular' view which asserts the reality of both God *and* the world of finite

things, see *Lectures on the History of Philosophy*, vol. 3, 280–1: 'Reason cannot remain satisfied with this 'also', with indifference like this' [*Die Vernunft kann bei solchem* auch, *solcher Gleichgültigkeit nicht stehenbleiben*]'.
27. *Novalis Schriften*, III 651.
28. Hegel, *Lectures on the History of Philosophy*, vol. 3, 282.
29. Among the British Idealists there was a tendency to moderate *some* aspects of the acosmist reading (Joachim, for example, occasionally claims that modes are only 'in part illusory' (*A Study of the Ethics of Spinoza*, 112)), but the general outline of this interpretation was endorsed by both Caird and Joachim. For Caird's and Joachim's Hegelian readings of Spinoza, see Parkinson, 'Spinoza and British Idealism.' The identification of Spinoza with Eleatic philosophy reaches its peak in Kojève's discussion of the 'acosmism of Parmenides–Spinoza' (*Introduction to the Reading of Hegel*, 106 (n. 3), 123–5).
30. 'So bekommt Parmenides mit dem Scheine und der Meinung, dem Gegenteil des Seins und der Wahrheit, zu tun; so Spinoza mit den Attributen, den Modis, der Ausdehnung, Bewegung, dem Verstande, Willen usf'. Hegel, *The Science of Logic*, 98 (Italics mine).
31. 'In Spinozism it is precisely the mode as such which is untrue; substance alone is true and to it everything must be brought back. But this is only to submerge all content in the void, in a merely formal unity lacking all content' (*Science of Logic*, 328). 'No truth at all is ascribed to finite things or the world as a whole in [Spinoza's] philosophy' (*Encyclopedia Logic*, 227 [§ 151a]). '[T]he understanding is ranked by Spinoza only among *affections*, and *as such has no truth*' (Italics mine. *Lectures on the History of Philosophy*, III 269. Cf. III 280–1, 288). Cf. *Lectures on the Philosophy of Religion*, I 377 and 432. On the unreality of attributes, see *Science of Logic*, 98 and 538.
32. We might still have to provide an explanation for the alleged *illusion* of the existence and flow of modes from the nature of God.
33. For consideration that provide prima facie support for the acosmist reading, see my 'Building Blocks of Spinoza's Metaphysics,' Part II. For an impressive contemporary defense of this reading, see Della Rocca, 'Rationalism, Idealism, Monism and Beyond.'
34. *'Nihil existit, ex cujus natura aliquis effectus non sequatur'*. This (mostly neglected) proposition states a principle that should properly be termed 'the principle of sufficient effect': everything must have an effect (and not only a cause, as the principle of sufficient reason stipulates).
35. See Parkinson ('Hegel, Pantheism and Spinoza', 455) for a similar argument. This argument is somewhat less conclusive since *natura naturans* could just cause itself and thus satisfy E1p16.
36. '[W]hether we conceive nature under the attribute of Extension, or under the attribute of Thought, or under any other attribute, we shall find one and the same order, or one and the same connection of causes, i.e., that the same things follow one another.'
37. Translation modified. Spinoza makes similar claims in several other texts. See, for example, E5p24.
38. On Spinoza's modes as God's *propria*, see my 'Spinoza's Metaphysics of Substance,' §6.
39. Furthermore, in E1p16d Spinoza insinuates that the intellect infers [*concludit*] the modes.
40. See Spinoza, Ep. 9 (IV/44/34–45/25), and Descartes, *Principles of Philosophy*, I 52.

41. See E1p10s and Ep. 9 (IV/44/34–45/25).
42. See TIE § 95 and Ep. 34.
43. 'With regard to the demonstration that I establish in the Appendix to my Geometrical Proof of Descartes' Principles, namely that God only be improperly called one or single, I reply that a thing can be called one or single only in respect of its existence, not of its essence. For we do not conceive things under the category of numbers unless they are included in a common class... It is clear that a thing cannot be called one or single unless another thing has been conceived which, as I have said, agrees with it. Now since the existence of God is his very essence, and since we can form no universal idea of his essence, it is certain that he who calls God one or single has no true idea of God, or is speaking of him very improperly' (Ep. 50). For a helpful discussion of this important passage, see Geach, 'Spinoza and the Divine Attributes', 21–23.
44. For Spinoza's view on the nature of mathematics and mathematical objects, see Ramon, *Qualité et quantité*, and Melamed, 'The Exact Science of Nonbeings.'
45. E1p4: 'Two or more distinct things are distinguished from one another, either by a difference in the attributes of substance or by a difference in their affections.' For a discussion of E1p4 and the Identity of Indiscernibles, see Della Rocca, *Representation*, 131–2.

Bibliography

Adams, Robert Merrihew. *Leibniz: Determinist, Theist, Idealist*. Oxford: Oxford University Press, 1994

Bayle, Pierre. *Dictionaire historique et critique par Mr. Pierre Bayle*. Amsterdam: Compagnie des Libraires.

——, 5 volumes. *The Dictionary Historical and Critical of Mr. Peter Bayle*. London: Routledge/Thoemmes Press, 1997.

Caird, John. *Spinoza*. Edinburgh: Blackwood, 1888.

Curley, Edwin. *Spinoza's Metaphysics: An Essay in Interpretation*. Cambridge Mass.: Harvard University Press, 1969.

Della Rocca, Michael. *Representation and the Mind-Body Problem in Spinoza*, Oxford: Oxford University Press, 1996.

——, *Spinoza* (New York: Routledge 2008).

——, 'Rationalism, Idealism, Monism and Beyond' in Fösrter and Melamed (eds.), *Spinoza and German Idealism* (Cambridge: Cambridge University Press, forthcoming).

Descartes, Rene. *Oeuvres de Descartes* [AT]. 12 volumes. Edited by Charles Adam and Paul Tannery. Paris: J. Vrin, 1964–76.

Franks, Paul W., *All or Nothing: Systematicity, Transcendental Arguments, and Skepticism in German Idealism*. Cambridge Mass.: Harvard University Press, 2005.

Geach, Peter T., 'Spinoza and the Divine Attributes' *Royale Institute of Philosophy Supplement* (1971), 15–27.

Hegel, G.W.F. *Gesammelte Werke (Kritische Ausgabe)*. Hamburg: Meiner, 1968.

——. *The Science of Logic*. Translated by A.V. Miller. London: Allen and Unwin, 1969.

——. *Lectures on the Philosophy of Religion*. Edited by Peter C. Hodgson. Berkeley and Los Angeles: University of California Press, 1984.

——, *Werke*. Frankfurt am Mein: Suhrkamp, 1986.

——. *The Encyclopedia Logic*. Translated and edited by T.F. Geraets, W.A. Suchtig and H.S. Harris. Indianapolis: Hackett, 1991.

——. *Lectures on the History of Philosophy*. 3 volumes. Translated by E.S. Haldane and F.H. Simson. London: University of Nebraska Press 1995.

Heidegger,Marin, *Einführung in die Metaphysik* (Tübingen: Niemeyer, 1953).

Heidenreich, Karl Heinrich. *Natur und Gott nach Spinoza*. Leipzig: Joh. Gottfr. Müllerschen, 1789 (*Aetas Kantiana*, Bruxelles 1973).

Jacobi, F.H., *Werke*. Edited by Klaus Hammacher and Walter Jaeschke. Hamburg: Meiner, 1998.

——, *The Main Philosophical Writings and the Novel Allwill*. Translated and edited by George di Giovanni. Montreal: McGill–Queen's University Press, 1994.

Joachim, Harold H. *A Study of the Ethics of Spinoza*. Oxford: Clarendon Press, 1901.

Kojève, Alexandre. *Introduction to the Reading of Hegel: Lectures on the Phenomenology of Spirit*. Translated by James H. Nicholas. Ithaca: Cornell University Press, 1969

Leibniz, G.W. *Die philosophischen Schriften von Gottfried Wilhelm Leibniz*. 7 volumes. Edited by C.J. Gerhardt. Berlin: Weidman, 1875–90. [Reprint, Hildsheim: Olms, 1965. Cited by volume and page].

——. *Philosophical Papers and Letters*. Translated an edited by Leroy E. Loemker. 2nd edition. Dordrecht: Kluwer, 1989.

——, *Philosophical Essays*, translated and edited by Roger Ariew and Dan Garber (Hackett: Indianapolis, 1989).

Maimon, Salomon. *Gesammelte Werke* [**GW**]. Edited by Valerio Verra. Hildshein: Olms 1965– 1976.

——. *Salomon Maimons Lebensgeschichte*. Edited by Zwi Batscha. Frankfurt a.M.: Insel Verlag, 1984. [Orig. 1792–3].

——. *Autobiography*. Translated by J. Clark Murray. Urbana and Chicago: University of Illinois Press, 2001.

——. *Hesheq Shelomo* (Hebrew: *Solomon's Desire*). Posen 1778. Manuscript 8^{0}6426 at the National and University Library, Jerusalem.

Melamed, Yitzhak Y., 'On the Exact Science of Nonbeings: Spinoza's View of Mathematics.' *Iyyun – The Jerusalem Philosophical Quarterly* 49 (2000): 3–22.

——, 'Salomon Maimon and the Rise of Spinozism in German Idealism,' *Journal of the History of Philosophy* 42 (2004), 79–80.

——, 'Spinoza's Metaphysics of Substance: The Substance–Mode Relation as a Relation of Inherence and Predication', *Philosophy and Phenomenological Research* 78 (2009), 17–82.

——, 'Acosmism or Weak Individuals? Hegel, Spinoza, and the Reality of the Finite', *Journal of the History of Philosophy*, 44 (January 2010), 77–92.

——, 'The Building Blocks of Spinoza's Metaphysics: Substance, Attributes and Modes' in Michael Della Rocca (ed.), *The Oxford Handbook of Spinoza* (Oxford: Oxford University Press, forthcoming).

——, 'Spinoza's Metaphysics of Thought', *Philosophy and Phenomenological Research*, forthcoming.

Melamed, Yitzhak and Lin, Martin, 'Principle of Sufficient Reason', *The Stanford Encyclopedia of Philosophy (Fall 2010 Edition)*, Edward N. Zalta (ed.), URL = <http://plato.stanford.edu/archives/fall2010/entries/sufficient-reason/>.

Nadler, Steven, 'Spinoza's Monism and the reality of the Finite' in Goff, Philip (ed.), Spinoza on Monism (Palgrave: 2011).

Normore, Calvin G., 'Accidents and Modes' in *The Cambridge History of Medieval Philosophy*, ed. Robert Pasnau (Cambridge: Cambridge University Press, 2010), vol. 2, 674–85.

Novalis. *Novalis Schriften*. Edited by Richard Samuel, Hans Joachim Mähl, and Gertrud Schulz. Stuttgart: Kohlhammer, 1960–1988.

Nozick, Robert, *Philosophical Explanations* (Oxford: Clarendon Press, 1981).

Ramond, Charles. *Qualité et quantité dans la philosophie de Spinoza*. Paris: Presses Universitaires de France, 1995.

Rundle, Bede, *Why There Is Something Rather Than Nothing* (Oxford: Oxford University Press, 2004).

Parkinson, G.H.R., 'Hegel, Pantheism and Spinoza.' *Journal of the History of Idea* 38 (1977): 449–59

——, 'Spinoza and British Idealism: The Case of H.H. Joachim.' *British Journal of the History of Philosophy* 1 (1993): 109–23.

Schaffer, Jonathan, 'Monism', *Stanford Encyclopedia of Philosophy (Fall 2008 Edition)*, Edward Zalta (ed.), URL= <http://plato.stanford.edu/archives/fall2008/entries/monism/>.

Schopenhauer, Arthur. *Parerga and Paralipomena*. Translated by E.F.J. Payne. Oxford: Oxford University Press, 1974.

Spinoza, *Opera* [G]. 4 volumes. Edited by Carl Gebhardt. Heidelberg: Carl Winter, 1925.

——, *The Collected Works of Spinoza* [C]. Vol. 1. Edited and translated by Edwin Curley. Princeton: Princeton University Press, 1985.

——, *Tractatus Theologico-Politicus*. 2nd ed. Translated by Samuel Shirley. Indianapolis: Hackett, 2001.

——, *The Letters* [S]. Translated by Samuel Shirley. Indianapolis: Hackett, 1995.

11
Spinoza's Monism and the Reality of the Finite

Steve Nadler

The label 'monism' is notoriously ambiguous. Its metaphysical ramifications depend essentially on that to which the 'oneness' is supposed to apply: Is there only one *thing*? Or is ontological uniqueness being ascribed only at the level of *type*? And if the latter, does this mean that there is only a single type of thing in the universe (e.g., Berkeley's and later Leibniz's claim that only mind-like things are real[1])? Or does it mean, less restrictively, that there are many types of thing but only one instance of each type (e.g., there is only one mind or thinking thing; only one body or material thing; etc.) And, to take the metaphysically more interesting, Eleatic scenario, if there is only one thing – what has been called 'existence monism'[2] – then what are we to make of the apparent reality and plurality of individual items that populate the world around us?

In this essay, I propose to address some of these questions on Spinoza's behalf by examining a long-standing and oft-debated problem in his metaphysics: Does Spinoza's monism have the consequence that the division of mundane reality into particular individual things is only illusory? I argue that Spinoza, while a monist about substance, nonetheless does not deny (nor is he inadvertently committed to denying) the reality of particular individual things, or what he calls 'finite modes.' I shall do this by showing that a plurality of finite things with ontological integrity is not merely a brute fact but can be made to fit into (and thus justified by) his deductive system. In this way, we will have fewer reasons to be tempted by the acosmic or phenomenalist interpretation of his metaphysics, most prominently promoted by Hegel but defended as well by some recent commentators, according to which the breaking up of reality into singular individuals is only a matter of perception.

I

Let us begin with a brief overview of the non-negotiable elements of Spinoza's metaphysics.

Definition Three of Part One (ID3[3]) of the *Ethics* is about substance (*substantia*), the most basic metaphysical category of all and one that would be familiar to his contemporary philosophical readers:

> By substance I understand what is in itself [*in se est*] and is conceived through itself, i.e., that whose concept does not require the concept of another thing, from which it must be formed.

When Spinoza defines a substance ontologically as that which is 'in itself', he is employing the classic self-subsistence criterion of substance common to both the Aristotelian and Cartesian philosophies. A substance, taken in the primary manner, is that which is truly ontologically independent and not in or dependent upon something else for its being. It is, in a word, an individual thing in the truest sense of the term. To use an example that Spinoza himself would ultimately – once the full implications of his definition are clear – have to reject, an individual horse can be seen as a substance because its being is independent of the being of any other creature. (By contrast, the colour of the horse cannot exist by itself, without a subject in which to inhere, but is dependent upon the thing whose colour it is.) Spinoza also introduces in his definition an epistemological or conceptual component that corresponds to the ontological requirement: a substance is that which can be conceived or understood on its own terms, without any appeal to the concept of anything else. If x is a substance, then one can have a complete idea of x – one that specifies exactly and fully what x is and why it is as it is – without recourse to the idea of some other substance y. The content of my concept of x does not include or refer to the concept of any substance y. Again, to use what will ultimately prove to be an un-Spinozistic example, one can have a complete concept of any particular horse without having to think of some other horse, or tree, or human being – or any other substantial thing.

ID4 concerns what Spinoza calls 'attributes': 'By attribute I understand what the intellect perceives of a substance as constituting its essence.' An attribute is the most general and underlying nature of a thing. It is, in fact, the thing itself conceived through its principal property – or, better, the nature that underlies all of its properties. (Descartes, for example, had claimed that the attribute of mind or spiritual substance is thought or thinking, and the attribute of body or material substance is extension or three-dimensionality.) The attribute of a substance, as its essence, might be thought of as the determinable nature of which all of the particular properties of the thing are determinate manifestations. Thought is a determinable nature of which particular thoughts or ideas are determinate expressions. Extension is a determinable nature of which particular shapes or figures are determinate expressions. To speak of the attribute of a substance is to refer to the most general *kind* of thing that it is. Indeed, the attribute is so important for making a substance what it is in the most basic sense that if two substances have different attributes, then, as Spinoza states in IP2, they have absolutely nothing in common with each other – neither as the kinds of things they are nor (since all of a thing's properties are simply determinations of its attribute) through their properties.

The third category of Spinoza's ontology is 'mode'. ID5 states: 'By mode I understand the affections of a substance, or that which is in another through which it is also conceived.' A mode or affection of a substance is like the property of a thing. It is a particular and determinate way in which the thing exists. The exact shape and size of an individual human body are modes (or modifications) of that body; specific thoughts or ideas in the human mind are modes of that mind. As such, the modes of a thing are concrete manifestations of the attribute or nature constituting the thing. They therefore cannot be conceived without also conceiving the attribute or nature that underlies them. One cannot understand the circularity of a compact disc without conceiving what it is to be a circle (or to be extended in a circular way), which in turn cannot be understood without conceiving what it is to be extended, or what extension itself is. In this way, the meaning of IP1 – 'A substance is prior in nature to its affections' – becomes clear. What Spinoza has in mind in this, the first proposition of the work, is the ontological and the epistemological priority of substance over its modes, since modes are dependent upon the substance to which they belong for their being and for their being understood.

As we shall see, there are, in fact, two ways in which modes can relate to substance for Spinoza. Some modes of substance follow directly and immediately from the substance's attribute alone. Other modes follow indirectly and mediately, from the attribute through one or more of its modes. This distinction between what follows immediately from a substance and its attribute and what follows only mediately is crucial for understanding the structure of Spinoza's universe, especially the status of finite things and the dynamic relations that govern them.

So much for the basic categories of Spinoza's ontology.

II

Ethics IP1–15 are dedicated to demonstrating a number of things about substance defined as that which is in-itself and conceived through itself: (a) that it exists necessarily (i.e., is self-caused) and thus is eternal (IP7); (b) that it is absolutely infinite (IP8) and thus has infinite attributes (IP9); and (c) that it is therefore unique (IP14). There is in the universe only one substance, only one self-subsisting, eternal, infinite thing, and it exists necessarily. But God is defined as 'an absolutely infinite being or substance' (ID6). Therefore, the one substance that necessarily exists is God – or, to use a formulation introduced later in the work (IV Preface, G II.206; C I.544), 'God or Nature [*Deus sive Natura*]'. Only God or Nature is in-itself. And because God is absolutely *infinite* substance, God contains infinite attributes. Thus, Thought is an attribute of God or Nature; Extension is an attribute of God or Nature; and so on, for infinitely many other attributes which are necessarily unknown to us. Everything else that exists in the universe – that is, everything whatsoever – is a mode of one of God's attributes. Or, as IP16 boldly proclaims, 'whatever is, is in God.' This is the fundamental principle of Spinoza's substance monism.

The next step in Spinoza's progression to the finite modes moves from the attributes of substance – the eternal, infinite and necessary foundations of Nature – to a number of other features of Nature that are also eternal, infinite and necessary, just because they follow necessarily from eternal, infinite and necessary causes. Some of these follow as a spontaneously generated and inseparable effect from the power of God or Nature (and its attributes) alone; these are God or Nature's first effects. Others follow from God or Nature only in conjunction with these first effects. They, too, are infinite, eternal and necessary (because such are their causes); but, unlike the first effects, they do not follow from substance and its attributes alone.[4]

This distinction is explained in IP21 through IP23. IP21 states that 'all things which follow from the absolute nature of any of God's attributes have always had to exist and be infinite, or are, through the same attribute, eternal and infinite'. IP22, by contrast, says that 'whatever follows from some attribute of God insofar as it is modified by a modification which, through the same attribute, exists necessarily and is infinite, must also exist necessarily and be infinite'. IP23 makes the same case but in the opposite direction: 'Every mode which exists necessarily and is infinite has necessarily had to follow either from the absolute nature of some attribute of God, or from some attribute, modified by a modification which exists necessarily and is infinite.'

The necessary and infinite things that follow from God's attributes, whether they follow from the absolute nature of the attribute itself or from the attribute in so far as it is modified by something, have come to be known as the 'infinite modes'. Those infinite modes that do follow directly from the absolute nature of an attribute are the 'immediate infinite modes'. Those infinite modes that follow from an attribute only in so far as it is already modified by some mode (that is, by an immediate infinite mode) are the 'mediate infinite modes'.

The immediate infinite modes include the most universal and basic principles that govern all of the other things that belong to that aspect of the universe represented by the attribute. To get some idea of what Spinoza has in mind here, it is useful to turn to his earlier writings. In the *Treatise on the Emendation of the Intellect* (*TIE*) Spinoza speaks of 'those fixed and eternal things [that]...because of their presence everywhere, and most extensive power, they will be to us like universals, or genera of the definitions of singular changeable things, and the proximate causes of all things' (G II.37; C I.41); while these 'fixed and eternal things' are at least the attributes, they may also include what follows absolutely and immediately from an attribute. In the *Short Treatise*, Spinoza says that these are the very first elements of *Natura naturata*, the principal and most proximate effects of God or substance's – i.e., of *Natura naturans*' – causal power: 'God is the proximate cause of those things that are infinite and immutable, and which we say he has created immediately' (I.3, G I.36/C I.81). 'Turning now to universal *Natura Naturata*, or those modes or creatures which immediately depend on, or have been created by God ... We say, then, that these have been from all eternity, and will remain to all eternity, immutable, a work truly as great as the greatness of the workman' (I.9, G I.48/C I.91).

Spinoza is frustratingly vague on the content of the immediate infinite modes and very sparing with examples. A plausible example of an immediate infinite mode for Extension might be the laws of Euclidean geometry, since Extension (the attribute) is geometric space. I shall return to this question below, as well as to an investigation of the content of the *mediate* infinite modes, as both of these topics are an important element in my case for the deductive justification within Spinoza's system of the reality of finite modes. Suffice it here to say that the mediate infinite modes are secondary effects of the power of God or Nature, that is, what that infinite power brings about through the mediation of its primary effects, the immediate infinite modes.

Finally, in contrast with the infinite modes, there are finite modes. What makes a finite mode finite is that it is a limited expression of a certain nature. A circle is a limited way of being extended, one that excludes other ways of being extended. Moreover, a finite mode, should it actually exist at a particular time, is causally bounded by other modes of that attribute, which in turn are causally bounded by other modes, and so on *ad infinitum*. Each finite mode is 'finite in its own kind' because there are other things of the same nature (that is, other modes of the same attribute) that determine and limit its reality and action. For example, two existing bodies (which are finite modes of Extension) cannot occupy the same part of space at the same time; and the power and motion of one body is affected, in both positive and negative ways, by the powers and motions of other bodies around it.

III

To recap so far, then: for Spinoza, Nature at its most basic ontological level is one eternal, infinite substance. It also has many (indeed, infinite) general aspects, each represented by an attribute. One aspect of Nature is physical reality, or Extension; another aspect of Nature is mental reality, or Thought. And each of these aspects has its own universal features, or immediate infinite modes, applicable to whatever belongs to that aspect of Nature. There should be no question that Spinoza considers all of this as constituting real and abiding (even necessary and eternal) features of the universe.[5]

But what happens when we descend to the level of finite modes? This is where the question of the reality of individual things – human beings, horses, trees – in Spinoza's metaphysics arises, since the familiar items populating the world around us are, for Spinoza, finite modes or determinate and limited expressions of an attribute of infinite substance. Spinoza defines 'singular things' as 'things that are finite and have a determinate existence' (IID7). The bodies we apprehend in nature are singular things *qua* determinate and limited expressions of Extension; and minds are singular things *qua* determinate and limited expressions of Thought.

In fact, as we shall see, the question of the reality of finite modes can arise at two levels. Finite modes can be either formal, eternal essences of singular things that may or may not actually exist at any given time (what we have seen Spinoza, in the *TIE*, call 'the definitions of singular and changeable things'); or they can be actually existing singular things (that is, 'singular and changeable things' themselves, instantiations in duration of those formal essences). 'We conceive things as actual in two ways: either insofar as we conceive them to exist in relation to a certain time and place, or insofar as we conceive them to be contained in God...The things we conceive in this second way as true, or real, we conceive under a species of eternity' (VP29s). The formal essence of a singular thing (such as the eternal essence or definition of a particular extended body, specified as a geometric formula) is as much a finite determination of its attribute (Extension) as that singular thing would be if it actually exists. In the case of the human body, for example, this distinction informs Spinoza's claim that 'God is the cause, not only of the existence of this or that human body, but also of its essence (by IP25), which therefore must be conceived through the very essence of God (by Ia4), by a certain eternal necessity (by IP16), and this concept must be in God (by IIP3)' (VP22d). (To add a little more detail, which will be explained below: an infinite series of finite modes understood as formal essences makes up an immediate infinite mode under each attribute, while an infinite series of finite modes understood as durationally existing entities makes up a mediate infinite mode under each attribute.)

But are singular things real? Is the world around us truly constituted by or broken up into a plurality of really existing individuals (bodies and minds) as finite modes? Or, on the other hand, is such division and diversity only illusory? Are human beings, horses and trees, while certainly not independent of substance and its eternal infinite modes – after all, everything is 'in' God or Nature – nonetheless authentic parcels of reality? Or are they merely subjective elements of experience, the product of one's perceptual apprehension of the one eternal, infinite thing that is 'really' real?

Put another way – and this is the more precise question with which I am concerned below – how can Spinoza descend deductively, via the *mos geometricus*, from Nature's infinite, eternal and necessary starting points (substance, attributes, infinite modes) to the conclusion that there are finite modes, either as formal essences of singular things or as actually existing (and changing) singular things in nature? How can one validly derive what is finite and durational from what is infinite, necessary and eternal? There seems, *prima facie*, to be an unbridgeable logical gap here.[6] If an attribute is a singular, infinite and eternal nature, then presumably whatever follows from it necessarily must also be singular, infinite and eternal. Spinoza himself is aware of the deductive chasm between the infinite and the finite; in IP21 and IP22, he establishes that whatever follows from what is infinite (either an attribute itself or an attribute modified by an infinite mode) must itself be infinite. At the same time, Spinoza concludes in IP16 that 'from the necessity of the divine nature there must follow infinitely many things in infinitely many modes', and it seems clear that what is supposed to 'follow' from the divine nature are not just infinite modes, but finite modes as well, since these too 'can fall under an infinite intellect' (i.e., be known by God). But how can an infinite nature give rise to finite entities?

This question first gets raised in one of the last extant letters we have from Spinoza's correspondence. When Walter Ehrenfried von Tschirnhaus, a friend of Spinoza who was living in Paris in the mid-1670s, wrote to Spinoza in the summer of 1676, he pressed him on just this issue. He insisted that from the simple definition of any thing considered in itself, one is able to deduce only one property – namely, its essential property; to be able to deduce more than one property, one must add to the definition to make it more complex and so be able to generate more implications. But, Tschirnhaus (who had with him a copy of the manuscript of the *Ethics*) goes on to say, this principle 'seems to be at variance to some extent with Proposition 16 of the *Ethics*... In this proposition [which states that 'infinitely many things' follow from each of the attributes of God, each of which represents a simple essence] it is taken for granted that several properties can be deduced from the given definition of any thing.'

Now Tschirnhaus may have in mind here the multiplicity of universal and general features of things constituting the infinite modes and how these are supposed to follow from the attribute. But it is certain that, like Spinoza himself, he also has in mind the multiplicity of individual finite modes falling under each attribute. For right at the beginning of his letter, he asks Spinoza to explain 'how, from Extension as conceived in your philosophy, the variety of things can be demonstrated a priori... how from an attribute considered only by itself, for example, Extension, an infinite variety of bodies can arise' (Ep. 82).

This problem of how Spinoza, committed as he is to the absolute certainty provided by the geometric method, can deduce that there is a plurality of finite things – even if they together constitute a single infinite Nature – from a unique and simple infinite starting point has long troubled commentators.

Tschirnhaus's Parisian acquaintance, Leibniz, for one, simply does not see how Spinoza can pull it off:

> He maintains ... that finite and durational things cannot be immediately produced by an infinite cause, but that they are brought about by other singular and finite causes. But how, ultimately, will they follow from God? For neither can they arise mediately in this case, since we would never arrive at the production of the finite by the finite.[7]

Spinoza's reply to Tschirnhaus is not very illuminating. He denies that the principle cited by Tschirnhaus regarding what can be deduced from a definition applies to real things (such as God, from whose essence one can deduce that God is infinite, unique, immutable, etc.), as opposed to abstract entities.[8] And yet, he also concedes that 'with regard to your question as to whether the variety of things can be demonstrated a priori solely from the conception of Extension, I think I have already made it quite clear that this is impossible' (Ep. 83). But what he adds to this suggests that Spinoza nonetheless believes that he *can* deduce the variety of things from *his* conception of the attributes of God: 'That is why Descartes is wrong in defining matter through Extension; it must necessarily be explicated through an attribute which expresses eternal and infinite essence.' He does not say anything further, however, and tells Tschirnhaus that they will have to discuss this at some later time, 'for as yet I have not had the opportunity to arrange in due order anything on this subject.' The opportunity never arose, as Spinoza died seven months after writing this letter.

The difficulty of filling in the blanks on Spinoza's behalf for a deduction of a diversity of finite modes from the simple nature of an eternal attribute has led many to conclude that they cannot, in fact, be filled in, and that the reality of finite individuals must remain either an inexplicable brute fact or an illusion. Solomon Maimon, for one, opts for the latter. He insists that 'in [Spinoza's] system, unity is real, but diversity is merely ideal'.[9] Similarly, Hegel claims that 'what constitutes the grandeur of Spinoza's manner of thought is that he is able to renounce all that is determinate and particular, and restrict himself to the One, giving heed to this alone.'[10] For Spinoza, Hegel says, 'the absolute is substance, and no being is ascribed to the finite; his position is therefore monotheism and acosmism. So strictly is there only God, that there is no world at all; in this [opinion] the finite has no genuine actuality.'[11] At the turn of the twentieth century, Harold Joachim was able to write that the world of finite, transitory things – the 'multiplicity of the phenomenal world ... the world of unscientific experience' – is 'largely illusory'.[12] For these commentators, only substance and its attributes (and, perhaps, infinite modes) are real; the finite is merely a conceptual or perspectival way in which we subjects apprehend reality.

I shall not pursue a lengthy and detailed case against the acosmic reading of Spinoza's monism.[13] In the scholarly literature, it has remained a minority view, and for the most part the reality of finite modes for Spinoza has been taken for granted.[14] However, even among those who insist on the reality of finite modes, their 'deduction' within the geometric ordering of Spinoza's system has been regarded as problematic at best, impossible at worst.[15] The upshot is that the reality of finite modes, if conceded, appears (prima facie) to be an inexplicable and unmotivated part of the Spinozistic cosmos.

What I do want to offer, then, is a particular argument in support of the idea that Spinoza's system not only allows for real finite individuals, but also that the reality of finite modes can be made to fit deductively into his metaphysics – that is, that there necessarily are finite modes in Spinoza's cosmos. One preliminary clarification is warranted, however. The question I am interested in is *not* about how Spinoza can defend the necessity of any particular finite mode. Nor is it about the necessity of the entire infinite series of finite modes (that is, the particular series of finite modes constituting the actual world). Both of these issues regarding Spinoza's 'necessitarianism' have been examined by a number of recent commentators[16]; and while certainly related to my project in this essay, they are distinct from it. Rather, the more general question I am concerned with is the justification of there being finite modes at all. It is one thing to ask whether Spinoza's metaphysics necessitates the reality of finite modes *per se*, and something different to ask whether it necessitates the reality of this or that finite mode or series of finite modes.

IV

There is a cheap and easy way to deal with this gap between the infinite and the finite – or, rather, to avoid dealing with it. Perhaps Spinoza is not troubled in the *Ethics* with the problem of how to derive a world consisting of a plurality and diversity of finite modes from starting points that are singular, simple and infinite because for him the universe of finite modes is simply a given. Experience tells us with certainty that there are finite things in the world around us. We see trees, dogs and human bodies. So the problem is not how to deduce that there *is* a plurality of finite things. Rather, the problem is to determine what exactly the ontological status of those finite things is. That is, given that (as we know from experience) there are finite things, and given that (as we know deductively from the propositions of Part One of the *Ethics*) there are infinite things, how can we connect the finite things up with their infinite causes and 'complete' the chain of explanation? The answer lies in showing how these singular things are not substances in their own right, but 'in God', or finite modes of one of the attributes of infinite substance. There is, of course, a great deal of debate over what it is for things to be 'in' God, over what exactly is the nature of the relationship between finite modes and infinite substance, but that is another question.[17]

The proponent of the idealist reading is unlikely to be satisfied by such a solution, however. He would argue that the alleged empirical evidence for the reality of finite things is illusory, and thus that this response begs the question.[18] Moreover, and perhaps more seriously, it leaves the plurality of finite things undetermined and unexplained – in short, a brute fact. And this would seem to run counter to Spinoza's causal rationalism. As Michael Della Rocca has shown in great detail, Spinoza's commitment to the principle of sufficient reason does not allow for any brute facts in his system.[19]

Fortunately, there is a more promising approach to integrating the reality of finite modes in Spinoza's deductive metaphysical system. It involves looking more closely at the content of the infinite modes, both immediate and mediate, since (as shall become clear below) the infinite series of finite modes *qua* formal essences of singular things constitutes for each attribute an immediate infinite mode, and the infinite series of finite modes *qua* actually (durationally) existing singular things constitutes for each attribute a mediate infinite mode.

Spinoza, to be sure, is not very forthcoming – in the *Ethics* or elsewhere – with details about the infinite modes.[20] It is thus extremely difficult to figure out what the precise content is of the immediate and the mediate infinite modes under each attribute. Commentators have long wrestled with this problem, and as yet no consensus has emerged. I shall concentrate on what I regard as the most plausible way of making sense of what Spinoza has in mind.[21] I shall also, for the sake of clarity and simplicity, focus primarily on the attribute of Extension.

One preliminary thing to bear in mind is Spinoza's claim that God's (or Nature's) essence is power (*potentia*). 'God's power is his essence itself' (IP34). Power is what constitutes the fundamental being of substance per se. It is what Nature (*Natura Naturans*) essentially is. All things that 'follow' from God or Nature do so because they are expressions of this infinite power in one way (through one attribute) or another and derive their being from it. 'God's power, by which he and all things are and act, is his essence itself.'

When Spinoza does get around to revealing the content of the immediate infinite mode under the attribute of Extension, he calls it 'motion and rest' (Ep. 64). It is not entirely clear what this means. One possibility is that what is entailed by the nature of extension (the attribute) is just mobility. Whatever is extended is necessarily mobile, capable of being put in motion or sitting at rest. And yet, Spinoza seems to have in mind something stronger than this. In the *Short Treatise* (I.9), he says that the immediate infinite mode in Extension is motion itself. Or, more precisely, the first effect (the immediate infinite mode) of the attribute of Extension generated by the power that is essential to Nature or substance is motion and rest – not motion and rest per se (since motion and rest need to be the motion and rest of *something*) but motion and rest *in* Extension. As God's (Nature's) active causal power is expressed through the attribute of Extension, what results, in the first instance, is extension modified by motion and rest. To put it somewhat metaphorically, motion and rest in extension is what you get when causal power mixes with Extension.

Now in a Cartesian schema such as Spinoza's, when motion and rest are introduced into infinite, undifferentiated extension, that extension is necessarily divided into finite parcels, each of which is individuated by its particular motion or rest relative to surrounding extension. Descartes himself insisted that God's organization of the cosmos of material things consisted simply in His adding motion to the bare extension or matter that He had created, which in turn (and according to the laws of motion) breaks that extension up into 'vortices' of matter, each differentiated from other vortices by its particular motion. In describing the origins of the world, Descartes postulates that the original matter:

> may be divided into as many parts having as many shapes as we can imagine, and that each of its parts is capable of taking on as many motions as we can conceive. Let us suppose, moreover, that God really divides it into many such parts, some larger and some smaller, some of one shape and some of another, however we care to imagine them. It is not that God separates these parts from one another so that there is some void between them: rather, let us regard the differences he creates within this matter as consisting wholly in the diversity of the motions he gives to its parts.[22]

The result of motion and rest being introduced into extension is a world of individual extended bodies. For Descartes, a body, whether simple or complex, is nothing but extension moving (or stationary) relative to its immediately contiguous surroundings – that is, extension moving (or stationary) in such a way that it can be distinguished from other moving (or stationary) extension. It is the relative motion alone that brings about such division of undifferentiated extension into individual, finite parcels. In *Principles of Philosophy* II.23, he notes that 'all the variety of matter, or the diversity of its forms, depends on motion.' He goes on to explain that:

> There is therefore but one kind of matter in the whole universe, and this we know only by its being extended. All the properties we distinctly perceive to belong to it are reducible to its capacity of being divided and moved according to its parts; and accordingly it is capable of all those affections which we perceive can arise from the motion of its parts. For the partition of matter in thought makes no change in it; but all variation of it, or diversity of form, depends on motion. The philosophers even seem universally to have observed this, for they said that nature was the principle of motion and rest, and by nature they understood that

by which all corporeal things become such as they are found in experience.

Spinoza is a faithful Cartesian on the question of the individuation of bodies (but not, of course, on their substantiality). 'Bodies are distinguished from one another by reason of motion and rest, speed and slowness, and not by reason of substance' (IIP13sLemma1, G II.97; C I.458). Any particular body is the body that it is, and is distinct from other bodies, because some matter is moving (or resting) in a certain way, different from the way in which surrounding matter is moving (or resting). And to the extent that its matter maintains that motion or rest (or, rather, its proportion of motion and rest, since most bodies are complex parcels of matter composed of smaller parcels of matter, each with its own motion and rest, standing in relationship to each other) in a relatively stable way, the body preserves its integrity and identity over time:

> When a number of bodies, whether of the same or different size, are so constrained by other bodies that they lie upon one another, or if they so move, whether with the same degree or different degrees of speed, that they communicate their motions to each other in a certain fixed manner, we shall say that those bodies are united with one another and that they all together compose one body or individual, which is distinguished from the others by this union of bodies. (IIP13sDef., G II.99-100; C I.460)

For Spinoza, as for Descartes, what you necessarily get when you introduce motion and rest into extension are individual bodies. And infinite motion and rest necessarily make possible the division of infinite extension into infinitely many finite parcels of extension. Here is the important point, then: the formal essence of *any* body specifies in conceptual terms only a quantity of extension distinguished by a certain proportion of motion and rest (what Spinoza calls 'a fixed pattern of motion and rest').

But if Extension (the attribute) plus 'motion and rest' (the immediate infinite mode) are the sole conditions for any particular body, they are alone sufficient to generate (conceptually) all possible bodies. And if, as Spinoza insists, there is necessarily 'motion and rest' following from God or Nature under Extension, then all possible bodies are necessarily contained (via their formal essences) in the immediate infinite mode of Extension. I am suggesting, that is, that the label that Spinoza uses for the immediate infinite mode in Extension, 'motion and rest', is shorthand for 'the formal essences of all finite bodies.' What Spinoza has called 'the definitions of singular and changeable things' are necessarily the content of the immediate infinite mode of Extension. This is because the definition of any singular body is constituted only by the concepts of extension and motion/rest, and therefore what Spinoza identifies as the immediate infinite mode of

Extension – 'motion and rest' – furnishes the conceptual materials for all possible bodies.

Thus, the first necessary consequence of God's (Nature's) active power being run through the attribute of Extension – that is, the immediate infinite mode of Extension – is really an infinite series of finite modes. It is not the series of actually (durationally) existing bodies, but the series of all possible bodies, that is, all formal essences of bodies, insofar as the essence of any particular body will be a kind of mathematical formula specifying some finite extension involving a degree of motion and rest.[23]

Notice, then, that we seem to have been able to generate a plurality of finite modes from infinite and eternal starting points. From God's infinite power running through the attribute of Extension, there necessarily follows motion and rest in extension (the immediate infinite mode of Extension) and, thus, the formal essences of finite extended bodies. Each bodily formal essence is a finite mode within the immediate infinite mode of Extension.

V

What, then, about actually existing bodies (that is, durational bodies)? What is their ontological status? Are the trees and animals and human beings we see around us authentic features of reality and nature? It would seem so. After all, actually existing bodies are simply the instantiations in duration of the formal essences of bodies, and thus their reality as finite modes should be no less than that of the formal essences (finite modes) they instantiate. If reality is broken up into actual finite modes at the level of formal essences, then it should be equally so at the level of duration. For detail, we need to turn to what Spinoza has to say about the *mediate* infinite mode of Extension.

If there is debate over what exactly the immediate infinite modes are, there is even more uncertainty surrounding the mediate infinite modes. These are the modes that follow not directly and immediately from the absolute nature of the attribute considered absolutely and in itself, but from 'some attribute of God insofar as it is modified by a modification which, through the same attribute, exists necessarily and is infinite'. The mediate infinite modes, that is, follow from the attribute taken together with its immediate infinite mode.

There is not a single hint in the *Ethics* itself as to what the mediate infinite modes in Extension and Thought might be. And when Spinoza does offer some information as to their respective contents, the mystery only deepens. In a letter from July, 1675, his friend Georg Hermann Schuller, acting on behalf of Tschirnhaus, asks Spinoza for some 'examples of those things immediately produced by God, and of those things produced by the mediation of some infinite modification' (Ep. 63). In reply, Spinoza offers only one example of a mediate infinite mode: 'the face of the whole universe [*facies totius universi*]' (Ep. 64). Although he does not tell Schuller whether this is an example of a mode in Extension or in Thought, it presumably lies in Extension, since he refers Schuller to the physical digression in Part Two of the *Ethics* (the scholium to Lemma 7 after IIP13) for some clarification.

'The face of the whole universe' is certainly an ambiguous phrase. But it is almost certain that what Spinoza means is the totality in space and time of all actually existing material things – all the finite modes of Extension in duration – taken as an infinite and eternal series. 'The face of the whole universe' refers to all of corporeal nature, in its infinite spatio-temporal variety. The mediate infinite mode in Extension, then, would be the entirety of the contents of the physical universe – all particular bodies and all their relations throughout all time – considered as an eternal, infinite set and as an individual in its own right, one that, as he remarks to Schuller, 'although varying in infinite ways, yet remains always the same.'

The actually existing bodies of this infinite series durationally realize as a causal sequence the eternal formal essences of bodies that, as we saw, are the necessary contents of the immediate infinite mode in Extension. Thus, it necessarily follows from the eternal and infinite 'premises' of Nature that there should be actually existing *finite* bodies – both collectively as an eternal infinite series and individually as durational finite modes.[24]

It remains somewhat of a mystery why there should necessarily be a series in *duration*. One might wonder how Spinoza does or can establish that from eternal starting points there should be *durational* consequences, a temporally realized sequence of physical things and events. But that is not my concern here.[25] Rather, I am addressing only the question of the *finite*. And it seems clear to me that, having shown how there can – indeed, must – follow finite modes within an immediate infinite mode of Extension, there is every reason why there should be finite modes within the mediate infinite mode that necessarily follows from it.

VI

The proponent of the acosmic reading still has one very effective trump card up his sleeve: IP21. This is the proposition in which Spinoza says that 'all things which follow from the absolute nature of any of God's attributes have always had to exist and be infinite, or are, through the same attribute, eternal and infinite.' This would seem to imply that it is indeed impossible within Spinoza's system to derive finite modes from an infinite attribute. This proposition can then be supplemented by IP28, which apparently says that a finite mode can follow only from another finite mode:

> Every singular thing, or any thing which is finite and has a determinate existence, can neither exist nor be determined to produce an effect unless it is determined to exist and produce an effect by another cause,

> which is also finite and has a determinate existence; and again, this cause also can neither exist nor be determined to produce an effect unless it is determined to exist and produce an effect by another, which is also finite and has a determinate existence, and so on, to infinity.

These two propositions would appear to undermine my argument in this chapter. However, regarding IP21, notice that what, even on my reading, first follows from the absolute nature of an attribute remains something that is itself eternal and infinite: the immediate infinite mode. In Extension, this is 'motion and rest'. But as I have shown, a closer investigation of the content of this immediate infinite mode of Extension reveals that it consists in the conceptual generative materials (extension plus motion and rest) of all possible bodies – that is, it consists in the series of the formal essences of bodies. This series, in keeping with IP21, has 'always had to exist and be infinite'. It is not the case that, on my reading, some single and determinate formal essence – some unique finite mode – taken by itself and to the exclusion of all others, or even a finite set of formal essences, is supposed to follow from the absolute nature of God's attribute of Extension. Rather, infinite finite modes *qua* eternal determinate essences are generable by what *does* follow immediately from the absolute nature of the attribute of Extension: 'motion and rest'.

IP28 is a more difficult proposition, and I can only make a tentative suggestion as to how to interpret it consistent with my reading. I propose that what Spinoza is talking about here is the *causal* order of bodies (or other things in other attributes) that actually exist. This proposition is *not* about the generation of finite modes as formal essences – which subsist *sub specie aeternitatis*, with each formal essence independent of any other formal essence and related only on a so-called 'vertical axis' to God (substance) and its attributes – but about the actualization of these essences in duration. Remember (from VP29s, examined above) that Spinoza distinguishes between two ways of being 'actual', and reserves the term 'existence' for what is actual 'in relation to a certain time and place'. According to IP28, then – which is about 'determinate *existence*' – the explanation for why any finite mode comes into actual existence at one durational moment rather than another lies not only in the infinite and eternal features of the cosmos but, just as importantly, in other finite features (a causal relation on what might be called the 'horizontal axis'). Finite modes, that is, have as their causes – both of their existence and of their power actually to produce effects – other, prior finite modes.[26]

VII

To turn briefly to the other attribute of which we have knowledge: The immediate infinite mode under the attribute of Thought is what Spinoza, responding to a request for clarification from Tschirnhaus, calls 'absolutely infinite intellect'.[27] This could be read as Spinoza's way of referring to God's power of thinking, or – since he rejects such abstractions as powers or faculties – God's infinite activity of thinking. Infinite thinking would thus be the first actualization (the immediate infinite mode) of the attribute of Thought generated by the power that is essential to Nature or substance. If you run (God's) infinite power through the attribute of Thought, what you get is, in the first instance, infinite active (divine) thinking. However, by itself this seems a little too spare to capture what Spinoza has in mind, since any thinking – even infinite thinking – would have to be a thinking *of* something.

A more plausible and fruitful reading is that the immediate infinite mode in Thought is God's actual thinking of everything. It is, in essence, a perfect and eternal knowledge of everything. A passage from the *Short Treatise* (I.9) suggests as much:

> As for Intellect in the thinking thing, this too is a Son, product or immediate creature of God, also created by him from all eternity, and remaining immutable to all eternity. Its sole property is to understand everything clearly and distinctly at all times. (G I.48; C I.92).

This might mean only that the infinite intellect is simply one infinite and eternal idea, a single thought whose content is infinite and all-encompassing; in fact, Spinoza often refers to the immediate infinite mode in Thought in the singular as 'God's idea [*idea Dei*]' (IP21). In this case we have not reached any diversity of finite modes. But a more likely interpretation is that the absolutely infinite intellect generated by God's power run through the attribute of Thought is an infinite and eternal set of finite thoughts – all possible thoughts of all possible things, with each thought distinguished from others by its particular object. If God, as Spinoza says, is to understand everything clearly and distinctly (that is, have infinite intellect), then God must have all possible adequate ideas. God's infinite intellect is therefore necessarily composed of infinitely many distinct adequate ideas.

What makes this interpretation so plausible is Spinoza's parallelism. For every mode of every attribute, there is a corresponding mode of Thought:

> IIP3: In God there is necessarily the idea not only of his essence, but also of all things which necessarily follow from his essence.
>
> Demonstration: God (by IP1) can think an infinite number of things in infinite ways, or (what is the same thing, by IP16) can form the idea of his essence, and of all things which necessarily follow therefrom. Now all that is in the power of God necessarily is (IP35). Therefore, such an idea as we are considering necessarily is, and in God alone.
>
> IIP7: The order and connection of ideas is the same as the order and connection of things.

> Demonstration: This proposition is evident from IAxiom4. For the idea of everything that is caused depends on a knowledge of the cause, whereof it is an effect.
>
> Corollary: Hence God's power of thinking is equal to his realized power of action – that is, whatsoever follows from the infinite nature of God in the world of extension (*formaliter*), follows without exception in the same order and connection from the idea of God in the world of thought (*objective*).

But we have already established that there is in the immediate infinite mode of Extension a plurality of finite modes (the formal essences of bodies). Thus, there must be in the infinite intellect a plurality of individual ideas *qua* finite modes, each having as its object a finite mode in Extension. Or, put another way, infinite intellect consists of an infinitude of finite ideas of the infinitude of finite formal essences of bodies. 'The ideas of singular things, or of modes, that do not exist must be comprehended in God's infinite idea in the same way as the formal essences of the singular things, or modes, are contained in God's attributes' (IIP8). Thus, just as the immediate infinite mode of Extension is made up of finite modes (formal essences of bodies), so the immediate infinite mode of Thought is made up of finite modes (ideas of formal essences of bodies). In a letter to Oldenburg (Ep. 32), Spinoza basically confirms this. He describes God's infinite intellect as 'an infinite power of thinking [*potentiam infinitam cogitandi*]', but not as a bare power that is not directed at some object. He says that this infinite power of thinking 'contains within itself the whole of Nature ideally, and whose thoughts proceed in the same manner as does Nature, which is in fact the object of its thought' (G IV.173–4/S 194–5).

If this is right, then we have arrived (albeit in a manner parasitic upon the division into finite modes necessitated within Extension) at a diversity of finite modes in the attribute of Thought, within its immediate infinite mode: the individual finite ideas composing infinite intellect. Each idea in the infinite intellect would be individuated by its (finite) object-content, and thus would be finite and distinct from other ideas. (Meanwhile, the mediate infinite mode of Thought would be the infinite set of actually existing finite ideas that instantiate in duration these finite ideas of the formal essences of bodies – that is, it would be the set of actually existing finite minds, which are ideas of actually existing finite bodies. 'The first element, which constitutes the actual being of the human mind, is the idea of some particular thing actually existing' [IIP11].)

VIII

Spinoza is clearly committed to the reality of finite modes. What I hope to have shown in this essay is that, by his own terms, he is entitled to them. Within the realm of our experience, which is the durational world constituting the mediate infinite mode that is the most causally remote from God or Substance, reality consists in discrete individuals. And there seems to be no reason why the deductive system of the geometric method of the *Ethics* cannot justify such a claim. Spinoza may have inherited certain problems of individuation from his philosophical mentor, Descartes. More particularly, motion may not be able to do the robust individuating work within extension that a faithful Cartesian physicist needs; and, in a plenum, where bodies are individuated only relatively, by motion alone, there will be some difficulty in determining whether and how two contiguous bodies at rest continue to remain two bodies instead of one. Be that as it may, Spinoza, at least, was in no doubt that physical reality really does come broken up into finite individuals.[28]

Notes

1. Strictly speaking, for Berkeley physical (non-thinking) objects are 'real', but they do not exist outside of the perceptions of a mind; whereas for the later Leibniz, incorporeal or 'soul-like' substances (monads) are real beings whether or not they are being perceived by some mind.
2. Jonathan Schaffer, 'Monism', *The Stanford Encyclopedia of Philosophy (Fall 2008 Edition)*, Edward N. Zalta (ed.), URL = <http://plato.stanford.edu/archives/fall2008/entries/monism/>.
3. I shall cite the *Ethics* using the standard abbreviation format of Part (using Roman numerals), Proposition (P), Axiom (A), Definition (D), and Scholium (S). I have used the translation by Edwin Curley, *The Collected Works of Spinoza*, vol. 1 (Princeton: Princeton University Press, 1985), henceforth abbreviated as 'C'.
4. A proponent of the acosmic or idealist reading might argue that the only real thing is substance and its attributes, and that these infinite effects of substance are no more real than finite modes. However, I do not see that this is an essential feature of the acosmic reading, which is really distinguished only by its emphasis on the reality of the infinite and denial of the reality of the finite. Be that as it may, since my concern in this chapter is with defending of the reality of the finite for Spinoza, I shall assume for the sake of my argument the reality of the infinite modes.
5. It has sometimes been argued that the attributes themselves are not real features of Nature, but only ways in which it is perceived; see, for example, Harry Wolfson, *The Philosophy of Spinoza* (Cambridge, MA: Harvard University Press, 1934), pp. 142–57. This seems, moreover, to have been an element of the acosmic or idealist reading. But this interpretation has been effectively refuted by Martial Gueroult (*Spinoza*, 2 vols. [Hildesheim: Georg Olms, 1968], vol. 1, pp. 428–61), among others. Again, since my concern in this chapter is with the reality of the finite, I shall assume for the sake of argument what is now the dominant reading on the reality of the attributes.
6. Gueroult (*Spinoza*, vol. 1, p. 327) insists that Spinoza provides 'une deduction des modes finis' only to establish 'qu'elles sont produites par Dieu' (that is, *that* they are modes of substance), not 'comment elles sont produites par Dieu.'
7. *Réfutation inedite de Spinoza*, M. de Gaudemar, ed.; L. A. Foucher de Careil, trans. (Paris: Actes Sud, 1999), p. 38.

8. Tschirnhaus had used the example of the definition of the circumference of the circle, from which only one property can be deduced: 'that it is everywhere alike or uniform'.
9. *Salomon Maimons Lebesgeschichte*, Zwi Batscha, ed. (Frankfurt: Insel, 1984), p. 217. For a study of Maimon's reading of Spinoza, see Yitzhak Melamed, 'Salomon Maimon and the Rise of Spinozism in German Idealism', *Journal of the History of Philosophy* 42 (2004): 67–96.
10. *Lectures on the History of Philosophy*, trans. E. S. Haldane and F. H. Simson, 3 vols. (Lincoln: University of Nebraska Press, 1995), vol. 3, p. 258. For a discussion of Hegel's reading of Spinoza, as well as of other thinkers (Bayle, Leibniz, Jacobi, Maimon) who, early on, attributed acosmism to Spinoza, see Kenneth L. Schmitz, 'Hegel's Assessment of Spinoza', in Richard Kennington, ed., *The Philosophy of Baruch Spinoza* (Washington, DC: Catholic University of America Press, 1980), pp. 229–43; Melamed, 'Salomon Maimon and the Rise of Spinozism in German Idealism', and 'Acosmism or Weak Individuals? Hegel, Spinoza, and the Reality of the Finite', *Journal of the History of Philosophy* 48 (2010): 77–92; and the essays in Manfred Walther, ed. *Spinoza und der Deutsche Idealismus* (Würzburg: Köningshausen & Neumann, 1991).
11. *Lectures on the Philosophy of Religion*, ed. Peter C. Hodgson, 2 vols. (Berkeley: University of California Press, 1984), vol. 1, p. 432.
12. *A Study of the Ethics of Spinoza* (New York: Russell and Russell, 1901 [1964]), pp. 79–80. Karolina Hübner has recently argued for an acosmic reading of Spinoza in *Spinoza on Substance and Cause* (Ph.D. Dissertation, 2010, University of Chicago). Michael Della Rocca seeks a more nuanced reading ('There is a grain – or more than a grain – of truth to the claim that finite modes, for Spinoza, do not exist.') in *Spinoza* (New York: Routledge, 2008), p. 289–90. Gueroult, meanwhile, dismisses the Hegelian acosmic reading, and says that its partisans 'ne font que projeter en [l'authentique doctrine de Spinoza] tout un monde de concepts nés ailleurs et sans rapport avec elle' (*Spinoza*, vol. 1, p. 468).
13. A full argument against the acosmic reading would be extremely complex, and have to take into account Spinoza's views on individuation, mereology, and other topics. For an important contribution to the more extended case, see Melamed, 'Acosmism or Weak Individuals?'. See also G. H. R. Parkinson, 'Hegel, Pantheism and Spinoza', *Journal of the History of Ideas* 38 (1977): 449–59.
14. See, for example, Jon Miller, 'Spinoza and the Stoics on Substance Monism', in Olli Koistinen, ed., *The Cambridge Companion to Spinoza's Ethics* (Cambridge: Cambridge University Press, 2009), pp. 99–117 (especially p. 110).
15. Margaret Wilson thus takes note of '[Spinoza's] deep difficulty in rationalizing the transition (in God) from infinite attribute (or its idea) to finite mode (or *its* idea)' (*Ideas and Mechanism: Essays on Early Modern Philosophy* [Princeton: Princeton University Press, 1999], p. 173). Edwin Curley notes that 'Spinoza never carries out the deduction of the finite from the infinite which his system (IP16) would seem to require to be possible. In my view a proper understanding of IP28 requires us to see that he would regard such a deduction as impossible even for an infinite intellect' (*Behind the Geometric Method* [Princeton: Princeton University Press, 1988], p. 151 n. 60). Jonathan Bennett, apparently agreeing, refers to 'that 'infinite and eternal' material from which particular facts cannot be extracted by logic alone' (*A Study of Spinoza's Ethics* [Indianapolis: Hackett, 1984], p. 118). What Curley and Bennett seem to be primarily concerned about,

however, is the deduction (or necessity) of the particular series of finite modes, not the establishment of finite modes per se (see also n. 14 below).

Joel Friedman does believe that 'the finite follows from the infinite in Spinoza's metaphysical system' with 'logico-metaphysical necessity'. But he limits his discussion to a very general level, showing only that with the proper distinctions in place we can see *that* Spinoza intends finite formal essences to follow deductively (in the immediate infinite mode) from the attributes. He does not, however, address the problem of how specifically they are supposed to so follow, and thus to that extent he ends up begging the question; see 'How the Finite Follows From the Infinite in Spinoza's Metaphysical System', *Synthese* 69 (1986): 371–407.

16. See, for example, Curley, *Spinoza's Metaphysics: An Essay in Interpretation* (Cambridge, MA: Harvard University Press, 1969), chapter 3; Don Garrett, 'Spinoza's Necessitarianism', in Yirmiyahu Yovel, ed., *God and Nature: Spinoza's Metaphysics* (Leiden: Brill, 1991), pp. 191–218; and Samuel Newlands, 'Spinoza's Modal Metaphysics', *The Stanford Encyclopedia of Philosophy (Spring 2010 Edition)*, Edward N. Zalta (ed.), URL = <http://plato.stanford.edu/archives/spr2010/entries/spinoza-modal/>.
17. Compare, for example, Curley's 'causal' account in *Spinoza's Metaphysics* with the 'inherence' account in John Carriero, 'On the Relationship Between Mode and Substance in Spinoza's Metaphysics', *Journal of the History of Philosophy* 33 (1995): 245–73; and Steven Nadler, ' 'Whatever is, is in God': Substance and Things in Spinoza's Metaphysics', in Charlie Huenemann, ed., *Interpreting Spinoza: Critical Essays* (Cambridge: Cambridge University Press, 2008), pp. 53–70.
18. My thanks to Karolina Huebner for bringing up this point.
19. This is one of the central themes of his *Spinoza*.
20. The references that do exist occur in the *Ethics* at IP21–23; the *Short Treatise* I.3, 8, 9; and Ep. 64.
21. I am indebted here to Gueroult's general reading of the immediate and mediate infinite modes (in *Spinoza*, vol. 1), which I think gets it just right. Gueroult, however, does not put this reading to service in arguing for the reality of the finite.
22. *Le Monde*, AT XI.34; CSM I.91.
23. Don Garrett, on the other hand, argues that formal essences are infinite modes, not finite modes; see 'Spinoza on the Essence of the Human Body and the Part of the Mind That is Eternal', in Koistinen, ed., *The Cambridge Companion to Spinoza's Ethics*, pp. 284–302. For Garrett, the formal essence of body is simply 'the omnipresent modification or aspect of an attribute of God that consists in the attribute's general capacity to accommodate – through the general laws of its nature as an attribute – the actual existence of a singular thing of a given specific structure whenever and wherever the series of actual finite causes should actually determine it to occur' (290). But why should this very specific capacity of an attribute to accommodate a particular and singular thing, or actually existing finite mode, not itself be a finite mode of the attribute? After all, such a specific capacity, indexed as it is to an actually existing finite mode, is a limited and determinate feature of the attribute, distinct from that attribute's capacity to accommodate other particular and singular things.
24. As I note above, however, this does not resolve the necessitarian question of why there should be *this* particular series of actually existing finite modes rather than some other.

25. Daniel Schneider has suggested to me that an answer to this question lies in Ep. 12, Spinoza's letter to Lodewijk Meijer on the infinite.
26. For an illuminating interpretation of this aspect of Spinoza's metaphysics, in terms of the respective causal contributions of laws and antecedent events to the bringing about of any state of affairs, see Curley, *Spinoza's Metaphysics*.
27. Ep. 64. In the *Short Treatise*, he simply calls it 'Intellect'.
28. I am grateful to Dominik Perler, Daniel Schneider, Eric Stencil, Yitzhak Melamed, Michael Della Rocca, Karolina Huebner, and Mogens Laerke for their helpful comments on an earlier version of this chapter.

12
Spinoza's Monism? What Monism?

Mogens Lærke

The claim that there is only *one* substance, namely God or Nature, is habitually considered central to Spinoza's philosophy.[1] For example, in his recent book on Spinoza, Michael Della Rocca opens the chapter on Spinoza's metaphysics of substance by writing: 'How many things are there in the world? Spinoza's answer: one' (Della Rocca 2008: 35). This is also a statement of what is commonly known as Spinoza's 'monism.' In an even stronger formulation, taking "one" in the sense of a property rather than as a quantifier, Jonathan Schaffer begins his entry on "Monism" in the *Stanford Encyclopedia of Philosophy* by noting that "there are many monisms. What they have in common is that they attribute *oneness*' (Schaffer 2007). He proceeds to classify Spinoza as a paradigmatic example of an 'existence monist' according to whom 'exactly one concrete object token exists (the One)' (ibid.).

Putting to one side the history of the term 'monism,' which could raise some terminological doubts about the propriety of such statements,[2] the conceptual point could appear indisputable. Already in the KV, Spinoza refers to God as 'the one, unique, all-encompassing being' (KV I, II, § 17n; trans. modified). He argues that 'God alone has being, and all other things have no being but are modes' (KV II, V, § 10) and that 'everything consists in one unique thing which is God himself' (KV II, XXIV, § 3).[3] Later, in the *Ethics*, Spinoza famously claims that 'in Nature there exists nothing but a unique substance' (EIP10S, G II 52: C 416; trans. modified), that 'except God, no substance can be or be conceived,' and 'that God is unique, i.e. (by D6), that in Nature there is only one substance' (EIP14&C1, G II 56: C 420). The last two passages constitute the focal point for most monist readings of Spinoza.[4]

Nonetheless, when taking a closer look at Spinoza's texts, it is far from clear that Della Rocca and Schaffer provide sufficiently nuanced answers on his behalf. Thus, in two passages that we will discuss further below, Spinoza enigmatically states that 'God is only very improperly called one and unique' (CM I, VI, G I 246: C 312) and that 'it is certain that he who calls God one or unique has no true idea of God, or is speaking of him very improperly' (Letter L, G IV 239: S 892; trans. modified). Hence, it seems that Spinoza both affirms and denies that God or substance is 'one' and 'unique.'

Such statements concerning the impossibility of counting God as one are not surprising to the extent that they reflect a general tendency in Spinoza to exclude numbers and numerical determinations from the foundations of metaphysics. Martial Gueroult even considers the 'depreciation of numbers' to be a very general feature of Spinoza's philosophy, referring mainly to the famous Letter 12 to Lodewijk Meyer (Gueroult 1968: 422–23, 514–19; cf. Melamed 2003: 3–22). Here, Spinoza writes that '[...] Measure, Time, and Number are nothing but Modes of thinking, or rather, of imagining' (G IV 57: C 203). He insists on 'the inability of numbers to determine all things' (G IV, 59: C 204) and on the fact that '[things] cannot be equated with any number' (G IV, 61: C 205). The theme also appears in the CM:

> We also have modes of thinking which serve to explain a thing by determining it through comparison to another. The modes of thinking by which we do this are called *time, number,* and *measure,* and perhaps there are other besides. Of these, time serves to explain duration, number discrete quantity, and measure continuous quantity. (CM I, I, G I 234: C 300)

The problem is to know just how far-reaching this depreciation of number is, and exactly how and why it affects Spinoza's conception of the unity of God or substance.

Some commentators have addressed the question over the last fifty years in greater or lesser detail. Gueroult argued that, for Spinoza, 'being *unique* is improperly said of God, if one understands this in its numerical sense.'[5] In his *Spinoza: Philosophie pratique,* Gilles Deleuze also notes cautiously that 'from the point of view of being, there is only one single substance for all the attributes (and, still, the term 'one' does not apply very well)' (Deleuze 1981: 148). In an article from 1994, Pierre Macherey mounts a frontal attack on 'monist' readings of Spinoza, arguing that they stem from a simplistic (and often unacknowledged, or even subconscious) use of Hegel's Spinoza reading. Hence, taking departure from the passages in CM I, VI, and Letter L quoted above, Macherey maintains that 'the 'monism' which is attributed to Spinoza is nothing but a turn of phrase, a disguise of his thought that we would be better off returning to the tool box, leaving it there to be forgotten' (Macherey 1994: 53). In *Leibniz lecteur de Spinoza* (2008), I have myself defended an interpretation close to Macherey's, here stressing the contrast between Leibniz and Spinoza concerning the nature of substantial unity (Lærke 2008: 671–78). These discussions among mainly Francophone commentators have received little attention or have not been deemed worthy of consideration in the Anglo-Saxon world.[6] In a recent article, Francesca Di Poppa notes the existence of the debates, but 'find[s] the dispute whether the substance is 'one' of little philosophical interest' (Di Poppa 2009: 933n). It seems to me, however, that a historian of philosophy must at a minimum take an interest in the issues that the philosopher studied took an interest in. The passages from CM and Letter L quoted above clearly demonstrate that Spinoza himself was interested. I will therefore allow myself to disregard Di Poppa's sweeping dismissal and ask once again whether we can in fact consider Spinoza as a monist in Schaffer's sense, i.e. as someone who ascribes *oneness* to substance.

I will focus on the three terms which, in Spinoza's texts, are immediately presented as having a bearing on whether the cardinal number 'one' can be assigned to God in any proper manner. These terms are *unity, uniqueness,* and *oneness*. Other terms would have to be studied in order to fully grasp the nature of substantial unity in Spinoza, including *simple, indivisible, individual, singular, whole, all, everything, immanent, internal, univocal, identical, the same, equal, first* and *prior*. I have, however, chosen not to touch upon Spinoza's implicit or explicit use of these notions here. The aim of this article is mainly negative, namely explaining why Spinoza did *not* think that divine unity could be properly understood in terms of *oneness* and *uniqueness* and pointing out that 'monist' readings of Spinoza must keep that in mind. How Spinoza thought divine unity should then be understood, I have not attempted to answer. In the following, through a discussion with Martial Gueroult, I develop two different aspects of Spinoza's conception of the determinations 'one,' which concern, respectively, the imaginary/intellectual and relative/absolute character of numerical determinations. I will use this discussion to determine exactly why Spinoza sometimes denies that being one and unique can be 'properly' predicated of God. I will in particular show that Spinoza's original conception of divine unity stems from his rejection of a common understanding according to which the conception of multitudes depends on the conception of unities and that there is a sense in which being and one are convertible terms (*ens et unum convertuntur*). Instead, for Spinoza, oneness is a relative property the conception of which depends on multitudes. For this reason, he denies that oneness properly pertains to God to whose absolute, substantial nature relative properties cannot apply. Finally, in conclusion, I will suggest a possible way of reconciling this interpretation with Spinoza's explicit statements to the effect that God is 'one' and 'unique.'

God as one and unique

In the passages quoted in the introduction, Spinoza both affirms and denies that substance is 'one' (*unum*) and that substance is 'unique' (*unicum*). He says nothing about 'unity' (*unitas*). In fact, the term *unitas* appears nowhere in the *Ethics*. Because unity in that way comes without conceptual 'baggage' in relation to Spinoza's main exposition of his metaphysics, I will in the following use it as a somewhat neutral analytical term expressing Spinoza's authentic conception of substance in this regard, whatever that conception may be.[7] I will thus restate my question as follows: What reasons could Spinoza have for putting into doubt the propriety of speaking of God's unity in terms of 'oneness' and 'uniqueness'? We should here note that the two determinations – one and unique – appear together in most of the relevant texts as if they were properties which are ascribed (properly or improperly) to God at one and the same time. It thus seems as if they are, if not identical, then at least intrinsically linked to each other. It is however by no means clear *how* they are linked. How 'oneness' and 'uniqueness' relate in the case of Spinoza's God is one crucial question we will have to answer in order to understand the specificity of his position.

Let us first consider the property of being 'unique.' We should here turn our attention to EIP8S2 and the Letter 34, where Spinoza provides another version of the argument contained in EIP8S2. In these texts, Spinoza argues that 'no definition ever envelops or expresses any determinate number of individuals' (EIP8S2, G II 50: C 415). He takes as an example the quantity '20 men.' If there are 20 men, there must be some reason or cause why there are 20 of them, no more and no less. Such cause or reason is either interior or exterior, depending on whether it is contained in the definition or concept of the thing or not. However, insofar as the definition of 'man' does not imply the concept of the quantity '20' (we can just as well conceive of two, three or six hundred men), the cause or reason for there being 20 of them must be extrinsic in relation to the definition or concept of man. From this it can be concluded that number 20 is a purely extrinsic denomination, in the sense that it adds nothing to the concept of the enumerated thing, i.e. 20 men are no more and no less men than 40 men are. The argument does, at first sight, seem to concern only the concept of individuals such as men, that is to say, *modes*. The argument, Spinoza argues, is however applicable to *all* concepts or definitions: '[A]ll things which are conceived to exist as a plurality are necessarily produced by external causes' and therefore 'no definition involves or expresses a plurality, or a fixed number of individuals [...]' (Letter 34, GP I 179–80: S 854–55). Therefore, the general lesson concerning number that we can derive from the example also has important consequences for the concept of God or substance. Spinoza writes:

> Now since it pertains to the nature of a substance to exist [...], its definition must involve necessary existence, and consequently its existence must be inferred from its definition. But from its definition (as we have shown [...]) the existence of a number of substances cannot follow (EIP8S2, G II 51: C 415–16).

We can unpack the argument as follows. Substance is by definition in itself and conceived through itself (EID3). That substance is in itself means that it pertains to its nature to exist, i.e. that it necessarily exists from itself. From EIP7, this follows from the fact that the essence of a substance involves existence, which, according to EID1, is equivalent to it being self-caused (*causa sui*). Correspondingly, since conceiving something (adequately) is conceiving it though its cause (EIA4), the fact that substance is conceived through itself means that conceiving of substance through itself is conceiving of it as *causa sui*. When conceived in this way, we see that substance is such that 'its concept does not require the concept of another thing, from which it must be formed,' as Spinoza alternatively defines substance in EID3. Consequently, since it is self-caused and conceived through this self-causation, substance cannot have its reason or cause from any other thing external to it, but it must be its own reason or cause (EIP11D2). In other words, substance has no extrinsic denominations. But as we have seen, in so far as all numerical determinations must have some reason or cause exterior to the enumerated thing – a reason or cause which consequently is not contained in the definition or concept of that thing – number cannot be ascribed to substance or God. Thus, Spinoza concludes in EIP8S2 that 'it follows necessarily from this that there exists only one of the same nature, as was proposed.' In Letter 34, he concludes that 'the definition of God as perfect Being includes nothing other than the nature [...] of God, and not a fixed number of [...] Gods' (G IV 179: S 854) from which follows 'the existence of one God only' (G IV 180: S 855). None of these conclusions involve the claim that God is not one (in fact, it seems, quite the contrary), but only the claim that, from his definition, it necessarily follows that God is not several.

Gueroult, however, argues that Spinoza is in fact denying the numerical unity of God in a stronger sense:

> All numbers, such as the notions of the *one*, the *unique*, and *several*, are nothing but 'modes of thinking' with no correlate in things, that is to say, artificial procedures invented by our minds in order to explain the things that it perceives imaginatively. To project them as real outside ourselves, is to corrupt the knowledge that we have of things. (Gueroult 1968: 155)

Consequently, 'being unique is improperly said of God, if one understands this in its numerical sense' (Gueroult 1968: 156). The texts Gueroult appeals to in this context are those also quoted partly in the introduction from the CM and from Letter L, written to Jarig Jelles in June 1674. Let us first consider the text from the CM. Spinoza writes:

> So let us begin with the first, viz. *One*. They [the Metaphysicians] say that this term signifies something real outside the intellect. But what this

> adds to being they cannot explain, which shows sufficiently that they confound being of reason with real being. We say, however, that Unity is not in any way distinguished from the thing itself, or that it adds nothing to the being, but is only a mode of thinking by which we separate the thing from others which are like it or agree with it in some way. To unity is opposed multiplicity, which, of course, also adds nothing to things, is nothing but a mode of thinking, as we understand clearly and distinctly. I do not see what more remains to be said about a thing so clear. All that need be noted here is that God can be called one. But insofar as we conceive that there cannot be more than one of the same nature, he is called unique. Indeed, if we wished to examine the matter more accurately, we could perhaps show that God is only very improperly called one and unique. (CM I, VI, G I 245–246: C 311–12)

It is not quite clear who are the 'metaphysicians' Spinoza is criticizing here. Unless he is not well informed, he cannot mean traditional Scholastic philosophy, since Spinoza's own argument here is quite similar to a line of reasoning concerning divine unity developed by Thomas Aquinas. Like Spinoza, Aquinas also denies that oneness adds anything to the being of the thing: '*One* does not add any reality to *being*; but is only a negation of division; for *one* means undivided *being*. This is the very reason why *one* is the same as *being* [...]' (*Summa Theol.*, p. I, q. 11, a. 1). For this reason, Aquinas maintains that 'one the principle of number' cannot be ascribed to God, but that oneness only pertains to God when 'one' is taken to mean 'metaphysical entity' which is 'convertible with being' (ibid.).[8] Despite what Spinoza himself affirms, his argument thus at first sight appears completely uncontroversial. In the second part of the argument, however, Spinoza cautions that if considered more closely, one might arrive at a stronger conclusion and conclude that in fact, God is neither unique nor one in *any* sense, presumably including the sense of 'metaphysical entity' which Aquinas still finds is a proper and acceptable (even essential) description of divine unity.[9] However, in the context of the CM, a text which is not dedicated to the exposition of his own views, but only to 'explain the more obscure things which are commonly treated by Writers on Metaphysic' (CM I, Preface, G I 233: C 299), Spinoza understandably chooses to leave the matter here.

The argument, however, is further developed in the letter L to Jarig Jelles (and I here leave out an example the importance of which will be discussed later):

> Further, with regard to the demonstration that I establish in the Appendix to my Geometrical Proof of Descartes' Principles, namely, that God can only improperly be called one or unique, I reply that a thing can be called one or single only in respect of its existence, not of its essence. For we do not conceive things under the category of numbers unless they are

> included in a common class. [...] Now since the existence of God is his very essence, and since we can form no universal idea of his essence, it is certain that he who calls God one or unique has no true idea of God, or is speaking of him very improperly. (Letter 50, G IV, 239: S 892; trans. modified)

Spinoza here appeals to the distinction between essence and existence to develop his point. At first sight, the reasoning however does not appear to justify a conclusion any stronger than the one he draws in EIP8S2 and in EIP14C2, namely that God is not several. It is relatively clear why the application of numbers such as 2, 3 or 20 would apply to existences and not to essences, namely because they are extrinsic denominations. As we have already seen Spinoza argue in EIP8S2, number does not apply to the essence of 'man' for instance, which does not involve any determinate number, but only to the existences which exemplify or instantiate that essence, such as existing '20 men.' It is also relatively clear why a determination such as '20 men' implies that the men involved are all considered as belonging to some common class, namely the class of 'man,' rather than as particular, individual men, such as Socrates, Napoleon, or Jacques Cousteau. Although Spinoza clearly claims that it does, it is not however clear why this principle applies to the number *one* as well, and why *one* individual thing, such as Cousteau, requires any (universal) idea other than the (particular) idea of Cousteau himself in order to be conceived as *one*, and even less clear what common class might be involved in the ideas of Cousteau *as* Cousteau, to the extent that 'common' could appear to involve two things, and not just one. In order to understand better what Spinoza had in mind, we will then have to compare more closely the two arguments contained, respectively, in EIP8S2 and Letter 34, and in CM II, II and Letter 50.

Imaginary and intellectual oneness

In the Appendix 17 of *Spinoza I: Dieu*, Gueroult proposes such an analysis. In this section, I will present and comment on Gueroult's analysis before moving on, in the next section, to my own interpretation. The first difference between Spinoza's two arguments which springs to mind is the presence of the notions of 'common class' (*commune genus*) and 'universal idea' (*universalis idea*) in Letter 50, notions which appear nowhere in EIP8S2 or in Letter 34. As Gueroult points out, our first problem is thus how we should understand these 'common classes' and 'universal ideas.' There are several options. The first option is the following. Common classes and universal ideas are like that which Spinoza in EIIP40S calls 'transcendental' or 'general' notions. These are abstract notions grounded in the imagination which are formed because 'the human Body, being limited, is capable of forming distinctly only a certain number of images at the same time' (G II 121: C

476). We are unable to form distinct images of (and thus also to imagine) very complex entities and small differences. For example, from perceiving many men, we form an abstract, universal notion of man, 'because so many images (e.g. of men) are formed at one time in the human Body that they surpass the power of imagining' (G II 121: C 477). Assigning numbers to things (2 pieces of money, 20 men) requires such abstract notions. Enumerating things therefore only refers to our incapacity to discern the real difference between these things, and consequently numbers are grounded in the imagination. Since this applies to the enumeration of things such as men and coins, *a fortiori*, it also applies to God. Thus, it could seem, Spinoza refuses to attribute a number to God, because there is something inherently imaginary about all numbers. Gueroult sees Letter 50 as arguing along these lines (cf. Gueroult 1968: 579).

If this is all that there is to numbers according to Spinoza, then his general 'depreciation of numbers' appears quite radical. It applies to both modes and substance, because number is always grounded in the abstraction from small, but real differences between individuals, allowing them to be subsumed under a common class. Numbers are purely imaginary. When looking closer at Spinoza's texts, however, it appears there may be a way in which number can be ascribed to things by the understanding and not by the imagination. Spinoza, as Gueroult notes, 'does not seem to confine number to the imaginary sphere,' and 'beyond the imaginative number, Spinoza seems in fact to use another number, having an objective nature and a necessary value, a clear and distinct concept produced *a priori* by the pure understanding and valid for things in themselves' (Gueroult 1968: 580, 581). Gueroult does not discuss EIP40S in this context, but the scholium provides a good pointer in that direction. Thus, after explaining how the formation of universal notions takes place because our power of imagining is surpassed, Spinoza adds: '[...] not entirely of course, but still to the point where the Mind can imagine neither slight differences of the singular [men] [...] *nor their determinate number*' (G II 121: C 477; my italics). The addition is revealing, since it appears that the formation of universal notions upon which the construction of (imaginary) numbers rely is grounded in the abstraction from... the determinate number of things enumerated! It could thus seem that there is number and there is number, that there are '20 men' in one sense and '20 men' in another. Hence, on the one hand, there are the imaginary numbers which are formed on the basis of imaginary universal notions. On the other, there are (presumably non-imaginary) numbers from which we abstract when forming these imaginary universal notions. The latter kind of numbers seem to have some ground in the nature of things, or to be, as Gueroult says it, 'ontologically grounded,' wherefore 'it is the pure understanding, and not the imagination which conceives this concrete and real multiplicity which belongs to the existences of singular modes' (Gueroult 1968: 580).

So how are we to understand these 'deeper' numbers which apparently are at least partly grounded in the nature of things? We should pay close attention to what Spinoza writes in EIP8S2 concerning the '20 men.' He does talk of 'the cause of human nature in general' (*causam naturae humanae in genere*), but also stresses that what is under consideration is 'the true definition of each thing' (*veram uniuscujusque rei definitionem*) and the 'true definition of man' (*vera hominis definitio*). Similarly, in Letter 34, he writes:

> A reason must be also be sought as to why twenty men, not more and not less, exist; for [...] a reason or cause must be assigned for the existence of every man. But this cause [...] cannot be contained in the nature of man himself, for the true definition [*vera ... definitio*] of man does not involve the number of twenty men. So [...] the cause of the existence of these twenty men, and consequently of each single man taken individually, must lie outside them. (Letter 34, G IV 180: S 854–55)

Clearly, in the argument concerning the '20 men,' Spinoza does not speak of 'men' in the imaginary sense of a universal notion described above, but relies on some 'true definition' of man. By such a 'true definition,' we can only understand an idea of the kind that Spinoza in EIIP40S1 calls a 'common notion' (*notio communis*). Common notions constitute the second kind of knowledge and they are always adequate. They differ from transcendental and universal notions in that they are not grounded in the observation of resemblances and the abstraction from differences between things, but in the way in which these thing affect and are affected by other things. Common notions are then notions which group together things which are similarly affected by the same things and therefore, as Spinoza says, 'agree' (*convenire*) with respect to those affective properties.[10] Since such affective properties are not, for Spinoza, imaginary, the common notions of things which they give rise to, are not imaginary either. I need not go into the intricate details of Spinoza's theory of common notions and how they are formed.[11] In this context, it suffices to note that Spinoza believes that numbers can in fact be adequately assigned to individual things, or modes, if only the enumeration is grounded in common notions.

Since the argument developed in EIP8S2 and Letter 34 is developed from the 'true definition' of man and not from allegedly imaginary 'common classes' and 'universal ideas,' one could conclude that this argument is in some way deeper than the one contained in Letter 50. Thus, Gueroult observes that, while the argument in Letter 50 is situated on the 'imaginative level,' the argument in EIP8S2 is situated on the 'ontological level' and is therefore 'better value for money' (Gueroult 1968: 581).[12] Concerning divine unity, this would then lead us to the conclusion that when Spinoza speaks of God as being 'one' and 'unique' in, for example, EIP14C2, the oneness he has in mind is of the *ontological* and not the *imaginary* kind.

In that case, Spinoza's argument concerning the impropriety of ascribing these properties to God could appear to turn on the distinction between inadequate, imaginary enumeration and adequate, intellectual enumeration, so that God can only improperly be called numerically 'one' in the first sense, but still be properly called numerically 'one' in the second sense. Thus, according to Gueroult, 'What is here [in the Letter L] denied of God, is the imaginative uniqueness [...]. The scholium to proposition 8, on the contrary, grants God uniqueness (ontological and not imaginative) by excluding ontological multiplicity from him' (Gueroult 1968: 518). On this reading, oneness, if understood rather than imagined, remains an essential property of God, adequately expressing his unity.

Absolute and relative oneness

Gueroult's analysis contains some essential insights. I fully agree that we must distinguish between numbers insofar as they are mere 'aids to the imagination,' and numbers insofar as they are formed on the basis of 'true definitions.' I have, however, some misgivings about his evaluation of the relative value of the *texts* in question.

First, it is not clear to me that the 'common classes' and 'universal ideas' that Spinoza speaks of in Letter 50 are necessarily *imaginary* general notions. Spinoza nowhere mentions their epistemological status. Apart from some terminological connotations, Spinoza's use of the expressions 'common kind' and 'universal idea' (none of which are found in EIP40S1 which only speaks of 'common notions,' 'transcendental terms,' and 'universal notions'), nothing prevents us from thinking that what Spinoza has in mind here includes *both* general notions grounded in the imagination *and* common notions grounded in the intellect. Moreover, when presenting the same argument in CM I, VI, Spinoza says that calling a thing 'one' is 'only a mode of thinking by which we separate the thing from others which are like it or agree with it in some way' (op.cit.). This determination, however, says nothing about the character of the relative 'likeness' or 'agreement' in question, and nothing indicates that these determinations are necessarily inadequate. After all, classifying things according to the way in which they 'agree' and do not 'agree' is the very foundation of the formation of common notions in Spinoza. This point taken into the consideration, I think there is no good reason to privilege the argument in EIP8S2 over the one given in Letter 50. Quite to the contrary, I believe there are important respects in which the argument in Letter 50 goes deeper than the one in EIP8S2.

This leads me to the second and more crucial point. While I am fully convinced by the point that, with regard to *modes* such as men and coins, there is a relevant distinction to be made between imaginary and intellectually grounded numbers, I am not at all convinced that the distinction between imaginary numbers and intellectually grounded numbers is at all relevant in the context of the argument concerning the unity of *substance*, i.e. *God's* unity. On Gueroult's reading, God *cannot* properly be called one and unique to the extent that such divine oneness is grounded in an imaginary 'universal idea' of God (as envisaged in Letter 50). God *can* however be called one and unique if the oneness ascribed is grounded in a 'true definition' of God (as envisaged in EIP8S2, and subsequently in EIP14C2). I believe, however, that Spinoza's refusal to ascribe oneness and uniqueness to God in Letter 50 does not in this way turn on the *imaginary* character of the 'common kinds' and 'universal ideas.' Quite to the contrary, as we shall see, it turns on the *relativity* of such determinations; a relativity which is common to both numbers grounded in the imagination *and* numbers grounded in the intellect.

Let us go back to the texts once again. We have seen that the arguments in EIP8S2 and Letter 34 aim at excluding only that one cannot speak of God as being numerically several, not that we cannot speak of him as numerically one. From this point of view, Spinoza's position is not substantially different from that found in a host of monotheistic philosophers. Excluding that God is numerically one is, however, exactly what Spinoza claims to do in Letter 50. If, then, the difference between the argument in Letter 50 and the one in EIP8S2/Letter 34 does not hinge on the distinction between imaginary and intellectually grounded oneness, what could the difference between the arguments be? The answer can be extracted from an example that Spinoza provides in the Letter 50, and which I omitted when rendering the argument above. Spinoza writes:

> For example, he who holds in his hand a penny and a dollar will not think of the number two unless he can apply one name to this penny and dollar, that is, pieces of money and coins. For then he can say that he has two pieces of money or two coins, because he calls both the penny and the dollar a piece of money or a coin. Hence it is clear that a thing can not be called one or unique unless another thing has been conceived which, as I have said, agrees with it. (Letter 50, G IV, 239: S 892; trans. modified)

The 'as I have said' (*ut sic dicam*) here refers to the statement in CM I, VI, according to which unity is just 'a mode of thinking by which we separate the thing from others which are like it or agree with it in some way.' As already noted above, the 'agreement' in question can be conceived both in terms of inadequate ideas of imaginary resemblances and in terms of adequate ideas of affective commonality. Indeed, I do not see how the argument would in any way be affected by referring to the one or the other kind of 'agreement.' The argument rather turns on the status of the number *one* in relation to *other numbers*. More precisely, it turns on the assumption that the number one does *not* have a special status different from that of other numbers: it is nothing but a *relation* between ideas. 'One' no less than any other numbers belongs among those 'modes of thinking which serve to explain a thing by determining it through comparison to another' (CM I, I, G I 234: C 300). Hence, when we say that a thing is *one*, we are only ascribing to that thing a relative property by means of which we distinguish *one* thing from *one other* thing.[13] Being *one* is inconceivable without the conception of several of the same nature and, *a fortiori*, inconceivable without the conceivability of several of the same nature.

This conception of oneness as a relative property is, as far as I can judge, fairly original. It certainly differs from the traditional view as found in for example Thomas Aquinas. Following Aquinas, just as it is axiomatically true that parts are prior to wholes, it is also axiomatically true that unities are prior to multitudes: '[...] multitude itself would not be contained under *being*, unless it were in some way contained under *one*' (*Summa theol*. p. I, q. 11, a. 1) and 'prior to all multitude we must find unity' (*Summa cont. gent.*, I, 18, a. 8). The kind of unities which metaphysically ground all such multitudes do, of course, not count as 'one' in the sense of 'one the principle of number,' which is a mere mathematical abstraction with no ontological content, but they do count as 'one' in the sense of 'metaphysical entities' the oneness of which is convertible with being. Moreover, while oneness does not *add* anything to being, beings are still susceptible to being *counted*, and properly so. The point is fairly intuitive: what is counted in a multitude like '20 men' is not *numbers*, but *beings*. Thus, in Aquinas, the priority of unity over multitude thus goes hand in hand with his conception of a metaphysical kind of 'oneness,' where *ens et unum convertuntur*. This is the kind of view which also transpires when a Scholastic thinker belonging to Spinoza's own intellectual context, such as Adriaan Heerebord, argues that '*numerus constat ex unitatibus*,' i.e. that 'number depends on unities,' meaning by this that the conception of multitudes depends on the conception of unities (Heerebord 1665: vol. II, disp. 4, 200). In Letter 50, however, Spinoza effectively holds the exact opposite, namely that unity (in the sense of 'one') depends on number (in the sense of 'several'). *Oneness* is a secondary property which is conceptually derived from the notions of *multitude* and *uniqueness*. Moreover, since multitude and uniqueness are nothing but the relative properties of being several and not being several, respectively, being one is no less a purely relative property than the multitude and/or uniqueness it is conceptually derived from. Thus, contrary to Aquinas, Spinoza holds that prior to numerical unity we must have multitude, and contrary to Heerebord, that unity in this sense depends on number: *Unitas constat ex numero*. Spinoza's argument concerning the number 'one' in Letter 50 is thus that, contrary to the traditional view, *uniqueness* is not a (relative) property grounded in some (absolute) *oneness*, but *oneness* is in fact a (relative) property grounded in (relative) *uniqueness*. The argument directly affects the conception of metaphysical entity as conceived by Aquinas. Not only does oneness not *add* anything to the being of a thing, but oneness does not *pertain to* any being except when considered in relation to other beings. Consequently, Spinoza's conception of the priority of multitude over numerical unity also implies the rejection of the notion of metaphysical entity, where *ens et unum convertuntur.* Considered in themselves, beings never count for one. In the case where several beings of a same nature are conceivable, one can however count beings as *ones* relative to other beings of the same nature, or *other ones.* It is perfectly proper to do so when we consider modes such as men or coins. However, in the case of God, there can be conceived *no other of the same nature.* Multiple Gods are inconceivable on account of God's very essence. Hence, since the conception of *one* of the same nature depends on the conception of *several* of the same nature, God cannot properly be ascribed the property *one.*[14]

Conclusion

The conception of the number 'one' that I have ascribed to Spinoza above explains his misgivings about attributing the properties 'oneness' and 'uniqueness' to God. It also explains why the label 'monism' cannot be properly applied to Spinoza, if indeed the concept of monism is, as Jonathan Schaffer argues, inseparable from 'ascribing oneness.' The interpretation is, however, not unproblematic and raises a number of issues. In the *Ethics,* Spinoza presumably develops his philosophy *in rigore metaphysico.* But how are we then to understand the famous statement in EIP14C1 according to which 'God is unique' and 'that in nature there is only one substance' (G II 56: C 420)? Should we conclude that Spinoza contradicts himself or is imprecise is his use of the term 'one' in the *Ethics*? Maybe we should. There is, however, another way around at least part of this problem which is both consistent with Spinoza's general philosophical practice and decidedly more interesting. I will conclude this chapter by briefly suggesting the alternative reading.

In fact, I do not think that there is a real conceptual contradiction between, on the one hand, CM II, VI, and Letter 50, and, on the other hand, EIP14C1 and the various passages from the KV quoted in the introduction where Spinoza explicitly affirms that God is 'one and unique.' There is instead a kind of terminological discrepancy, i.e. a difference in the meaning of the term 'one' between these texts. Furthermore, this discrepancy can be explained from a difference in status and aim of the texts in question, i.e. whether they are didactic, polemical, demonstrative, or other. Hence, I believe that we are dealing with a problem of *genre,* and ultimately with a problem of *words.* Spinoza himself seems to suggest something like this when, in CM II, VI, he contends that finally the question of God's unity 'does not matter greatly, or even at all, to those who care about things and not about words' (G II 246: C 312).

Let us disregard Spinoza's advice for a brief moment and care a bit about 'words,' or more precisely about the status and aim of the texts concerned. The Letter 50 expands on a remark from the CM. The PPD and the CM were originally written for a student named Casearius to whom Spinoza found it imprudent to unveil his real philosophy just yet (Letter VIII, in G IV 39: S 778). While the PPD was dedicated to Descartes' philosophy, the primary aim of the CM was to clarify a series of common philosophical terms used by metaphysicians, in conformity with the didactic purpose of the entire publication from 1663. The *Ethics*, on the contrary, is not a didactic work. It is Spinoza's own system as deduced from original definitions and axioms. The aim is not to elucidate previously used philosophical terms, but to develop a new set of concepts which do not suffer from the 'more obscure things' with which 'common Logic and Philosophy' is fraught (CM I, Preface, G I 233: C 299). Admittedly, in the *Ethics*, Spinoza employs many traditional-sounding philosophical terms, including terms that he explicitly addresses in the CM. But, contrary to the CM, he now redefines them specifically for his own purposes, and many of them are in this context only intelligible if understood independently of tradition and according to the systemic sense that the internal conceptual structure of Spinoza's metaphysics bestows upon them. It is therefore not surprising if we detect terminological discrepancies between the CM and the *Ethics*, or that the CM rule improper the use of a term that the *Ethics* adopts.

Bearing this in mind, let us now finally take Spinoza's advice and pay attention to things and not to words in EIP14C1, and consider how the notion of 'one' substance is elaborated within Spinoza's deductive framework. We notice that, according to Spinoza, EIP14C1 allegedly follows 'very clearly' from EIP14. This proposition states that 'no substance except God can be given nor be conceived' (G II 56: C 420). It is patently clear, however, that it does *not* follow 'very clearly' from this proposition that substance is *one* in the traditional sense of 'metaphysical entity,' i.e. a unity convertible with being and ontologically prior to multitudes. What *does* clearly follow from it, on the contrary, is the negative, relational property of 'not being several,' i.e. uniqueness. Moreover, there is nothing in the way in which Spinoza subsequently uses EIP14C1 which indicates that we should understand by God being *one* anything stronger than this purely relative notion according to which God is not several, i.e. that there is *not another one*.[15] Even in EIP14C1, oneness does not come out as an essential feature of Spinoza's God, but rather as a secondary, relational property derived from another relational property.

No wonder then that Spinoza only states God's oneness in a *corollary*, i.e. a derived or secondary proposition which figures as a mere supplement to a main proposition. Recall that the Latin noun *corollarium* also signifies something which is given free of charge. The connotations are appropriate. In a sense, 'oneness' and 'monism' come free of charge in EIP14C1, being clearly and derived from EIP14 in a completely transparent and immediate manner. But as almost always with such complimentary benefits, they are not worth much and do not add much value to what has already been purchased. Hence, none of these determinations give us more than what is already stated in EIP14, namely that God is unique, that is to say, *not several*. This relative and merely negative property, however, is clearly not an adequate concept of divine unity. Consequently, that 'there is one substance' cannot pass for the quintessential Spinozist statement that monist readings make of it.

Notes

1. For this chapter, I have much profited from various exchanges with Ohad Nachtomy over recent years. Earlier versions were presented at Bar Ilan University, the University of Chicago and the University of Leiden. I am grateful for the invitations and for all the helpful comments I received on those occasions. I am also grateful to Gonzalo Rodriguez-Pereyra for some helpful comments. Unless otherwise indicated, translations are my own.
2. The term 'monism' does not appear anywhere in Spinoza's texts. The first to use 'monism' as a philosophical term was Christian Wolff, namely in the preface to the second edition of the *Vernünfftige Gedancken von Gott, der Welt und der Seele des Menschen, auch allen Dingen überhaubt*. This book was published in 1721, that is, some 44 years after Spinoza died. In his *Psychologia Rationalis* (1740), Wolff gives the following succinct definition of a monist philosopher: 'I call that philosopher a monist who admits only of only one kind of substance [*Monistae dicuntur philosophi, qui unum tantummodo substantiae genus admittunt*]' (Wolff 1740: Sect. 1, chap. 1, § 32, 24.) Spinoza, however, held that substance is constituted by an infinity of attributes and, from EID6Exp, it is clear that attributes can in some way be construed as such distinct kinds (*genera*). Taken in its original meaning, it is thus clear that Spinoza was *not* a monist. The meaning of the term 'monism' has however been subject to considerable variation throughout the history of philosophy since it was first introduced by Wolff. Most importantly, monism has come to signify also a doctrine according to which all things are *one*, or which allows for *only one substance*. More careful commentators here speak of 'substance monism' in order to distinguish it from the kind of monism described by Wolff (see for example Kulstad 2003: 63–82). R.J. Delahunty makes a similar distinction between 'attributival monism' and 'substantival monism,' classifying Spinoza as a monist of the latter variety (cf. Delahunty 1985: 105–107.) The historical origins of this second, more recent use of the notion 'monism' is, I believe, Hegelian. The term 'monism' was rarely employed by philosophers after its invention by Wolff until it was reintroduced by a certain Karl F. Göschel in *Der Monismus des Gedankens* from 1832. Göschel describes monism (as opposed to dualism) as a doctrine which 'is based on an original *unity*, and this *unity* is the origin [*der Anfang*] or the first [*das Erste*], from which the two [*die Zwei*] which is in it, develops' (Göschel 1832: 40). As should be clear enough from the jargon, Göschel was a fervent Hegelian. Monism of this variety is very frequently attributed to Spinoza. For a good example, see Russell 2004: 521–31. See also the remarks on Russell by Macherey 1994: 39–41.

3. Other texts hinting at, or directly stating, the oneness or uniqueness of God include EIP15S, G II 57–60: C 421–24; Letter 12, G IV 56: C 203; Letter 35, G IV 181: S 855; TIE 76; KV I, I, Note I; KV II, 17; KV I, Dial. I, 9; KV Appendix II, 10; KV I, II, 27; KV II, XX, 4.
4. See for example Charlton 1981: 503; Bennett 1984: 70; Kulstad 1996: 299; Kulstad 2003: 65; Schmidt 2009: 72, etc. An exception is R.J. Delahunty, who takes the passage quoted above from KV II, XXIV, § 3, according to which 'everything consists in one unique thing which is God himself,' to state 'the essence of [Spinoza's] philosophical system' (Delahunty 1985: 105).
5. Gueroult 1968: 156, 578.
6. There are exceptions. See in particular Nachtomy [forthcoming], passim.
7. God's unity (*unitas*) is however explicitly discussed in a section in the CM entitled *De unitate Dei*. Spinoza here develops an argument in favor of divine unity from a consideration of divine omniscience: 'Among the attributes of God we have numbered also supreme understanding, and we have added that he has all his perfection from himself ad not from another. If now you say that there are many Gods, or supremely perfect beings, they will all have to understand, in the highest degree. To satisfy that condition, it is not sufficient that each one should understand only himself, he will have to understand both himself and the rest. From this it would follow that the perfection of each one's intellect would depend partly on himself and partly on another. Therefore, there could not be any supremely perfect being, i.e., as we have noted, any being that has all its perfection from itself and not from another. Nevertheless we have already demonstrated that God is a supremely perfect being and that he exists. From this we can now conclude that he is unique [*unicum*]' (CM II, II, G I 253: C 318–19). We note that the conclusion of the argument only mentions *uniqueness*. In fact, there are reasons to think that Spinoza found the argument unsatisfactory as an argument in favor of *unity*. Thus, a passage which can be found only in the Dutch version of the CM states that 'although this proof is completely convincing, nevertheless it does not explain God's *Unity* [*eenheit*]' (CM II, II, G I 253: C 319). The same argument appears in the PPD, but here as showing that there 'are not more than one [*non datur plures*]' God, i.e. as a demonstration of *uniqueness* (PPD I P10, G I 169: C 254–55). The argument does not figure in Descartes. Curley traces it back to Duns Scotus' *Quaestiones in quattuor libros sententiarum*, I, ii, 3 (C 318, note).
8. The aim is here to exclude that numbers in themselves have ontological weight. '*Numerum non esse ens reale*,' as Heerebord puts it (Heerebord 1665: vol. II, disp. 4, 199).
9. I will here leave aside complications related to the fact that Aquinas considers God to be not only one, but *supremely* one (*Summa theol*. p. I, q. 11, a. 4). On the reasoning from analogy and eminence which underlies this conception, see Klima 2000: 195–215.
10. An important occurrence in this context is in EPDL2: 'All bodies agree [*convenient*] in certain things.' The term also appears frequently in EIV, when Spinoza is explaining how 'agreement' among things (such as human beings) is a source of joy (see EIVP18S, EIVP31–37, and EIV Chap. 7 and 9.) In Letter 32, *consentire* and *convenire* seem to be used as equivalent (G IV 173: S 849). The *Ethics* does not employ the term *consentire*. Note however, that *convenire* has several meanings in the *Ethics*. The term also often appears in Spinoza's discussions of truth, to the extent that in EIA6, he lays down the basic truth requirement that '*Idea vera*

debet cum suo ideato convenire.' This latter use of the term is not, as far as I can see, relevant in the present context.

11. For an illuminating account, see Deleuze 1968: 252–67, and Deleuze 1981: 80–81, 154–63.
12. Gueroult uses the expression, difficult to translate, '*de meilleur aloi.*' In Letter 34, Spinoza refers to the argument here developed as 'the best way' of proving the proposition, which could provide some support for thinking of the demonstration in EIP8S2 and Letter 34 as the superior arguments (Letter 34, G IV 180: S 855). The fact, however, that Spinoza still reproduces the *other* argument from essence and existence eight years after the Letter 34, namely in the Letter 50, does not permit us to lend much credence to this particular evaluation.
13. We find a very interesting parallel reflection in Letter 32, concerning the relation between *parts* and *wholes*: 'On the question of whole and parts, I consider things as parts of a whole to the extent that their natures adapt themselves to one another so that they are in closest possible agreement. Insofar as they are different from one another, to that extent each one forms in our mind a separate idea and is therefore considered as a whole, not a part' (Letter 31, G IV 170–71: S 848). Exactly as is the case with unities and multitudes, Spinoza here suggests that the conception of wholes and parts depends on the conception of some 'agreement' between natures, i.e. that the mind conceives of some general or common notion under which all the parts would fall. More importantly, however, Spinoza also argues that the conception of what is a separate whole depends on this whole being conceived as different from *some other whole*. Being a 'whole' is thus a relative property exactly like being 'one' is a relative property.
14. Jonathan Bennett has hinted at something similar, suggesting that at least in some cases we should understand Spinoza's term 'substance' as a 'mass noun' rather than as a 'count noun,' so that for Spinoza, there is substance rather than there is *a* substance (Bennett 1984: 104). However, Bennett immediately drops further discussion of the issue, not under the pretext that it is uninteresting *per se* (quite to the contrary), but arguing that it just did not seem to have crossed Spinoza's mind (ibid.). This paper should make it clear that it did.
15. In EIP17C2, EIP14C1 is used (with EIP11) to demonstrate that 'God alone exists only from the necessity of his own nature'; in EIP24C, it taken as equivalent to saying that 'to [God's] nature alone it pertains to exist'; in EIP29S, it is taken (along with EIP17C2) to demonstrate that the expression 'such attributes of substance as express an eternal and infinite essence' is equivalent to the expression 'God, insofar as he is a free cause'; in EIP30D, it is glossed as 'in nature (by P14C1) there is only one substance, viz. God,' when demonstrating that 'there are no affections other than those which are in God [...],' i.e. that affections can be of no *other* substance than God; in EIP33D, it used to prove 'absurd' the idea that 'there could have been two or more Gods'; finally, in EIIP4D, it is used to state that 'God is unique.'

Bibliography

Aquinas, Thomas, *Summa theologica*, New York: Benziger 1920
——, *Summa contra gentiles*, New York: Hanover House 1955–57
Bennett, Jonathan, *A Study of Spinoza's Ethics*, Indianapolis: Hackett 1984

Charlton, William, 'Spinoza's Monism,' in *The Philosophical Review* 90/4 (1981), 503–529
Delahunty, R.J., *Spinoza*, London: Routledge and Kegan 1985
Deleuze, Gilles, *Spinoza et le problème de l'expression*, Paris: Minuit 1968
——, *Spinoza. Philosophie pratique*, Paris: Minuit 1981
Di Poppa, Francesca, 'Spinoza's Concept of Substance and Attribute: A Reading of the Short Treatise,' in *British Journal for the History of Philosophy* 17/5 (2009), 921–38
Göschel, Karl F., *Der Monismus des Gedankens. Zur Apologie der gegenwärtigen Philosophie am Grabe ihres Stifters*, Naumberg: Eduard Zimmerman 1832
Heerebord, Adriaan, *Meletemata philosophica*, Neomagi [=Nijmegen]: Andreae ab Hoogenhuysen 1665
Klima, Guyla, 'Aquinas on One and Many,' in *Documenti e studi sulla tradizione filosofica medievale* 11 (2000), 195–215
Kulstad, Mark, 'What Spinoza, in company with Leibniz and Descartes, can bring to Light about Important Varieties of Substance Monism,' in Andreas Bächli and Klaus Petrus (eds.), *Monism*, Frankfurt and London: Ontos Verlag 2003, 63–82
——, 'Spinoza's Demonstration of Monism: A New Line of Defense,' in *History of Philosophy Quarterly* 13:3 (1996), 299–316
Lærke, Mogens, *Leibniz lecteur de Spinoza. La genèse d'une opposition complexe*, Paris : Champion 2008
Macherey, Pierre, 'Spinoza est-il moniste?,' in. Revault d'Allones et H. Rizk (eds.), *Spinoza. Puissance et Ontologie*, Paris: Kimé 1994, 39–53
Melamed, Yizhak, 'On the Exact Science of Nonbeings. Spinoza's view of Mathematics,' in *Iyyun. The Jerusalem Philosophical Quarterly* 49 (2000), 3–22
Nachtomy, Ohad, 'Infinité de l'être et infinité du nombre chez Leibniz et Spinoza,' in P.-F. Moreau, M. Lærke, et R. Andrault (eds.), *Spinoza/Leibniz*, Lyon: ENS Editions, [forthcoming]
Russell, Bertrand, *History of Western Philosophy*, London: Routledge 2004
Schaffer, Jonathan, 'Monism,' in the *Stanford Encyclopaedia of Philosophy*, on URL: http://plato.stanford.edu. First published March 2007. Entry: August 2010
Wolff, Christian, *Psychologia rationalis*, Marburg 1740

13
Spinoza's Demonstration of Monism: A New Line of Defense

Mark Kulstad

Introduction

> P14: Except God, no substance can be or be conceived.
>
> Dem.: Since God is an absolutely infinite being, of whom no attribute which expresses an essence of substance can be denied (by D6) and he necessarily exists (by P11), if there were any substance except God, it would have to be explained through some attribute of God, and so two substances of the same attribute would exist, which (by P5) is absurd. And so except God, no substance can be or, consequently, be conceived, q.e.d. (IP14D; Curley, p. 420)

Two of the best-known features of Spinoza's *Ethics* are its monism – the view that there is only one substance – and its geometrical method – the demonstration, *more geometrico,* of all the propositions of the *Ethics* from its definitions and axioms. A persistent concern about these two elements of the *Ethics* is whether Spinoza can maintain them both. Specifically, the concern – indeed, typically the criticism – is that Spinoza has not satisfied his own demand relating to these two items, namely, the demand for a geometrical demonstration of monism from the definitions and axioms of the *Ethics*. Many, indeed, have felt that Spinoza's demonstrations in this regard are hopelessly inadequate. But such a view is too harsh. Here an interpretation of Spinoza's demonstration will be presented which embodies a defense – admittedly not a complete defense – of the claim that Spinoza's monism does indeed follow validly from the definitions and axioms of Part I of the *Ethics*.

Of course, it is not enough to provide an interpretation that makes sense of the logic of proposed demonstrations – however much this side of the interpretive enterprise recommends itself in virtue of the principle of charity. So it will also be argued here that the proposed interpretation does a reasonable job of plausibly construing important passages in Spinoza's demonstration, sometimes in interesting new ways. In short, the present interpretation of Spinoza's demonstration is based on grounds of both validity and textual plausibility. In this way a defense of Spinoza's demonstration of monism from the definitions and axioms of the *Ethics* is provided. Along the way, there are suggestions of possible relevance for the interpretation of Spinoza's metaphysics more generally.

To be sure, only a limited defense of Spinoza's demonstration of monism is proposed. What are the limitations? One is implicit in what is said above. The assertion that Spinoza's demonstration of monism is sound – an assertion which would of course entail that Spinoza's monism is true – is not defended here. Rather, what is defended – and even here only partially – is the thesis that Spinoza's monism can be derived validly from the definitions and axioms of Part I of the *Ethics*.

Here a bit of explanation is in order. The passage quoted above, including IP14 and IP14D, is of course critical for our purposes. But, as with most of Spinoza's explicit demonstrations of particular propositions, IP14D does not explicitly take the derivation of Proposition 14, Spinoza's monism, all the way back to the definitions and axioms of the *Ethics*; that is, to the theses on which the demonstration, in theory, ultimately and exclusively rests. To be sure, IP14D explicitly invokes one definition, that of God, ID6. But the other two official premises of IP14D are not definitions or axioms, but rather earlier propositions of Part One, specifically, Propositions 5 and 11. With respect to Proposition 5, we are in luck. We are preceded by the brilliant work of Don Garrett on this subject, who has argued that proposition 5 does indeed follow validly from the definitions and axioms of Part I.[1] While a good deal of Garrett's fine work is accepted, this chapter nonetheless departs from him on both the question of the proper reading of IP5 and on the proper response to what Garrett calls the Bennett–Leibniz objection to Spinoza's demonstration of IP5.[2] With respect to proposition 11, however, which is crucial in bringing an existence claim to Spinoza's metaphysics – the claim of the existence of God – things are more problematic. There is no attempt, in this chapter, to defend the demonstration of proposition 11 from the axioms and definitions of Part I, although some important features of its demonstration are considered. This is a key respect in which the present defense of the demonstration of monism must be termed limited.

There are, finally, two issues – one major, one less so – that are not addressed in this chapter. The minor one is that the last three words of Spinoza's formulation of monism are not addressed: 'Except for God no substance can be *or be conceived*' (IP14; Curley, p. 420; emphasis added). The major one concerns an issue that becomes central in Part II of the *Ethics*, namely, that, according to Spinoza, 'the thinking substance and the extended substance are one and the same substance, which is now comprehended under this attribute, now under that' (IIP7S; Curley, p. 451). This notoriously difficult aspect of Part II of Spinoza's metaphysics cannot be dealt with here, although it is to be hoped that the interpretation presented in these pages may provide a new perspective from which to grapple with this important topic.

The chapter has the following divisions. In section 13.1, a preliminary reconstruction of the explicit demonstration of monism, that is, of IP14, is developed. It turns out that there is a significant objection to this reconstruction, presented in section 13.2; namely, that analysis of it reveals an implicit contradiction. This leads to reconsideration, in section 13.3, of some crucial aspects of Spinoza's demonstration and the presentation of an interpretation that would not force Spinoza into this contradiction. Unfortunately, this interpretation is in turn subject to the objection that a contradiction can be derived from it also, as is outlined in section 13.4. Finally, section five provides a revised interpretation that handles the problems of both contradictions and another leading interpretive problem as well, the Bennett–Leibniz objection to the demonstration of IP5. This solution, which leads also to a revision of Garrett's defense of the demonstration of IP5, contains as a subpart a second reconstruction of Spinoza's demonstration of monism, which is claimed to be a valid deduction of monism – bracketing questions about the deduction of IP11 – from the axioms and definitions of Part One of Spinoza's *Ethics*.

13.1 First reconstruction of the demonstration of monism

The first reconstruction of the demonstration of monism is as follows:

(1) God is a substance having all attributes (Df. 6).
(2) God exists (IP11).
(3) There are no two substances having the same attribute (IP5).
(4) Every substance has at least one attribute (suggested in the course of Spinoza's demonstration of IP14).
(5) So, if God exists and some substance other than God exists, then there are two substances having the same attribute (1,4).
(6) So, it is not the case that God exists and some substance other than God exists (3,5).
(7) So, either God does not exist or no substance other than God exists (6).
(8) So, no substance other than God exists (2,7).

A few comments are in order here. First, premise (1) is not a simple statement of Definition 6. It is an interpretation of what that definition says or implies. Although the interpretation is plausible, it is not defended here beyond citing Jonathan Bennett's persuasive work in defending the critical move from the actual definition to the insertion of 'all attributes' above.[3] Secondly, premise (4) is not an official, explicitly-cited premise of Spinoza's argument, as ID6, IP5, and IP11 clearly are. In fact, it is not even explicitly stated in Spinoza's demonstration. More exactly, what Spinoza says is that 'if there were any substance except God, it would have to be explained through some attribute of God' (IP14D; Curley, p. 420). But this would seem to imply premise (4), an essential premise of the argument in the present reconstruction.[4] This still leaves the question of whether premise (4) could in principle be derived from the axioms and definitions of the *Ethics*. It is not implausible that Spinoza would have thought that it could be, given the close links between substance, essence and attribute in his thought. (IP4 would obviously be critical here.) But this question will not be taken up in detail in what follows. This too, then, will be a limitation of the present defense.

Despite the initial plausibility of the reconstruction above, there seems to be a problem with the argument for monism reconstructed in this way. To get a different perspective on how the argument works, and hence to see how the problem arises, it may be helpful to consider just one non-monistic – that is, pluralistic – state of affairs; namely, a state of affairs in which God exists and some other substance – say a substance of exactly one attribute, the attribute of extension (call this Ed) – also exists. How does Spinoza's demonstration of IP14, as reconstructed above, rule out this state of affairs? First, we apply Proposition 5 and Definition 6, the definition of God, to get the result that only one or the other of God and Ed can exist; they cannot both exist, for then there would be two substances having the same attribute – the attribute of extension, contra Proposition 5. We can put this by saying that if God necessarily exists, then Ed cannot exist; but we can also put this, equivalently but more worrisomely, by saying that if Ed necessarily exists, then God cannot exist. The first of these provides the most obvious entrée for Proposition 11, God necessarily exists. Putting the first together with Proposition 11, a simple application of modus ponens gives us the result that Ed cannot exist. And the same sort of argument would, given the implicit premise that every substance must have an attribute, yield the same result for every other substance not identical to God, so that, granting God's necessary existence, no other substance could exist. But the very power of this procedure – along with the simplicity of the first demonstration of Proposition 11 – gives rise to a serious concern about the argument. Might not one use the logic of Proposition 11 to arrive at a very different result?

Let's look at the first demonstration of Proposition 11, that God necessarily exists:

> Dem.: If you deny this, conceive, if you can, that God does not exist. Therefore (by A7) his essence does not involve existence. But this (by P7) is absurd. Therefore God necessarily exists, q.e.d.

The most interesting thing about this demonstration is that its two official premises, A7 and P7, are perfectly general – they are about things and substances, not exclusively about God. This means that Spinoza's version of the ontological argument is quite different from more traditional versions, which clearly do turn on distinctive features of God (e.g., that God is the most perfect being, or a being than which none is greater, or a being having all perfections). In the demonstration of P11 just quoted, the only features of God that are required for the argument to proceed are that God is a thing and that God is a substance – both extremely non-distinctive features, at least before the demonstration of monism. In short, any substance – being both thing and substance – can be shown to exist necessarily by the logic of this argument.[5]

It may be granted that this is very different from the logic of traditional ontological arguments, but how does the difference relate to the demonstration of monism? Well, recall our finding, relative to that demonstration and the sample case of Ed and God, that if Ed necessarily exists, then God cannot exist. Now imagine a kind of anti-Spinoza turned loose on this sample case and given the ammunition of the demonstration of IP11 just considered. Our anti-Spinoza knows that the logic of the demonstration of IP11 yields the result that the substance, Ed, necessarily exists. Given this result, an application of modus ponens to the conditional above yields for our anti-Spinoza the result that God cannot exist.

This result would, obviously, be a problem for a Spinozist. But the real problem would not be that someone opposed Spinozist views. More strictly, the problem looming for Spinozists is rather that the theses of the *Ethics* up through Proposition 14 and its demonstration seem to provide the basis for a contradiction; that is, to imply a contradiction; that is, to be logically inconsistent. If the existence of a substance having exactly one attribute, that of extension, can be deduced by the logic of the demonstration of IP11, and the existence of God – who is such that no attribute can be denied him – can also be so deduced, then it appears that there will be a contradiction with one of the official premises of IP14D; namely, IP5 – that there cannot be two or more substances of the same nature or attribute. God and Ed, both of whom (we are supposing) demonstrably exist, have the attribute of extension.

It should not be thought that this problem marks the end of the road for Spinoza's demonstration of monism. But the problem does force us to rethink the steps of reasoning leading to Spinoza's monism, and perhaps to see his thought in a new way. Let us consider some steps of dialectic proceeding from this problem.

13.2 A resolution of the first contradiction problem, based on the Guéroult–Loeb interpretation

An interesting first step is provided by an unusual interpretation of Spinoza's views on the relation of substance and attribute. It comes from such interpreters as Martial Guéroult and Louis Loeb and will here be called the Guéroult–Loeb interpretation.[6] There are two key theses involved, both of which are at least somewhat controversial. The first is that God is a compound substance, a substance consisting of multiple simple substances, each 'having' exactly one attribute.[7] The second is that each simple substance, or each substance 'having' exactly one attribute, just is that attribute; attributes and simple substances are identical. (Of course, we can still say that this simple substance 'has' the attribute of extension, thus verbally suggesting a difference between the simple substance and the attribute. But in fact there is, on the Guéroult–Loeb interpretation, no metaphysical difference here: the attribute of extension just is the simple substance in question.) Proceeding from these theses, and examining more closely the different shades of meaning possible in the interpretation of Spinoza's statement of monism and IP5, one can find an escape from the threatening contradiction.

Putting this differently – and more contentiously – the Contradiction Problem may arise on many interpretations of Spinoza's *Ethics*, but, granting a certain not unreasonable hypothesis, it does not go through on the Guéroult–Loeb interpretation. This may be taken as providing one reason for favouring that interpretation over many others.

To see how the Guéroult–Loeb interpretation might lead to a resolution of the contradiction problem, let us return to the test case of God and Ed (our substance having exactly one attribute, that of extension). An assumption of the argument for contradiction above is that God and Ed are 'distinct' substances. For many this will be seen as a well-grounded assumption: God is a substance who has multiple attributes; Ed is a substance who, having exactly one attribute, does not have multiple attributes; therefore, God and Ed are 'distinct' substances. But on the Guéroult–Loeb interpretation, things take on a different look, suggesting a reconsideration of some central concepts.

Consider the two following cases, sketched in accordance with the Guéroult–Loeb interpretation: (1) there is just one substance – the compound substance, God, consisting of infinitely many attributes, each of which is itself a (simple) substance and one of which is the simple substance consisting of (identical with) an attribute of extension; and (2) there are two substances – the compound substance, God, described just as above, and, over and above this, a simple substance consisting of an attribute of extension. Note that in case (2) there are *two* simple substances consisting of an attribute of extension; in case (1) there is only one.

Now consider IP5, that 'in the universe there cannot be two or more substances of the same nature or attribute.' The not unreasonable hypothesis mentioned above is that Spinoza intends this to apply only to something like case (2) – not to case (1), where just God, with his infinitely many attributes, exists. Let us bring in the case of God and Ed to explore this a bit more. Ed, it will be recalled, is a substance having exactly one attribute, the attribute of extension. On the Guéroult–Loeb interpretation, of course, Ed is just a simple substance, not at all distinct from the attribute it 'has.' But as cases (1) and (2) reveal, this simple description of Ed leaves us with an important question unanswered. For all we know about Ed, Ed could be the simple substance with the attribute of extension that is, as in case (1), just one of the simple substances constituting the compound substance God, rather than being the simple substance with the attribute of extension that in case (2) is supposed to exist over and above God and all the constituent simple substances of God. The fact that there is an ontological argument for Ed – that is, for the existence of a substance having exactly one attribute, that of extension – as well as an ontological argument for the existence of God, in no way shows that case (2) obtains rather than case (1).[8] But by the not unreasonable hypothesis about IP5 presented above, it would only be case (2) that contradicts IP5.

Let me put this another way. The contradiction problem is supposed to be that IP11 can be used to prove not only the existence of God, but also the existence of a substance having exactly one attribute – that of extension – and that this leads to a contradiction of IP5. The question is, what state of affairs is supposed to be demonstrated by this double proof? Is it supposed to show that case (2) obtains? Not necessarily, since the double proof is perfectly consistent with case (1), with the existence of a simple substance having the attribute extension being proved twice over: once via the ontological proof of God, once via the ontological proof of a substance having exactly one attribute – that of extension. Nothing about the two ontological proofs shows that the existence of *two* simple substances having the single attribute extension has been demonstrated. Keep in mind that, given the hypothesis mentioned above, only case (2) contradicts IP5.

But, some will reply, is it not the case that God is nonetheless numerically distinct from Ed, even granting the points made above? For Ed is a simple substance, and God is a compound substance. They must be numerically distinct. Hence, the present line of thought, based on the Guéroult–Loeb interpretation, also contradicts Spinoza. Specifically, it contradicts his monism. There is no gain here via the Guéroult–Loeb interpretation. We get inconsistency either way.

Do we? The preceding discussion brings to the fore an important question about monism in relation to difference or distinctness. What precisely is Spinoza claiming in saying that 'except for God no substance can be or be conceived' (Curley, p. 420), or, as another translator puts it, 'no substance can be or be conceived *external to* God?'[9] Is Spinoza saying that there is no substance numerically distinct from God? Or is Spinoza saying that there is no substance distinct from God in another sense, the sense appealed to above in saying that the proof of the existence of Ed proves the existence of nothing over and above – nothing in some second sense distinct from – what is already proved to exist by the ontological proof of the existence of God?

It turns out that very much the same idea involved in the hypothesis above about IP5 will help answer this question too. But at this point we need to refine the idea, spelling out explicitly the notion of distinctness involved there. Here then is a definition of a notion of distinctness different from numerical distinctness. (The label, 'distinct1', will be used to refer to numerical distinctness; the label, 'distinct2', to refer to the second sense of distinctness.)

> x and y are distinct2 = df. (i) x and y are distinct1, i.e., numerically distinct, and (ii) neither x nor y is a constituent of the other.[10]

It will help in explaining this concept of distinctness if we apply it to cases (1) and (2) above. In case (1), we supposed the compound substance God, one of whose constituent substances was a simple substance having the attribute of extension. So as not to beg any questions about the relationship of this simple substance to the substance named earlier – Ed – let us name this simple substance Elvis. Again, this newly-named Elvis is a simple substance, a constituent of the compound substance God, and has the attribute of extension. We may grant that God and Elvis are distinct1, that is, numerically distinct – since one is a compound substance and the other is simple – while nonetheless holding that they are not distinct in another sense, that of distinctness2. For Elvis is a constituent of God (v. condition (ii) of the definition above), one of the simple substances that together constitute the compound substance God. More informally, Elvis is not a substance existing over and above what exists once the existence of God is granted, and so is not distinct from God in this sense. Or, again informally – and adopting the language of one of the translations presented above of Spinoza's statement of monism – we can say that Elvis, while not being numerically identical to God, is not 'external' to God either (since Elvis is a constituent of God), so that the existence of Elvis does not contradict the monistic thesis that 'no substance can be or be conceived external to God.'[11]

Applying this now to the substance named Ed, we get the following results. If Ed is numerically identical to Elvis, then, obviously, Ed is not distinct2 from God any more than Elvis is. And this is true even if we grant that Ed is numerically distinct from God. But if Ed is numerically distinct from Elvis, then if Ed and God (hence also Elvis) exist, we would have two substances, Ed and Elvis, being of the same attribute, the attribute of extension. And this, of course, would violate IP5. But in the case of just Elvis and God, or, if you wish, the case of Elvis (=Ed) and God, we are just in case (1), and, we have asserted, this constitutes no violation of IP5.

At this point some may be desirous of a fuller defense of the claim that the existence of the numerically distinct substances, God and Elvis – both in some sense 'having' the attribute of extension – does not violate IP5. We are now in a position to give this defense. Again, the second sense of distinctness is central. IP5 asserts that 'In nature there cannot be two or more substances of the same nature or attribute.' The present suggestion is that this be taken as asserting, in essence, that there cannot be two distinct2 substances of the same attribute. God and Elvis, while numerically distinct, are not distinct2, since Elvis is a constituent of God, so the case of Elvis and God does not violate IP5 as it has just been interpreted. And on the Guéroult–Loeb interpretation this reading is not altogether implausible. For, in the first place, on the Guéroult–Loeb interpretation, God's 'having' the attribute of extension is really a quite different thing from Elvis's 'having' that attribute of extension: the compound substance God 'has' the attribute of extension solely in virtue of having Elvis as a constituent simple substance, which substance, in turn, 'has' the attribute of extension in virtue of simply being numerically identical with it. One is tempted to say that in this case it is only verbally, but not actually, that the attribute is instantiated twice, and that this has some relevance to what Spinoza was getting at in IP5. And, in the second place, in a sense God and Elvis are not really two substances, any more than we would want to say, without qualification, that my body and my heart are two substances. (In a sense they are; in a sense they are not. Perhaps it was the second sense – the sense of distinctness2 – that Spinoza had in mind in talking about two substances in IP5.)

Even if it is granted that the preceding provides a strong response to the contradiction problem of the preceding section, some may be uneasy about the response's reliance on an interpretation, the Guéroult–Loeb interpretation, that has been acknowledged to be controversial. Where, it may be asked, is the argument for this interpretation? It may surprise the reader that there is no direct argument for this interpretation in the present chapter, despite the fact that the interpretation does in fact figure in the final version of the defense of the demonstration of monism proposed in this chapter. Rather, the present chapter offers an indirect argument, while also referring the reader to Guéroult and Loeb themselves for the direct arguments these two offer for the interpretation.[12] Briefly, the indirect argument will take this form: the Guéroult–Loeb interpretation makes possible a defense of Spinoza's demonstration of monism, a defense that frees it from some serious difficulties. If there is no equally plausible model that also makes possible a defense of that demonstration from these difficulties, then, by the Principle of Charity, we would seem to have a significant, albeit indirect, argument in support of the Guéroult–Loeb interpretation as a viable interpretation of Spinoza. Again, no claim is made that such an indirect argument would by itself be decisive. Not only would direct arguments have to be considered, but also counterarguments, including arguments in support of models inconsistent with the Guéroult–Loeb interpretation. Such a complete survey will not be attempted here. Rather, the argument is restricted to developing a particular line of defense, incorporating the Guéroult–Loeb interpretation, in support of Spinoza's demonstration of monism.

But it should not be thought that the procedure adopted here is uncritical, or that any claim has been made that the exposition of the intended line of defense is already essentially complete. In fact, even though the defense so far (which at base consists of the adoption of the Guéroult–Loeb interpretation, along with an interpretation of P14 and P5 in terms of distinctness2 instead of distinctness1) is a genuine answer to what will be called the First Contradiction Problem, it is not itself free of difficulties. In what follows, an important criticism will be raised and a response to it will be given. To be sure, the response requires a revision of what has been presented so far in this defense of Spinoza's demonstration of monism, but it retains the Guéroult–Loeb interpretation as a central element.

13.3 The second contradiction problem

We have seen above that the derivation of the original contradiction, that is, the contradiction allegedly brought about by the assertion of IP5 and the logic of IP11D – the latter implying, contra the former, both the existence of God and the existence of a substance of exactly one attribute, extension – could be blocked by adopting the Guéroult–Loeb interpretation along with an interpretation of IP5 and IP14 in terms of distinctness2. But of course the entailment of any contradiction by any valid route is sufficient to show the inconsistency of a set of propositions. And it might be argued that a second contradiction seems derivable from the newly interpreted IP5 and IP11, even granting that the first is not.[13]

Consider the following two substances: S1 is a compound substance constituted by two attributes (or simple substances), the first being the attribute of thought, the second, one of those attributes that surpass human comprehension – call it attribute *X*; and S2 is a compound substance also constituted by two attributes, but this time by the attribute of extension, not thought, along with, again, mysterious attribute *X*. Pretty clearly, (a) the logic of the first demonstration of IP11 should apply to these two substances as well as it did to Ed and Elvis, so that both necessarily exist, and (b) S1 and S2 are two numerically distinct substances, since one has an attribute that the other lacks, and (c) S1 and S2 are of the same attribute, since they both have or involve attribute *X*.

A quick look at these results suggests that these two points already give rise to a contradiction: the existence of substances S1 and S2 contradicts IP5. But our work above with the case of God and Elvis reveals that we must proceed with care here before drawing such a conclusion. For God and Elvis met conditions (a), (b) and (c). And yet the existence of both of those substances could be handled on the Guéroult–Loeb interpretation, without contradiction, assuming that IP5 asserts only that no two distinct2 substances are of the same attribute.

But the problem raised by this new case, of substances S1 and S2, is that a similar resolution will not work in this case. S1 and S2 *are* distinct2, whereas

God and Elvis were not: (i) S1 and S2 are numerically distinct and (ii) neither is a constituent of the other; in the case of God and Elvis only the first condition was satisfied. So, after all, it appears that the existence of S1 and S2 will lead to a contradiction, even on the assumption of the Guéroult–Loeb interpretation and the interpretation of IP5 in terms of distinctness2.

To some this may look like an overly technical difficulty. But it should be taken seriously. In what follows, a solution to the difficulty, via a modification of the Guéroult–Loeb approach adopted above, is proposed.[14]

13.4 A resolution of the second contradiction problem and more

A key part of the approach mentioned above was the emphasis on a special sense of distinctness, one that we called distinctness2, different from numerical distinctness. This sense was invoked in giving an interpretation of both IP14 and IP5. Of these two applications, the one to IP5 is probably the more controversial.[15] Most scholars have interpreted IP5 in terms of distinctness1 – that is, numerical identity – rather than in terms of distinctness2. Of course, the interpretation of IP5 in terms of distinctness2 was an essential part of our earlier solution to the first contradiction problem, and so is not something to be given up easily in constructing a defense of Spinoza's demonstration of monism from threatening contradictions. Nonetheless, we should indeed explore the option of giving up this interpretation of IP5, and set about constructing a reading in terms of this option – one that satisfies the following conditions, or desiderata, if you will, of a satisfactory interpretation of Spinoza's demonstration of monism: (i) the problem of the first contradiction must be resolved; (ii) the problem of the second contradiction must be resolved; (iii) the Leibniz–Bennett objection to IP5 must be avoided.

The third desideratum warrants further explanation. One of the oldest objections to Spinoza's system is that of Leibniz to IP5 and its demonstration. Leibniz felt that there was nothing in Spinoza's demonstration that ruled out the possibility – made pressing by Spinoza's own embrace of the decidedly uncartesian idea of a substance with multiple attributes – that two substances, each having two attributes, might share a single attribute but nonetheless be distinguished by other of their attributes. His example was of two substances, A and B, the former having attributes c and d; the latter, attributes d and e, with d being the shared attribute, and c and e being the attributes which distinguish substances A and B.[16] This simple example seemingly undercuts one of the key moves of Spinoza's demonstration. Details will not be presented here, but it will be assumed that this is a genuine difficulty for Spinoza's demonstration of IP5 – as is assumed also by Garrett in the article referred to above.

But Garrett's attempted resolution of this problem will not be followed. Rather, in the present defense of Spinoza's demonstration of monism, a theory will be proposed that solves both of the contradiction problems of this chapter, plus the problem the Leibniz–Bennett objection poses for the demonstration of IP5 – with the final point being obviously critical for any defense of the full demonstration of monism. One reason why Garrett's attempted resolution is not followed here is that, while his ingenious defense of the demonstration of IP5 as successful against the problems he addresses, it does not provide a promising base for the broader defense of monism against the difficulties raised in the present chapter. Again, an attempt is made to provide a defense that both resolves his difficulties and resolves the ones presented in the present chapter.

What, then, is the proposed resolution? The key modifications from the resolution presented in section 13.2 have to do with IP5. First, as indicated above, we return to the more traditional idea that IP5 concerns numerical distinctness, rather than distinctness2. Secondly, we adopt an idea that several commentators have mentioned at one point or another,[17] namely, that IP5 is in fact restricted to substances of one attribute. On this interpretation, the demonstration of IP5 seems to leave gaps in the case of substances of more than one attribute for the very good reason that it was never meant to be a demonstration that covers such a case. Putting these two ideas together, we get the following interpretation of IP5: there cannot exist two numerically distinct substances of one attribute that are of the same attribute. Here again, the argument for this interpretation will not be direct, but rather indirect: taken together with the Guéroult–Loeb interpretation and certain other features of the interpretation presented above, it allows for a reasonable defense of Spinoza's demonstration of monism. A challenge for rival interpretations would be to show that they too can provide the basis for a reasonable defense in the face of the kinds of difficulties we have raised.

To begin in mounting this indirect argument, let us examine whether these two changes in our interpretation of IP5 undercut our ability to deal successfully with the first contradiction problem, or whether they too allow for a resolution of that problem. Recall the contradiction involving God and Ed, with Ed being a substance having exactly one attribute, the attribute of extension. The existence of both God and Ed was proved via the logic of the first demonstration of IP11. But the existence of both of these substances appeared to contradict IP5.

Now one might be tempted by the view that the existence of these two substances poses even less of a problem on the new interpretation of IP5 – restricted as it is, on this interpretation, to substances of one attribute – than it did on the previous interpretation of IP5 (in terms of distinctness2). For God is obviously a substance of *multiple* attributes.

But such a view would be too hasty. For the newly interpreted IP5 still does apply to the case of God and Ed, albeit indirectly. To see this, one needs to follow out a bit the consequences of the proof of the existence of God. We know from the definition of God that God is a substance having infinite (that is, on Spinoza's unusual use of 'infinite', *all)* attributes, so we know – assuming the Guéroult–Loeb interpretation – that the proof of the existence of God brings with it a proof of the existence of the simple substances of one attribute which constitute God, including – since extension is an attribute – a simple substance having an attribute of extension, or a simple substance which just is identical to this attribute of extension. As before, we call this simple substance of the attribute of extension Elvis.

Once this is seen, it becomes clear that we can – indeed, must – apply the newly-interpreted Proposition 5 to the case of God and Ed. The question is, of course, whether this case violates the principle that there can be no two numerically distinct simple substances of the same attribute. And this in turn reduces to the question of whether Ed is numerically distinct from Elvis. Now it is no part of our purpose here to prove that Ed and Elvis are or are not numerically distinct. Rather, we argue only that nothing in the case so far presented forces the conclusion that they are numerically distinct. To put this differently, nothing in the 'first contradiction problem' *forces* us to acknowledge a contradiction in Spinoza's metaphysics once we have adopted the interpretations that make up the present approach. The present approach allows for a reading that yields consistency, namely, that the proof of Ed just provides a second proof of the numerically identical simple substance, Elvis, implicitly proved in the proof of God. In sum, the modified interpretation does not undercut our ability to respond to the first contradiction problem.

What about the second contradiction problem? As it turns out, there are some obvious analogues between the analysis of this case and the analysis of the case above. First, the newly-interpreted IP5 does not apply directly to the case of the two numerically distinct substances S1 and S2 (approximately in the way it did not apply directly to the case of God and Ed), since S1 and S2 are substances of two attributes each (with one being shared and one not); they are not substances of a single attribute. Secondly, the newly-interpreted IP5 does nonetheless apply indirectly to the case of S1 and S2, since – according to the Guéroult–Loeb interpretation – each is constituted by two simple substances, i.e., substances of exactly one attribute, and the newly-interpreted IP5 applies specifically to such substances. Thirdly, in considering whether any contradiction arises when applying the newly-interpreted IP5 in this indirect way to substances S1 and S2, we get a result similar to what we found above: no contradiction is forced. To be sure, there would be a contradiction *if* the simple substance of mystery attribute *X* that is a constituent of S1 were numerically *distinct* from the simple substance of mystery attribute *X* that is a constituent of S2. But nothing about the proposed ontological argument for substances S1 and S2, or about the newly-interpreted IP5 forces such a conclusion. Again, our present approach allows for a consistent reading – namely, that the proof of S2 simply provides a second proof of the numerically identical simple substance of the mystery attribute *X*, already demonstrated in the proof of S1.

What about desideratum (iii), that a proposed interpretation should provide an answer to the Leibniz–Bennett objection? In a way things are easy here; in a way hard. The easy response with respect to the Leibniz–Bennett objection is that on the newly-interpreted IP5 the Leibniz–Bennett objection simply disappears: the objection assumes that IP5 is intended to apply to substances of more than one attribute; but on the present interpretation it does not. Again, it applies (directly, one should add[18]) only to substances of just one attribute.

What is the hard part of the response to the Leibniz–Bennett objection? As it turns out, both Bennett and Garrett[19] address, more or less directly, the feature of the present interpretation of IP5 here under discussion – namely, that it applies only to substances of a single attribute. And both claim something that would be utterly devastating from the point of view of the present project: they claim that such an interpretation totally undercuts the demonstration of monism in IP14. It will not do to respond to the Leibniz–Bennett objection in such a way that there can be no defense of the demonstration of monism. Obviously, we must respond to this kind of objection.

To begin with, we note the two pieces of good news for our interpretation of IP5 that Bennett includes in his discussion: (i) he grants that the Leibniz–Bennett objection would indeed be blocked by this interpretation, and (ii) he acknowledges that there is some textual basis for adopting such an interpretation, given that Spinoza does not mention the possibility of a substance of multiple attributes until after the presentation of IP5, specifically, in IP9.[20] But Bennett proceeds immediately from these points to what he clearly views as the decisive objection against an interpretation of IP5 that would restrict its application to substances of one attribute:

> [A]re we to suppose that Spinoza intended his argument [for IP5] in that way, and simply forgot to review it in the light of his later thesis that substances can have more than one attribute? That is not credible, given how the pivotal p14d depends on combining 'There is a substance which has every attribute' with (p5) 'Two substances cannot share any attribute'. Surely in *this* context Spinoza could not just forget that p5d assumed that no substance has more than one attribute![21]

The point is clear: on Bennett's understanding of Spinoza's demonstration of monism, an interpretation of IP5 that restricted its application to substances of one attribute would completely undercut that demonstration.

How can such a powerful objection be handled? A first step is to say that while the objection may well be decisive within the framework of Bennett's own interpretation of Spinoza's metaphysics, it does not follow that it is decisive within the framework of other interpretations of Spinoza's metaphysics. So the real question for the purposes of the present project is whether the objection is decisive within the interpretative framework we are presently in. And with respect to that question, the answer is that the objection is not decisive.

To see this, let us revise our initial reconstruction of the demonstration of IP14 in accordance with our current interpretations. Naturally, a key element in this reconstruction will be the interpretation of IP5 as applying solely to substances of one attribute and being simply about numerical distinctness. But the Guéroult–Loeb interpretation and the interpretation of IP14 in terms of distinctness2 will also be essentially involved. We shall see if such an interpretation leaves Spinoza's argument hopelessly unable to reach the conclusion of monism. The steps are:

(1) God is a substance having all attributes, that is, a compound substance constituted by simple substances of every attribute (Df. 6).
(2) God exists (IP11).
(3) There are no two numerically distinct substances of one attribute having the same attribute (IP5).
(4) Every substance has at least one attribute (introduced in the course of Spinoza's demonstration of IP14).
(5) So, if God exists and some substance distinct2 from God exists, then there are two numerically distinct substances of one attribute having the same attribute (1,4).
(6) So, it is not the case that God exists and some substance distinct2 from God exists (3,5).
(7) So, either God does not exist or no substance other than God exists (6).
(8) So, no substance other than God exists (2,7).

The steps of this second reconstruction have been intentionally kept in strict parallel with the steps of the first reconstruction, to make it easier to see precisely what has changed and what has stayed the same. One disadvantage of this approach is that it leaves obscure an additional, very significant, change in the final reconstruction. That change comes in the inference to line (5). This is the further point that needs to be explained.

Fortunately, the basic idea has already emerged in what has gone before: in some cases IP5 is applied indirectly rather than directly. Suppose, as Spinoza does in his demonstration, that there is a substance other than God. Of course, on the present interpretation of IP14, this means supposing that a substance exists that is distinct2 from God. Keeping things simple, at least to start, we first suppose that this distinct2 substance is a substance of a single attribute, say extension. For old times' sake, call this substance Ed. Obviously, since God is constituted by simple substances of every attribute, and since, by P11, God exists, we know that there is a simple substance – that is, a substance of a single attribute – that is a constituent of God and is of the attribute of extension. Again, for old time's sake, call this substance Elvis. Now, by our supposition, Ed cannot be numerically identical with Elvis. For the supposition was that there exists a substance distinct2 from God; and if Ed were numerically identical with Elvis, Ed would of course be what Elvis is, namely, a constituent of the compound substance God, which would contradict Ed's being distinct2 from God. But if Ed is not numerically identical with Elvis, then IP5 is contradicted. So the supposition must be rejected.

Now the same line of argument would obviously apply also for a simple substance of any attribute other than extension. And, though things would be more complicated, it is clear that it would also apply for any compound substance that was not a constituent of God.[22] So, on the hypothesis (more than plausible from the point of view of the Guéroult–Loeb interpretation) that all substances are simple or compound, the argument applies to all substances distinct2 from God. Thus, the claim that interpreting IP5 as applying solely to substances of one attribute undermines the demonstration of monism is shown to be incorrect, at least within the framework of the interpretation we are here presenting.

But we are now in a position to say that all three of our desiderata have been attained in the context of giving a defense of Spinoza's demonstration of monism: (i) we are not forced to the conclusion that Spinoza's principles entail the first contradiction; (ii) we are not forced to the conclusion that Spinoza's principles entail the second contradiction; and (iii) we can avoid the Leibniz–Bennett objection to the demonstration of IP5. And we have done this, it bears repeating, on the assumption of the two central theses of the Guéroult–Loeb interpretation, on the assumption that Spinoza's monism is the thesis that there can be no substance that is distinct2 from God, and on the assumption that Spinoza's IP5 is to be interpreted as stating that in nature there can be no two numerically distinct substances that are of the same nature or attribute. This result is evidence that the constellation of interpretative theses just stated deserves serious consideration as expressing Spinoza's metaphysical intent in presenting his demonstration of monism.

Notes

This chapter is reprinted from Kulstad, Mark, A. 1996 'Spinoza's Demonstration of Monism: A New Line of Defense', *History of Philosophy Quarterly*, 13: 4, 299–316.

1. Don Garrett, '*Ethics* IP5: Shared Attributes and the Basis of Spinoza's Monism,' in *Central Themes in Early Modern Philosophy: Essays Presented to Jonathan Bennett*, J. A. Cover and Mark Kulstad (eds.), (Indianapolis: Hackett, 1990), pp. 69–108.
2. What the Bennett–Leibniz objection is will be explained below.
3. What Definition 6 actually says is that God is 'a substance consisting of an *infinity* of attributes ... ,' (*The Collected Works of Spinoza*, vol. 1, ed. and trans. by Edwin

Curley, [Princeton: Princeton University Press, 1985] p. 409; emphasis added; hereinafter cited as Curley) not of all attributes. However, Bennett gives a nice argument that Spinoza's text warrants the move from the former to the latter. See his *A Study of Spinoza's* Ethics, (Indianapolis: Hackett, 1984), pp. 75–76.

4. Jonathan Bennett also seems to view this premise as necessary for the argument. See his *A Study of Spinoza's* Ethics, p. 70.
5. Don Garrett makes a similar point in '*Ethics* IP5,' *op. cit.*, p. 85, as does Louis Loeb in *From Descartes to Hume: Continental Metaphysics and the Development of Modern Philosophy*, (Ithaca: Cornell, 1981), p. 165, n. 4.
6. For more on this interpretation see Martial Guéroult, *Spinoza I, Dieu (Ethique, I)* (Paris: Aubier-Montaigne, 1968), pp. 47ff, and Louis Loeb, *From Descartes to Hume*, pp. 161–66.
7. There are perhaps two main reasons for the controversial nature of this thesis. First, many view it as flatly contradicting Spinoza's monism, since it allows multiple substances. We shall address this question below. Secondly, it seems also to contradict Spinoza's insistence that substances cannot be divided, or have parts (v. IP12, IP12D, and IP13). Loeb responds to this second point in an interesting way. See Louis Loeb, *From Descartes to Hume*, pp. 170–71.
8. One might be tempted, à la Caterus, by other ontological arguments, e.g., by an argument starting from the following definition: SuperEd =df. a substance that (i) consists of exactly one attribute, extension, and (ii) is not a constituent of any compound substance of multiple attributes. Arguably, it is both the case that the logic of IP11D yields the existence of SuperEd as much as it yields the existence of God, and that the pair of ontological arguments, for God and SuperEd, does indeed force a situation of the type of case (2). In short, it might be argued that while the details of the section on the Contradiction Problem do not themselves prove that a contradiction can be derived from the resources of Spinoza's Part One, a refinement of those details does in fact lead to the derivation of a contradiction. To be sure, as Leibniz has taught us, one must not attempt an ontological argument from a definition that involves a contradiction. But it would appear that the challenge here would be to show that the definition of SuperEd does indeed involve a contradiction, while the definitions of God and Ed – or perhaps just of God – do not. Another route, this time following Descartes, in the Replies to Objections I, would be to argue that the concept of SuperEd does not involve a true and immutable nature, but only a fictitious one, due to a mental synthesis (*The Essential Descartes*, Margaret Wilson (ed.) [New York: Mentor, 1969], p. 229), while the definitions of God and Ed – or perhaps just of one of these two – do not. Interestingly, Spinoza seems to adopt something of this sort at one point. Bennett discusses it, but not sympathetically (v. *A Study of Spinoza's* Ethics, p. 75).
9. IP14D, in a translation by Samuel Shirley, *Baruch Spinoza:* Ethics, Treatise on the Emendation of the Intellect, *and Selected Letters*, edited with an introduction by Seymour Feldman (Indianapolis: Hackett, 1992), p. 39, emphasis added.
10. In turn one might request a definition of 'constituent'. While no formal definition will be offered here, some assistance may be given. A paradigm case of constituency for present purposes is the relation of simple substances to the compound substance that they constitute: each of these simple substances is a constituent of the compound substance. For compound substances, the key assertion is that (x)(y)(if x and y are compound substances, then x is a constituent of y just in case (z)(if z is a simple substance and z is a constituent of x, then z is a constituent of y)). (Perhaps some would qualify this a bit, saying that a

constituent compound substance must lack a simple substance that the other compound substance has to rule out the verbally awkward result of a compound substance being a constituent of itself.) Finally, it is stipulated that one thing can be a constituent of another without being a part of the other. Thus, a simple substance could be a constituent of the compound substance God without being a part of it. This provides a terminological equivalent to Loeb's advocacy of what may be called the Guéroult–Loeb Interpretation of substances and attributes combined with Loeb's denial that the Guéroult–Loeb Interpretation conflicts with Spinoza's assertion that a substance cannot have parts into which it can be divided. (See IP12 and IP12D and also Loeb, *From Descartes to Hume*, pp. 165–66.)

11. Feldman, *Ethics, op. cit.*, p. 39.
12. See note 6 above.
13. The difficulty here is due to Darien Lynx, who has also provided useful comments on other points in this chapter. I am indebted to him for his insights.
14. There are some interesting questions here that will be mentioned but, for reasons of space, not pursued. One is whether there could be such substances as S1 and S2 on Spinozistic premises. Another is whether the difficulty takes on a different colour depending on whether S1 and S2 share a numerically identical simple substance (a simple substance of mystery attribute *X*) – as opposed to having in common that one of their constituent simple substances is 'of the same attribute' as a constituent of the other, while not being numerically identical with a constituent of the other.
15. At least it can be said that others have supported a similar reading of IP14. See, for instance, Loeb, *From Descartes to Hume*, pp. 170–71.
16. See C. J. Gerhardt (ed.), *G. W. Leibniz: Die philosophischen Schriften*, 7 vol. (Berlin: Weidmann, 1875–90; reprint, Hildesheim: Olms, 1978), volume I, p. 142; translation from Leroy Loemker, ed., *G. W. Leibniz: Philosophical Papers and Letters*, 2nd ed. (Dordrecht: Reidel, 1969), p. 199. (For Jonathan Bennett's statement of the objection, see his *A Study of Spinoza's* Ethics, p. 69.) Notice the similarity between this and the case that gave rise to the second contradiction problem. One of the reasons for adding desideratum (iii) to the list above is that this similarity virtually forces recognition that there is a danger here of robbing Peter to save Paul, that is, as applied to this case, of solving the second contradiction problem while leaving unsolved the very similar problem of the Leibniz–Bennett objection. If the solution we offer satisfies all three conditions, we will have avoided this danger.
17. See, for instance, Jonathan Bennett, *A Study of Spinoza's Ethics*, p. 69. It should be noted that he mentions the idea only to reject it. Since the idea is retained in the present defense of Spinoza's demonstration of monism, it will be defended against Bennett's line of attack later in this chapter.
18. One might think that there is still the problem of an indirect application. But here the Leibniz–Bennett objection differs from what we saw in the analysis of the second contradiction problem. To be sure, indirect application is possible in the case of the two two-attribute substances mentioned by Leibniz – and the results would be perfectly analogous to what we saw in the case of substances S1 and S2. But – and here is the difference – this is of no relevance to what is being argued in the Leibniz–Bennett objection. That objection is supposed to show that the demonstration of IP5 is invalid for substances of two or more attributes. But, on the present interpretation, Spinoza is *not* presenting a demonstration for

such a conclusion: he is arguing only that there are no two numerically distinct substances *of one attribute* that are of the same nature or attribute.

19. See Bennett, *A Study of Spinoza's* Ethics, p. 69, and Don Garrett, '*Ethics* IP5,' p. 94.
20. Bennett, *A Study of Spinoza's* Ethics, p. 69. On the same page Bennett adds that up until IP9, Spinoza 'is thinking in terms of the concept of a one-attribute substance, a concept which explicitly appears in [I]p8d.'
21. Bennett, *A Study of Spinoza's* Ethics, p. 69. Garrett makes a similar point in his '*Ethics* IP5,' *op. cit.*, p. 94.
22. For reasons of space, this subargument is not given in full detail. The full version would make use of the explanation of a constituent given in an earlier note.

14
Explanatory Completeness and Spinoza's Monism

Rebecca Newberger Goldstein

So many monisms

Spinoza's zest for unification is isotropic. He is everywhere intent on dissolving disparities, reconciling polarities, denying dualities. Conceptual domains collide, and terms usually assigned to quite distinct categories are fused. The divine is collapsed into the natural, the ethical into the psychological, the mental and physical into each other, and, most startlingly of all, the ontological into the logical, a collapse which gives the eccentric deductive form to the *Ethics*.

Paired with each of these collapses, save one, there is an obvious statement of identity. The collapse of the divine into the natural yields the identification of God with nature[1]; the collapse of the ethical into the psychological yields the identification of the good with that which is in harmony with human nature[2]; and the collapse of the mental and the physical into each other yields the identification of minds and bodies.[3] Each of these identity statements can be expressed as a variety of monism: theological monism, ethical monism, and mind–body monism.

But, dramatic (and ambiguous) as these statements of identity are, they are not usually what we mean when we speak of Spinoza's monism. Rather that term is generally reserved for Spinoza's assertion that there is only one substance,[4] with all other things demoted to the status of modifications of the one substance. In particular, minds[5] and bodies, themselves identified with one another, are reduced to modifications, a reduction which does not undermine their status as individual things.[6]

Thinginess, then, is not the same as substancehood. There are many things, there is only one substance. Things – bodies and minds – are subjects of predication, so it is not enough, to qualify as a substance, to be the subject of predication. Things – bodies and minds – persist over time even as they change.[7] So diachronic identity is not sufficient to qualify as a substance. In short, Spinoza's notion of substance is not Aristotle's. It is not Descartes'.

What then is it, Spinoza's notion of substance, and precisely what is he saying about the world in asserting the existence of only one? Can his assertion of substance monism be illuminatingly linked with any of the four conceptual collapses, which, taken together, qualify him as a monist most supreme?[8] Spinoza's one substance is identified with that denseness of infinity which can be viewed alternatively as God or as nature, *Deus sive natura*, and *Deus sive natura* is itself an expression of the collapse of the theological into the natural.

But more light is shed on his substance monism if we relate it to the collapse between the ontological and the logical. In terms of shock value, Spinoza's deductive ontology is up there with his substance monism. These, the two most extreme aspects of his system, are intimately connected with one another. A most natural place to begin then, in explaining his substance monism – what it asserts and why it is asserted – is with his logicizing of ontology.

Logic power

The collapse of the ontological into the logical is what makes Spinoza the sort of rationalist he is, one who asserted that 'the eyes of the mind, whereby it sees and observes things, are none other than proofs'.[9] For Spinoza, a thing is known to exist if and only if it is logically derived, the derivation coming either from beside[10] or from above.[11] We can only see and observe by way of proofs precisely because we cannot know *that* something is unless we know *why* it must – logically – be. We do not even know *what* a thing is, what its nature is, unless we know *why* it is, which knowledge can only come to us through derivation. Basic conceptions – of substance, of causality[12], of God, of minds, of bodies – are remolded to fit the shape imposed on them by the deductions, which is why, as Spinoza readily acknowledges,[13] he is often forced to change the meanings of words.

Spinoza's collapse of the ontological into the logical (where the logical relationships hold primarily between concepts[14]) is what gives the eccentric form to the *Ethics,* setting itself up as a picture of nature, including human nature, that is as strictly deductive as Euclidean geometry. And because ontology is logicized, there can be, for Spinoza, no logically alternative world to the one which we have.[15] There is only one logically possible world, and this (tautologically) is it.

Why would Spinoza make so radical a claim? How bizarre it is to think that every feature of the world is logically determined, meaning that there is some sort of logical fallacy (out-and-out contradiction?) engendered in negating any descriptive fact, no matter how paltry, such that I am, at this precise moment, sitting with a laptop on my lap and typing this sentence. What possible intuition could have led Spinoza to so counterintuitive a position?

The intuition behind Spinoza's logicizing of ontology is the very same intuition behind his substance monism. It is no accident at all that these two most radical features of his system are intimately connected with each other (which makes for a parsimony of outrages to commonsense). Both are expressions of one and the same fundamental intuition, an intuition which Spinoza endows with the status of a logical principle, treating it as belonging to the general stock of those presumptions of reason to which a rationalist is entitled to help himself without proof. So the next question, of course, is: what is this methodologically and metaphysically loaded intuition?

A presumption of reason yielding explanatory completeness

The rationalist project, Spinoza's no less than Descartes's and Leibniz's, is perhaps best viewed as an experiment, seeking to test how far we could get were we to rely on reason alone.[16] We do not start out on such an experiment empty-minded. We do not have to prove everything, otherwise with what would we prove anything? If the project is to determine how far we can get relying on reason alone, then we are entitled to help ourselves to the presumptions of reason, those truths without which reason cannot itself function and which can, in that sense at least, be dubbed 'logical.'[17] The reliance on reason provides us with a select number of truths – certainly including the Law of Non-Contradiction, without which reason could not prove a thing, for then, having reached a conclusion, reason could not rule out the negation of the conclusion. A rationalist experimenter rightfully feels himself entitled to presumptively use the Law of Non-Contradiction without first proving it. To what other presumptions of reason, if any, does Spinoza feel entitled?

We are used to regarding the presumptions of reason as restricted to logical principles which are strictly formal in nature. They do not tell us anything about how the world actually is, do not yield us any knowledge of facts of the matter or existence (in Hume's terminology), but rather set out the array of possible combinations of truths. Their factual vacuity is the price of their aprioricity.

Spinoza, however, does not acknowledge this restrictive claim about the presumptions of reason. For Spinoza, there is at least one presumption of reason – a truth to which reason is entitled to help itself, for its negation renders thought itself incoherent – which also comes packed with descriptive content; in fact, it comes packed with all the descriptive content that there is, more than we are capable of unpacking. Like the other presumptions of reason – the Law of Non-Contradiction, for example – it is not explicitly listed among the axioms of the *Ethics*,[18] but rather – as befits a proper presumption of reason – it makes its presence known in its functioning, flitting beneath the surface of inferences, swelling the meanings of axioms and the designs of definitions.[19] In fact, it makes itself very busy, especially in the early sections of the *Ethics,* in which the existence of the one and only substance is being established.

So, for example, consider this passage, which occurs in Spinoza's first discussion of the singularity of substance:

> [I]f a given number of individual things exist in nature, there must be some cause for the existence of exactly that number, neither more nor less. For example, if twenty men exist in the universe (for simplicity's sake, I will suppose them existing simultaneously, and to have had no predecessors), and we want to account for the existence of these twenty men, it will not be enough to show the cause of human existence in general; we must also show why there are exactly twenty men, neither more nor less; for a cause must be assigned for the existence of each individual. Now this cause cannot be contained in the actual nature of man, for the true definition of man does not involve any consideration of the number twenty. Consequently, the cause for the existence of these twenty men, and consequently of each of them, must necessarily be sought external to each individual. Hence we may lay down the absolute rule, that everything which may consist of several individuals must have an external cause.[20]

Or consider this passage:

> Of everything whatsoever a cause or reason must be assigned, either for its existence, or for its non-existence – e.g. if a triangle exist, a reason or cause must be granted for its existence; if, on the contrary, it does not exist, a cause must also be granted, which prevents it from existing, or annuls its existence.... But the reason for the existence of a triangle or a circle does not follow from the nature of those figures, but from the order of universal nature in extension. From the latter it must follow, either that a triangle necessarily exists, or that it is impossible that it should exist. So much is self-evident. It follows therefrom that a thing necessarily exists, if no cause or reason be granted which prevents its existence.[21]

Spinoza is here relying, in the course of his inference, on the claim that all facts must be accounted for, and he is showing himself in both of these passages to hold to this principle in a radically strong form. Consider: If several things of a particular kind exist in a precise quantity, then this fact – the precise number of this sort of thing – needs to be accounted for. If something exists then the fact of its existence must be accounted for, and if something *doesn't* exist then this fact, too – the fact of its non-existence – must be accounted for. If the fact of its non-existence has no accounting then it is no fact at all – the thing in question not only exists, it necessarily exists; which, of course, entails that everything that exists necessarily exists, and everything that doesn't exist necessarily doesn't exist. Existence comes in only two flavours: necessary or impossible. We are denizens of the only possible world.[22] An alternative to it cannot be and cannot be conceived. The collapse of the ontological into the logical has already begun, with this demand that all facts come with an accounting so complete as to rule out the very possibility that they might not have been facts. This is his fundamental intuition (FI) – a version of what Leibniz would eventually dub the Principle of Sufficient Reason – although Spinoza differs from Leibniz as to what sorts of considerations count as sufficient reasons, and this is a difference that makes all the difference between these two robust rationalists.

Spinoza seems to regard FI as itself having the status of a logical principle,[23] requiring no special statement as an axiom but rather being utilized in the course of deductions, as it is in the passages quoted above. His deductive use of FI carries the presumption that the very idea of a fact which is a fact for no reason other than that it is a fact is as preposterous a supposition as a violation of the Law of Non-Contradiction. The notion of the arbitrarily true – it just *is*, end of story – is an affront to reason as insufferable as inconsistency (or perhaps even one with inconsistency). The world, for him, is surfeited with explanations – the very notion of the inexplicable rejected as incoherent. The presumption is that the world itself is reasonable, that the trail of explanations does not abruptly end in *tohu vavohu*. For Spinoza, it is not turtles all the way down, but rather explanations. The world is explanatorily complete, with arbitrariness as impermissible as inconsistency.

But must explanatory completeness commit one to a logicizing of reality? Leibniz, for one, thought not, distinguishing between 'the principle of contradiction, in virtue of which we judge to be false anything that involves contradiction, and as true whatever is opposed or contradictory to what is false' and 'that of sufficient reason, in virtue of which we hold that no fact could ever be true or existent, no statement correct, unless there were a sufficient reason why it was thus and not otherwise – even though those reasons will usually not be knowable by us.'[24] Spinoza, in contrast, appears to reduce these two principles to one, so that in his version, the Principle of Sufficient Reason (PSR) is more like the Principle of Sufficient Logical Reason (PSLR). Because FI leads him to a different standard of what counts as a sufficient reason – with only self-accounting logic capable of filling the bill – Spinoza is led, as Leibniz is not, to claim that the world itself offers up its own complete explanation, crowding out the very possibility of a transcendent God, a God whose choices offer explanations for the world from *outside* the world. 'Such a doctrine might well have sufficed to conceal the truth from the human race for all eternity, if mathematics had not furnished another standard of verity in considering solely the essence and properties of figures without regard to their final causes.'[25]

For Spinoza, nothing less than the sort of accounting that we get in mathematics, all corners squarely tucked into deduction, will do. It is logical deduction alone that can provide the full accounting that his understanding of FI demands. The reasoning seems to be something like the following: It is not enough to say that the world is necessary, if this necessity cannot itself be accounted for (brute necessity!), and it is only logic – one thing deductively following from another – that provides the kind of accounting to end all accountings. Explanatory completeness must therefore complete itself in logical entailments. FI is Spinoza's demand for explanatory completeness. PSLR is Spinoza's understanding of what alone constitutes explanatory completeness. Spinoza's assertion (II, p VII) that the order and connection of ideas – which is constituted by logical entailments – is the same as the order and connection of things, should be read as his most explicit statement of the collapse of the ontological into the logical. It is an explicit statement of PSLR.

Spinoza's FI is disseminated throughout the *Ethics,* since the work largely consists of its implications. This means that his intuition must be built into the definitions and axioms of Part I; and indeed it is. Consider, for example, Axiom I: *Everything which exists, exists either in itself or in something else.* This might sound simply like a recap of Aristotelian metaphysics – all is either substance or substance's modifications, understanding these terms in Aristotelian fashion. But swelled by FI, Axiom I is asserting that everything which exists, has its necessary existence derivable either from itself or from something else. And whence the necessity of this necessary existence? From FI, of course. Definition III states: '*By* substance, *I mean that which is in itself and is conceived through itself; in other words that of which a conception can be formed independently of any other conception.*' We form the conception of a thing, any thing – whether substance or modification – by grasping the explanation for that thing's necessary existence.[26] So substance is that which, in being conceived through itself, provides its own accounting of its necessary existence. In that sense, it cannot be conceived without conceiving of its necessary existence. It, therefore, meets the definition of the self-caused (Def. I): *By that which is self-caused, I mean that of which the essence involves existence, or that of which the nature is only conceivable as existent.* They are, of course, all tangled together, these axioms and definitions, and all of them brimful with FI. That's what makes Spinoza's fundamental intuition fundamental.

Pre-science and prescience

These definitions – of *substance,* of *the self-caused* – prepare the wary reader to anticipate some re-warmed version of the logically unappetizing Ontological Argument. Spinoza seems to be manoeuvring himself precisely into place to serve up such an argument, depositing the predicate of *existence,* or – even better – the predicate of *necessary existence* into the very definition of a thing, and then cheerily proceeding to deduce that the thing so defined must, by definition, exist. And Spinoza's formal proofs of the necessary existence of substance (I, p VII) and the necessary existence of God

(I, p XI) really do look like reproductions of the arguments of Anselm and Descartes, arguments that giddily spin around on nothing more substantive than definitions.

But Spinoza's derivation of the one and infinite substance is, in fact, based on something far more substantive than mere definition. Here's the reasoning:

If it is explanations all the way down – and it must be if FI is true – then we can consider the whole infinite set of these explanations *in toto*, bound all together by the internal necessity connecting causes and effects by way of laws which are themselves ultimately explicable, meaning logically necessary. We can consider the whole vast implicate order,[27] consisting of the whole complete network of logical implications, all the necessary causal laws and all the infinite number of things that follow from them. Since all is explicable, we know that this vast system, consisting of all things bound by necessary explanations, exists. Let us call this whole implicate order *the world*.

The world, too – the vast implicate order considered *in toto* – must, of course, be accounted for. Three possible candidates for world-accounter present themselves:

1. Something, traditionally known as *God*, that exists outside the world
2. Something that exists within the world
3. The world itself

Can anything outside of the world account for the world's nature and existence? Certainly not, since the world consists of the whole vast system of all things explicable. If something exists outside of the world, it is ipso facto inexplicable and – according to FI – the inexplicable is the incoherent, is the non-existent. Outside of the world, at least the world so conceived, nothing can be nor even be conceived (since we conceive of each thing in terms of its derivational accounting). To be is either to be identical with the whole implicate order or to be implied by the implicate order. So scratch that one, or rather That One.

What about candidate two? Surely any such candidate suffers from serious delusions of grandeur in even presenting itself for consideration. Some single implication of the implicate order, a humbly specific implication of which the conception cannot even be formed without dragging in a massive tangle of entailments, offering itself up for explanation of the whole infinite totality? Please.

That leaves us with candidate three as the only possible choice. This gives us an exquisite solution, with a mathematical elegance devoutly to be desired. The thing which accounts for the world itself is the world itself. It is the world, understood as the infinite implicate order containing all explanations, that qualifies as substance. The singularity of substance is nothing more nor less than the singularity of this world, outside of which nothing can be nor be conceived. FI demands that this singularly self-explanatory substance exists. This is not an argument which runs on definitions. It runs on FI.

The world consists of an infinite implicate order, and to be is either to be identical with this infinite implicate order (substance) or to be entailed by this infinite implicate order (modification). To be is to be explicable, meaning logically derivable, although not necessarily derivable by us, since we are finite and therefore can grasp only limited aspects of the infinite explanatory nexus. The full and complete representation of the implicate order is equivalent to what Spinoza calls the infinite intellect of God.

Spinoza intuited an implicate order of a complexity so vast, involving abstractions so subtle, that it is, in its absolute being, hidden to our incurably finite and concrete minds. What we know of it is that it is so compelling as to bring about its own existence. This compellingness is what constitutes its essence, a coiled necessity that explodes in an infinity of consequences. We can grasp this essence because it is one with FI.

But to conceive with more completeness of the essence of substance, we must cast specific explanatory nets over the implicate order, representing its internal causality in terms of either (what we would now call) physics or (what we would now call) psychology. Those are the two explanatory schemata available to us – finite creatures that we are – the ways we have of conceiving the necessary connections of existence, its infinite generative power; even though, according to Spinoza, the bare implicate order, in the purity of its abstractions, admits of an infinity of ways in which its explosive existence could be represented concretely.[28] Spinoza's mind–body monism – the assertion that physics and psychology are two mutually irreducible ways of formulating one and the same implicate order – follows directly from his substance monism, which is itself an implication of FI.[29]

So what, then, does Spinoza's assertion of the one and only substance amount to? What is he saying about the nature of the world by this startlingly monist statement? Scrape away the language of substance and its modifications, the muddying suggestions of Aristotelian ontology that cling to the terms, and Spinoza is asserting something rather startlingly modern. To put it in the language of some contemporary physicists, Spinoza is asserting that there is a Final Theory of Everything, which, accounting, as it promises, for *everything*, will also account for why it itself is the Final Theory of Everything. It provides the explanation for itself. It is, in Spinoza's language, the *causa sui*. If arbitrariness is ultimately to be expelled from the universe, then there must, in theory, be a Final Theory of Everything, in which everything – even itself – is neatly folded and tucked into place. And there can be only one such Final Theory of Everything, outside of which nothing explicable can be nor be conceived, since the Final Theory of Everything exhausts all things explicable. This one self-explanatory Final Theory of Everything alone qualifies as substance, with all other things – those individual existences that find their explanatory places within it – relegated to modifications.

It is revealing to quote Steven Hawking, speaking of Einstein (thus roping two great physicists into the Spinozist orbit):

> 'Einstein once asked the question: 'How much choice did God have in constructing the universe?' Even if there is only one possible unified theory, it is just a set of rules and equations. What is it that breathes fire into the equations and makes a universe for them to describe? Why does the universe go to all the bother of existing? Is the unified theory so compelling that it brings about its own existence?'[30]

A theory just that compelling, bringing about its own existence, is precisely what Spinoza had in mind with his concept of substance. Just as Aristotle had introduced the term 'substance' to bear the weight of his ontology, so Spinoza takes over the term and radically transforms its meaning so that it might bear the weight of *his* ontology. 'I am aware that these terms are employed in senses somewhat different from those usually assigned,' he remarks apropos of some psychological terms he is defining in Part III, 'But my purpose is to explain, not the meaning of words, but the nature of things.'[31]

This remark is relevant to Spinoza's treatment of other terms as well, most especially the metaphysically-fraught notion of *substance*. Etymologically speaking, his choice of the word *substance* is perfect. Substance stands beneath all being. It offers the explanation for what it is to be. He preserves the ancient sense of the term. It is the reference which is so radically different.

Spinoza's FI, most especially as expressed (in PSLR) as the collapse of ontology into logic, might strike one as a violation of commonsense too extreme for sustained consideration, and so it might be. Nevertheless, if we hold that the usefulness of an intuition's consequences are relevant to judgments of truth, then it might be harder to dismiss Spinoza's FI, since it led him, in the infancy of modern science, to affirm the existence of something very close to that Final Theory of Everything of which physicists only began to speak in the late twentieth century. Einstein himself, whose admiration for Spinoza expressed itself not only in prose but in poetry,[32] seemed to discern in the philosopher intuitions in accord with his own.

On the other hand, one might be inclined to say that, if Spinoza is justified in drawing the consequences he does out of FI – including his logical determinism, then his system is best viewed as a reductio ad absurdum of FI, which might otherwise seem not so unreasonable, since it is simply the intuition that it is reasons all the way down.

But whatever one's reaction to Spinoza's version of the world, if we want to understand what Spinoza meant by asserting his one and only substance, and why it was that he believed that this one substance must necessarily exist, then FI provides the answer. FI is how Spinoza gets ontos out of logos.

Okay, but why God?

Speaking of philosophically loaded terms which get deformed in the process of Spinoza's explaining not 'the meaning of words, but the nature of things,' consider, if you will, *God*.

What kind of name is that for a Final Theory of Everything? Why start using that term to refer to the implicate order?[33] Well, why not, just so long as one carefully guards against illegitimately smuggling in any extra-substantial characteristics associated with more conventional notions of God. (One runs the risk of this by categorizing Spinoza as a pantheist, a habit to be fastidiously avoided.)

The notion of the whole vast sweep of existence, itself necessarily existing and providing in itself the complete explanations for everything, is sufficiently impressive to be appropriately called God, if you're hankering to call something or other God. The substitution of the word 'God' for 'substance,' which starts occurring in *Ethics* I pXI, doesn't add anything substantive – nothing over and above what is already implied by FI; but perhaps Spinoza thought the use of the term 'God' for substance would do some good, underlining the fact that no *other* God – a transcendent God, with all sorts of inscrutable designs, making us all half-mad with desperation to discover what his intentions for us are and thereby save ourselves – was possible: the position of God has already been filled; no others need apply.

With the identification of God with substance – itself identified with the implicate order – all matters divine are merged with matters natural, which, in turn, are merged with matters logical.[34] The fundamental intuition that all facts have a complete accounting is, in Spinoza's hands, a presumption of remarkable potency. Deny this intuition, Spinoza claims, and you are denying reason itself. Assume it and the entire nature of existence spills forth.

Notes

I am grateful to Michael della Rocco for his helpful comments on this chapter.

1. The expression *Deus sive natura*, implying the identification of God and nature, is first introduced in *Ethics* IV, the preface, and repeated in pIV, Corollary. See also *The Theological-Political Treatise*, p. 28, pp. 45–46, p. 82 (The pagination refers to Gebhardt, *Spinoza Opera*, Heidelberg, n.d.)
2. *Ethics* IV, Preface, as well as IV pXXXI.
3. II pVII, Note. Also II, p XXI, including *Note*. Additionally, within the psychological sphere, Spinoza denies the bifurcation between cognition and the emotions.
4. I pXIV.
5. Or, more strictly speaking, ideas. Ideas are the more primitive notion for Spinoza; minds are constituted of ideas. See II, pXV.
6. I, pXXV, *Corollary*
7. The aim of the *Ethics*, after all, is to get us to change our own minds over time, to change what we think and care about, according to the dictates of reason.

8. Spinoza also rejects, as one would expect, a dualism between universals and particulars. See *Ethics* II p40 s1.
9. V, pXXIII, Note. All translations of the *Ethics* are by R.H.M. Elwes.
10. This corresponds to *knowledge of the second kind*, the nature and existence of an individual thing deduced from the nature and existence of another individual thing which is its cause, by way of scientific laws utilizing properties 'common to all things.' In particular, we explain individual bodies via the mathematical laws of science that capture the essence of extension in terms of mathematical equations. See II, p XXXVIII–XL, including, most especially Note II.
11. This corresponds to knowledge of the third kind, or *intuition*. where our knowledge of an individual thing does not come from its necessary connection to another individual thing, its proximate cause, but rather from a grasp of the thing's place in the infinite whole. See II, p XXXVIII, Note II, and V, p XXV–XXXII.
12. Spinoza holds the causal relation to be analytically true. See I, AXIOM IV: *The knowledge of an effect depends on and involves the knowledge of its cause.* He understands this potent axiom as entailing that the causal connection is the logical connection, as he explicitly deduces in II, p VII. Spinoza asserts the 'backwards analyticity' of causal relations, as it were, asserting that the concept of an effect entails the concept of a cause, whereas Hume, denying causal analyticity, concentrates on arguing against 'forward analyticity': 'In a word, then, every effect is a distinct event from its cause. It could not, therefore, be discovered in the cause, and the first invention or conception of it, *a priori*, must be entirely arbitrary. And even after it is suggested, the conjunction of it with the cause must appear equally arbitrary, since there are always many other effects which, to reason, must seem fully as consistent and natural.' *Inquiry Concerning Human Understanding*, IV. For a defense of the claim that Spinoza construes causal relations as analytically true, see Michael della Rocca, 'A Rationalist Manifesto: Spinoza and the Principle of Sufficient Reason,' *Philosophical Topics*, Vol. 31, 2003 pp. 75–93.
13. See I, p XVII, Corollary II, Note, and also III, p XX, *Explanation*, where Spinoza acknowledges using words 'in some significations quite different from what they usually bear.'
14. Cf. *The Treatise on the Intellect*, section 62: 'If by chance we should say that men are changed in a moment into beasts, that is said very generally, so that there is in the mind no concept, i.e. idea, or connection of subject and predicate. For if there were any concept, the mind would see together the means and causes, how and why such a thing was done.'
15. I pXXXIII.
16. The result of Descartes' experiment – a rather restrained rationalism which holds that empirical knowledge, receiving rational certification, is also required in order to know the nature of the world – is quite different from Spinoza's and Leibniz's bulked-up rationalism. These differing outcomes of the rationalist experiment are explained by Spinoza's and Leibniz's resorting to the presumption of reason I discuss in this section, while Descartes does not.
17. There are, of course, other more formal senses of 'logical.'
18. But see I, p VII, Note II, Premise 3.
19. Spinoza's using the presumption in an inferential capacity underlines my claim that he regards it as a logical principle, even if the incoherence that results from its negation is not regarded by him as the incoherence of out-and-out contradiction, (although maybe it is).

20. I, p VIII, *Note II.* Translation R.H.M Elwes.
21. I. p XI, *Another proof.*
22. For an interesting discussion of whether Spinoza is (as I claim here) committed to there being only one possible world, see Don Garrett, 'Spinoza's Necessitarianism,' and Edwin Curley and Gregory Walski, 'Spinoza's Necessaritarianism Reconsidered,' in *New Essays on Rationalism,* ed. Rocco J Gennaro and Charles Huenemann (New York: Oxford University Press, 1999) 241–62.
23. That he uses FI in the course of deductions, and in this sense treats it as a logical principle, does not altogether answer the question of whether he thinks that it is logically, or analytically, true, in the more narrow sense that its negation involves a contradiction. I'm not sure if he does or does not. He might regard FI as being necessarily true without being analytically true, even though its truth implies, according to him, that all other truths are analytically true. Can a truth, itself not analytic, imply analytic truths, or is such a logical situation impossible?
24. *Monadology,* 31–32.
25. I, APPENDIX.
26. An endless task, as it turns out, only completed in the infinite intellect of God. Still, the more we grasp of the explanation of x, the more adequate our conception of x. Falsity consists of *privation* (II, p XXXV); it is a matter of how much of the explanation is left out. Since the explanation is, in fact, infinite, everything that we believe is to some extent necessarily false. Spinoza, such a rationalist optimist, who believes we can save ourselves through reason, does not seem to want to stress this rather depressing consequence of his system.
27. This wonderful phrase comes from the physicist David Bohm. See David Bohm's *Wholeness and The Implicate Order,* Routledge, 2002.
28. I, p X, Note.
29. His ethical monism – merging ethics into psychology – also follows straightaway from FI. Spinoza is unswervingly strict about his self-explanatory world. Nothing at all about it can be explained by appeal to something outside of it. This means that our answers to ethical questions cannot inhabit a plane apart. If there are facts of the matter about which actions are better than others, which ways of life are better than others, then these facts are going to have to be located within the implicate order.
30. *A Brief History of Time* (Bantam, 1998) p. 190.
31. III, pXX, *Explanation.*
32. Einstein's poem, 'Zu Spinozas Ethik,' can be found in Jammer, Max, *Einstein and Religion* (Princeton University Press, 1999).
33. These two phrases, 'the implicate order' and 'The Final Theory of Everything,' seem to me to nicely catch the nuanced difference Spinoza offers us in his two phrases *natura naturata* and *natura naturans.*
34. Spinoza's conception of God blocks the problem of evil. The world was not created with a view toward human well-being. Logic entails what it does. It is not surprising that out of the vastness of logical implications there are many which do not particularly suit us. See I, *Appendix.*

Index

the ultimate whole, the atomist attributes ultimate priority to the ultimate parts. I will argue (§2.4) that *Atomism* is the best form of *Pluralism*, but I don't build *Atomism* into the definition of *Pluralism*.

Monism and *Pluralism* are exclusive theses. One doctrine holds that the cosmos is basic, while the other denies it. Given the tiling constraint, they are also exhaustive. There are no other possible answers to the question of fundamental mereology. This follows from the fact that *Monism* is equivalent to ~B*u* given tiling, and *Pluralism* is equivalent to B*u* given tiling – which are exhaustive conditions. Metaphorically speaking, *Monism* is the view that one leaves the whole pie intact, while *Pluralism* is the view that one cuts the pie (and *Atomism* is the version of this view on which one cuts down to the smallest crumb).

By way of concluding this section, it may be worth clarifying five points about *Monism* and *Pluralism*. First, the debate is not over what exists. Both sides can and should agree that the world exists and has parts (§1.1). The debate is rather over what is basic – it is about how to answer the question of fundamental mereology.

Second, none of the views as defined say anything about the relative priority ordering among derivative entities. Thus *Monism* allows that the whole is prior to its parts all the way down the mereological hierarchy. But it also allows that all of the many parts are equally secondary. And it even allows that the many ultimate parts come second in the priority ordering, with metaphysical explanation snaking upward from there. Likewise, *Pluralism* – at least in its atomistic form – allows that the parts are prior to their whole all the way up the mereological hierarchy. But even *Atomism* allows that all but the ultimate parts are equally secondary. And even *Atomism* allows that the one whole comes second in the priority ordering, with metaphysical explanation dangling downward from there. The thematic versions of *Monism* and *Pluralism* treat whole-to-part priority *with constancy* all the way along the mereological hierarchy, but I do not require either the monist or the pluralist to be thematic in this respect.

Third, *Monism* and *Pluralism* are both claims about the actual world. Neither says anything about any other worlds. I will argue (§2.2) that whichever of these views of fundamental mereology is actually true should hold with metaphysical necessity. But I do not build this into the definitions of these doctrines.

Fourth, the only assumption that is essential to the debate as a whole is the assumption that there is a priority ordering among actual concrete objects (§1.2). Without that there is no notion of basicness to debate. The remaining assumptions are inessential. The assumption that there is a world helps make *Monism* viable, and the assumption that it has parts helps make *Pluralism* viable. Either of these assumptions could be waived, though the debate would at that point be decided. The assumption that composition is not identity and the *No Overlap* aspect of the tiling constraint both help render *Monism* and *Pluralism* exclusive. These could be waived, though then one would need to consider the prospect that *both* the one whole and some of its many parts are basic. Furthermore, the assumption of a well-founded partial ordering and the *Covering* aspect of the tiling constraint both help to render *Monism* and *Pluralism* exhaustive. These could be waived, though then one would need to consider the prospect that *neither* the one whole nor a complete plurality of its parts are basic.

Fifth, I have made little attempt yet to argue that these doctrines deserve their labels (see appendix). I am interested in the doctrines themselves. I will be defending the thesis that the cosmos is the one-and-only fundamental actual concrete object, prior to all of its proper parts. The reader who would not call that *Monism* is welcome to find another label.[20]

This concludes my attempt to clarify the debate. The debate concerns the question of fundamental mereology, which is the question of which actual concrete objects are basic. *Monism* and *Pluralism* – given assumptions that I have tried to articulate – emerge as exclusive and exhaustive possible answers. For the monist, there is one and only one basic object, and it is the whole cosmos. For the pluralist, there are many basic objects, and they are all proper parts of the cosmos.

1.2 Monism: the priority of the whole

Which objects are fundamental? Is the one whole – the cosmos – the one and only fundamental object, as per *Monism*; or are some of the many parts fundamental instead, as per *Pluralism*? What is the metaphysically correct way to carve up the cosmos? I will now discuss what I consider to be the four main arguments in the debate and maintain that the monistic side has the better of the arguments.

1.2.1 Common sense: parts as arbitrary abstractions

It will prove useful to begin with Russell's claim that pluralism is favoured by *common sense* since this claim is the source of the contemporary dismissal of monism as being obviously false. So Russell (1985, 36) declares: 'I share the common-sense belief that there are many separate things; I do not regard the apparent multiplicity of the world as consisting merely in phases and unreal divisions of a single indivisible Reality.' Russell (1985, 48) then frames the debate as a debate between the commonsensical empiricist pluralist who can see that 'there are many things' and the wildeyed rationalistic monist who would argue a priori that there is only one thing. Here is the birth story of analytic philosophy and what has sounded like the death knell for monism.[21]

But analytic philosophy – for all of its many virtues – was born in sin. Russell misinterpreted monism. *Monism* is not the doctrine that exactly one thing exists but rather the doctrine that the one whole is fundamental (§1.4, appendix). Or at least, both the monistic and the pluralistic views under discussion accept the existence of the one whole and its many parts (§1.1). Thus the advocate of *Monism* and Russell's 'empirical person' are in perfect agreement over Russell's claim that 'there are many things.'

If there is to be an argument from common sense against *Monism*, it must be an argument for the *priority* of the parts to their whole. That is, it must be an argument that it is commonsensically obvious that the cosmos is not fundamental. In this vein consider the grains of sand and the heap. Intuitively, the grains seem prior to the heap. Thus Leibniz (1989, 213) – with his plurality of fundamental monads – claimed that in general 'a composite is nothing else than a collection or *aggregatum* of simple substances' and wrote to Arnauld, 'Every being derives its reality only from the reality of those beings of which it is composed' (1989, 85).

On the other hand, the monist may offer a general conception of the *partialia* as abstract, in the etymologically correct sense of being a partial aspect. Wholes are complete and concrete unities. Parts may be conceived of as aspects of wholes, isolated through a process that Bradley (1978, 124) describes as 'one-sided abstraction.' The priority of the one whole to its many parts is thus of a piece with the priority of the substance to its modes, both being instances of the general priority of the concrete entity to its abstract aspects.[22]

In my view, common sense has a more nuanced opinion on the priority question. I think common sense distinguishes *mere aggregates* from *integrated wholes*: 'that which is compounded out of something so that the whole is one – not like a heap, but like a syllable ' (Aristotle 1984b, 1644). Common sense probably does endorse the priority of the parts in cases of mere aggregation, such as with the heap. Yet common sense probably endorses the priority of the whole in cases of integrated wholes, such as with the syllable. Thus, consider the circle and its semicircles (or even more gerrymandered divisions of the circle). Intuitively, the circle seems prior – the semicircles represent an arbitrary partition of the circle.[23] Or consider an organism and its organs. According to Aristotle at least, the organism is prior, and the organs are defined by their functional integration within the organism.[24] Or consider the myriad details of a percept. Here it seems that the percept is prior – the details are just particulars of the overall gestalt.[25] So it seems that, at the very least:

1. According to common sense, integrated wholes are prior to their arbitrary portions.

Further, common sense tends to view the cosmos as an integrated whole (not like a heap, but like a syllable). As Brand Blanshard (1973, 180) declaims, the conviction 'of the plain man' and 'of most thoughtful minds' is that 'the world is not in the final account a rag-bag of loose ends.'

Such an intuition echoes through many religious traditions. It is present in Plato's Timaean picture of the cosmos as constructed by the demiurge in the pattern of 'one visible animal comprehending within itself all other animals' (Plato 1961, 1163). And it resurfaces from reflection on the patterns of nature. Thus Paul Davies (1983, 145) writes, 'That the universe is ordered seems self-evident. Everywhere we look, from the far-flung galaxies to the deepest recesses of the atom, we encounter regularity and intricate organization.' Indeed the very term 'cosmos' is derived from the Greek term for order. Thus:

2. According to common sense, the cosmos is an integrated whole.

Finally, common sense tends to view the many parts of the cosmos it is concerned with – such as animals and artifacts – as arbitrary parts, in at least two respects. The first arbitrariness concerns *partitions*. Common sense appreciates that there are many ways to carve the world. Consider all the ways that one may slice a pie, or all the ways of drawing lines on a map. There seems no objective ground for carving things in just one way.[26]

The second sort of arbitrariness that common sense recognizes with common objects like animals and artifacts concerns *boundaries*. Common sense recognizes that common objects are all like clouds, blurry at the edges. As D. Lewis (1999c, 165) explains, 'There are always outlying particles, questionably parts of the thing, not definitely included and not definitely not included' (compare Unger 1980). So even if there were some objective reason to prefer drawing a line on the map, say, between mountain and valley, there would still be arbitrariness concerning where exactly the mountain begins. Given the arbitrariness of partitions and boundaries and the focus of common sense on animals, artifacts, and their ilk:

3. According to common sense, the many proper parts are arbitrary portions of the cosmos.

From 1–3, and assuming the consistency of common sense on these matters, it follows that:

4. According to common sense, the cosmos is prior to its many proper parts.

So if anything, it is *Monism* that can claim the mantle of common sense. As confirmation of 4, note that the monistic side has long been the ascendant position in metaphysics and that many of the world's religions have a monistic character.[27] So – peering beyond the provinces of twentieth-century analytic metaphysics – the overall pull of intuitions across cultures and ages favours the monistic view. Not for nothing did James (1975, 65) acknowledge monism to be 'part of philosophic common sense' and pen the following apologetics for his pluralism, which may be worth repeating at length:

> It is curious how little countenance radical pluralism has ever had from philosophers. Whether materialistically or spiritually minded, philosophers have always aimed at cleaning up the litter with which the world apparently is filled. They have substituted economical and orderly conceptions for the first sensible tangle; and whether these were morally elevated or only intellectually neat, they were at any rate always aesthetically pure and definite, and aimed at ascribing to the world something clean and intellectual in the way of inner structure. As compared with all these rationalizing pictures, the pluralistic empiricism which I profess offers but a sorry appearance. It is a turbid, muddled, gothic sort of an affair, without a sweeping outline and with little pictorial nobility. Those of you who are accustomed to the classical constructions of reality may be excused if your first reaction upon it be absolute contempt – a shrug of the shoulders as if such ideas were unworthy of explicit refutation. (1977, 26)

I thus conclude that it is *Monism* – properly understood as the claim that the cosmos is an integrated whole – that best fits intuitions about priority. Though I should hasten to add that I think this counts for little. At best *Monism* can lay claim to being the default view. Common sense – what Einstein called 'a deposit of prejudices laid down in the mind before you reach eighteen' (quoted in Bell 1951, 42) – may favour *Monism*, but it matters little either way.

Glancing back to Russell's argument from the start of this section, one finds a further puzzling step. Russell claims that the issue is empirical and then invokes what the empirical person would 'naturally say'. But why does it matter what the empirical person would 'naturally say'? Empirical issues are to be settled, not by appeal to common sense, but by empirical inquiry.

1.2.2 Quantum entanglement and emergence: the asymmetry of supervenience

So what does empirical inquiry reveal? It might seem that current empirical inquiry favours *Pluralism* insofar as physics purports to tell the complete causal story of the world in terms of particles. Thus Paul Oppenheim and Hilary Putnam (1991, 409) speak of a hierarchy of *scientific levels*, where 'any thing of any level except the lowest must possess a decomposition into things belonging to the next lower level,' and on which 'there must be a unique lowest level,' which they label 'Elementary Particles'. As Jaegwon Kim (1998, 15) explains, 'The bottom level is usually thought to consist of elementary particles, or whatever our best physics is going to tell us are the basic bits of matter out of which all material things are composed.' If there is to be a good argument for *Pluralism* over *Monism*, it will not be Russell's argument from common sense (§2.1) but rather Kim's argument from physics.

That said, there is a gap in the argument from physics. For it is one thing to assume that physics is fundamental, and another to assume that fundamental physics will deal in particles or other wee 'bits of matter' (Schaffer 2003; Hüttemann and Papineau 2005). The monist can and should allow that physics will tell the complete causal story of the world. The monist will maintain that this physical story is best told in terms of fields pervading the whole cosmos, rather than in terms of local particles. What is at issue is not the success of physics, but rather its content.

I will now argue that quantum mechanics is holistic in a way that supports *Monism*. I begin with a description of *entangled systems* in quantum mechanics. An entangled system is one whose state vector is not factorizable into tensor products of the state vectors of its *n* components:

$$\psi_{\text{system}} \neq \psi_{\text{component-1}} \otimes \psi_{\text{component-2}} \otimes \ldots \otimes \psi_{\text{component-n}}$$

Thus the quantum state of an entangled system contains information over and above that of the quantum states of its components.[28]

To illustrate, consider the Einstein, Podolsky, and Rosen (EPR) thought experiment, in which two electrons are produced in the singlet state:

$$[\psi\rangle_{\text{EPR}}=1/\sqrt{2}[\uparrow\rangle_1[\downarrow\rangle_2 - 1/\sqrt{2}[\downarrow\rangle_1[\uparrow\rangle_2$$

Here '$[\uparrow\rangle n$' means that electron$_n$ is in a spin-up state (strictly speaking an up state with respect to some chosen component of spin) and '$[\downarrow\rangle_n$' means that electron$_n$ is in a spin-down state. An electron pair in the singlet state is *anti-correlated* with respect to spin. The total spin of the entire system is zero. If one reads the correlation coefficients ($1/\sqrt{2}$) as square roots of the chances of outcomes (Born's Rule), then electron pairs in the singlet state have a .5 chance of measuring out as electron$_1$ being spin-up and electron$_2$ being spin-down, and a .5 chance of measuring out as electron$_1$ being spin-down and electron$_2$ being spin-up. Crucially, this system affords zero chance of both electrons measuring out as spin-up, or both electrons measuring out as spin-down. This is the sense in which the electron pair is anti-correlated with respect to spin.

The singlet state seen in ψ_{EPR} is entangled, and as such is not derivable from the state vectors of its two electrons. A pure spin state can be attributed to neither electron individually. A pure spin state can be attributed to the electron pairs only collectively, as a system. As Michael Esfeld (2001, 252) puts the point: 'These properties of the whole contain *all* that can be said about the local properties of the parts, and *only* these properties of the whole contain all that can be said about the local properties of the parts.'

Such entanglement has results that Einstein famously described as 'spooky action at a distance.' No matter how far apart the particles are, a spin measurement on one will immediately set the spin state of the other to the opposite (since the spins are anti-correlated). Entangled particles seem as if telepathic. They act as a unit. As Tim Maudlin (1998, 56) concludes: 'The physical state of a complex whole cannot always be reduced to those of its parts, or to those of its parts together with their spatiotemporal relations.... The result of the most intensive scientific investigations in history is a theory that contains an ineliminable holism.'

So far I have only tried to convey what entangled systems are like. Now the argument from quantum entanglement to *Monism* begins from the premise that the cosmos forms *one vast entangled system*. This can be argued for both physically and mathematically. Physically, one gets initial entanglement from the assumption that the world begins in one explosion (the Big Bang) in which everything interacts.[29] This initial entanglement is then preserved thereafter on the assumption that the world evolves via Schrödinger's equation.[30] More precisely, the initial singularity is virtually certain (measure 1) to produce universal entanglement, and the Schrödinger dynamics are virtually certain (measure 1) to preserve it. In fact Schrödinger evolution tends to spread entanglements, so that even without initial entanglement, 'eventually every particle in the universe must become entangled with every other ' (Penrose 2004, 591).

Mathematically, one needs only to suppose that there *is* a wave-function of the universe. Then it is virtually certain that it will be entangled since measure 1 of all wave-functions are entangled. So unless there is a specific form of evolution – such as some form of wave-function collapse – that promotes disentanglement, one should expect universal entanglement. Thus – absent wave-function collapse – it seems virtually certain that:

5. The cosmos is in an entangled state.[31]

It remains to be argued that the entangled universe displays what David Bohm and B. J. Hiley (1993, 352) call an 'unbroken wholeness,' in a way that supports monism. It will prove useful to start with a Democritean pluralist picture, featuring particles with intrinsic physical properties in external spatiotemporal relations,[32] and generalize from there. Democritean pluralism cannot provide an adequate basis for entangled systems (see Teller 1986, 71–73; Healey 1991, 405–6). It fails the completeness requirement (§1.3). Thus consider the EPR system's intrinsic correlational property of having total spin zero. This property is not fixed by the Democritean base – it is not fixed by fixing the quantum states of the two particles, along with their spatiotemporal arrangement. In general, duplicating the intrinsic properties of the particles, along with the spatiotemporal relations between the particles, does not metaphysically suffice to duplicate the cosmos and its contents. The intrinsic correlational properties of entangled wholes would not be duplicated. So on the assumption that the basic actual concrete objects must be complete, Democritean pluralism is ruled out.

Lifting the Democritean supposition, it should be obvious that no movement to larger molecules or further intrinsic properties will help the pluralist find a complete basis for the entangled cosmos. The physical properties of the whole are not fixed by the total intrinsic properties of any subsystems. The only move that seems to help the pluralist attain completeness is to add new fundamental external relations: *entanglement relations*. The pluralist might still maintain that particles are fundamental but now would have them laced together by both spatiotemporal arrangements and correlational entanglements (compare Teller 1986). So, for instance, the EPR particles would not merely be at such-and-such distance, they would also be thus-and-so correlated.

There are, however, at least two main problems with a move to entanglement relations. The first problem is that it is not obvious that the fundamental theory will retain particles – the relata of these proposed entanglement relations – especially when one looks beyond quantum mechanics to relativistic quantum field theory (see Halvorson and Clifton 2002; Kuhlmann 2006, §5). In quantum field theory, 'particle number' is just an operator on the field and as such need not have a definite whole number expectation value. How could particles be fundamental if there is not even a fact about how many of them the system has? Moreover, 'particle number' is not frame invariant. For instance, there is the Unruh effect in which an inertial observer will observe a vacuum state (fields at lowest energy), while a uniformly accelerated observer will observe many particles. So particles in relativistic quantum field theory seem to assume the same nonobjective status as simultaneity does in special relativity. Thus H. D. Zeh (2003, 330) recommends that we 'abandon a primordial particle concept entirely, and ... replace it with fields only,' noting 'this is indeed what has always been done in the *formalism* of quantum field theory.' The formalism looks, on the surface, to be treating worldwide fields as fundamental.

The second problem with entanglement relations – purely internal to quantum mechanics, and even granting the presence of particles – is that the unity of properties gets lost. If one treats entangled systems holistically, then one accords them basic intrinsic spin properties, and crucially one can attribute *the very same property* to different systems with different numbers of components. For instance, a single electron, and various systems, might each have the same spin property. But if one treats entangled systems via parts in entanglement relations, then one cannot attribute *the same relation* with different numbers of components. This represents a loss of empirically important unity, as Healey (1991, 420) explains:

> As far as its spin goes, it is irrelevant whether or not a system is composed of subsystems: quantum mechanics applies to the spin of a system in just the same way in either case. This is important, since it permits one to treat the total spin of a complex system like a silver atom just as one would that of a spin 1/2 system with no nontrivial subsystems.

I conclude that an entangled system is best treated as a fundamental unit:

6. Entangled systems are fundamental wholes.

From 5 and 6, it follows:

7. The cosmos is a fundamental whole.[33]

And so, given that quantum mechanics (or better, relativistic quantum field theory) represents our best current guide to the structure of reality, it seems that empirical inquiry now favours the holism of the monistic view.

A second argument to *Monism*, the argument from *the possibility of emergence*, lurks behind this first argument. I have argued that quantum entanglement is a case of emergence, in the specific sense of a property of an object that has proper parts, which property is not fixed by the intrinsic properties of its proper parts and the fundamental relations between its proper parts. However the empirical questions ultimately get resolved, it seems clear that this sort of emergence – at the level of the cosmos – is at least metaphysically possible:

8. It is metaphysically possible for the cosmos to have emergent properties.

So consider a world in which the cosmos has such emergent properties. The concrete realm at such a mereologically complex world cannot be completely characterized in terms of any plurality of its proper parts. That is, duplicating any plurality of these proper parts, while preserving their fundamental relations, would not metaphysically suffice to duplicate this possible cosmos. Indeed nothing will suffice to completely characterize an object with emergent properties short of that whole object, or any wider whole that object is part of. And so, given that the basic objects of a world must be complete for that world (this is the natural modal generalization of the completeness requirement: §1.3), among the concrete objects of an emergently propertied world *w*, the whole cosmos of *w* must be basic. So there is a metaphysically possible monistic scenario:

9. It is metaphysically possible for the cosmos to have proper parts but be a fundamental whole.

Now I take it that *Monism* and *Pluralism*, though defined as doctrines about the actual world (§1.4), are metaphysically general theses, in the sense that whichever doctrine is true, is true with metaphysical necessity (compare van Inwagen 2002, 28). Just as the dispute as to whether properties are universals, tropes, or nominalistic constructions is thought to concern a metaphysical necessity, so the dispute over the priority of the whole seems to concern a comparable necessity. Indeed, I take the realm of metaphysical possibility to concern what is compossible with *the laws of metaphysics*, which govern what grounds what.[34] *Monism* and *Pluralism* are rival doctrines about the laws of metaphysics, with respect to the grounding of mereological structure. Thus:

10. Either it is metaphysically necessary for the cosmos to be a fundamental whole, or it is metaphysically necessary for the cosmos (if it has proper parts) to be derivative.

The parenthetical clause in 10 serves to cover the case of a one-atom cosmos, which is the one case in which the pluralist will allow the cosmos to be fundamental.

Together 9 and 10 entail *Monism*, as a thesis about the actual world:

11. The cosmos is a fundamental whole.

In short, if *Pluralism* is true, then it is necessarily true, by 10. But by 9, *Pluralism* is not necessarily true. So it is not true.

An underlying mereological asymmetry comes to light: *the asymmetry of supervenience*. The asymmetry is that the proper parts must supervene on their whole (§1.3), but the whole need not supervene on its proper parts. In other words, though emergence is metaphysically possible, *submergence* – the converse of emergence – is metaphysically impossible. For submergence, the intrinsic properties of the proper parts, along with the fundamental relations between these parts, must fail to supervene on the intrinsic properties of the whole. This is impossible because (i) any intrinsic property of the proper parts ipso facto correlates to an intrinsic property of the whole, namely, the property of having-a-part-with-such-and-such-intrinsic-property, and (ii) any relations between the parts also correlates with an intrinsic property of the whole, namely, the property of having-parts-thus-and-so-related. Fix the whole, and all of its parts are fixed.

Given the asymmetry of supervenience, the monist can guarantee a complete inventory of basic objects. The impossibility of submergence guarantees that the cosmos is complete unto itself. But the pluralist cannot guarantee a complete inventory, for no roster of proper parts can be guaranteed complete, given the possibility of emergence. In this sense the whole may well be – and by the lights of our best physics actually is – more than the sum of its parts.

1.2.3 Heterogeneity: configuring the many

There is a very general sort of empirical information, however, that might be thought to favour *Pluralism*. The very general sort of empirical information is that the world is *heterogeneous*, in the sense of featuring qualitative variegation. Some parts are discernible from others.

Heterogeneity is a classic problem for the monist, prefigured in the Parmenidean vision of a perfect homogeneous sphere, which 'is all alike; nor is there more here and less there' (Kirk and Raven 1962, 275) and which is 'like the bulk of a well-rounded sphere, from the centre equally balanced in every direction;... [B]eing equal to itself on every side, it rests uniformly within its limits' (Kirk and Raven 1962, 276).[35] Plotinus (1991, 353) saw this problem:

> From such a unity as we have declared The One to be, how does anything at all come into substantial existence, any multiplicity, dyad, or number? Why has the Primal not remained self-gathered so that there be none of this profusion of the manifold which we observe in existence and yet are compelled to trace to that absolute unity?

And Joachim labeled it 'the fundamental difficulty' for the monist:

> For any monistic philosophy the fundamental difficulty is to find intelligible meaning within its system for the relative independence of the differences of the One.... [W]e have One, and find it difficult to reconcile with its Unity the being of a variety or plurality within it. (Joachim 1906, 48–49; compare Ritchie 1898, 469–70)

(Note that Plotinus and Joachim – monists both – are evidently not denying the existence of a plurality but rather trying to account for a diverse plurality from a fundamental One.)

What exactly is the argument? Presumably the key premise is that any basic entity must be homogeneous. From this premise it would follow that the monist, with one basic cosmos, must have a homogeneous cosmos. And it would follow that the pluralist, with many basic parts, could still have heterogeneity in virtue of these parts *differing from each other.* Thus the pluralist might argue that the heterogeneity of the world can be due only to external differences between *many* internally homogeneous basic bits of being.

More precisely, the key premise would be:

12. Fundamental objects must be homogeneous.

From 12, the refutation of *Monism* would follow swiftly, for it would follow that:

13. If the cosmos were fundamental, then the cosmos would be homogeneous.

When evidently:

14. The cosmos is not homogeneous.[36]

And given 13 and 14, the refutation of *Monism* is at hand:

15. Therefore the cosmos is not fundamental.

But why think that any basic entity must be homogeneous, as per the key premise 12? I can think of two *bad* reasons. First, one might think that a heterogeneous basic entity would in some sense 'differ from itself.' But (i) if this were objectionable, the objection would apply equally to the pluralist's heterogeneous derivative entities – they too would 'differ from themselves.' This objection does not succeed in picking out anything special about *basic* objects that requires them to be homogeneous. Also (ii) the thought that heterogeneous basic entities are objectionable may arise from a conflation of numerical difference with qualitative variegation. What is true is that nothing can be nonidentical to itself. What is false is that nothing can be internally qualitatively variegated.

Second, one might think that any heterogeneity demands metaphysical explanation in terms of an arrangement of homogeneous parts. But this is just a demand for an explanation of a particular type of whole from a particular type of part. As such it begs the question against the monist. If there is to be an objection to *Monism* in the offing, there must be an argument against the prospect of explaining heterogeneity by starting from a fundamental heterogeneous whole.

Indeed, the monist can reply that heterogeneous basic entities must be allowed by everyone. For it is metaphysically possible for there to be *heterogeneity all the way down*, in the sense of a cosmos every part of which has heterogeneous proper parts. I will argue for the possibility of gunk (matter every part of which has proper parts) in §2.4. If gunk is possible, heterogeneity all the way down should be possible since such constitutes a consistent distribution of properties over gunk.